SOIL
AND WATER
CONSERVATION
SOCIETY

**About the Soil and Water
Conservation Society**

The Soil and Water Conservation Society (SWCS) is a nonprofit scientific and educational organization that serves as an advocate for environmental quality professionals and for science-based conservation policy. SWCS seeks to advance the science and art of soil, water, and related natural resource conservation to achieve sustainability. Members practice and promote an ethic that recognizes the interdependence of people and their environment.

Environmental Management Glossary

Soil and Water Conservation Society

Edited by:
Debra A. Happe

Soil and Water Conservation Society
Ankeny, Iowa, USA

Published by the Soil and Water Conservation Society
945 SW Ankeny Road
Ankeny, Iowa 50023-9723
800-THE-SOIL (843-7645)
www.swcs.org

Environmental Management Glossary
Fourth Edition

First Edition, 1970
Second Edition, 1976
Third Edition, 1982

Library of Congress Cataloging-in-Publication Data
Happe, Debra A. (ed)
ENVIRONMENTAL MANAGEMENT GLOSSARY
p. cm.
ISBN 0-9769432-2-0
1. Environmental sciences. 2. Glossary. 3. Reference. 4. Conservation

Table of Contents

Preface . . . . *vii*

List of acronyms . . . . *viii*

Conversion tables . . . . *xi*

Area of plane figures . . . . *xxi*

Glossary of environmental science terms 1

Preface

The Soil and Water Conservation Society's *Soil and Water Conservation Glossary* was first published in 1952 under the direction of Arnold J. Baur. It has been revised, expanded, and reprinted as the *Resource Conservation Glossary* in 1970, 1976, and 1982. This fourth edition sees a name change to *Environmental Management Glossary*, which reflects the expansion of the soil and water conservation field of study.

This edition represents an increase in the number of entries and technologies represented. It includes over 4,000 terms commonly used in over 50 technologies. This glossary is for the practitioner, student, and layman. While most professionals and researchers have specialized glossaries, this glossary will be useful to them as they encounter interdisciplinary activity. The technologies represented in this edition, include agronomy, air resources, anthropology, acquaculture, biology (fish and wildlife), cartography, conservation, conservation education, conservation computer science, ecology, economics, engineering, environmental management, erosion and sedimentation, fertilizers, forestry, geography, geology, horticulture, hydrology, irrigation, land use planning, mining, outdoor recreation, plant materials, range science, remote sensing, salinity control, soils, tillage, urban planning, water resources, waste management, and weather modification.

This edition of the *Environmental Management Glossary* was prepared with the help of interns Lisa D'Amico, Kala King, and Kari Sampson, and Suzi Case, administrative assistant at the Soil and Water Conservation Society.

List of Acronyms

AFO	animal feeding operations
AGNPS	AGricultural Non-Point Source
ASA	American Society of Agronomy
ASAE	American Society of Agricultural Engineers
ASCE	American Society of Civil Engineers
AVSWAT	ArcView GIS - SWAT model system
BASINS	Better Assessment Science Integrating Point and Nonpoint Sources
CAFO	concentrated animal feeding operations
CERL	Construction Engineering Research Laboratory
CNMP	comprehensive nutrient management plans
CREAMS	Chemicals, Runoff, and Erosion from Agricultural Management Systems
CREP	Conservation Reserve Enhancement Program
CRP	Conservation Reserve Program
CSEP	Climatic Index for Soil Erosion Potential
CSREES	Cooperative State Research Education and Extension Service
CTIC	Conservation Technology Information Center
DEM	Digital Elevation Models
EGS-AGU–EUG	European Geophysical Society- American Geophysical Union - European Union of Geosciences
EPA	Environmental Protection Agency
EPIC	Environmental Policy Integrated Climate
ERS	Economic Research Service
ESRI	Environmental Systems Research Institute
EUROSEM	European Soil Erosion Model
FGDC	Federal Geographic Data Committee
FTP	file transmission protocol
GCTE	Global Change and Terrestrial Ecosystems
GIS	Geographical Information Systems
GLEAMS	Groundwater Loading Effects of Agricultural Management Systems
GPS	Global Positioning System
GRASS	Geographic Resources Analysis Support System
IAHS	International Association of Hydrological Sciences

IGBP	International Geosphere-Biosphere Programme
JSWC	Journal of Soil and Water Conservation
KINEROS	Kinematic Runoff and Erosion Model
LCTA	Land Condition-Trend Analysis
LISEM	LImberg Soil Erosion Model
MEDALUS	Mediterranean Desertification and Land Use
N	Nitrogen
NASIS	National Soil Information System
NASS	National Agricultural Statistics Service
NLCD	National Land Cover Data
NRCS	Natural Resources Conservation Service
NSERL	National Soil Erosion Research Laboratory
NCSS	National Cooperative Soil Survey
NOAA	National Oceanographic and Atmospheric Administration
NLEAP	Nitrate Leaching and Economic Analysis Package
OTA	Office of Technology Assessment
OM	organic matter
P	Phosphorus
PRISM	Parameter-elevation Regressions on Independent Slopes Model
RUSLE	Revised Universal Soil Loss Equation
SAS	Statistical Analysis Systems
SCS	Soil Conservation Service
SDR	Sediment Delivery Ratio
SEDD	Sediment Delivery Distributed
SoLIM	Soil Land Inference Model
SSSA	Soil Science Society of America
SSSD	State Soil Survey Database
SSURGO	Soil Survey Geographic Database
STATSGO	State Soil Geographic
STP	Soil Test Phosphorus
SWCS	Soil and Water Conservation Society
TMDL	Total Maximum Daily Load
USDA-ARS	U.S. Department of Agriculture-Agricultural Research Service

USDA-ERS	U.S. Department of Agriculture–Economic Research Service
USDA-NRCS	U.S. Department of Agriculture–Natural Resources Conservation Service
USDA-SCS	U.S. Department of Agriculture–Soil Conservation Service
USGS	U.S. Geological Survey
USLE	Universal Soil Loss Equation
UTM	Universal Transfers Mercator
WEPP	Water Erosion Prediction Project
WMI	Wildlife Management Institute

Conversion Tables

Table 1. Conversion factors.

Multiply:	by:	to get
	LENGTH	
in	0.0833	ft
in	0.028	yd
ft	12	in
ft	0.33	yd
ft	0.06	rods
yd	36	in
yd	3	ft
yd	0.18	rods
rods	198	in
rods	16.5	ft
rods	5.5	yd
mi	5280	ft
mi	1760	yd
mi	320	rods
	AREA	
in^2	0.007	ft^2
ft^2	144	in^2
ft^2	0.11	yd^2
yd^2	1296	in^2
yd^2	9	ft^2
yd^2	0.03	rods^2
rods^2	272.25	ft^2
rods^2	30.25	yd^2
acres	43560	ft^2
acres	4840	yd^2
acres	160	rod^2
	VELOCITY	
miles/hr	88	ft/min
miles/hr	1.47	ft/sec
	FORCE	
ounces	0.06	pounds
pounds	16	ounces
tons (short)	2000	pounds
tons (metric)	2205	pounds
	VOLUME	
ft^3	1728	in^3
ft^3	0.04	yd^3
ft^3	7.48	gallons
yd^3	27	ft^3
yd^3	202	gallons
Quarts	2	pints
Quarts	0.25	gallons
Gallons	8	pints
Gallons	4	quarts
Gallons	0.13	ft^3

Table 2. Multiple and submultiple units of the metric system.

Multiplication factor	Prefix	Symbol
1 000 000 000 000 000 000 = 10^{18}	exa	E
1 000 000 000 000 000 = 10^{15}	peta	P
1 000 000 000 000 = 10^{12}	tera	T
1 000 000 000 = 10^{9}	giga	G
1 000 000 = 10^{6}	mega	M
1 000 = 10^{3}	kilo	k
100 = 10^{2}	hecto*	h
10 = 10^{1}	deka*	da
0.1 = 10^{-1}	deci*	d
0.01 = 10^{-2}	centi*	c
0.001 = 10^{-3}	milli	m
0.000 001 = 10^{-6}	micro	μ
0.000 000 001 = 10^{-9}	nano	n
0.000 000 000 001 = 10^{-12}	pico	p
0.000 000 000 000 001 = 10^{-15}	femto	f
0.000 000 000 000 000 001 = 10^{-18}	atto	a

*Avoid when possible.

Table 3. Less common conversion factors.

Multiply:	By:	To get:
DENSITY		
lb/ft³	16.0185	kg/m³
lb/yd³	0.5933	kg/m³
PRESSURE		
psi	6894.8	Pa
ksi	6.8948	MPa
lb/ft³	47.88	Pa
VELOCTIY		
ft/sec	0.3048	m/sec
mph	0.4470	m/sec
mph	1.6093	km/hr

Water constants
Freezing point of water 0 = °C (32°F)
Boiling point of water under pressure of one atmosphere = 100°C (212°F)
The mass of one cu. meter of water is 1000 kg
The mass of one liter of water is 1 kg (2.20 lbs)
1 c. ft. of water @ 60°F = 62.37 lbs (28.29 kg)
1 gal of water @ 60°F = 8.3377 lbs (3.78 kg)

Cement constants
1 sack of cement (appx.) = 1 ft³ = 0.028 m³
1 sack of cement = 94 lbs = 42.64 kg
1 gallon water = 8.3453 lbs @ 39.2°F
1 gallon water = 3.7854 kg @ 4°C

Table 4. Conversion factors for U.S. and metric units commonly used in natural resources.

Multiply by to convert metric units to U.S. units ↓			To Convert U.S. units to metric units multiply by: ↓
LENGTH			
0.0394	inch (in)	millimeter (mm)	25.4000
00.3937	inch	centimeter (cm)	2.5400
0.0328	foot (ft)	meter (m)	30.4800
1.0936	yard (yd)	meter	0.9144
0.5468	fathom	meter	1.8288
0.1988	rod (rd)	meter	5.0292
00.004971	furlong	meter	201.1680
0.0006214	mile (U.S. statute) (mi)	meter	1,609.3440
0.6214	mile (U.S. statute)	kilometer (km)	1.6093
MASS			
0.0353	ounce (avoirdupois) (oz)	gram (g)	28.3495
2.2046	pound (avoirdupois) (lb)	kilogram (kg)	0.4536
0.0197	hundredweight (cwt)	kilogram	50.8023
1.12	ton (t)	metric ton (t)	0.8929
MASS/AREA			
0.893	pound per acre (lb/ac)	kilogram per hectare	1.12
893	pound per acre (t/ac)	metric ton per hectare (t/ha)	0.00112
0.4461	ton per acre (t/ac)	metric ton per hectare	2.2417
0.0149	bushel per acre (60 lb bu) (bu/ac)*	kilogram per hectare	67.2540
0.0159	bushel per acre (56 lb bu)	kilogram per hectare	62.7704
MASS/VOLUME			
.0624	pound per cubic foot (lb/ft³)	kilogram per cubic meter (kg/m³)	16.0185
1.3600	ton per acre-foot (t/ac-ft)	kilogram per cubic meter	0.7353
AREA			
0.1550	square inch (in²)	square centimeter (cm²)	6.4516
1,550.0031	square inch	square meter (m²)	0.000645
0.00108	square foot (ft²)	square centimeter	929.0304
10.7639	square foot	square meter (m²)	0.0929
1.1960	square yard (yd²)	square meter	0.8361
0.0002471	acre (a)	square meter	4,046.8564
2.4710	acre	hectare (ha)	.4047
247.1054	acre	square kilometer (km²)	0.004047
0.3861	square mile (section) (mi²)	square kilometer	2.5900
0.003861	square mile	hectare	258.9988
0.0107	township (36 mi²)	square kilometer	93.2396
0.0001073	township	hectare	9,323.9570

*A bushel is a unit of volume. To convert that volume measure to a weight measure, you must know what a bushel of a particular crop weighs. The two bushels shown in the conversion table are for standard weights of shelled corn (56 lb bu) and soybeans (60 lb bu).

Table 5. Conversion factors for U.S. and metric units commonly used in natural resources.

Multiply by to convert metric units to U.S. units ↓			To Convert U.S. units to metric units multiply by: ↓
VOLUME			
.0610	cubic inch (in³)	cubic centimeter (cm³)	16.3871
61,023.74	cubic inch	cubic meter (m³)	.0000164
.0000353	cubic foot (ft³)	cubic centimeter	28,316.8467
35.3146	cubic foot	cubic meter	.0283
1.3079	cubic yard (yd³)	cubic meter	.7646
423.3823	board foot (bd ft)	cubic meter	.00236
.2759	cord (cd)	cubic meter	3.6246
28.3777	bushel (bu)	cubic meter	.0352
.0008107	acre-foot (ac-ft)	cubic meter	1,233.4818
6.2898	barrel (oil, 42 U.S. gal)	cubic meter	.1590
(Liquid Measure)			
.0338	fluid ounce (fl oz)	milliliter (ml)	29.5735
33.8140	fluid ounce	liter (l)	.0296
2.1134	pint (pt)	liter	.4732
1.0567	quart (qt)	liter	.9464
.2642	gallon (gal)	liter	3.7854
(Dry Measure)			
1.8162	pint	liter	.5506
1,816.1660	pint	cubic meter	.0005506
908.1003	quart	cubic meter	.0011
227.0199	gallon	cubic meter	.0044
FLOW RATE			
35.3146	cubic food per sec. (ft³/sec)	cubic meter per second (m³/s)	.0283
2,118.880	cubic foot per minute (ft³/sec)	cubic meter per second	.00047
15,850.3220	gallon per minute (gal/min)	cubic meter per second	.0000631
78.4769	cubic yard per minute (yd³/min)	cubic meter per second	.0127
TEMPERATURE			
$t_f = 1.8t_c + 32$	degrees Fahrenheit	degrees celsius (°C)	$t_c = (t_f - 32)/1.8$
$t_f = 1.8t_k - 459.67$	degrees Fahrenheit	degrees kelvin (°K)	$t_k = (t_f + 459.67)/1.8$

Table 6. Steel tape temperature corrections.

$$C = 11.66 \cdot 10^{-6} (T_C - 20) L_m$$
$$C = 6.45 \cdot 10^{-6} (T_F - 68) L_f$$

where:
  C = Correction
  T_C = Temperature in degrees Celsius
  L_M = Length in meters
  T_F = Temperature in degrees Fahrenheit
  L_f = Length in feet

Table 7. Factors for converting domestic and metric weights and measures commonly used for agricultural commodities.

Domestic Weight		Equivalent	Metric Weight		Equivalent
1 ounce	=	28.3495 grams	1 gram	=	0.035274 ounce
1 pound	=	453.5924 grams	1 gram	=	0.0022046 pound
1 pound	=	0.455924 Kilograms	1 kilogram	=	2.204622 pounds
1 pound	=	0.0045359 m quintal	1 m quintal	=	220.4622 pounds
1 pound	=	0.0005 short ton	1 short ton	=	2,000 pounds
1 pound	=	0.0004536 metric ton	1 metric ton	=	2,204,622 pounds
1 pound	=	0.0004464 long ton	1 long ton	=	2,240 pound
1 short ton	=	0.907185 metric ton	1 metric ton	=	1.102311 short tons
1 long ton	=	1.016047 metric tons	1 metric ton	=	0.984206 long ton
1 short ton	=	0.892857 long ton	1 long ton	=	1.12 short tons
1 million pounds =		500 short tons	1 short ton	=	0.002 million pounds
1 million pounds =		453.5925 metric tons	1 metric ton	= 0.0022046 million pounds
1 million pounds=		446.4286 long tons	1 long ton	=	0.00224 million pounds

60-pound bushel of wheat, white potatoes and soybeans

1 bushel	=	0.03 short ton	1 short ton	=	33.333 bushels
1 bushel	=	0.0272155 metric ton	1 metric ton	=	36.7437 bushels
1 bushel	=	0.0267857 long ton	1 long ton	=	37.333 bushels
1 bushel	=	0.272155 metric quintal	1 metric quintal=		3.67437 bushels
1 bushel	=	27.2155 kilograms	1 kilogram	=	0.036744 bushels

56-pound bushel of shelled corn, rye, sorghum grain, and flaxseed

1 bushel	=	0.028 short ton	1 short ton	=	41.667 bushels
1 bushel	=	0.025 4 metric ton	1 metric ton	=	39.368 bushels
1 bushel	=	0.025 long ton	1 long ton	=	40 bushels

48-pound bushel of barley, buckwheat, and apples

1 bushel	=	0.024 short ton	1 short ton	=	35.714 bushels
1 bushel	=	0.021772 metric ton	1 metric ton	=	45.9296 bushels
1 bushel	=	0.021429 long ton	1 long ton	=	46.667 bushels

32-pound bushel of oats

1 bushel	=	0.016 short ton	1 short ton	=	62.5 bushels
1 bushel	=	0.014515 metric ton	1 metric ton	=	68.8944 bushels
1 bushel	=	0.014286 long ton	1 long ton	=	70 bushels

38-pound bushel of oats

1 bushel	=	0.019 short ton	1 short ton	=	52.63 bushels
1 bushel	=	0.01724 metric ton	1 metric ton	=	58.016 bushels
1 bushel	=	0.01696 long ton	1 long ton	=	58.94 bushels

Table 8. Units of the metric system.

Quantity	Unit	Symbol
acceleration	meter per second squared	m/sec²
angle, plane	radian	rad
	degree	°
angle, solid	steradian	sr
angular acceleration	radian per second squared	rad/sec²
angular velocity	radian per second	rad/sec
area	square meter	m²
density	kilogram per cubic meter	kg/m³
electric capacitance	farad	F
electric field strength	volt per meter	V/m
electric inductance	henry	H
electric potential difference	volt	V
electric resistance	ohm	Ω
electric current*	ampere	A
electromotive force	volt	V
energy	joule (Newton meter)	J
entropy	joule per kelvin	J/K
force	Newton	N
frequency	hertz	Hz
illumination	lux	lx
length*	meter	m
luminance	candela per square meter	cd/m²
luminous flux	lumen	lm
luminous intensity*	candela	cd
magnetic field strength	ampere per meter	A/m
magnetic flux	weber	Wb
magnetic flux density	tesla	T
magnetomotive force	ampere	A
mass*	gram	g
power	watt	W
pressure	Pascal (Newton/square meter)	Pa
quantity of electricity	coulomb	C
quantity of heat	joule	J
radiant intensity	watt per steradian	W/sr
specific heat	joule per kilogram-kelvin	J/kg·K
stress	pascal	Pa
thermal conductivity	watt per meter-kelvin	W/m·K
temperature*	kelvin	K
	celsius	C
time*	second	sec
velocity	meter per second	m/sec
viscosity, dynamic	newton second per square meter	N·sec/m²
viscosity, kinematic	square meter per second	m²/sec
voltage	volt	V
volume	cubic meter	m³
wave number	reciprocal meter	(wave)/m
work	joule	J

*Basic units of the metric system; all other units are derived.

Table 9. Conversion factors for U.S. and metric units with yield and rate.

To convert column 1 into column 2 multiply by: ↓	Column 1 acceptable unit	Column 2 SI unit	To convert column 2 into column 1 multiply by: ↓
35.84	32 lb bushel per acre bu/ac	kilogram per hectare kg/ha	2.79×10^{-2}
53.75	46-lb bushel per acre bu/ac	kilogram per hectare kg/ha	1.86×10^{-2}
62.71	56-lb bushel per acre bu/ac	kilogram per hectare kg/ha	1.59×10^{-2}
67.19	60-lb bushel per acre bu/ac	kilogram per hectare kg/ha	1.49×10^{-10}
9.35	gallon per acre gal/ ac	liter per hectare l/ha	0.107
1.12×10^{-2}	hunderedweight per acre cwt/ac	kilogram per hectare	0.892×10^{2} or 893
1.12	pound per acre lb/ac	kilogram per hectare kg/ha	0.893
1.12×10^{-1}	pound per acre, lb/ac	megagram per hectare Mg/ha	893
12.87	pound per acre lb/ac	kilogram per cubic meter kg/cu m	7.77×10^{-2}
16.02	pound per cubic foot lb/ft	kilogram per cubic meter kg/cu m	$6.25\ 10^{-2}$
2.24	ton (2000 lb) per acre t/ac	megagram per hectare Mg/ha	0.446

Table 10. Weights of a bushel of various agricultural commodities.

Commodity	Weight of 1 Bushel* Pounds	Weight of 1 Bushel* Kilograms	Commodity	Weight of 1 Bushel* Pounds	Weight of 1 Bushel* Kilograms
Alfalfa seed	60	27.2	Parsnips	50	22.7
Apples	48	21.8	Peaches	50	21.8
Barley	48	21.8	Peanuts, unshelled		
Beans			Virginia type	17	7.7
lima, dry	56	25.4	Spanish type	25	11.3
other, dry	60	27.2	Pears	48-50	21.8-22.7
Beets	50	25.4	Peas, dried	60	27.2
Bluegrass seed	14-30	6.4-13.6	Plums	48	21.8
Bromegrass seed	14	6.4	Popcorn, shelled	56	25.4
Buckwheat	48	21.8	Potatoes, Irish	60	27.2
Carrots	50	22.7	Potatoes, sweet	55	25.0
Castor beans	41	18.6	Rape seed	50	22.7
Cherries	40	18.1	Red top seed	14	6.4
Clover seed	60	27.2	Rice, rough	45	20.4
Corn			Rutabaga	50-56	27.2
shelled	56	25.4	Rye	56	25.4
meal	50	22.7	Ryegrass seed	22	10.0
Cottonseed	32	14.5	Sorghum grain	56	25.4
Cowpeas	60	27.2	Soybeans	60	27.2
Cucumbers	48	21.8	Sudangrass seed	40	18.1
Flax seed	56	25.0	Sweet corn	50	22.7
Grapes with stems	40	18.1	Timothy seed	45	20.4
Hemp seed	44	20.0	Tomatoes	53	25.4
Millet seed	48-50	21.8-22.7	Turnips	55	24.9
Oats	32	14.5	Vetch	60	27.2
Onions	57	25.9	Wheat	60	27.2
Orchardgrass seed	1	46.4			

* These are common weights. Legal weights may vary from state to state.

Table 11. Names applied to coarse fragments in soils.

Fragments		Descriptive terms applied to fragments that have:		
Shape	Material	Diameters less than 3 inches	Diameters from 3 to 10 inches	Diameters more than 10 inches
rounded or sub-rounded	all kinds of rock	pebble gravelly	cobblestone cobbly	stony*
irregular and angular	chert	chert fragment cherty	coarse chert fragment	stony*
	other than chert	angular pebble gravelly	angular cobblestone cobbly	stony*
		Lengths up to 6 inches	**Lengths from 6 to 15 inches**	**Lengths over 15 inches**
thin and flat	limestone, sandstone, or schist	fragment channery	flagstone flaggy	stony
	slate	slate fragment slaty	flagstone flaggy	stony
	shale	shale fragment shaly	flagstone flaggy	stony

*Bouldery is sometimes used when stones are larger than 24 inches.

Table 12. Relationship between orders of the present soil classification system used in the United States and their approximate equivalents used prior to 1996.

Present order	Approximate equivalents
1. Entisols	Azonal and some Low-Humic Gley soils
2. Vertisols	Grumusols
3. Inceptisols	Ando, Sol Brun Acide, some Brown Forest, Low-Humic Gley, and Humic Gley soils
4. Aridisols	Desert, Reddish Desert, Sierozem, Solonchak, some Brown and Red-dish Brown soils, and associated Solonetz
5. Mollisols	Chestnut, Chernozem, Brunizem (Prairie), Rendzina, some Brown, Brown Forest soils, and associated Solonetz, and Humic Gley soils
6. Spodosols	Podzols, Brown Podzolic soils, and Groundwater Podzols
7. Alfisols	Gray Brown Podzolic, Gray Wooded soils, Non-Calcic Brown soils, Degraded Chernozem, and associated Planosols, and some Half-Bog soils
8. Ultisols	Red Yellow Podzolic soils, Reddish Brown Lateritic soils of the United States, and associated Planosols and Half-Bog soils
9. Oxisols	Laterite soils, Latosols
10. Histosols	Bog soils

Table 13. Slope equivalents in grade (ratio), degree, and percent.

Grade	Degree	Percent
1/2:1	76	—
1/4:1	64	—
3/4:1	53.5	—
1:1	45	100
1 ?:1	39	80
1 ?:1	34	67
1 ?:1	31	57
2:1	27	50
2 ?:1	24.5	45
2 ?:1	22	40
2 ?:1	20	36
3:1	18.5	33
3 ?:1	17	31
3 ?:1	16	29
3 ?:1	15	27
4:1	14	25
5:1	11	20
6:1	9.5	17
7:1	8	14
8:1	7	12
9:1	6.5	11
10:1	5.5	10
15:1	4	7
20:1	3	5

Areas of Plane Figures

Figure 1.
Areas of plane figures.

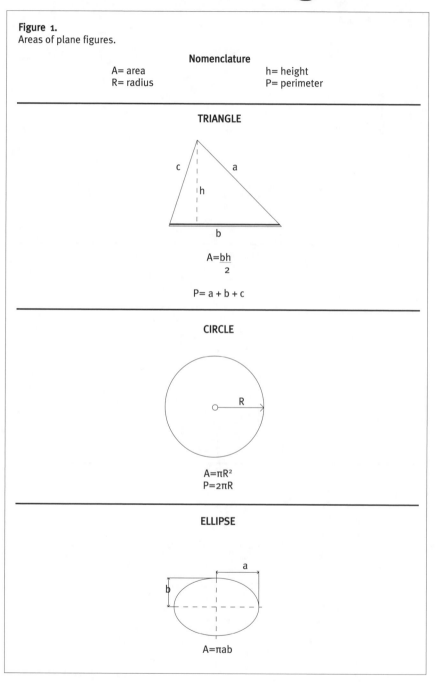

Nomenclature

A= area   h= height
R= radius   P= perimeter

TRIANGLE

$$A=\frac{bh}{2}$$

$$P= a + b + c$$

CIRCLE

$$A=\pi R^2$$
$$P=2\pi R$$

ELLIPSE

$$A=\pi ab$$

Figure 1 continued.

SEGMENT

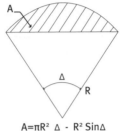

$$A = \pi R^2 \frac{\Delta}{360°} - \frac{R^2 \; Sin\Delta}{2}$$

SECTOR

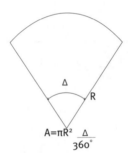

$$A = \pi R^2 \frac{\Delta}{360°}$$

$$P = 2R + \frac{\Delta}{360°} (2\pi R)$$

FILLET

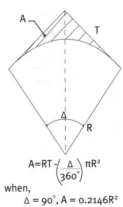

$$A = RT - \left(\frac{\Delta}{360°}\right) \pi R^2$$

when,

$$\Delta = 90°, A = 0.2146R^2$$

Figure 1 continued.
Areas of plane figures.

PARALLELOGRAM

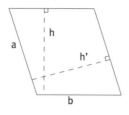

A=bh
A=ah'
P=2(a+b)

TRAPEZOID

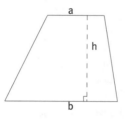

$$A=\frac{(a+b)h}{2}$$

POLYGON

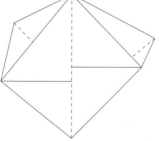

Divide into triangles
A=Sum of all triangles

Figure 1 continued.
Areas of plane figures.

ANNULUS
(CIRCULAR RING)

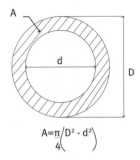

$$A = \frac{\pi}{4}\left(D^2 - d^2\right)$$

IRREGULAR FIGURE

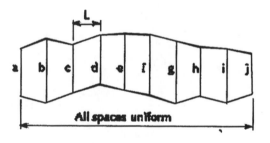

$$A = L\left(\frac{a+j}{2} + b+c+c+d+e+f+g+h+i\right)$$

A

AASHTO classification: The official classification of soil materials and soil aggregate mixtures for highway construction used by the American Association of State Highway Transportation Officials.

abatement: The process of reducing pollution levels by modifying flow of residuals into the environment.

abatement debris: Waste from remediation activities.

ABC soil: A soil that has a profile including A, B, and C master horizons. See *soil horizon.*

aberrant: Atypical, departing from the normal type or structure.

abiotic: Non living, basic elements and compounds of the environment.

abiotic factor: A physical, meteorological, geological, or chemical aspect of environment.

ablate: To remove by wearing away as by erosion.

ablation: The process of wearing away, such as the gradual removal of a surface layer in erosion or sandblasting.

abney level: An instrument suitable for direct leveling or for measuring angles or percent of slope; consists of a simple hand level, on one side of which is mounted a reversible graduated arc with pivoted bubble tube.

abrasion: The wearing away by friction, the chief agents being currents of water or wind laden with sand or other rock debris and glaciers.

abrasion test: A test made on rock materials to determine their resistance to wear during construction operations or their suitability for riprap. The Los Angeles abrasion test (ASTM No. C131) involves tumbling the dry material in a cylindrical drum with 1 7/8 inch diameter steel balls for 500 or 1,000 revolutions. Material that breaks down to smaller than No. 12 sieve size is considered the weight loss. The Deval abrasion test (ASTM No. D289) uses a similar machine, using 10,000 revolutions.

abscission: The natural process by which leaves, fruit, or other parts of plants become detached.

absorbed light: Light rays that are neither reflected nor transmitted when directed toward opaque or transparent materials.

absorbed water: Water held mechanically in a soil or rock mass and having physical properties not substantially different from ordinary water at the same temperature and pressure.

absorption: The penetration of a substance into or through another, such as the dissolving of a soluble gas in a liquid.

absorption factor: The fraction of a chemical making contact with an organism that is absorbed by the organism.

absorption loss (irrigation): The initial loss of water from a canal or reservoir by wetting of the soil when water first enters the structure.

absorption trench: A trench not over 36 inches wide with at least 12 inches of clean, coarse aggregate and a distribution pipe, covered with at least 12 inches of earth.

abutment: That part of the valley wall against which the dam is constructed. The part of a dam that contacts the riverbank. A structure that supports the ends of a dam or bridge. An artificial abutment is sometimes constructed, as a concrete gravity section, to take the thrust of an arch dam where there is no suitable natural abutment. Action or place of abutting; the part of a structure that is the terminal point or receives thrust or pressure. Defined in terms of left and right as looking away from the reservoir, looking downstream (i.e., left abutment, right abutment).

accelerated erosion: See *erosion*.

acceleration: In terms of flow, acceleration is the time rate of change of the velocity vector, either of magnitude or direction or both.

accent plant: Any plant, placed in contrast to its surroundings, that by reason of distinctive form, foliage, texture, or color attracts special attention.

accession: Plant material (plant, seed, or vegetative part) collected and assigned a number to maintain its identity during evaluation and storage.

access road: A vehicular travelway constructed to provide entry to an area.

access tube: Small diameter tube (about 50 millimeters) inserted through the soil root zone to provide passage of a neutron probe to determine the water content of soil at various depths.

acclimation: Physiological and behavioral adjustments of an organism in response to a change in environment.

acclimatization: The acclimation or adaptation of a particular species over several generations to a marked change in the environment.

accretion: The gradual addition of new land to old by the deposition of sediment carried by a stream.

acetate: A non-flammable plastic sheeting used as a base for photographic films or as a drafting base for color separation manuscripts and overlays.

acid: Any substance that yields to its solution or other substances hydrogen ions; a compound that can react with a base to form a salt.

acid deposition: A complex chemical and atmospheric phenomenon that occurs when emissions of sulfur and nitrogen compounds and other substances are transformed by chemical processes in the atmosphere, often far from the original sources, and then deposited on earth in either wet or dry form. The wet forms, popularly called "acid rain," can fall as rain, snow, or fog. The dry forms are acidic gases or particulates.

acid-forming material: Material containing sulfide minerals or other materials, which if exposed to air, water, or weathering processes will form sulfuric acid that may create acid mine drainage.

acidity, active: The activity of hydrogen ions in the aqueous phase of a soil, measured and expressed as a pH value.

acid mine drainage: Drainage discharged from an active, inactive, or abandoned mining operation containing free sulfuric acid, mainly due to the weathering of iron pyrites, and having a pH of less than 6.0.

acid gas: The anhydrous gaseous form of an acid (i.e., hydrogen chloride).

acid rain: Atmospheric precipitation that is composed of the hydrolyzed by products from oxidized halogen, nitrogen, and sulfur substances.

acid soil: A soil with a preponderence of hydrogen ions, and probably of aluminum in proportion to hydroxyl ions. Specifically, soil with a pH value less than 7.0. For most practical purposes, a soil with a pH value less than 6.6. The pH values obtained vary greatly with the method used; consequently, there is no unanimous agreement on what constitutes an acid soil. The term is usually applied to the surface layer or to the root zone unless specified otherwise.

acid spoil: Spoil material with a pH less than 6.9, containing sufficient pyrite so that weathering produces acid water. See also *spoil, toxic spoil, acid-forming material.*

acre foot: The volume of water that will cover 1 acre to a depth of 1 foot.

acre inch: The volume of water that will cover 1 acre to a depth of 1 inch.

acre value (wildlife): A value measurement of wildlife habitat; the existing wildlife habitat value of plant, water, or other cover on an acre of land compared to the maximum value of such cover if managed as wildlife habitat. Values range from a low of 0 to a high of 1.0.

AC soil: A soil having a profile containing A and C horizons with no clearly developed B horizon. See *diagnostic horizons, soil horizons.*

actinomycetes: A large group of moldlike microorganisms that give off an odor characteristic of rich earth and are the significant organisms involved in the stabilization of solid wastes by composting.

action memorandum: A document authorizing and outlining the cleanup plan that will be followed as part of a short-term cleanup.

activated carbon: A highly absorbent form of carbon, used to remove odors and toxic substances from gaseous emissions.

activated sludge: Sludge that has been aerated and subjected to bacterial action.

activated sludge process: The process of using activated sludge to hasten breakdown of organic matter in raw sewage during secondary waste treatment.

active capacity: The reservoir capacity normally usable for storage and regulation of reservoir inflows to meet established reservoir operating requirements. It extends from the highest of either the top of exclusive flood control capacity, the top of joint use capacity, or the top of active conservation capacity, to the top of inactive capacity. It is also the total capacity less the sum of the inactive and dead capacities. The reservoir capacity that can be used for irrigation, power, municipal and industrial use, fish and wildlife, recreation, water quality, and other purposes.

active conservation capacity (active storage): The reservoir capacity assigned to regulate reservoir inflow for irrigation, power, municipal and industrial use, fish and wildlife, navigation, recreation, water quality, and other purposes. It does not include exclusive flood control or joint use capacity. It extends from the top of the active conservation capacity to the top of the inactive capacity (or dead capacity where there is no inactive capacity).

active earth pressure: The minimum value of earth pressure. This condition exists when a soil mass is permitted to yield sufficiently to cause its internal shearing resistance along a potential failure surface to be completely mobilized.

active fault: A fault that has undergone movement in recent geologic time (the last 10,000 years) and may be subject to future movement.

active floodplain: The level area with alluvial soils adjacent to streams that is flooded by stream water on a periodic basis and is at the same elevation as areas showing evidence of flood channels free of terrestrial vegetation, recently rafted debris or fluvial sediments newly deposited on the surface of the forest floor or suspended on trees or vegetation, or recent scarring of trees by material moved by flood waters.

active transport: An energy-expending mechanism by which a cell moves a chemical across the cell membrane from a point of lower concentration to a point of higher concentration, against the diffusion gradient.

activity day: The measure of recreation use by one person on one facility or area for one day or part of a day.

actual use (range): The actual grazing use of a grazing unit, usually expressed as animal months or animal unit months.

acute exposure: A single exposure to a hazardous material for a brief length of time.

acute toxicity: Any toxic effect that is produced within a short period of time, usually 24 to 96 hours. Although the effect most frequently considered is mortality, the end result of acute toxicity is not necessarily death. Any harmful biological effect may be the result. See *chronic toxicity, direct toxicity.*

adaptive management: Adaptive management is based upon the premise that managed natural systems are complex and unpredictable. While there are numerous definitions of adaptive management, most include adaptive management is the process of adjusting management actions and/or directions as new and better information emerges about the ecosystem.

additive effects (pollution): The combined toxic effects of several air pollutants, acting together or independently, to cause a total response equal to the sum of the separate reactions.

adequate size farm: A farm with enough resources and productivity to generate enough income to:1) provide an acceptable level of family living; 2) pay current operating expenses; 3) pay interest on loans; and 4) allow for capital growth to keep in step with technological growth.

adhesion: Molecular attraction which holds the surfaces of two substances in contact, such as water and rock particles.

ad hoc: To establish for a specific purpose or situation.

adiabatic lapse rate: The theoretical rate at which the temperature of the air changes with altitude. In a dry atmosphere the adiabatic lapse rate is 1 degrees C per 100 meters.

adit: A horizontal or nearly horizontal passage, driven from the surface, for the working, or dewatering of a mine. See also *drift, shaft, portal.*

adjusted normalized prices: Priced used in water and related land resource development to reflect the real exchange values expected to prevail over the period of analysis; relative price

relationships and the general level of prices prevailing during the planning study will be assumed to hold generally for the future; as agricultural prices and costs are influenced by highly variable factors, such as weather, insect infestations, or sudden demand changes, it is desirable to correct for the effects of these factors by the use of a normalizing procedure.

adobe: Clayey and silty deposits found in the desert basins of southwestern North America and in Mexico; used extensively for making sun-dried brick.

absorbent (pollution): Any of several substances used to collect gaseous pollutants, either for measurement or control.

adsorption: The adhesion of a substance to the surface of a solid or liquid; often used to extract pollutants by causing them to be attached to such adsorbents as activated carbon or silica gel. Hydrophobic, or water repulsing adsorbents, are used to extract oil from waterways in oil spills.

adulterants: Chemicals or substances that by law do not belong in a food, plant, animal, or pesticide formulation. Adulterated products are subject to seizure by the Food and Drug Administration.

advanced waste treatment: Waste water treatment, beyond the secondary or biological state, that includes removal of nutrients such as phosphorus and nitrogen and a high percentage of suspended solids.

See *tertiary waste treatment.*

advance time: The time it takes water to travel the length of an irrigation furrow.

advection: The flow of air masses in a horizontal pattern due to pressure gradients.

adventitious bud: A bud product in a unusual place or part of a plant.

adverse slope: An uphill incline for hauling or skidding of logs or other loads.

advisory level: A level of chemical concentration in fish or shellfish whereby consumption of the fish would pose a human health risk. Levels may be determined by various federal or state agencies and may lead to advisories such as restricted consumption or consumption bans. Typical chemicals for which advisories exist include PCBs, chlordane, and dioxins.

advocacy planning: The preparation of plans or planning proposals and their advocacy by professional planners on behalf of an organization, interest group, or community as an alternative or in opposition to plans or planning proposals prepared by an official agency.

aeolian deposits: Wind-deposited material such as dune sands and loess deposits.

aeolian soil material: See *eolian soil material.*

aerate: To impregnate with gas, usually air.

aeration: The process of being supplied or impregnated with air; in waste treatment, the process used to foster biological and chemical purification; in soils, the process by which air in the soil is replenished by air from the atmosphere. In a well aerated soil, the soil air is similar in composition to the atmosphere above the soil. Poorly aerated soils usually contain a much higher percentage of carbon dioxide and a correspondingly lower percentage of oxygen. The rate of aeration depends largely on the volume and continuity of pores in the soil. The zone of aeration is the zone between the land surface and the water table.

aerial camera: A camera specifically designed for use in aircraft.

aerial cover: Ground area circumscribed by the perimeter of the branches and leaves of a given plant or group of plants (generally used as a measure of relative density).

aerial film: Specially designed roll-film supplied in many lengths and widths and with various emulsion types for the use in aerial cameras.

aerial photograph: A photograph of the earth's surface taken from airborne equipment, sometimes called aerial photo or air photograph. See *remote sensing.*

oblique: An aerial photograph taken with the camera axis directed between the horizontal and vertical; high oblique, the apparent horizon is shown; low oblique, the apparent horizon is not shown.

vertical: An aerial photograph made with the optical axis of the camera approximately perpendicular to the earth's surface and with the film as nearly horizontal as practicable.

aerial reconnaissance: The collection of information by visual, electronic, or photographic means from the air. See *remote sensing*.

aerial survey: A survey using photographic, electronic, or other data obtained from an airborne station.

aerial triangulation: See *phototriangulation*.

aerobic: Having molecular oxygen as a part of the environment; growing only in the presence of molecular oxygen, as aerobic organisms; occurring only in the presence of molecular oxygen (said of certain chemical or biochemical processes, such as aerobic decomposition). See *anaerobic*.

aeronautical chart: A specialized representation of mapped features of the earth, or some part of it, produced to show selected terrain, cultural, and hydrographic features and supplemental information required for air navigation, pilotage, or for planning air operations.

aerosol: Solid or liquid particles, usually less than 1 micron in diameter, suspended in a gaseous state.

aerospace: Of or pertaining to both the earth's atmosphere and space; the earth's envelope of air and space above it; the two are considered as a single realm for the flight of air vehicles and in the launching, guidance, and control of ballistic missiles, earth satellites, dirigible space vehicles, and the like.

aesthetics: The appeal or beauty of objects, animals, plants, scenes, natural or improved areas to the viewer and his appreciation for such items.

aestivate: To pass the summer in

a dormant state.

affected environment: Existing biological, physical, social, and economic conditions of an area subject to change, both directly and indirectly, as the result of a proposed human action. Also, the chapter in an environmental impact statement describing current environmental conditions.

afforestation: The artificial establishment of forest crops by planting or sowing on land that has not previously, or recently, grown trees.

afterbay (tailrace): The body of water immediately downstream from a powerplant or pumping plant. A reservoir or pool that regulates fluctuating discharges from a hydroelectric power plant or a pumping plant.

afterbay dam (reregulating dam): A dam located downstream from a large hydroelectric powerplant used to regulate discharges downstream.

afterburner: A device composed of an auxiliary fuel burner and a combustion chamber used to dissipate combustible air wastes into the atmosphere.

aftermath: The regrowth of forage crops after harvesting.

after-ripening: A curing process sometimes required by seeds, bulbs, and related structures of various plants before germination will take place.

aggradation: The process of building up a surface by deposition; a long term or geologic trend in sedimentation.

aggregate: Crushed rock or

gravel screened to sizes for use in road surfaces, concrete, or bituminous mixes.

aggregated retention: Retaining trees in patches throughout a cut-block or cutting unit.

aggregation, soil: The cementing or binding together of several to many soil particles into a secondary unit, aggregate, or granule. Water stable aggregates, which will not disintegrate easily, are of special importance to soil structure.

agitated pit: A reservoir, pit, or pond that ordinarily is not stirred or aerated, but which is mixed just before emptying to suspend any settled solids. See *holding pond*.

agribusiness: The sum of all operations involved in the production, storage, processing and wholesale marketing of agricultural products.

agrichemicals: Chemical materials used in agriculture; sometimes used erroneously to emphasize a supposed difference between "chemical materials" and "natural materials."

agricultural drainage: The process of directing excess water away from root zones by natural or artificial means, such as by using a system of pipes and drains placed below ground surface level (also called subsurface drainage). The water drained away from irrigated farmland.

agricultural economics: The application of economic principles to the agribusiness sector of the economy.

agricultural ladder: The classic path to farm ownership, that is, working as a hired hand, acquir-ing equity in livestock and equipment, renting a farm, buying a farm, and finally owning an unencumbered farm.

agricultural land: Land in farms regularly used for agricultural production; all land devoted to crop or livestock enterprises, for example, farmstead lands, drainage and irrigation ditches, water supply, cropland, and grazing land of every kind on farms.

agricultural pollution: Liquid and solid wastes from all types of farming, including runoff from pesticides, fertilizers, and feedlots; erosion and dust from plowing; animal manure and carcasses; and crop residues and debris.

Agricultural Market Transition Act (AMTA): Title I of the 1996 Act allowed farmers who participated in the wheat, feed grain, cotton, and rice programs in any one of the previous five years to enter into seven year production flexibility contracts for 1996-2002. Total production flexibility contract payment levels for each fiscal year were fixed. The AMTA allowed farmers to plant 100 percent of their total contract acreage to any crop, except for limitations on fruits and vegetables, and receive a full payment. Land had to be maintained in agricultural uses, including idling or conserving uses. Unlimited haying and grazing was allowed, as was the planting and harvesting of alfalfa and other forage corps—with no reduction in payments.

agricultural waste: Residues produced from the raising of plants and animals for food; including such things as animal manure, plant stalks, hulls, and leaves. See *waste*.

agricultural use: The use of any tract of land for the production of animal or vegetable life; uses include, but are not limited to, the pasturing, grazing, and watering of livestock and the cropping, cultivation, and harvesting of plants.

agrochemical: Synthetic chemicals (pesticides and fertilizers) used in agricultural production.

agroecosystem: Land used for crops, pasture, and livestock; the adjacent uncultivated land that supports other vegetation and wildlife; and the associated atmosphere, the underlying soils, groundwater, and drainage networks.

agronomic practices: Soil and crop activities employed in the production of farm crops, such as selecting seed, seedbed preparation, fertilizing, liming, manuring, seeding, cultivation, harvesting, curing, crop sequence, crop rotations, cover crops, stripcropping, pasture development, and others.

A horizon: See *soil horizon*.

air binding: Situation where air enters the filter media and harms both the filtration and backwash processes.

air-bound: Condition in a pipeline wherein air trapped in a summit prevents the free flow of the material in the pipeline.

air curtain: A method for mechanical containment of oil spills in which air is bubbled through a perforated pipe, causing an upward water flow that retards the spreading of oil; also used as barriers to prevent fish from entering a polluted body of water.

air drainage (soil): Renewal of soil

air by diffusion and meteorological factors, such as soil temperature changes, barometric variations, and wind action.

air dry weight: Weight of a substance after it has been allowed to dry to equilibrium with the atmosphere.

air layering: A propagation technique used to induce certain plants to produce roots above ground. See *propagation*.

air monitoring: Continuous sampling and measuring of contamination in the atmosphere.

air pollution: The presence of contaminants in the air in concentrations that prevent the normal dispersive ability of the air and that interfere directly or indirectly with man's health, safety, comfort, or the full use and enjoyment of his property.

air pollution episode: The occurrence of abnormally high concentrations of air pollutants, usually due to low winds and temperature inversion, and accompanied by an increase in illness and death. See *inversion*.

air porosity: The proportion of the bulk volume of soil that is filled with air at any given time or under a given condition, such as a specified soil water pressure; usually the large pores, that is, those drained by a tension of less than approximately 100 cm of water. See *water tension*.

air quality: Measure of the health-related and visual characteristics of the air, often derived from quantitative measurements of the concentrations of specific injurious or contaminating substances.

air quality control region: Geographical areas wherein two or more communities establish and enforce air quality standards.

air quality criteria: Levels of pollution and lengths of exposure at which adverse effects on health and welfare occur.

air quality standards: The prescribed level of pollutants in the outside air that cannot be exceeded legally during a specified time in a specified geographical area.

air resources: Those naturally occurring constituents of the atmosphere, including those gases essential for human, plant, and animal life.

airshed: A common air supply demarcated by arbitrary or convenient borders, such as an urban area.

air slaking: The process of breaking up or sloughing when an indurated soil is exposed to air.

air-space ratio: Ratio of volume of water that can be drained from a saturated soil or rock under the action of force of gravity to total volume of voids.

air sparging: Injecting air or oxygen into an aquifer to strip or flush volatile contaminants as air bubbles up through the groundwater and is captured by a vapor extraction system.

air stripping: A treatment system that removes volatile organic compounds (VOCs) from contaminated groundwater or surface water by forcing an airstream through the water and causing the compounds to evaporate.

air valve: A device to admit or release air from a pipeline automatically without permitting loss of water.

air-void ratio: The ratio of the volume of airspace to the total volume of voids in a soil mass.

air waves: Air borne vibrations caused by explosions.

Aitoff equal-area map projection: See *map projection*.

albedo: The percentage of incident global radiation reflected by a surface.

Alber conical equal-area map projection: See *map projection*.

alfalfa valve: A screw type valve placed on the end of a pipe to regulate the flow of water.

Alfisols: See *soil classification*.

algae (sing., alga): Simple plants, many microscopic, containing chlorophyll; forming the base of the food chain in aquatic environments. Some species may create a nuisance when environmental conditions are suitable for prolific growth.

algae bloom: A heavy growth of algae in and on a body of water as a result of high phosphate concentration from farm fertilizers and detergents.

algal bloom: Proliferation of living algae on the surface of lakes, streams, or ponds; stimulated by phosphate enrichment.

algicide: One of a group of plant poisons used to kill filamentous algae and phytoplankton.

algorithm: A series of well-defined steps used in carrying out a specific process; e.g., the classification algorithm. An algorithm may be in the form of a word description, an explanatory note, or a diagram or labeled flow chart.

alidade: A part of a surveying instrument, consisting of a sighting device, with index, and reading or recording accessories.

aliquot: Portion of a sample.

alkali: Any substance capable of furnishing to its solution or other substances the hydroxyl ion (OH negative); a substance having marked basic properties in contrast to acid. The important alkali metals are sodium and potassium; the term is applied less scientifically to the soluble salts, especially sulfates and chlorides of sodium, potassium, and magnesium and the carbonates of sodium and potassium, which are present in some soils of arid and semiarid regions in sufficient quantities to be detrimental to ordinary agriculture.

alkali-aggregate reaction (AAR): A deterioration of concrete by which the alkali in the cement paste in the concrete reacts chemically with the silica or carbonate present in some aggregates. In the presence of free moisture, the gel (product of the reaction) will expand and manifest into cracking and differential movement in structures as well as other deleterious effects such as reduction in freeze-thaw durability and compressive and tensile strength. Three forms of alkali-aggregate reaction have been identified, see alkali-silica reaction, the slow/late-expanding type of reaction referred to as alkali-silicate reaction, and the alkali-carbonate reaction.

alkali-silica reaction (ASR): Reaction of alkalis with aggregate with various forms of poorly crystalline reactive silica:

opal, chert, flint and chalcedony and also tridymite, crystoblite and volcanic glasses. Aggregate containing such materials (e.g., some cherty gravels) may cause deterioration of concrete when present in amounts of 1 percent to 5 percent. Concrete made of these aggregates is characterized by the early onset of a relatively rapid expansion. Cracking of structures is often observed within 10 years of construction.

alkali-silicat/silica reaction (ASSR): Reaction of alkalis with strained quartz is thought to be one reactive component of aggregates causing this reaction. A wide variety of quartz-bearing rocks have been found to be reactive including graywackes, argillites, quartzwackes, quartzarenites, quartzites, hornfels, quartz biotite, gneiss, granite, phyllite, arkose and sandstone. This type of reaction is characterized by a delayed onset of expansion and cracking may not become evident for up to 20 years after construction.

alkaline: Having the properties of an alkali; opposite of acidic.

alkaline soil: A soil that has a pH value greater than 7.0, particularly above 7.3, throughout most or all of the root zone, although the term is commonly applied to only the surface layer or horizon of a soil.

alkalinity: The quality or state of being alkaline; the concentration of OH negative ions.

alkalinity, soil: The degree or intensity of alkalinity in a soil, expressed by a value greater than 7.0 for the soil pH.

alkalinity, total: The total measurable bases (OH, HCO_3, CO_3) in a volume of water; a measure of the material's capacity to neutralize acids.

alkali soil: 1. A soil with a high degree of alkalinity (pH of 8.5 or higher) or with a high exchangeable sodium content (15 % or more of the exchange capacity) or both. 2. A soil that contains sufficient alkali (sodium) to interfere with the growth of most crop plants. See *saline alkali soil, sodic soil.*

all-aged forest: A stand that contains trees of all, or almost all, age classes including those of harvestable size.

allelopathy: Any direct or indirect harmful effect of one plant on another through production and release of chemical compounds into the environment.

allochthonous: Formed elsewhere than in situ; of foreign origin. See *autochthonous.*

allopatric: Having separate and mutually exclusive areas of geographical distribution.

allowable bearing capacity: The maximum pressure that can be permitted on foundation soil, giving consideration to all pertinent factors, with adequate safety against rupture of the soil mass or movement of the foundation of such magnitude that the structure is impaired.

allowable pile bearing load: The maximum load that can be permitted on a pile with adequate safety against movement of such magnitude that the structure is endangered.

allowable use: The degree of use of range or pastureland considered desirable and attainable, considering the present nature and condition of the resource, the management objective, and the level of investment.

alluvial: Pertaining to material that is transported and deposited by running water.

alluvial aquifer: A water-bearing deposit of unconsolidated material (sand and gravel) left behind by a river or other flowing water.

alluvial fan: A sloping, fan shaped mass of sediment deposited by a stream where it emerges from upland onto a plain.

alluvial land: Areas of unconsolidated alluvium, generally stratified and varying widely in texture, recently deposited by streams, and subject to frequent flooding; a miscellaneous land type.

alluvial valley floor: A valley bottom resulting from deposition of alluvium by water; (irrigation). Unconsolidated stream-laid deposits holding water in sufficient quantity for subirrigation or flood irrigation agricultural activity.

alluvium: A general term for all material deposited or in transit by streams, including gravel, sand, silt, clay, and all variations and mixtures of these; unless otherwise noted, alluvium is unconsolidated.

alpha particle: A positively charged particle emitted by certain radioactive materials; the least penetrating of the three common types of radiation (alpha, beta, and gamma) and usually not dangerous to plants, animals, or man.

alpine: That portion of mountains above tree growth or organisms living there.

alpine garden: A garden in which the plants used are largely derived from Alpine regions.

alternating current (AC): An electric current that reverses its direction (positive/negative values) at regular intervals.

alternatives: Courses of action that may meet the objectives of a proposal at varying levels of accomplishment, including the most likely future conditions without the project or action.

altitude: The vertical distance of a level, a point, or an object considered as a point, measured from mean sea level; angular distance above the horizon; the arc of a vertical circle between the horizon and a point on the celestial sphere, measured upward from the horizon.

altocumulus: See *cloud*.

altostratus: See *cloud*.

amalgamation: The dissolving or blending of a metal (commonly gold and silver) in mercury to separate it from its parent material.

ambient: Surrounding natural conditions or environment at a given place and time. Environmental or surrounding conditions.

ambient air: Any unconfined portion of the atmosphere; the outside air.

ambient air quality standard: A legal limit on the amount of a given pollutant that is permitted in the ambient air.

ambient temperature:

Temperature of the surrounding air (or other medium).

ambursen dam: A buttress dam in which the upstream part is a relatively thin flat slab usually made of reinforced concrete.

amenity: The preservation and enhancement of a pleasing and agreeable urban and rural environment, including attractive open spaces and landscape features, social and recreational provisions, and technical improvements designed to increase the pleasantness of life.

amides: The family of herbicides designed to retard root and shoot growth, causing stunted and malformed seedlings; most effective on grassy weeds; commercial names include Lasso, Dual, Ramrod, Bexton, Propachlor, and Alnap. See *herbicide*.

ammonia: The gaseous compound of nitrogen and hydrogen (NH_3), commonly known as anhydrous ammonia in the fertilizer industry.

ammonification: The biochemical process whereby ammoniacal nitrogen is released from nitrogen containing organic compounds.

ammonium: One form of nitrogen that is usable by plants.

ammonium fixation: The adsorption or absorption of ammonium ions by the mineral or organic fractions of the soil in such a manner that they are relatively insoluble in water and relatively unexchangeable by the usual methods of cation exchange.

amperage: The strength of an electric current measured in amperes. The amount of electric current flow, similar to the flow of water in gallons per minute (gpm).

ampere (amp): A unit of electric current or rate of flow of electrons. One volt across 1 ohm of resistance causes a current flow of 1 ampere.

amphibian: Vertebrate animals that have life stages both in water and on land (e.g., salamanders, frogs, and toads). Animals capable of living either in water or land.

amplification: Modification of the input bedrock ground motion by the overlying unconsolidation materials. Amplification causes the amplitude of the surface ground motion to be increased in some range of frequencies and decreased in others. Amplification is a function of the shear wave velocity and damping of the unconsolidated materials, its thickness and geometry, and the strain level of the input rock motion.

anabolism: Synthesis or manufacture of organic compounds within an organism. See *metabolism*.

anadromous fish: Fish that ascend rivers from the sea at certain seasons for breeding, for example, salmon, steelhead, and shad. See *catadromous*.

anaerobic: The absence of molecular oxygen; growing in the absence of molecular oxygen (such as anaerobic bacteria); occurring in the absence of molecular oxygen (as a biochemical process). See *aerobic*.

anaerobic decomposition: Dissolution process of organic matter caused by bacterial and other microbes that do not require free or dissolved oxygen for metabolism but substances such as carbohydrates, nitrates, or sulfate.

anaglyph: A stereogram in which the two views are printed or projected superimposed in complementary colors, usually red and blue. By viewing through filter spectacles of corresponding complementary colors, a stereoscopic image is formed.

analog computer: A computer that represents variables by physical analogies, using mechanical or electrical equivalent circuits as an analog for physical phenomenon, such as flow or temperature.

anatomy: The structure of a plant or animal.

ancillary data (remote sensing): Secondary data pertaining to the area or classes of interest, such as topographic, demographic, or climatological date; may be digitized and used in the analysis process in conjunction with the primary remote sensing data.

ancillary services: Other energy-related services that are required to control system frequency, to meet changing scheduling requirements, to react to changing loads and unexpected contingencies, and to ensure system stability (i.e. preventing blackouts).

andesite: Fine-grained, medium gray volcanic rock of intermediate composition between rhyolite and basalt.

angiosperm: A plant whose seeds are enclosed in a pod or seed case.

angle count method (forestry): (Angle gauge method, variable radius or plot method, point sampling, prism count method, plotless sampling, Bitterlich method.) A method used to estimate the basal area of a stand by use of an instrument (e.g., an angle gauge or prism wedge) incorporating a fixed angle, with which a 360° sweep is made from a series of sampling points, counting at each point the number of stems whose breastheight diameter appears larger than the fixed angle they subtend. The average stem number multiplied by a factor appropriate to both the fixed angle and the units of measurement chosen gives the basal area per unit of the stand. The probability of selection is proportional to the size of the variable being measured.

angle of external friction (angle of wall friction): Angle between the abscissa and the tangent of the curve representing the relationship of shearing resistance to normal stress acting between soil and surface of another material.

angle of internal friction (angle of shear resistance): The angle between the axis of normal stress and the tangent to the Mohr envelope at a point representing a given failure-stress condition for solid material.

angle of obliquity: The angle between the direction of the resultant stress or force acting on a given plane and the normal to that plane.

angle of repose: Angle between the horizontal and the maximum slope that a soil assumes through natural processes.

angle of wall friction: Angle between the abscissa and the tangent of the curve representing the relationship of shearing resistance to normal stress acting between soil and surface of another material.

angler-day: The time spent fishing by one person for any part of a day.

animal unit (AU): A measurement of livestock numbers based on the equivalent of a mature cow (approximately 1,000 pounds or 454 kilograms live weight); roughly one cow, one horse, one mule, five sheep, five swine, or six goats.

animal unit month (AUM): A measure of forage or feed requirement to maintain one animal unit for a period of 30 days.

anion: Negatively charged ion; ion which during electrolysis is attracted to the anode.

anisotropic mass: A mass having different properties in different directions at any given point.

anisotropy: Flow conditions vary with direction. Most aquifers are anisotropic.

annual energy costs: Variable costs relating to energy production in a year, usually espressed in mills per kilowatt-hour.

annual failure probability: The probability of the load multiplied by the probability of failure.

annual flood: The highest peak discharge in a water year.

annual (growth) layer: A growth layer produced in one year; or viewed on the cross section of a stem, branch, or root. In the temperate zone, layer and year generally coincide.

annual inspection (AI): Annual inspections of a dam and appurtenant facilities are conducted by the local operating office. These examinations address both O&M and dam safety issues and use an "Annual Inspection Checklist" to aid in the examination and formal documentation of the inspection.

annual load factor: This factor is equal to energy generated in a year divided by the product of the peak demand for that year and the number of total hours in a year.

annual plant: A plant that completes its life cycle and dies in 1 year or less.

annualized loss of life: The sum of the probability of dam failure multiplied by the annual probability of the loading and the estimated number of lives that would be lost (consequences) for each dam failure scenario under a particular loading category (i.e. probability of failure, probability of load, potential loss of life).

annular: Ring-shaped.

annular space: A ring-shaped space located between two circular objects, such as two pipes.

annuity: A series of equal payments made at equal intervals of time.

anomalies: As related to fish, externally visible skin or subcutaneous disorders, including deformities, eroded fins, lesions, and tumors.

anoxic: Without oxygen.

antagonsim (pollution): The combined toxic reaction of several air pollutants, acting simultaneously or independently, to cause a total response less than their separate effects.

antecedent flood: A flood or series of floods assumed to occur prior to the occurrence of an inflow design flood (IDF).

antecedent soil water: Degree of wetness of a soil prior to irrigation or at the beginning of a runoff period, expressed as an index or as total inches soil water.

anterior end: The shorter end of the shell as measured from the umbo; also considered the front end.

anthropogenic: Human-created.

anthropogenic heat: Anthropogenic heat is man-made heat generated by buildings, people, or machinery. Estimates of anthropogenic heat generation can be made by totaling all the energy used for heating and cooling, running appliances, transportation, and industrial processes. Anthropogenic heat is small in rural areas, becoming larger in dense urban areas. It is not usually large enough to be a significant factor in summertime heat island formation, but has a more significant impact on wintertime heat islands.

anticline: A fold in rocks that curves upward in a convex way. Upward fold in rock layers that creates an arched or domelike uplift of sedimentary layers. See *syncline.*

anti degradation clause: A provision in air quality standards that prohibits deterioration of air quality in areas where the pollution levels are presently below those allowed by the standards.

ap: The surface layer of a soil disturbed by cultivation or pasturing.

aphotic zone: That portion of a body of water to which light does not penetrate with sufficient intensity to have any biological significance. See *euphotic zone.*

application efficiency: See *water application efficiency.*

appraisal, range: An evaluation of

the capacity of range lands to produce income, which includes not only consideration of grazing capacity, but also facilities for handling livestock, accessibility, and relation to other feed sources. The classification and evaluation of a range from an economic and production standpoint.

approach channel: The channel upstream from that portion of the spillway having a concrete lining or concrete structure. Channel upstream from intake structure of an outlet works. Channel is generally unlined, excavated in rock or soil, with or without riprap, soil cement or other types of erosion protection.

appropriated rights, water: See *water rights.*

appropriation: Amount of water legally set apart or assigned to a particular purpose or use.

appropriative: Water rights to or ownership of a water supply which is acquired for the beneficial use of water by following a specific legal procedure.

appurtentant structures: Outlet works, spillways, bridges, drain systems, tunnels, towers, etc.

apron (soil engineering): A floor or lining to protect a surface from erosion, for example, the pavement below chutes, spillways, or at the toes of dams.

aquatic: Growing in, living in, or dependent upon water.

aquatic algae: Microscopic plants that grow in sunlit water containing phosphates, nitrates, and other nutrients.

aquatic barrier: Any obstruction to fish passage.

aquatic ecosystems: Basic ecolog-ical unit composed of living and non-living elements interacting in an aqueous environment.

aquatic guidelines: Specific levels of water quality which, if reached, may adversely affect aquatic life. These are nonenforceable guidelines issued by a governmental agency or other institution.

aquatic plants: Plants growing in or near water with true roots, stems, and leaves; other than algae.

aqueduct: Man-made canal or pipeline used to transport water.

aqueous: Something made up of water.

aqueous solubility: The maximum concentration of a chemical that will dissolve in pure water at a reference temperature.

aquic: A mostly reducing soil moisture regime nearly free of dissolved oxygen due to saturation by groundwater or its capillary fringe and occurring at periods when the soil temperature at 50 cm is above 5 degrees C.

aquiclude: A layer of clay which limits the movement of groundwater.

aquifer: A geologic formation or structure that transmits water in sufficient quantity to supply the needs for a water development; usually saturated sands, gravel, fractures, and cavernous and vesicular rock. The term water bearing is sometimes used synonymously with aquifer when a stratum furnishes water for a specific use.

aquitard: A rock unit with relatively low permeability that retards the flow of water.

arable land: Land so located that

production of cultivated crops is economical and practical.

arboretum: A collection of plants, trees, and shrubs grown for public exhibition; for public enjoyment, recreation, education, or research.

arboriculture: The planting, care, and tending of trees and shrubs, individually or in small groups, for shade or landscape effects.

arch dam: Curved masonry or concrete dam, convex upstream, that depends on arch action for its stability. The load is transferred by the arch to the abutments.

archeological area: Any location containing significant relics and artifacts of past cultures that is set aside for preservation, study, or public exhibition.

archimedean screw: An ancient water-raising device attributed to Archimedes, made up of a spiral tube coiled about a shaft or of a large screw in a cylinder, revolved by hand. A pump consisting of an inclined, revolving, corkscrew-shaped shaft tightly enclosed in a pipe.

arching: The transfer of stress from a yielding part of a soil or rock mass to adjoining less-yielding or restrained parts of the mass.

area curve (channel hydraulics): Commonly used to describe a plotting of stage or elevation versus cross sectional area. (reservoir): A plotting of stage or elevation versus the associated water surface area.

area mining: Surface mining that is carried on in level to gently rolling topography on relatively large tracts.

area source: Geographic source from which air pollution originates.

argillan: See *clay film.*

argillic horizon: See *diagnostic horizons.*

arid climate: Regions that lack sufficient moisture for crop production without irrigation. The limits of precipitation vary considerably according to temperature conditions, with an upper annual limit for cool regions of 10 inches (25.4 cm) or less and for tropical regions as much as 15 to 20 inches (38.1-50.8 cm)

aridic: A soil moisture regime that has no moisture available for plants for more than half the cumulative time that the soil temperature at 50 cm is above 5 degrees C, and has no period as long as 90 consecutive days when there is moisture for plants while the soil temperature at 50 cm is continuously above 8 degrees C.

aridisols: See *soil classification.*

arroyo: A gully, usually of ephemeral flow and with two or more feet of unconsolidated alluvium forming vertical walls.

artesian water: Water confined under enough pressure to cause it to rise above the level where it is encountered in drilling. Flowing artesian wells are produced when the pressure is sufficient to force the water above the land surface.

artesian well: Water held under pressure in porous rock or soil confined by impermeable geologic formations. An artesian well is free flowing.

artificial drains: Man-made or constructed drains.

artificial recharge: Addition of surface water to a groundwater reservoir by human activity, such as putting surface water into spreading basins.

artifical regeneration: Establishing a new forest by planting seedlings or by direct seeding (as opposed to natural regeneration).

artificial substrate: A device placed in the water for a specified period of time that provides living spaces for a multiplicity of organisms (e.g., glass slides, concrete blocks, multiplate samplers, or rock baskets); used primarily to collect organisms in areas where the physical habitat is limiting or cannot be adequately sampled using conventional methods.

A scale sound level: The measurement of sound approximating the auditory sensitivity of the human ear; used to measure the relative noisiness or annoyance of common sounds.

ash: The incombustible material that remains after a fuel or solid waste has been burned.

ash-free basis: The method whereby the weight of ash in a fuel sample is subtracted from its total weight and the adjusted weight is used to calculate the percent of certain constituents present, e.g., the percent of fixed carbon (FC) on an ash-free basis is computed as follows:

FC (weight) x 100= ash-free FC Sample (weight) − ash (weight)

ash sluice: A trench or channel in which water transports residue from an ash pit to a disposal or collection point.

aspect: The viewing direction from or to an object, such as the southern aspect or view from a scenic overlook, and what would be seen from that aspect.

aspect (forestry): The direction that a slope faces.

assemblage: In conservation biology, a predictable and particular collection of species within a biogeographic unit. (e.g., ecoregion or habitat)

assimilation: In biology, the conversion or incorporation of absorbed nutrients into protoplasm; in water pollution, the ability of a body of water to purify itself of organic pollution.

associated costs (water resources): In water resource development projects, the value of goods and services needed over and above project costs to make the immediate products or services of a project available for use or sale.

association: A climax plant community identified by the combination of dominant species present. See *soil association*.

astrometry: The branch of astronomy dealing with the geometric relations of the celestial bodies and their real and apparent motions; used in tracking satellites and space probes.

at-rest earth pressure: The value of the earth pressure when the soil mass is in its natural state without having been permitted to yield or without having been compressed.

atlas grid: A reference system that permits the designation of the location of a point or an area on a map, photo, or other graphic in terms of numbers and letters; also called alphanumeric grid.

atmosphere: The layer of air surrounding the earth.

atmospheric area: An air shed in

which all environmental conditions influence the capacity of the atmosphere to dilute and disperse air pollutants.

atmospheric deposition: The transfer of substances from the air to the surface of the Earth, either in wet form (e.g., rain, fog, snow, dew, frost, hail) or in dry form (e.g., gases, aerosols, particles).

atmospheric pressure: Pressure of air enveloping the earth, averaged as 14.7 psi at sea level, or 29.92 inches of mercury as measured by a standard barometer.

atmospheric windows: Those wavelength ranges where radiation can pass through the atmosphere with relatively little attenuation; in the optical portion of the spectrum, approximately 0.3 to 2.5, 3.0 to 4.0, 4.2 to 5.0, and 7.0 to 15.0 micrometers.

atom: The smallest portion of an element that can take part in a chemical reaction.

atomic pile: A nuclear reactor.

Atterberg limits: Atterberg limits are measured for soil materials passing the No. 40 sieve. They include:

shrinkage limit (SL): The maximum water content at which a reduction in water content will not cause a decrease in the volume of the soil mass. This defines the arbitrary limit between the solid and semisolid states.

plastic limit (PL): The water content corresponding to an arbitrary limit between the plastic and semisolid states of consistency of a soil.

liquid limit (LL): The water content corresponding to the arbitrary limit between the liquid and plastic states of consistency of a soil.

plasticity index (PI): The numerical difference between the liquid limit and plastic limit.

shrinkage index (SI): The numerical difference between the plastic and shrinkage limits.

attitude (geology): The relation of some directional features to a rock in a horizontal surface.

attractant: A chemical or agent that lures insects or other pests by olfactory stimulation. See *pheromone*.

attribute sampling: Sampling where the characteristics under consideration are attributes.

aufwuchs: See *periphyton*.

auger: Any drilling device in which the cutting are mechanically and continuously removed from a borehole without the use of fluids.

auger mining: Mining that utilizes a machine designed on the principle of the auger, boring into an exposed coal seam, and conveying the coal to a storage pile or bin for loading and transporting.

autecology: The study of the individual, or members of a species collectively, in relation to environmental conditions.

autochthonous: Pertaining to those substances, materials, or organisms originating within a particular waterway and remaining in that waterway. See *allochthonous*.

automatic data processing system (ADP): An electronic system that includes an electronic data processing system plus auxiliary and connecting communications equipment.

automated system (irrigation): An irrigation system using timers or self propulsion to reduce labor requirements in the application of irrigation water.

automatic system pumping: A system whereby the pumping unit starts and stops automatically in response to an automatic control, such as a float switch.

autotroph: An organism that manufactures its own food, such as a plant.

autotrophic: Self nourishing; denoting those organisms that do not require an external source of organic materials such as green plants, pigmented flagellates. See *heterotrophic*.

auxiliary spillway: A dam spillway built to carry runoff in excess of that carried by the principal spillway.

available capacity: The amount of water held in the soil that is available to the plants.

available forage: Forage that is accessible for animal consumption.

available nutrient: That portion of any element or compound in the soil that readily can be absorbed and assimilated by growing plants. Not to be confused with exchangeable.

available volumes: The portion of total inventory volumes that is available for harvesting after all management constraints on timber harvesting have been considered, including definition of the timber harvesting land base, age of tree merchantability, deferrals and any other priorities or constraints on timber harvesting.

available water: The portion of water in a soil that can be absorbed by plant roots; usually that water held in the soil against a soil water pres-

sure of up to approximately 15 bars. See *field capacity*.

available water capacity (soils): The capacity to store water available for use by plants, usually expressed in linear depths of water per unit depth of soil; the difference between the percentage of soil water at field capacity and the percentage at wilting point. This difference multiplied by the bulk density and divided by 100 gives a value in surface inches of water per inch depth of soil. See *field capacity, wilting point*.

average annual runoff: For a specified area, the average value of annual runoff amounts calculated for a selected period of record that represents average hydrologic conditions.

average degree of consolidation: The ratio of the total volume change in a soil mass at a given time to the total volume change anticipated in the soil mass due to primary consolidation.

average long term yield: The annual average of the total yield over the next 200 years minus unsalvaged losses. This figure is generally greater than the long run sustained yield due to the influence of cutting old growth timber in the first few decades.

average year water demand: Demand for water under average hydrologic conditions for a defined level of development.

average year supply: The average annual supply of a water development system over a long period.

avoidable waste: The volume of timber left on the harvested area that should have been removed in accordance with the utilization standards in the cutting authority. It does not include the volume of timber that could not be removed because of physical impediments, safety considerations, or other reasons beyond the control of the licensee. Avoidable waste volumes are billed monetarily, as well as for cut control.

axil: The angular space between a plant stem and the base of a leaf growing out of the stem.

axillary bud: A bud found in the axil of a leaf.

azimuth: The direction of a line given as an angle, measured clockwise from a reference direction, usually true north.

B

back blade: To drag the blade of a bulldozer or grader in the down position as the machine moves backward, as opposed to pushing the blade forward.

backfill: The material used to refill a ditch or other excavation, or the process of doing so.

backfire: A fire started intentionally ahead of an advancing fire to remove flammable material by controlled burning and thus stop or control the main fire.

backflow: A reverse flow condition, created by a difference in water pressures, which causes water to flow back into the distribution system.

backfurrow: The first cut of a plow, from which the slice is laid on undisturbed soil.

background concentration: A concentration of a substance in a particular environment that is indicative of minimal influence by human (anthropogenic) sources.

background level: Amounts of pollutants present in the ambient air due to natural sources, such as marsh gases, pollen.

backhoe tamping: A processing step, often used in direct dump transfer systems, in which a conventional backhoe is used to compact waste contained in an open top transfer trailer.

backlog: A Ministry of Forests term applied to forest land areas where silviculture treatments such as planting and site preparation are overdue. Planting is considered backlog if more than five years have elapsed since a site was cleared (by harvesting or fire) in the interior and more than three years on the coast of British Columbia.

back pressure: A pressure that can

cause water to backflow into the water supply when a user's waste water system is at a higher pressure than the public system.

back scatter: The scattering of radiant energy into the hemisphere of space bounded by a plane normal to the direction of the incident radiation and lying on the same side as the incident ray; the opposite of forward scatter; also called backscattering. In radar usage, backscatter generally refers to that radiation reflected back toward the source.

backsight: A sight on a previously established survey point or line; (traverse) a sight on a previously established survey point, which is not the closing sight of the traverse; (leveling) a reading on a rod held on a point whose elevation has been previously determined and which is not the closing sight of a level circuit; any such rod reading used to determine height of instrument prior to making a foresight; also called plus sight.

backsiphonage: A form of backflow caused by a negative or below atmospheric pressure within a water system.

backwashing: Reversing the flow of water back through the filter media to remove entrapped solids.

backwater: A small, generally shallow body of water with little or no current of its own. Stagnant water in a small stream or inlet. Water moved backward or held back by a dam, tide, etc.

bacteria: Single cell, microscopic organisms that possess rigid cell walls. They may be aerobic, anaerobic, or facultative; they can cause disease; and some are important in

the stabilization of solid wastes.

badlands: Areas of steep or very steep barren land, usually broken by an intricate maze of narrow ravines, sharp crests, and pinnacles resulting from serious erosion of soft geologic materials. Most common in arid or semiarid regions. A miscellaneous land type.

baffles: Vanes, guides, grids, grating, or similar devices placed in a conduit to deflect or regulate flow and effect a more uniform distribution of velocities.

bagasse: The fibrous residue that remains after juice is extracted from sugar cane or sugar beets.

baghouse: An air pollution abatement device used to trap particulates by filtering gas streams through large fabric bags, usually made of glass fibers.

bailer: A pipe with a valve at the lower end, used to remove slurry from the bottom or side of a well as it is being drilled, or to collect groundwater samples from wells or open boreholes; a tube of varying length.

balanced head condition: The condition in which the water pressure on the upstream and downstream sides of an object are equal (such as an emergency or regulating gate).

baler: A machine used to compress and bind solid waste or other materials.

baling: A means of reducing the volume of solid waste by compaction.

ball-milling: The repeated churning action of cobbles, gravel, and sand caused by the force of water in a stilling basin or other structure by which severe concrete abrasion can occur.

balled and burlapped: Nursery plant stock dug for transplanting, in which the soil around roots is undisturbed; the ball of earth is then bound in burlap or similar mesh fabrics.

ballistic separator: A machine that separates inorganic from organic matter in a composting process.

band: Any number of sheep or goats handled as a single unit under range conditions, usually considered synonymous with herd.

band application: The application of a chemical pesticide over or next to each row of plants in a field.

band seeding: Seeding of grasses and legumes in a row one to two inches directly above a band of fertilizer.

band, spectral: An interval in the electromagnetic spectrum defined by two wavelengths, frequencies, or wave numbers.

bandwidth: In an antenna, the range of frequencies within which its performance, in respect to some characteristic, conforms to a specified standard; in a wave, the least frequency interval outside of which the power spectrum of a time-varying quantity is everywhere less than some specified fraction of its value at a reference frequency; the number of cycles per second between the limits of a frequency band.

bank: The sloping ground that borders a stream and confines the water in the natural channel when the water level, or flow, is normal.

bank full: An established river stage at a given location along a river which is intended to represent the maximum safe water level that will not overflow the river banks or cause any significant damage within the river reach.

bank storage: Water absorbed by the bed and banks of a stream, reservoir, or channel and returned in whole or in part as the water level falls.

bare-rooted: Nursery plant stock dug for transplanting from which the soil is removed from around the roots.

barrage (gate-structure dam): A barrier built across a river, comprising a series of gates which when fully open allow the flood to pass without appreciably increasing the flood level upstream of the barrage.

barrel: A liquid-volume measure commonly used in expressing quantities of petroleum products; equal to 42 US gallons or 15.9 decaliters.

barrel sampler: Open-ended steel tube used to collect soil samples.

barrier island: Refers to a long, narrow island running parallel to the mainland, built up by waves and currents and protecting the coast from erosion by surf and tidal surges.

bar scale: See *graphic scale.*

bar screen: In waste water treatment, a screen that removes large floating and suspended solids.

basal area: In forestry, the area of the cross section (measured inside or outside the bark, usually the latter) of a single tree or of all trees in a stand, usually expressed in square feet; in range, the area of ground surface covered by the stem or stems of a range plant, usually measured one inch above the soil, in contrast to the full spread of the foliage.

basal application: The application of a pesticide on the stems or trunks of plants just above the soil line.

basalt: Fine-grained, dark-colored volcanic rock rich in iron-bearing minerals.

base course: A layer of specified or selected material of planned thickness constructed on the subgrade or subbase for the purpose of serving one or more functions such as distributing load, providing drainage, minimizing frost action, etc.

base exchange capacity (obsolete): See *cation exchange capacity*.

base flow: The stream discharge from groundwater runoff.

base level: The theoretical limit toward which erosion constantly tends to reduce the land. Sea level is the general base level, but in the reduction of the land there may be many temporary base levels which, for the time being, the streams cannot reduce. These temporary base levels may be controlled by the level of a lake or river into which the stream flows or by a particularly resistant stratum of rock that the stream has difficulty in removing.

base line: A surveyed line established with more than usual care, to which surveys are referred for coordination and correlation.

base map: A map showing certain basic data to which other information may be added.

base period: A period of time from which comparisons of other time periods are made, normally used with reference to price, population, production, or other statistics.

base saturation percentage: The extent to which the adsorption complex of a soil is saturated with exchangeable cations other than hydrogen; expressed as a percentage of the total cation exchange capacity.

baseloading: Running water through a powerplant at a roughly steady rate, thereby producing power at a steady rate.

basic crops: Crops such as corn, wheat, and cotton that are most important in the agricultural economy due to acreage, value, or climate.

basic fixed sites: Sites on streams at which streamflow is measured and samples are collected for temperature, salinity, suspended sediment, major ions and metals, nutrients, and organic carbon to assess the broad-scale spatial and temporal character and transport of inorganic constituents of streamwater in relation to hydrologic conditions and environmental settings.

basic intake rate: The nearly constant infiltration rate of soil after the soil has been thoroughly wetted. See *infiltration*.

basic silviculture: Harvesting methods and silviculture operations including seed collecting, site preparation, artificial and natural regeneration, brushing, spacing and stand tending, and other operations that are for the purpose of establishing a free growing crop of trees of a commercially valuable species and are required in a regulation, pre-harvest silviculture prescription or silviculture prescription.

basin: In hydrology, the area drained by a river; in irrigation, a level plot of field, surrounded by dikes, which may be flood irrigated.

basin and range physiography: A region characterized by a series of generally north-trending mountain ranges separated by alluvial valleys.

basin irrigation: A method of irrigation in which a level or nearly level area, surrounded by an earth ridge or dike, is flooded with water.

basin lister: See *lister*.

bathyal zone: That region of the sea that extends from the euphotic zone to the bottom of the continental slope. Density of life in this zone depends on organic material settling from the euphotic zone and is generally inversely proportional to the depth.

batter board: One of a series of horizontal boards set across or to one side of a trench line to indicate a desired level of reference grade from which ditch or trench elevations are determined.

beaching: The action of water waves by which beach materials settle into the water because of removal of finer materials.

bearing capacity: The maximum load that a material can support before failing.

Beccari process: A composting process in which anaerobic fermentation is followed by a final stage in which decomposition proceeds under partially aerobic conditions.

bedding: In soil engineering, a method of surface drainage consisting of narrow width plowlands in which the dead furrows run parallel to the prevailing land slope and are used as field drains; also known as crowning or ridging; in engineering, the process of laying a drain or other conduit in its trench and tamping earth around the conduit to form its bed; in geology, the arrangement of sediment and sedimentary rock in layers, strata, or beds more than 1 centimeter thick. See *lamination*. In agriculture, a method of preparing seedbeds for row crop culture; also used for irrigation or drainage.

bedding, animal: Material, usually organic, that is placed on the floor of livestock quarters for animal comfort and to absorb excreta.

bedding plane: The division that separates the individual layers in a sedimentary or stratified rock or sediment.

bedding ground: An area where animals sleep and rest.

bed elevation: Height of streambed above a specified level.

bed layer: The flow layer, several grain diameters thick (usually taken as two grain diameters thick), immediately above the bed.

bedload: The sediment that moves by sliding, rolling, or bounding on or very near the streambed; sediment moved mainly by tractive or gravitational forces or both but at velocities less than the surrounding flow.

bedload discharge: The quantity of bed load passing a cross section of a stream in a unit of time.

bed material: Unconsolidated material, or sediment mixture, of which a streambed is composed.

bed-material discharge: That part of the total sediment discharge which is composed of grain sizes found in the bed. The bed-material discharge is assumed equal to the transport capability of the flow.

bed planting: A method of crop planting in which several rows; sometimes no wider than two crop rows, are planted on an elevated bed, with bed being separated by furrows or ditches.

bedrock: The solid rock underlying soils and the regolith in depths ranging from zero (where exposed by erosion) to several hundred feet.

bed sediment: The material that temporarily is stationary in the bottom of a stream or other watercourse.

bed sediment and tissue studies: Assessment of concentrations and distributions of trace elements and hydrophobic organic contaminants in streambed sediment and tissues of aquatic organisms to identify potential sources and to assess spatial distribution.

bench (mining): The surface of an excavated area at some point between the material being mined and the original surface of the ground on which equipment can be set, moved, or operated; a working road or base below a highwall, as in contour stripping for coal.

bench flume: Flume built on constructed benches or terraces along hillsides or around mountain slopes when the ground is too rough or too steep to permit the use of an excavated canal.

benchmark: In economics, data for a specific time period that is used as a base for comparative purposes with comparable data; a fixed reference, usually placed on or near the ground, giving the measurement in elevation of that point in relation to mean sea level or some other reference datum.

bench terrace: See *terrace*.

benefit–cost ratio: An economic indicator of the efficiency of a proposed project, computed by dividing benefits by costs, usually, both the benefits and costs are discounted so that the ratio reflects efficiency in terms of the present value of future benefits and costs. See *discount rate*.

benthic: Refers to plants or animals that live on the bottom of lakes, streams, or oceans.

Benthic invertebrates: Insects, mollusks, crustaceans, worms, and other organisms without a backbone that live in, on, or near the bottom of lakes, streams, or oceans.

benthic region: The bottom of a body of water, supporting the benthos.

benthos: The plant and animal life whose habitat is the bottom of a sea, lake, or river.

bentonite: A highly plastic clay consisting of the minerals montmorillonite and beidellite that swells extensively when wet.

benzoics: A family of herbicides that cause abnormal shoot and root growth by upsetting plant hormone (auxin) balance; when soil applied, uptake is through roots or seeds; applied post-emergence, uptake can be through leaves; commercial names include Amiben, Banvil. See *herbicide*.

berm: A shelf or flat area that breaks the continuity of a slope.

best management practice (BMP): A practice or combination of practices that are determined by a state or designated areawide planning agency to be the most effective and practicable (including technological, economic, and institutional considerations) means of controlling point and nonpoint pollutants at levels compatible with environmental quality goals.

beta particle: A high-speed electron or positron, especially one emitted in radioactive decay; intermediate in its ability to penetrate of the three common types of radiation (alpha, beta, gamma).

B horizon: See *soil horizon*.

bicarbonate alkalinity: Alkalinity caused by the bicarbonate ions.

biennial plant: A plant that requires two years to complete its life cycle.

binary: A numbering system based on 2s rather than 10s and that uses only the digits 0 and 1 when written.

binomial: Scientific name of plants or animals which has two parts: a genus and a species name.

bioaccumulation: A build up of specific organic compounds within tissues of given organisms; usually applied to certain heavy metals, pesticides, or metabites.

bioassay: The employment of living organisms to determine the biological effect of some substance, factor, or condition.

bioassimilation: The accumulation of a substance within a habitat.

bioavailability: The capacity of a chemical constituent to be taken up by living organisms either through physical contact or by ingestion.

biodiversity: The variety of life and its processes and includes the variety of living organisms, the genetic differences among them, and the communities and ecosystems in which they occur.

biochemical: Refers to chemical processes that occur inside or are mediated by living organisms.

biochemical oxidation: The process by which bacteria and other microorganisms feed on complex organic materials and decompose them. Self purification of waterways and activated sludge and trickling filter wastewater treatment processes depend on this principle.

biochemical oxygen demand (BOD): A measure of the oxygen used in meeting the metabolic needs of aerobic microorganisms in water rich in organic matter; also called biological oxygen demand.

biocoenosis: The plants and animals comprising a community.

bioconverision: Conversion of one form of energy into another by plants or microorganism.

biodegradable: The significant breakdown by microorganisms of the physical and/or chemical structure of a compound.

biogenic hydrocarbons: Biogenic hydrocarbons are naturally occurring compounds, including VOCs (volatile organic compounds) that are emitted from trees and vegetation. High VOC-emitting tree species like eucalyptus can contribute to smog formation. Species-specific biogenic emission rates may be an important consideration in large-scale tree plantings, especially in areas with high ozone

concentrations.

biogeoclimatic classification system: A hierarchical classification system of ecosystems that integrates regional, local and chronological factors and combines climatic, vegetation and site factors.

biogeoclimatic unit: Part of the biogeoclimatic ecosystem classification system. The recognized units are a synthesis of climate, vegetation and soil data and defined as classes of geographically related ecosystems that are distributed within a vegetationally inferred climatic space.

biogeoclimatic zone: A geographic area having similar patterns of energy flow, vegetation and soils as a result of a broadly homogenous macroclimate.

biological availability: That portion of a chemical compound or element that can be taken up readily by living organisms.

biological control: A method of controlling pest organisms by means of introduced or naturally occurring predatory organisms, sterilization, the use of inhibiting hormones, or other methods, rather than by mechanical or chemical means.

biological diversity: The variety of life and life processes, and includes the levels of landscape, community, species, and genetics.

biological herbicide: A naturally occurring substance or organism which kills or controls undesirable vegetation. Preferred over synthetic chemicals because of reduced toxic effect on the environment.

biological integrity: The biotic composition, structure, and functioning at genetic, organism, and community levels consistent with natural conditions, including the natural biological processes that shape genomes, organisms, and communities.

biological legacies: Features which remain on a site or landscape after a natural disturbance. These legacies include live and dead trees, coarse woody debris, soil organic matter, plants, fungi, micro-organisms and seeds.

biological magnification: The increasing concentration of a substance along succeeding steps in a food chain.

biological oxidation: See *biochemical oxidation.*

biological oxygen demand (BOD): See *biochemical oxygen demand.*

biology: The scientific study of life.

biomass: The total amount of living material in a particular habitat or area; an expression of the total weight of a given population of organisms.

biome: A major biotic unit consisting of plant and animal communities having similarities in form and environmental conditions.

biomonitoring: Continuous surveillance of an effluent (or dilution thereof) by using living organisms to test its suitability for discharge into a receiving water; use of living organisms to test the quality of a receiving water downstream from a waste discharge. See *bioassay.*

biosphere: The term "Biosphere" was coined by the Russian scientist Vladimir Vernadsky in 1929. It refers to the relatively thin vertical zone of air, soil, and water that extends from the deepest ocean floor up roughly six miles in to the atmosphere. The biosphere is often divided into distinct biomes that represent the interactions between groups of organisms forming a trophic pyramid and the environment or habitat in which they live.

biostabilizer: A machine used to convert solid waste into compost by grinding and aeration.

biota: The flora and fauna of a region.

biota influence: The influence of animals and plants on associated plant or animal life as contrasted with climatic influences and edaphic (soil) influences.

biotechnology: Techniques that use living organisms or parts of organisms to produce a variety of products (from medicines to industrial enzymes) to improve plants or animals or to develop microorganisms to remove toxics from bodies of water, or act as pesticides.

biotic community: A general term to designate biotic sociological units of all degrees, from the simplest (as unrooted mat of algae) to the most

complext ecosystem (as a mul-
tistoried rain forest).

biotic factors: In ecology, those
environmental factors which are
the result of living organisms and
their activities, distinct from
physical and chemical factors,
such as competition and predation. See *ecological factor.*

biotic potential: Inherent
capacity of an organism to
reproduce and survive, which
is pitted against limiting influences of the environment.

biotype: A group of individuals
occurring in nature, all with
essentially the same genetic
constitution. A species usually
consists of many biotypes. See
habitat.

bituminous: Containing asphalt
or tar.

blackbody (remote sensing):
An ideal body, which if it
existed, would be a perfect
absorber and a perfect radiator, absorbing all incident radiation, reflecting none, and
emitting radiation at all wavelengths. Emittance curves of
black blues at various temperatures can be used to model
naturally radiation and terrestrial emiissivty.

blackwater: Water that contains
animal, human, or food waste.

blade: The cutting part of an
instrument; as, the blade of a
tractor propelled earthmoving
vehicle for clearing land, building roads, airfields, and the like.
Types used in earthmoving
include:

earth: A heavy, broad plate that
is connected to the front of a
tractor and is used to push and

spread soil or other material.

landfill: A U blade with an
extension on top that increases the volume of solid wastes
that can be pushed and spread,
and protects the operator from
any debris thrown out of the
solid waste.

u blade: A dozer blade with
an extension on each side;
they protrude forward at an
obtuse angle to the blade and
enable it to handle a larger
volume of solid waste than a
regular blade.

blaze: A shallow excision made
by an axe or other cutting tool
that removes part of the bark or
wood from a tree stem or log,
to designate trees to be cut or
to mark the location of some
point, such as along a boundary, trail, or survey line.

bleed: That edge of a map or
chart on which the carto-
graphic detail is extended to
the edge of the sheet; also
called bi-margin format; bleed-
ing edge.

blind: In soil engineering, the
placement of loose soil around
a tile or conduit to prevent
damage or misalignment when
the trench is backfilled and
allowing water to flow more
freely to the tile.

blind drain: A type of drain
consisting of an excavated
trench refilled with pervious
materials, such as coarse sand,
gravel, or crushed stones,
through whose voids water
percolates and flows toward an
outlet. Often referred to as a

French drain.

blinding material: Material placed on top of and around a closed drain to improve the flow of water to the drain and to prevent displacement during back filling of the trench.

blind inlet: Inlet to a drain in which entrance of water is by percolation rather than open flow channels.

block cut method: A surface mining method in which overburden is removed from and placed around the periphery of a box shaped cut. After coal is removed, the spoil is pushed back into the cut and the surface blended into the topography.

blocky soil structure: See *soil structure, types*.

bloodworms: Midge fly larvae. Many of the species have meoglobin in the blood causing a red color and are often accosiated with rich organic deposits. Also, the common name for certain marine segmented worms (class polychaeta). See *sludgeworms*.

bloom: A readily visible concentrated growth or aggregation of minute organisms, usually algae, in bodies of water.

blowdown (windthrow): Uprooting by the wind. Also refers to a tree or trees so uprooted.

blown-out land: Areas from which all or almost all of the soil and soil material has been removed by wind erosion; usually barren, shallow depressions with a flat or irregular floor consisting of a more resistant layer and/or an accumulation of pebbles, or a wet zone immediately above a water table; usually unfit for crop production. A miscellaneous area.

blowout: An excavation in areas of loose soil, usually sand, produced by wind; a break or rupture of a soil surface attributable to hydraulic pressure, usually associated with sand boils.

blueline: A nonreproducible blue image or outline, usually printed photographically n paper or plastic sheeting, and used as a guide for drafting stripping, or layout; also called blind image.

boardfoot: A unit of measure of the wood in lumber, logs, bolts, or trees; the amount of wood in a board 1 foot wide, 1 foot long, and 1 inch thick before surfacing or other finishing.

boat launch: Man made device for launching watercraft. May be a mechanical "lift" or a ramp structure where a boat trailer may be backed into the water to a depth sufficient to float the boat.

BOD5: The amount of dissolved oxygen needed or consumed in five days by biological processes that break down the organic matter in an effluent.

bog: A poorly drained area rich in plant residues, usually surrounded by an area of open water, and having characteristic flora.

bole: The trunk of a tree.

boom: A floating device used to

contain oil on a body of water; a piece of equipment used to apply pesticides from a tractor or truck.

border: In wildlife management a strip of low growing vegetation, herbaceous or woody, usually more than 10 feet wide, established along the edges of fields, woodlands, or streams.

border dikes: Earth ridges built to guide or hold irrigation water within prescribed limits in a field; a small levee.

border ditch: A ditch used as a border of an irrigated strip or plot, water being spread from one or both sides of the ditch along its entire length.

border irrigation: A surface method of irrigation by flooding between border dikes.

border strip: The area of land bounded by two border ridges or dikes that guide the irrigation stream from the point or points of application to the ends of the strips. Cross slope between ridges or dikes is usually eliminated.

bore (hydraulics): A rapidly varied flood wave front generated by grossly unsteady flow; resembles a hydraulic jump but faces upstream and normally does not move.

borrow: Material excavated from one area to be used as fill material in another area.

borrow pits: Specific site(s) within a borrow area from which material is excavated for use.

botanical forest products: Prescribed plants or fungi that occur naturally on Crown forest land. There are seven recognized categories: wild edible mushrooms, floral greenery, medicinal products, fruits and berries, herbs and vegetables, landscaping products and craft products.

botanical garden: See *arboretum*.

bottom ash: The non-airborne combustion residue from burning pulverized coal in a boiler; the material which falls to the bottom of the boiler and is removed mechanically; a concentration of non-combustible materials, which may include toxics.

boulder: A rock fragment, usually rounded by weathering or abrasion, with an average dimension of 12 inches or more: will not pass a 12-inch screen. A particle of rock that will not pass a 12-inch (300-mm) square opening. A rock which is too heavy to be lifted readily by hand.

boulder clay: A geological term used to designate glacial drift that has not been subjected to the sorting action of water and therefore contains particles from boulders to clay sizes.

boundary screen: Plant or construction materials on the boundary of a site that provides protection on concealment.

box cut: The initial cut driven in a property, where no open side exists; resulting in a highwall on both sides at the cut.

brackish: Slightly salty; applied to water with a saline content that is intermediate between that of freshwater streams and sea water; neither fresh nor salty.

breach: A gap, rift, hole, or rupture in a dam; providing a break; allowing water stored behind a dam to flow through in an uncontrolled and unplanned manner. An eroded opening through a dam which drains the reservoir. A controlled breach is a constructed opening. An uncontrolled breach is an unintentional opening which allows uncontrolled discharge from the reservoir.

break grade: To change grade, as in a tile line, ditch, or field.

breakdown product: A compound derived by chemical, biological, or physical action upon a pesticide. The breakdown is a natural process which may result in a more toxic or a less toxic compound and a more persistent or less persistent compound.

breccia: A rock consisting of consolidated granular rock fragments larger than sand grains.

brecciated: A rock made up of highly angular, coarse fragments.

breeding herd: Livestock retained for breeding purposes to provide for the perpetuation of the herd or band; excludes animals being prepared for market.

briquetter: A machine that compresses a material, such as metal turnings, charcoal, or coal dust, into small pellets.

British thermal unit (Btu): The quantity of head required to raise the temperature of the one of water 1 degrees F at or near 39.2 degrees F; equals 252 calories, 1,055 joules, or 0.293 watt-hours.

broad base terrace: See *terrace*.

broadcast burning: A controlled burn, where the fire is intentionally ignited and allowed to proceed over a designated area within well-defined boundaries, for the reduction of fuel hazard after logging or for site preparation before planting. Also called slash burning.

broadcast seeding: Scattering seed on the surface of the soil, in contrast to drill seeding, in which seeds are placed in rows in the soil.

broadcast tillage: Cropping system in which the entire field surface is tilled, in contrast to partial tillage in bands or strips, also called total surface tillage.

broad crested weir: An overflow structure for measuring water, often rectangular in cross section, in which the water adheres to the surface of the crest rather than springing clear.

brownfields: Real property, the expansion, redevelopment, or reuse of which may be complicated by the presence or potential presence of a hazardous substance, pollutant, or contaminant.

browse: Twigs or shoots, with or without attached leaves, of shrubs, trees, or woody vines available as forage for domestic and wild browsing animals.

browse line: The line on woody plants marking the height to which browsing animals have removed browse.

brush: A growth of shrubs or small trees.

brush management: Management and manipulation of stands of brush by mechanical, chemical, or biological means or by prescribed burning.

brush matting: A matting of branches placed on badly eroded land to conserve moisture and reduce erosion while trees or other vegetative covers are being established; a matting of mesh wire and brush used to retard streambank erosion.

bucket: An open container affixed to the movable arms of a wheeled or tracked vehicle to spread solid waste and cover material, and to excavate soil.

bucket wheel excavator: A continuous digging machine with a boom on which is mounted a rotating vertical wheel having buckets on its periphery. As the rotating wheel is pressed into the material to be dug, the buckets cut, gather, and discharge onto a conveyor belt where the material is moved to a transport system.

budding: Grafting by inserting a bud having a small amount of tissue at its base, into a slit in the bark of a rootstalk, so that, after union, the portion of the rootstalk above the bud may be removed, leaving a shoot to develop entirely from the bud.

bud scale: One of the scalelike leaves that form the external covering of a bud during the dormant period.

buffer species: A nongame species that serves as food for

predators and thus relieves predation on a game species.

buffer strips: Strips of grass or other erosion resisting vegetation between or below cultivated strips or fields.

buffer zones: Land bordering and protecting critical babitats or water bodies by reducing runoff and nonpoint source pollution loading; areas created or sustained to lessen the negative effects of land development on animals, plants, and their habitats.

building code: Regulations adopted by state or local government which establish minimum standards of construction related to building materials, hazards, and structural collapse.

built-up area: An area mainly occupied by buildings; broadly synonymous with urban in its physical sense.

bulk blending: Mixing dry, individually granulated materials to form a mixed fertilizer.

bulk density: In soils, the mass of dry soil per unit bulk volume, determined before drying a constant weight at 105° C.

bulkhead: A one-piece fabricated steel unit which is lowered into guides and seals against a frame to close a water passage in a dam, conduit, spillway, etc. An object used to isolate a portion of a waterway for examination, maintenance, or repair. A wall or partition erected to resist ground or water pressure.

bulk fertilizer: Commercial fertilizer delivered to the purchaser, either in the solid or liquid state, in a non packaged form to which a label cannot be attached.

bulkhead gate: A gate used either for temporary closure of a channel or conduit before dewatering it for inspection or maintenance or for closure against flowing water when the head difference is small (e.g., for diversion tunnel closure).

bulk specific gravity: The ratio of the bulk density of a soil to the mass of unit volume of water.

bulk volume: The volume, including the solids and the pores, of an arbitrary soil mass.

bulking: The increase in volume of a material due to manipulation. Rock bulks upon being excavated; damp sand bulks if loosely deposited, as by dumping, because the apparent cohesion prevents movement of the soil particles to form a reduced volume.

bulky waste: Large items of waste material, such as appliances, furniture, large auto parts, trees, branches, stumps, and others.

bull clam: A tracked vehicle that has a hinged, curved bowl on the top of the front of the blade.

bulldozer: A tracked vehicle equipped with an earth blade.

bunchgrass: A grass that does not have rhizomes or stolons and forms a bunch or tuft.

buried soil: A soil once exposed but now overlain by more recently formed soil.

burl: A hard, woody outgrowth or bulge on the trunk of a tree.

burn: The degree of heat treatment to which refractory bricks are subjected when manufactured.

burner: a kind of furnace where a flame is produced to consume combustible materials. Types include:

concial: A hollow, cone-shaped combustion chamber that has an exhaust vent at its point and a door at its base through which waste materials are charged; aire is delivered to the burning solid waste inside the cone; also called a teepee burner.

primary: A burner that dries out and ignites materials in the primary combustion chamber.

refuse: A device for either central or on-site volume reduction of the solid waste by burning; it is of simple construction and all the factors of combustion cannot be controlled.

residential: A device used to burn the solid wastes generated in an individual dwelling.

secondary: A burner installed in the secondary combustion chamber of an incinerator to maintain a minimum temperature and to complete the combustion of incompletely burned glass; also called afterburner.

bushel: A volume measure of agricultural commodities; equal to eight dry gallons. See *table (page 19) for weight conversations for a bushel of various crops.*

buyers market: A market situation in which the supply (availability of goods and services) is high in relation to demand.

C

cable logging: A yarding system employing winches, blocks, and cables.

cadastral control (surveying): Lines established and market on the ground by suitable, permanent monuments, which are used as starting and closing points in the land surveys of the public domain of the United States.

cairn: A pile of stones used as a marker.

caisson: A box or chamber used in construction work under water. A structure or chamber which is usually sunk or lowered by digging from the inside. Used to gain access to the bottom of a stream or other body of water.

calcareous soil: Soil containing sufficient free calcium carbonate or magnesium carbonate to effervesce carbon dioxide visibly when treated with cold 0.1 normal hydrochloric acid.

calcic horizon: See *diagnostic horizons.*

calcite: Light-colored mineral composed of calcium carbonate that often fills veins in igneous rocks and forms the sedimentary rock limestone.

caldera (crater): Large circular depression formed by explosion or collapse of a volcano.

Caliche: A soil layer near the surface, more of less cemented by secondary carbonates of calcium or magnesium precipitated from the soil solution; may occur as a soft, then soil horizon, as a hard, thick bed just beneath the solum, or as a surface layer exposed by erosion. Not a geologic deposit; alluvium cemented with sodium nitrate, chloride, and/or other soluble salts in the nitrate deposits of Chile and Peru. See *hardpan.*

California bearing ratio (CBR): The load supporting capacity of a soil as compared to that of a standard crushed limestone, expressed as a ratio and multiplied by 100; first standardized in California. A soil with a ratio of 16 will support 16 percent of the load that would be supported by the standard crushed limestone per unit area crushed limestone per unit area and with the same degree of distortion.

caliper (landscape architecture): The diameter of a tree measured six inches above ground line for trees up to a four-inch caliper, 12 inches above ground line for larger trees.

callus: A tissue of thin-walled cells developed on plant wound surfaces; most evident, in time, after cutting off a tree limb flush with a main trunk or limb.

cambium: A single layer of cells between the woody part of the tree and the bark. Division of these cells results in diameter growth of the tree through formation of wood cells (xylem) and inner bark (phloem).

camera: A lightproof chamber or box in which the image of an exterior object is projected upon a sensitized plate or film, through an opening usually equipped with a lens or lenses, shutter, and variable aperture.

multiband: A camera that exposes different areas of one film, or more than one film, through one lens and a beam splitter or through one lens and a beam splitter or through two or more lenses equipped with different filters to provide two or more photographs in different spectral bands.

multiple lens: A camera with two or more lenses, the axes of the lenses being systematically arranged at a fixed angle to cover a wide field by simultaneous exposures in all chambers; in most

such cameras the oblique lenses are arranged symmetrically around a central lens.

cambic horizon: See *diagnostic horizons*.

cambium: A layer of delicate tissue between the inner bark of a tree and wood that produces secondary growth; responsible for the annual rings of wood.

camping: A form of recreation in which living out of doors in a more or less close relationship with the natural environment is significant.

canal: A constructed open channel for transporting water from the source of supply to the point of distribution.

canker: A localized lesion on a stem in which the bark of the tree, and sometimes the underlying cambium and wood, is killed.

canopy: The cover of leaves and branches formed by the tops or crowns of plants as viewed from above the cover.

canopy angle: Generally, a measure of the openness of a stream to sunlight. Specifically, the angle formed by an imaginary line from the highest structure (for example, tree, shrub, or bluff) on one bank to eye level at midchannel to the highest structure on the other bank.

canopy closure: The progressive reduction of space between crowns as they spread laterally, increasing canopy cover.

capability, land: See *land capability*.

capacity curve, pump: A graph showing the relationship of pump speed, discharge, pumping and friction head, and efficiency for a specific pump. Also called head

capillary action: Movement of water through very small spaces due to molecular forces called capillary forces.

capillary attraction (capillary force): The tendency of water to move into fine spaces, as between soil particles, regardless of gravity.

capillary forces: The molecular forces which cause the movement of water through very small spaces.

capillary fringe: A zone just above the water table (zero guage pressure) that remains almost saturated The extent and the degree of definition of the capillary fringe depends upon the size distribution of pores.

capillary head: The potential, expressed in head of water, that causes the water to flow by capillary action.

capital: All the durable and non-durable items used in production.

capital goods: Tangible economic goods, other than land, that are used in production.

capitalized cost: The first cost of an asset plus the present value of all renewals expected within the planning horizon.

capital recovery period: The period of time required for the net returns from an outlay of capital to equal the investment.

capture efficiency: The fraction of organic vapors generated by a process that are directed to an abatement or recovery device.

carbonaceous: Pertaining to or containing carbon derived from plant and animal residues.

carbonaceous matter: Pure carbon or carbon compounds present in the fuel or residue of a combustion process.

carbonate alkalinity: Alkalinity caused by carbonate ions.

carbonate hardness: Water hardness caused by the presence of carbonate and bicarbonates of calcium and magnesium.

carbonate rocks: Rocks (such as limestone or dolostone) that are composed primarily of minerals (such as calcite and dolomite) containing the carbonate ion (CO_3^{2-}).

carbon absorber: An add-on control device that uses activated carbon to absorb volatile organic compounds from a gas stream. (The VOCs are later recovered from the carbon.)

carbon adsorption: A treatment system that removes contaminants from groundwater or surface water by forcing it through tanks containing activated carbon treated to attract the contaminants.

carbon balance: The concentration of carbon released into the atmosphere compared to the amounts stored in the oceans, soil and vegetation.

carbon cycle: The sequence of transformations whereby carbon dioxide is fixed as carbon or carbon compounds in living organisms by photosynthesis or chemosynthesis, liberated by respiration and/or death and decomposition of the fixing organism, used by heterotrophic species, and ultimately returned to its original state to be used again.

carbon dioxide (CO₂): A colorless, odorless, nonpoisonous gas that forms carbonic acid when dissolved in water; produced during combustion and microbial decomposition.

carbon monoxide (CO): A colorless, poisonous gas that has an exceedingly faint metallic odor and taste; produced during combustion and microbial decomposition when the oxygen supply is limited.

carbon nitrogen ratio (C:N): The ratio of the weight of organic carbon to the weight of total nitrogen in the soil or in organic material obtained by dividing the percentage of organic carbon (C) by the percentage of total nitrogen (N).

carbon tetrachloride (CC$_{14}$): Compound consisting of one carbon atom ad four chlorine atoms, once widely used as a industrial raw material, as a solvent, and in the production of CFCs. Use as a solvent ended when it was discovered to be carcinogenic.

carcinogenic: Tending to produce or incite cancer.

cardinal lines: A general term applying, collectively, to base lines and principal meridians. See *base line, principal meridian.*

cardinal points: (surveying) Any of the four principal astronomical directions on the surface of the earth; north, east, south, west; (optics) those points of a lens used as reference for determining object and image distances.

carnivore: A flesh eating animal, or a plant that eats insects.

carrion: The putrifying dead body of an animal.

carry over: The quantity of water which continues past an inlet.

carrying capacity: In recreation, the amount of use a recreation area can sustain without detrioration of its quality; in wildlife, the maximum number of animals an area can support during a given period of the year. See *grazing capacity.*

cartographic feature: The natural or cultural objects shown on a map or chart.

cartographic scanner: A device for strip by strip scanning of two dimensional copy and for digital registration of the light/dark (black/white) parts as rectangular coordinates.

cartography: The art and science of making maps and charts.

cash-grain farm: A farm on which corn, sorghums, small grains, soybeans, or field beans, and peas account for at least 50 percent of the value of farm products sold.

cash renting: A type of land rental agreement between a landlord and tenant. Typically, the tenant rents the land for a fixed amount per acre that is pre-specified in the agreement.

catabolism: The breakdown of organic compounds within an organism. See *metabolism.*

catadromous: Pertaining to fish that spend most of their life in freshwaters, but migrate to the sea to spawn, such as the American eel. See *anadromous.*

catalyst: A substance that changes the speed or yield of a chemical reaction without being consumed or chemically changed by the chemical reaction.

catalytic converter: An air pollution abatement device that removes organic contaminates by oxidizing them into carbon dioxide and water through chemical reaction; can be used to reduce nitrogen oxide emissions from motor vehicles.

catalytic incinerator: A control device that oxidizes volatile organic compounds (VOCs) by using a catalyst to promote the combustion process. Catalytic incinerators require lower temperatures than conventional thermal incinerators, thus saving fuel and other costs.

catastrophic drift: Massive drift of bottom organisms under conditions of stress, such as floods or toxicity. See *drift organisms, periodic drift.*

catch crop: A crop produced incidental to the main crop of the farm and usually occupying the land for a short period; a crop grown to replace a main crop which has failed.

catchment: A reservoir or basin developed for flood control or water management for livestock and/or wildlife.

category (soils): Any one of the ranks of the system of soil classification in which soils are grouped on the basis of their characteristics.

catena: A sequence of soils of about the same age, derived from similar parent material, and occurring under similar climatic conditions but having different characteristics due to variation in relief and in natural drainage. See *clinosequence, toposequence.*

cathode ray tube (CRT): a vacuum tube capable of producing a black-and-white or color image by beaming electrons onto a sensitized screen.

cation: Positively charged ion; ion which, during electrolysis, is attracted to the cathode. Common soil cations are calcium, magnesium, sodium, potassium, and hydrogen.

cation exchange: The interchange between a cation in solution and another cation on the surface of any surface active material, such as clay colloid or organic colloid.

cation exchange capacity (CEC): The sum total of exchangeable cations that a soil can adsorb; expressed in milliequivalents per gram or 100 grams of soil (or of other exchanges, such as clay.)

catkin: A drooping flower cluster, suggesting a cat's tail in shape, usually a scaly spike; typical of such trees as willow, hickory, and birch.

cattle walkway: An earth fill or embankment constructed on marsh range or range areas subject to overflow.

cavitation: The formation and collapse of gas pockets or bubbles on the blade of an impeller or the gate of a valve; collapse of these pockets or bubbles drives water with such force that it can cause pitting of the gate or valve surface.

cavitation damage: Damage caused when partial vacuums formed in a liquid by a swiftly moving solid body (e.g. a propeller) pit and wear away solid surfaces (e.g. metal or concrete). The attack on surfaces caused by the implosion of bubbles of water vapor.

cell (waste management): Compacted solid wastes that are enclosed by natural soil or cover material in a sanitary landfill.

cell height: The vertical distance between the top and bottom of the compacted solid waste enclosed by natural soil or cover material in a sanitary landfill.

cell thickness: The perpendicular distance between the cover materials placed over the last working faces of two successive cells in a sanitary landfill.

cellulose: A complex carbohydrate occurring in wood and all other vegetable material. Wood cellulose fibers are basic components of lumber and wood pulp and many other useful products.

cellustic waste: Byproducts from the processing of wood and other vegetative material.

cementation: Weakly cemented, strongly cemented, and indurated.

cemented: Indurated; having a hard, brittle consistency because the particles are held together by cementing substances such as humus, calcium carbonate, or the oxides of silicon, iron, and aluminum. The hardness and brittleness persist even when wet.

census: A complete counting, with classification, of a population or group at a point in time, as regards some well defined characteristic(s) (e.g., of traffic on particular roads); usually has a governmental and economic social connotation; often used in wildlife surveys.

Census of Agriculture: A census taken by the Bureau of Census every five years; includes number of farms, land in farms, crop acreage and production, livestock numbers and production, farm spending, farm facilities and equipment, farm tenure, value of farm products sold, farm size, and other data given for states and counties.

Census of Population and Housing: A census taken by the Bureau of Census every 10 years; includes number of people and housing units and various population and housing characteristics.

center pivot irrigation: See *irrigation system, center pivot*.

centrifugal collector: Any of several mechanical systems using centrifugal force to remove aerosols from a gas stream.

centrifugal pump: A device that converts mechanical energy to pressure or kinetic energy in a fluid by imparting centrifugal force on the fluid through a rapidly rotating impeller.

cesspool: A lined and covered excavation in the ground which receives the discharge of domestic sewage or other organic wastes from a drainage system, so designed as to retain the organic matter and solids ... but permitting the liquids to seep through the bottom and sides.

C-factor: (Soil erosion) See *universal soil loss equation*; (remote sensing) An empirical value that expresses the vertical measuring capability of a given stereoscopic system; generally defined as the ratio of the flight height to the smallest contour interval accurately plotable; used to determine the flight height required for a specified contour interval, camera, and instrument system; also called altitude-contour ratio.

chain: A device used by surveyors for measuring distance; the length of this device as a unit of distance; the usual chain is 66 feet (20.117 meters), and consists of 100 links, each 7.92 inches (20.117 centimeters).

chalk: Composed mainly of the calcareous shells of various marine microorganisms, but whose matrix consists of fine particles of calcium carbonate, some of which may have been chemically precipitated.

channel: A natural stream that conveys water; a ditch or channel excavated for the flow of water.

channel capacity: Flow rate of a ditch, canal, or natural channel when flowing full or at design flow.

channel density: Ratio of the length of stream channels in a given basin to the area of the basin; expressed in feet per acre (meters/hectare).

channel improvement: The improvement of the flow characteristics of a channel by clearing, excavation, realignment, lining, or other means in order to increase its capacity; sometimes used to connote channel stabilization.

channel modification: The modification of the flow characteristics of a channel by clearing, excavation, realignment, lining, or other means to increase its capacity; sometimes used to connote channel stabilization.

channel realignment: The construction of a new channel or a new alignment; may include the clearing, snagging, widening, ,and/or deepening of the existing channel.

channel stabilization: Erosion prevention and stabilization of velocity distribution in a channel using jetties, drops, revetments, vegetation, and other measures.

channel storage: Water temporarily stored in channels while enroute to an outlet.

channel terrace: See *terrace*.

channelization: The straightening and/or deepening of a river channel.

channery: In Scotland and Ireland, gravel; in the United States, thin, flat fragments of limestone, sandstone, or schist up to six inches in major diameter. See *coarse fragments*.

chaparral: A brush community composed of evergreen, sclerophyllous species.

character plant: Unique, atypical, or distinctly different plants, either in form or density, created by pruning or other cultural manipulation. See *specimen plant*.

check (hydraulics, irrigation): A structure, permanent or portable, designed to raise or control the water surface in a channel or ditch.

check dam: Small dam constructed in a gully or other small watercourse to decrease the streamflow velocity, minimize channel scour, and promote deposition of sediment.

check irrigation: A method of irrigation in which an area is practically or entirely surrounded by earth ridges.

chelates: Organic compounds used as carriers for polyvalent metals, such as iron, copper, or zinc, to improve their availability in soils.

chemical fallow: Period of rest of land to enchance moisture storage, using contact and/or residual chemicals for vegetation control rather than tillage, also called chemical tillage or no-till fallow.

chemical oxygen demand (COD): A measure of the amount of oxygen required to oxidize organic and oxidizable inorganic compounds in water. The COD test, like the BOD test, is used to determine the degree of pollution in an effluent.

chemosterilant: A pesticide chemical that controls pests by destroying their ability to reproduce.

cherty: An adjective incorporated into the soil textural class designations of horizons when the soil mass contains between 15 and 90 percent by volume of chert fragments. See *chert fragments and coarse chert fragments as defined under coarse fragments.*

chilling effect: Phenomenon in which the increase in atmospheric particulates inhibits penetration of the sun's energy, thus gradually lowering the temperature of the earth.

chimera: A plant part containing tissues of differing genetic make-up. Some new varieties originate from this natural phenomenon.

Chinook: A warm, dry southwest wind blowing from the sea onto the coast of Oregon and Washington in the winter and spring; a warm, dry wind blowing down the eastern slope of the Rocky Mountains.

chiseling: Breaking or loosening the soil, without inversion, with a chisel cultivator or chisel plow.

chisel planting: Seedbed preparation by chiseling without inversion of the soil, leaving a protective cover of crop residue on the surface for erosion control. Seedbed preparation and planting may or may not be in the same operation.

chisel plowing: Cropland preparation by a special implement (chis-el) that avoids complete inversion of the soil (as occurs with conventional moldboard plowing). Chisel plowing can leave a protective cover of crop residues on the soil surface that helps prevent erosion and improve infiltration.

chlorinated hydrocarbon: A class of generally long-lasting, broad-spectrum insecticides, of which the best known is DDT; first used for insect control during the World War II. See *herbicides.*

chlorinated solvent: A volatile organic compound containing chlorine. Some common solvents are trichloroethylene, tetrachloroethylene, and carbon tetrachloride.

chlorination: The addition of chlorine to drinking water, sewage, or industrial waste for disinfection of oxidation of undesirable compounds.

chlorinator: A device for adding a chlorine containing gas or liquid to drinking or wastewater.

chlorine contact chamber: In a waste treatment plant, a chamber in which effluent is disinfected by chlorine before it is discharged to the receiving waters.

chlorine residual: The quantity of chlorine remaining in water or wastewater at the end of a specified contact period. The demand for any given water or waste varies with the amount of chlorine applied, time of contact, and temperature.

chlorofluorocarbons: A class of volatile compounds consisting of carbon, chlorine, and fluorine. Commonly called freons, which have been used in refrigeration mechanisms, as blowing agents in the fabrication of flexible and rigid foams, and, until several years ago, as propellants in spray cans.

chlorophenoxy: A class of herbicides that may be found in domestic water supplies and cause adverse health effects.

chlorophyll: Green photosynthetic pigment present in many plant and some bacterial cells. There are seven known types of chlorophyll; their presence and abundance vary from one group of photosynthetic organisms to another.

chlorosis: An abnormal yellowing of plant foliage, usually a symptom of some mineral deficiency, a virus infection, root or stem girdling, or extremely reduced light.

Chopped hay: Forage that is dried to less than 25 percent moisture and chopped to lengths of two inches (5.1 cm) or less.

C horizon: See *soil horizons.*

chroma: The relative purity, strength, or saturation of a color; directly related to the dominance of the determining wavelength of the light and inversely related to grayness; one of the three variables of color. See *Munsell color system, hue, value.*

chronic exposure: Continuous or repeated exposure to a hazardous substance over a long period of time.

chronic toxicity: Toxicity, marked by a long duration, that produces an adverse effect on organisms. The end result of chronic toxicity can be death, although the usual effects are sublethal, such as inhibiting reproduction or reducing growth. These effects are reflected by changes in the productivity and population

structure of the community. See *acute toxicity.*

chronosequence: A sequence of related soils that differ one from the other in certain properties primarily as a result of time as a soil forming factor.

chute: A high velocity, open channel for conveying water to a lower level without erosion.

Cipolletti weir: A trapezoidal weir with one to four side slopes. See *measuring weir.*

circulation road (recreation): A vehicular travelway within a recreation area.

cirocululus: See *cloud.*

cirrostratus: See *cloud.*

cistern: Small tank or storage facility used to store water for a home or farm; often used to store rain water.

clamshell bucket: A vessel used to hoist and convey materials; having two jaws that clamp together when the vessel is lifted by specially attached cables.

clarifer: In wastewater treatment, a settling tank which mechanically removes settleable solids from wastes.

clarification: The removal of turbidity and suspended solids from wastewater by settling, and often aided by centrifugal action or chemically induced coagulation.

classification: The assignment of objects or units to groups within a system of categories distinguished by their properties or characteristics.

classification map (remote sensing): The map-like representation that shows the class assignment of each data vector, often taking the form of a CRT image or computer line-printer output.

class of animal: Age and/or sex groups of a kind of animal, for example, cows, calves, yearlings, ewes, does, fawns.

clastic: Composed of broken fragments of rocks and minerals.

clay (soils): A mineral soil separate consisting of particles less than 0.002 millimeter in equivalent diameter; a soil textural class; (engineering) a fine grained soil that has a high plasticity index in relation to the liquid limits.

clayey: See *particle size classes for family groupings.*

clayey skeletal: See *particle size classes for family groupings.*

clay film: A thin coating of well oriented clay particles on the surface of a soil aggregate, particle, or pore.

clay mineral: Naturally occurring mineral crystalline material found in soils and other earthy deposits, the particles being of clay size, that is, less than 0.002 millimeter in diameter; material as heretofore described but not limited by particle size.

claypan: A dense, compact layer in the subsoil having a much higher clay content than the overlying material from which it is separated by a sharply defined boundary; formed by downward movement of clay or by synthesis of clay in place during soil formation. Claypans are usually hard when dry, and plastic and sticky when wet. They usually impede movement of water and air, and the growth of plant roots. See *hardpan.*

clay seal: A barrier constructed of impermeable clay that stops the flow of water or gas.

clay tile: Shore lengths of pipe made from clay and used for subsurface drainage.

Clean Air Act (CAA): A Federal law that gives EPA authority to set standards for air quality and to control the release of airborne chemicals from industries, power plants, and cars.

clean tillage: Cultivation of a field so as to cover all plant residues and to prevent the growth of all vegetation except the particular crop desired.

Clean Water Act (CWA): A Federal law that regulates the pollution that will reach surface waters (rivers, lakes, ponds, and streams). The law prohibits a point source from discharging pollutants into the water unless the discharge meets certain permit requirements.

clearcutting: A method of cutting that removes the entire timber stand on the area cut. See *selective cutting.*

clearcutting silvicultural system: Defined as a silvicultural system that removes an entire stand of trees from an area of one hectare or more, and greater that two tree heights in width, in a single harvesting operation. A new evenaged stand is obtained by planting, natural or advanced regeneration or direct seeding. The opening size and dimensions created are generally large enough to limit significant microclimatic influence from the surrounding stand.

clearcutting with researves: A variation of the clearcut silvicultural system in which trees are retained, either uniformly or in small groups, for purposes other than regeneration.

clearing: The removal of all vegetation such as trees, shrubs, brush, stumps, exposed roots, down timber, branches, grass, and weeds. The removal of all rubbish and all other objectionable material.

clearing and snagging: The removal of brush, log jams, snags, and other material from a stream or river where significant blockage of the stream flow occurs.

cleavage: The splitting or tendency to split along crystallographic planes of minerals. As applied to rocks, it is the property of splitting into thin parallel sheets which may be highly inclined to the bedding planes, as in slate.

climate: The sum total of all atmospheric or meteorological influences, principally temperature, moisture, wind, pressure, and evaporation, which combine to characterize a region and give it individuality by influencing the nature of its land forms, soils, vegetation, and land use. See *weather*.

climate change: Climate change is sometimes used to refer to all forms of climatic inconsistency. But because the Earth's climate is never static, the term is properly used to imply a significant change from one climatic condition to another. In some cases, climate change has been used synonymously with global warming. Scientists, however, tend to use climate change in the wider sense to include both human-induced and natural changes in climate.

climate, continental: The type of climate characteristic of land areas separated from the moderation influence of oceans by distance, direction, or mountain barriers;

marked by relatively large daily and seasonal change in temperature.

climate, oceanic: The type of climate characteristic of land areas near oceans which contribute to the humidity and at the same time have a moderating influence on temperature and range of temperature variation.

climatic year: A continuous 12 month period arbitrarily selected for the analysis and presentation of climatological or streamflow data, generally beginning March 1 or April 1. See *water year*.

climatology: The study of climate.

climax: The highest ecological development of a plant community capable of perpetuation under the prevailing climatic and edaphic conditions.

climax community: The highest ecological development of a plant community capable of perpetuation under the prevailing climatic and edaphic conditions.

climax culture: The point of maximum intensity of a culture.

climosequence: A sequence of related soils that differ, one from the other, in certain properties primarily as a result of the effect of climate as a soil forming factor.

clinkers: Hard, sintered, or fused pieces of residue formed in a fire by the agglomeration of ash, metals, glass, and ceramics.

clinosequence: A group of related soils that differ, one from the other, in certain properties primarily as a result of the effect of the degree of slope on which they were formed. See *toposequence*.

clod: A compact, coherent mass of

soil ranging in size from five to 10 millimeters (.2 to .4 inches) to as much as 200 to 250 millimeters (eight to 10 inches); produced artificially, usually by the activity of man by plowing, digging, etc., especially when these operations are performed on soils that are either too wet or too dry for normal tillage operations.

clone: A group of organisms derived by asexual reproduction from a single parent. Such organisms are therefore of the same genetic constitution.

closed drain: Subsurface drain, tile, or perforated pipe that receives surface water through surface inlets.

cloud: A mass of vapor or an aggregate of watery or icy particles floating in the atmosphere; clouds have been classified in four families and ten genera according to height and formation.

cloud, cirrus: Very high, white, wispy, clouds, usually consisting of ice crystals and seen as tufts or feathery bands across the sky; average height, seven miles (11.3 km).

cloud, cirrostratus: A thin, whitish veil of cloud that does not blur the outline of the sun or mood; the result of evaporation and recondensation at upper levels; average heigh, six miles (9.7 km).

cloud, cirrocumulus: A mass of fleecy, globular cloudlets in contact with one another; result of small, local convection currents at high altitudes; average height, five miles (8 km).

cloud, altostratus: A somewhat high level, blue to grayish blue cloud that forms a sheet or layer, average height, 3.5 miles (5.6 km)

cloud, altocumulus: A fleecy cloud, usually a rounded mass, but which can change radically and unexpectedly, producing intermediate forms, average height, 2.5 miles (4 km).

cloud, stratus: A very low, sheet or layer cloud that resembles fog; may settle to become fog or be q fog that has risen; average height, .25 miles (.4 km).

cloud, stratocumulus: Large globular masses of cloud, gray to black in color, arranged in waves, groups, or bands; often cover the whole sky; average height, 1 mile (1.6 km).

cloud, nimbostratus: A low, amorphous, dark gray cloud layer; the familiar rain cloud; precipitating continuous rain or snow; average height, .25 miles (.4 km).

cloud, cumulus: Thick, billowy, usually white cloud formation with relatively flat bases and dome-shaped upper surfaces; the fair weather cloud; average height, two miles (3.2 km).

cloud, cumulonimbus: A heavy massive cumulus cloud with striking vertical development, at times reaching great heights and rising to form an anvil-shaped top; generates thunder and rain showers; average height, four miles (6.4 km).

cloud modification: Any process by which the natural course of development of a cloud is altered by artificial means.

cloud seeding: Any process of injecting a substance into a cloud for the purpose of influencing the cloud's subsequent development.

closed canopy: The description given to a stand when the crowns of the main level of trees forming the canopy are touching and intermingled so that light cannot reach the forest floor directly.

cluster development: A variation in subdivision design which permits building lots to be made smaller and grouped on part of a site, thereby leaving the remaining land open for recreational or conservation purposes. Such a plan generally maintains the same overall density as the conventional subdivision design.

cluster sampling: Sampling (commonly attribute sampling) in which the unit of observation is a group of individuals, e.g., the trees in a sample plot; the unit value is the proportion of the individuals in the group having the same specified attribute.

coal: A solid, brittle, more or less distinctly stratified, combustible, carbonaceous rock, formed by the partial to complete decomposition of vegetation

coal, anthracite: A hard, black, lustrous coal containing a high percentage of volatile matter: often called hard coal.

coal, bituminous: A coal that is high in carbonaceous matter, having between 15 to 50 percent volatile matter; often called soft coal.

coal, lignite: A brownish-black coal of low rank with high inherent moisture and volatile matter; alternation of vegetal matter has proceeded further than peat, but not so far as subbituminous coal.

coal, subbituminous: A coal similar to bituminous, but softer and high in moisture.

coal gasification: Conversion of coal to a gas, suitable for use as a fuel.

coal processing waste: Earth materials that are combustible, physically unstable, or acid-forming or toxic-forming, which are wasted or otherwise separated from product coal and slurried or otherwise transported from coal preparation plants after physical or chemical processing, cleaning, or concentrating of coal.

coal seam: A layer, vein, or deposit of coal; a stratigraphic layer of the earth's surface containing coal.

coagulation: The clumping of particles in order to settle out impurities; often induced by chemicals such as lime or alum.

coarse cherty: Similar to cherty but fragments are coarse chert in size. See *coarse fragments.*

coarse fragments: Rock or mineral particles greater than 2.0 mm in diameter.

coarse gravel protection: Gravel generally placed in a layer upon a finished surface to protect the finished surface from deterioration or erosion.

coarse loamy: See *particle size classes for family groupings.*

coarse sand: See *soil separates, soil texture.*

coarse sandy loam: See *soil texture.*

coarse silty: See *particle size classes for family groupings.*

coarse texture: The soil texture exhibited by sands, loamy sands, and sandy loams, except very fine sandy loam; a soil containing large quantities of these textural classes (US usage). See *sand, moderately coarse texture, soil texture.*

Coastal zone: Coastal waters and adjacent lands that exert a measurable influence on the uses of the seas and their resources and biota.

cobblestone: See *coarse fragments*.

cobbly: An adjective incorporated into the soil textural class descriptions of horizons when the soil mass contains between 15 and 90 percent by volume of cobblestones. See *cobblestone as defined under coarse fragments*.

COBOL: Acronym for Common Business Oriented Language used on digital computers; a problem oriented, high level language in which the source program is written using statements in English.

co-dominant trees: Trees with crowns forming the general level of the forest canopy and receiving full light from above but comparatively little from the sides; usually with medium sized crowns more or less crowded on the sides.

coefficient discharge: Ratio of observed to theoretical discharge.

coefficient of consolidation: A coefficient that relates the change in excess pore pressure with time to the excess pore pressure diffusion in the soil mass in terms of soil mass and pore fluid characteristics.

coefficient of haze (COH): Unit of measurement for determining visibility based on the amount of particles in 1,000 linear feet.

coefficient of linear extensibility (COLE): The ratio of the difference between the moist and dry lengths of a clod to its dry length; (Lm Ld)/Ld, wherein Lm is the moist length (at 1/3 bar) and Ld is the air dry length. The measurement correlates with the volume change of a soil upon wetting and drying.

coefficient of roughness: See *roughness coefficient*.

coefficient of runoff (irrigation): Factor in the rational runoff formula expressing the ratio of peak runoff rate to rainfall intensity.

coefficient of variation or variability: The standard deviation of a statistic expressed as a fraction of the mean or a percentage.

cohesion: Holding together; force holding a solid or liquid together, owing to attraction between like molecules; decreases with rise in temperature.

cohesionless materials: Soil materials that when unconfined have little or no strength when air-dried and that have little or no cohesion when submerged. Soil that has little tendency to stick together whether wet or dry, such as sands and gravels.

cohesive soil: Predominantly clay and silt soil, fine-grained particles, that sticks together whether wet or dry. A soil that, when unconfined, has considerable strength when air-dried, and that has significant cohesion when submerged.

coldwater fish: A fish that requires relatively cool water for survival; optimum temperatures for species vary, but most are found in water where temperatures are 20 degrees C or less.

coliform: A group of bacteria used as an indicator of sanitary quality in water. The total coliform group Is an indicator of sanitary significance, because the organisms are normally present in large numbers in the intestinal tracts of humans and other warm blooded animals.

An index of the bacteriological quality of water, based on a count of the numbers of coliform bacteria.

collapsible soil: A soil that undergoes reorientation of particles and reduction in volume under constant load when the moisture content is increased; most applicable to in situ soil having a loose particle arrangement and a moisture content considerably less than saturation.

collector: A mechanical device designed to remove suspended particles from gaseous emissions arising from industrial processes.

collector, bag-type: A filter in which the filtering medium is a fabric cylindrical bag.

collector, cyclone: A collector in which an inlet gas stream is made to move vertically; its centrifugal forces tend to drive suspended particles to the wall of the cyclone.

collector, dust: Any device used to remove dust from exhaust gases.

collector, fly ash: Equipment used to remove fly ash from combustion gases.

collector, mechanical: A device in which inertial and gravitational forces separate dry dust from gas.

collector, multicyclone: A dust collector consisting of a number of cyclone collectors that operate in parallel; the volume and velocity of combustion gas can be regulated by dampers to maintain efficiency over a given load range.

colloid: A substance that, when apparently dissolved in water, diffuses not at all or very slowly through a semi-permeable membrane and usually has little effect on freezing point, boiling point,

or osmotic pressure of the solution; a substance in a state of fine subdivision with particles from .00001 to .0000001 centimeter; in soil, organic or inorganic matter having very small particle size and a correspondingly large surface area per unit of mass. Most colloidal particles are too small to be seen with the ordinary compound microscope.

colloidal particles: Soil particles that are so small that the surface activity has an appreciable influence on the properties of the aggregate. Particles smaller than 0.001 mm.

colloidal suspension: Suspension in water of particles so finely divided that they will not settle under the action of gravity, but will diffuse, even in quiet water, under the random impulses of Brownian motion; particle sizes range from about one micron to about one millimicron; however, there is no sharp differentiation by size between coarse ("true") suspension and colloidal suspension or between colloidal suspension and solution.

colluvial: In geology, material consisting of alluvium in part and also containing angular fragments of the original rock; also talus and cliff debris; material of avalanches; in soils, material that has moved downhill and has accumulated on lower slopes and/or at the bottom of the hill; moved downhill by the force of gravity and to some extent by frost action and local wash. Also called colluvium. See *soil creep*.

colluvium: A general term applied

to loose and incoherent deposits, usually at the foot of a slope and brought there chiefly by gravity.

color: See *Munsell color system.*

color composite (remote sensing): A color picture produced by assigning a color to a particular spectral band. For Landsat data, ordinarily blue is assigned to band 1 (~500 to 600 nm), green to band 2 (~600 to 700 nm, and red to band 3 (~700 nm to 1 um) or band 4 (~800 nm to 1.1 um) to form a picture approximating a color infrared photograph.

colorimetric method: Process for determining the levels of air pollutants in the atmosphere by quantifying their transmission of wave length of lights in chemical solutions.

color infrared film: Photographic film which is sensitive to energy in the visible and near-infrared wavelengths, generally from 0.4 to 0.9 micrometers.

colormetric method: Process for determining the levels of air pollutants in the atmosphere by quantifying their transmission of wavelength of lights in chemical solutions.

color infrared film: photographic film which is sensitive to energy in the visible and near-infrared wavelengths, generally from 0.4 to 0.9 micrometers.

color proof: A single or composite copy of each color of a polychrome (multicolor) printing.

color separation: The process of preparing a separate drawing, engraving, or negative for each color required in the production of a lithographed map or chart; a photographic process or electronic scanning procedure using color filters to separate multicolored copy into separate images of each of the three primary colors.

columnar (forestry-horticulure): A straight narrow habit of growth of various trees and shrubs.

columnar soil structure: See *soil structure types.*

combined sewer overflow: A discharge of untreated sewage and stormwater to a stream when the capacity of a combined storm/sanitary sewer system is exceeded by storm runoff.

combustion: Act or instance of burning; commonly the union of substances with oxygen, accompanied by the evolution of light and heat. The side processes (i.e. formation of carbon monoxide and sulfur dioxide) in turn contribute to air pollution.

combustion chamber: The part of an incinerator or furnace where combustion or burning takes place. Types include:

primary: The chamber in an incinerator where waste is ignited and burned.

secondary: The chamber of an incinerator where combustible solids, vapors, and gases from the primary chamber are burned and fly ash is settled.

commercial thinning: A silviculture treatment that 'thins' out an overstocked stand by removing trees that are large enough to be sold as products such as poles or fence posts. It is carried out to improve the health and growth rate of the remaining crop trees.

comminutor: A device that grinds solids, making them easier to treat.

committed use: Either a current public use; or a planned public use of a natural resource for which there is a documented legal, administrative, budgetary, or financial commitment established before the discharge of oil or release of a hazardous substance is detected.

Commodity Credit Corporation (CCC): A federally owned and operated corporation within the USDA created to stabilize and support agricultural prices and farm income by making loans and payments to producers, purchasing commodities, and engaging in various other operations. The CCC handles all money transactions for agricultural price and income support and related programs.

common excavation: All materials excavated not considered as rock. Boulders or detached pieces of solid rock less than 1 cubic yard in volume are classified as common excavation.

common material: All earth materials which do not fall under the definition of rock.

common outlet: An outlet used in common by several drains.

common use (range): Grazing use by more than one kind of animal, either at the same time or at different times within the same growing season.

community: An aggregation of organisms within a specified area; people living within the same district, city, etc., under the same laws.

community air: The ambient environment in the immediate vicinity of a community.

community building (recreation):

Building in a recreation area which provides services such as showers, restrooms, laundry, store, and covered area for group activities.

community water system: A public water system which serves at least 15 service connections used by year-round residents or regularly serves at least 25 year-round residents.

compacted backfill: Backfill which has been reduced to bulk by rolling, tamping, or soaking.

compacted embankment: Embankment which has been reduced in bulk by rolling, tapping, or soaking.

compaction: To unite firmly; the act or process of becoming compact; (in geology) the changing of loose sediment into hard, firm rock; (soil engineering) the process by which the soil grains are rearranged to decrease void space and bring them into closer contact with one another, thereby increasing the weight of solid material per cubic foot; (solid waste disposal) the reducing of the bulk of solid waste by rolling and tamping.

compactor: A mechanical device used to reduce the void space in solid wastes. Types include:

mobile: A vehicle with an enclosed body containing mechanical devices that convey solid waste into the main compartment of the body and compress it.

sanitary landfill: A vehicle equipped with a blade and with rubber tires sheathed in steel or hollow steel cores; both types of wheels are equipped with load concentrations to provide compaction and a crushing effect.

stationary: A machine that reduces the volume of solid waste by forcing it into a container.

companion crop: A crop sown with another crop. Used particularly for small grains with which forage crops are sown. Preferred to the term nurse crop.

comparative advantage: The idea that producers at each locality tend to use their resources to produce those goods which they can produce at the lowest relative costs and use the proceeds from these goods to purchase those goods produced under greater advantage elsewhere.

comparator: An instrument or apparatus for measuring a dimension in terms of a standard; a precision optical instrument used to determine the rectangular coordinates of a point with respect to another point on any plane surface, such as a photographic plate; (surveying) an instrument for comparing standards of length; for subdividing such standards; or for determining a standard length of measuring devices.

compatible: (grafting) Scions and rootstalks that grow together satisfactorily; (pollination) flowering plants that are interfertile; (landscape design) ecologic or esthetic harmony in land development.

competing vegetation: Vegetation that seeks and uses the limited common resources (space, light, water, and nutrients) of a forest site needed by preferred trees for survival and growth.

compensable regulation: Regulation of land use that compensates the owner for any drop in the land value that can be attributed to the regulation; value is determined just before imposition of the regulation; payment is due only when the land is sold.

competition: The general struggle for existence within a trophic level in which the living organisms compete for a limited supply of the necessities of life.

compilation: The production of a new or revised map or chart, or portion thereof, from existing maps, aerial photographs, surveys, new data, and other sources.

complete treatment: A method of treating water that consists of the addition of coagulant chemicals, flash mixing, coagulation-flocculation, sedimentation, and filtration. Also called conventional filtration.

composite map: A map that portrays information of two or more general types; usually a compiled map, bringing together on one map, for purposes of comparison, data that were originally portrayed on separate maps.

composite sample: A series of water samples taken over a given period of time and weighted by flow rate.

compost: Organic residues or a mixture of organic residues and soil that have been piled and allowed to undergo biological decomposition, until relatively stable.

composting: A controlled process of degrading organic matter by microorganisms. Techniques include:

mechanical: A method in which the compost is continuously and mechanically mixed and aerated.

ventilated cell: the compost is

mixed and aerated by being dropped through a vertical series of ventilated cells.

windrow: An open air method in which compostable material is placed in windrows, piles, or ventilated bins or pits and is occasionally turned or mixed. The process may be anaerobic or aerobic.

Comprehensive Environmental Response, Compensation, and Liability Act (CERCLA): A Federal law, enacted in 1980 and nicknamed "Superfund," that provides the authority through which the Federal government can compel people or companies responsible for creating hazardous waste sites to clean them up. It also created a public trust fund, known as the Superfund, to assist with the cleanup of inactive and abandoned hazardous waste sites or accidentally spilled or illegally dumped hazardous materials.

comprehensive plan: A report from a governmental planning agency that describes how its area of jurisdiction should be developed, expressing both policies and a coordinated plan for public and private land use, a transportation system, and public services, and facilities. Also called comprehensive development plan, general plan, master plan.

comprehensive planning program: A continuing process Which includes research on the conditions and trends in physical, social, and economic development; preparation and adoption of a comprehensive plan; programming of capital improvements; and initiation of the regulatory and administrative measures for

implementation and maintenance of the plan.

compressed natural gas (CNG): An alternative fuel for motor vehicles; considered one of the cleanest because of low hydrocarbon emissions and its vapors are relatively non-ozone producing. However, vehicles fueled with CNG do emit a significant quantity of nitrogen oxides.

compression: A system of forces or stresses that tends to decrease the volume or compact a substance, or the change of volume produced by such a system of forces.

concentrates: Feed with high total digestible nutrient and low fiber content, for example, grain and grain by products.

concentration: The amount of suspended particles in a unit volume as specified for a given temperature and pressure.

concessionaire: A person or agency that receives a grant or lease of a portion of a premises for some specific use such as the selling, renting, or leasing of a commodity or equipment.

concretion (soils): A local concentration of a chemical compound, such as calcium carbonate or iron oxide, in the form of an aggregate or nodule of varying size, shape, hardness, and color.

condensation: The physical process by which a vapor becomes a liquid or solid; the opposite of evaporation.

condensation nucleus: A particles, natural or man-made, liquid or solid, upon which water vapor condenses in the atmosphere. See *nucleation.*

condominium: A form of ownership in which the property owner has fee simple ownership of a unit within a structure, in the land and shared building facilities.

conduction: The transfer of heat by physical contact between two or more objects.

conductimetric method: The process for determining concentrations of air pollutants based on their electrical conductivity in chemical solutions.

conduit: Any channel intended for the conveyance of water, whether open or closed.

cone (botany): A more or less conical multiple fruit or, in the staminate (male) flower, a mass of pollen-bearing scales in the staminate flower of the pine, fir, or other related trees. The pistillate (female) cone consists of scales bearing naked seeds.

cone of depression: Depression, roughly conical in shape, produced in a water table or piezometric surface by the extraction of water from a well.

conformal map projection: See *map projection.*

confined aquifer: An aquifer in which groundwater is confined under pressure which is significantly greater than atmospheric pressure.

confining layer: A layer of sediment or lithologic unit of low permeability that bounds an aquifer.

confluence: The place where two streams meet, or the stream formed from two joining streams.

conic map projection: See *map projection.*

conglomerate: The consolidated equivalent of gravel.

conifer: A tree belonging to the order Coniferae with cones and evergreen leaves of needle shape or "scale like." The tree is harvested to produce wood known commercially as "softwood."

coniferous: Pertaining to conifers, which bear woody cones containing naked seeds.

conjunctive water use: The joining together of two sources of irrigation water, such as groundwater and surface water, to serve a particular piece of land.

conk: A hard, fruiting body containing spores of a wood-decaying fungus.

conservation: The protection, improvement, and use of natural resources according to principles that will assure their highest economic or social benefits.

conservation biology: The discipline that treats the content of biodiversity, the natural processes that produce it and the techniques used to sustain it in the face of human-caused environmental disturbance.

conservation plan for farm, ranch or nonagricultural land unit: The properly recorded decisions of the cooperating landowner or operator on how he plans, within practical limits, to use his land in an operating unit within its capability and to treat it according to its needs for maintenance or improvement of the soil, water, and plant resources.

Conservation of Private Grazing Land Initiative: The 1996 Farm Act authorized a coordinated technical, educational, and related assistance program for owners and managers of non-Federal grazing lands, including rangeland, pasture land, grazed forest land, and hay land. The purpose of the program is to enhance water quality and wildlife and fish habitat, address weed and brush problems, enhance recreational opportunities, and maintain and improve the aesthetic character of non-Federal grazing lands.

Conservation Reserve Enhancement Program (CREP): This program was initiated following the 1996 farm bill. CREP is a State-Federal conservation partnership program targeted to address specific State and nationally significant water quality, soil erosion, and wildlife habitat issues related to agriculture. The program offers additional financial incentives beyond the CRP to encourage farmers and ranchers to enroll in 10 to 15 year contracts to retire land from production. CREP is funded through CCC.

Conservation Reserve Program (CRP): Established in its current form in 1985 and administered by USDA's Farm Services Agency, this is the latest version of long-term land retirement programs used in the 1930s and 1960s. CRP provides farm owners or operators with an annual per-acre rental payment and half the cost of establishing a permanent land cover, in exchange for retiring environmentally sensitive cropland from production for 10 to 15 years. In 1996, Congress

reauthorized CRP for an additional round of contracts, limiting enrollment to 36.4 million acres at any time. The 2002 Farm Act increased the enrollment limit to 39 million acres. Producers can offer land for competitive bidding based on an Environmental Benefits Index during periodic signups or automatically enroll more limited acreages in such practices as riparian buffers, field windbreaks, and grass strips on a continuous basis. CRP is funded through the Commodity Credit Corporation.

Conservation Reserve Program (CRP) Continuous Sign-up: This program was initiated following the 1996 farm bill. Continuous sign-up allows enrollment of land in riparian buffers, filter strips, grass waterways, and other high priority practices without competition. Eligible land is automatically accepted into the program. A total of four million acres (under the CRP acreage cap) are reserved for continuous sign-up enrollment.

Conservation Security Program (CSP): This newly created program will provide payments to producers for maintaining or adopting structural and/or land management practices that address a wide range of local and/or national resource concerns. As with Environmental Quality Incentives Program, a wide range of practices can be subsidized. But CSP will focus on land-based practices and specifically excludes livestock waste handling facilities.

Producers can participate at one of three tiers; higher tiers require greater conservation effort and offer higher payments. The lowest cost practices that meet conservation standards must be used.

Conservation Technical Assistance (CTA): Since 1936, CTA, administered by USDA's Natural Resources Conservation Service (NRCS) and local conservation districts, has provided technical assistance to farmers for planning and implementing soil and water conservation and water quality practices. Farmers adopting practices under USDA conservation programs and other producers requesting assistance in adopting approved NRCS practices can receive technical assistance. In recent years, CTA has prepared conservation plans for highly erodible lands to help farmers maintain eligibility for USDA program benefits.

conservation district: A public organization created under state-enabling law as a special-purpose district to develop and carry out a program of soil, water, and related resource conservation, use, and development within its boundaries; in the United States usually a subdivision of state government with a local governing body; often called a soil conservation district or a soil and water conservation district.

conservation easement: An agreement negotiated on privately owned lands to preserve open space or protect certain natural resources.

conservation education: A comprehensive concept that spans curricula from kindergarten through adult, post-graduate programs and links that subject to natural resource conservation, stressing the characteristics and interrelationships in management and use of our natural resources that will result in knowledgeable citizenry with attitudes of responsibility toward conservation of those natural resources.

conservation plan: A collection of material containing land user information requested for making decisions regarding the conservation of soil, water, and related plant and animal resources for all or part of an operating unit.

conservation plan map: A portion of an aerial photograph or a composite mosaic of two or more aerial photos covering a farm or ranch with planned land use, field boundaries, fences, etc., portrayed thereon.

conservation practice: A technique or measure used to meet a specific need in planning and carrying out soil and water conservation programs for which standards and specifications have been developed.

conservation standards: Standards for various types of soils and land uses, including criteria, techniques, and methods for the control of erosion and sediment resulting from land disturbing activities.

conservation tillage: Any tillage system which reduces loss of soil or water compared to unridged or clean tillage.

consistence (soil): The resistance of a material to deformation or rupture; the degree of cohesion or adhesion of the soil mass. Terms used for describing consistence of soil materials at various soil moisture contents and degrees of cementation are:

wet soil: nonsticky, slightly sticky, sticky, very sticky, nonplastic, slightly plastic, plastic, and very plastic.

moist soil: loose, very friable, friable, firm, very firm, and extremely firm.

dry soil: loose, soft, slightly hard, hard, very hard, and extremely hard.

consumers (biology): Heterotrophic organisms, chiefly animals, that ingest other organisms or particle organic matter.

consolidate: Any or all of the processes whereby loose, soft, or liquid earth materials become firm and hard.

constituent: A chemical or biological substance in water, sediment, or biota that can be measured by an analytical method.

construction waste: Waste materials produced in the construction of homes, office buildings, dams, industrial plants, schools, etc., including used lumber, miscellaneous metal parts, packaging materials, cans, boxes, wire, excess sheet metal, etc. See *waste, demolition waste, rubble.*

consumers: Heterotrophic organisms, chiefly animals, that ingest other organisms or particulate organic matter.

consumer waste: Materials which have been used and discarded by the buyer, or consumer, as opposed to "in-plant waste," or waste created in the manufacturing process.

consumptive irrigation requirement: The centimeters per hectare of irrigation water, exclusive of precipitation, stored soil moisture, or groundwater, needed consumptive-

ly for crop production.

consumptive use: The quantity of water used and transpired by vegetation plus that evaporated. See *evapotranspiration.*

contact grouting: Filling, with cement grout, any voids existing at the contact of two zones of different materials, e.g., between a concrete tunnel lining and the surrounding rock. The grout operation is usually carried out at low pressure.

contact herbicide: A herbicide that kills primarily by contact with plant tissue rather than as a result of translocation.

contact load: Sediment particles that roll or slide along in almost continuous contact with the streambed.

contact point (outdoor recreation): The physical location where an audience is exposed to an interpretive message.

containment levee: A dike or embankment to contain stream flow.

contaminant: An impurity in the environment that may be toxic to sensitive organisms.

contamination: The act of polluting or making impure, used to indicate chemical, sediment, or bacteriological impurities.

continental climate: A continental climate is a climate lacking oceanic influence and characterized by more extreme temperatures than marine climates. Therefore, a continental climate has a high annual temperature range for its latitude relative to a climate with marine influence.

continuous delivery (irrigation): A system by which an irrigator receives his allotted quantity of water at a continuous rate throughout the irrigation season.

continuous-flow irrigation: System of irrigation water delivery where each irrigator receives their allotted quantity of water at a continuous rate.

continuous grazing: Domestic livestock grazing a specific area throughout the grazing season. Not necessarily synonymous with year long grazing.

continuous sample: A flow of water, waste or other material from a particular place in a plant to the location where samples are collected for testing. May be used to obtain grab or composite samples.

continuous tone (lithography): An image that has not been screened and contains unbroken, gradient tones from black to white, and may be either in negative or positive form.

contour: An imaginary line on the surface of the earth connecting points of the same elevation; aline drawn on a map connecting points of the same elevation.

contour ditch: Irrigation ditch laid out approximately on the contour.

contour farming: Conducting field operations, such as plowing, planting, cultivating, and harvesting, on the contour.

contour flooding: Method of irrigating by flooding from contour ditches.

contour furrow irrigation: Applying irrigation water in furrows that run across the slope with a forward grade in the furrows.

contour furrows: Furrows plowed approximately on the contour on pasture and rangeland to prevent runoff and increase infiltration. Also, furrows laid out approximately on the contour for irrigation purposes.

contour interval: The vertical distance between contour lines.

contour level irrigation: Areas bounded by small contour levels and cross levels are completely flooded.

contour map: See *map, topographic.*

contour plowing: Plowing done in accordance with the natural outline or shape of the land by keeping the furrows or ditches at the same elevation as much as possible to reduce runoff and erosion.

contour stripcropping: Layout of crops in comparatively narrow strips in which the farming operations are performed approximately on the contour. Usually strops of grass or close-growing crops are alternated with those in cultivated crops or fallow.

contour stripping: The removal of overburden and mining from a coal seam that outcrops or approaches the surface at approximately the same elevation, in steep or mountainous areas.

contour surface mining: See *mining.*

contracted weir: The crest and sides of a retangular weir are far enough from the bottom and sides of the channel so that their effect on flow is negligible.

contraction joint: Contraction joints are joints placed in concrete to provide for volumetric shrinkage of a monolithic unit or movement between monolithic units. Contraction joints have no bond between the concrete surfaces forming the joint. Except as otherwise provided for dowels, reinforcement is never continuous across a contraction joint. Contraction joints will not transfer moment and will not transfer shear unless keyed.

contrails: Long narrow clouds caused by the disturbance of the atmosphere during passage of high flying jets. Proliferation of contrails may cause changes in the weather.

contrasting textures (As used in the Soil Classification System of the National Cooperative Soil Survey in the United States): If two widely different particle size classes occur within a vertical distance of five inches in the control section from which the soil family is derived, both particle size classes are listed in the name. For example, if the upper part of the control section is loamy sand and the lower part is clay, the particle size class is sandy over clayey.

contributing area: The area in a drainage basin that contributes water to streamflow or recharge to an aquifer.

control: In research, something under study, either untreated or given a standard treatment, which is used as a standard for comparison against the results of other treatments.

controlled burning: The deliberate use of fire where the burning is restricted to a predetermined area and intensity. See *prescribed burning*.

controlled drainage (irrigation): Regulation of the water table to maintain the water level at a depth favorable for optimum crop growth.

control point: A reference point precisely located on a photograph and on the ground; used in assembling photographs for map compilation.

control section (As used in the Soil Classification System of the National Cooperative Soil Survey in the United States): Arbitrary depths of soil material within which certain diagnostic horizons, features, and other characteristics are used as differentiae in the classification of soils. The thickness is specific for each characteristic being considered but may be different for different characteristics.

control strategy: The combination of measures, such as emission limitations, land use plans, emission taxes, designed to reduce levels of a specific pollutant in the ambient air.

control structure: A regulating structure to maintain water at a desired elevation, usually installed in gravity flow systems.

control techniques (pollution): Methods, equipment, and devices applicable to the prevention and control of air pollutants at their sources, such as process changes, fuel use limitations, and plant location, rules, etc.

convection: The transfer of heat through a gas or solution because of molecular movement.

convective clouds: Clouds generated by the rising of air over relatively warm ground. See *cloud*.

conventional signs (cartography): Symbols used in map margins to explain certain structures or other details that, because of map scale, cannot be shown in the true shape on the map itself.

conventional tillage: The combined primary and secondary tillage operations normally performed in preparing a seedbed for a given crop grown in a given geographical area.

coverage: Used much the same as data layer; an example of a coverage is the road information or NWI information for any given area; may also be called a theme.

conversion: A resource recovery method using chemical or biological processes to change waste materials into other useful forms, for example incineration to produce heat; pyrolysis to produce gas, oil, and char; and composting to produce a humus like soil conditioner. See *reuse, recycling.*

conveyance loss (water): Loss of water from delivery systems during conveyance, including operational losses and losses due to seepage, evaporation, and transpiration by plants growing in or near the channel.

cooling sprays: Water sprays directed into flue gases to cool them and, in most cases, to remove some fly ash.

cooling tower: A device to remove excess heat from water used in industrial operations.

cool season plant: A plant that makes its major growth during the cool portion of the year, primarily in the spring but in some

localities in the winter.

coordinate: An ordered set of data values, either absolute or relative, which specifies a location.

coordinated resource plan: A conservation plan including privately-owned land and public land; generally developed on the land by the private landowner and representatives of all appropriate land-administering agencies, and includes an entire operating unit, allotment, or other resource unit.

coordinatopgraph: An instrument used to lot in terms of plane coordinates; it may be an integral part of a stereoscopic plotting instrument whereby the planimetric motion (x and y) or the floating mark are plotted directly; also called rectangular coordinate plotter.

cooperative housing: A form of ownership in which each occupant family owns a share in the entire development, including land and buildings.

coppice (coppicing): The tendency of certain tree and brush species (such as red alder and bigleaf maple) to produce a large number of shoots when a single or few stems are mechanically removed but the root system left intact.

copy (lithography): Any furnished material (typewritten manuscript, pictures, artwork, etc.) to be used in the production of printing.

cord: A unit of measurement of stacked wood containing 128 cubic feet within its outside surfaces. The standard cord is a pile of wood four feet by eight feet, made up of sticks four feet long, containing about 80 solid cubic feet of wood.

cordon: A tree, usually of a fruiting variety, trained to a single or double stem without side branches.

corduroy: Logs placed transversely along a road, usually with branches intact, and covered with fill material, to "float" the road over soft subsoils.

core (energy): The part of a nuclear reactor where energy is released from the radioactive material.

core drilling: The process by which a cylindrical sample of soil or rock is obtained through the use of a hollow drilling bit that cuts and retains a section of the strata penetrated.

core trench: Excavation for a core wall in the construction of an earth embankment.

core wall: Wall of masonry, sheet piling, or compacted earth placed near the center of a dam or embankment to reduce seepage.

corona effect: Electrical charging (ionization) of air near pointed objects or conductors.

corrasion: The wearing away of earth materials through the cutting, scraping, scratching, and scouring effects of solid material carried in the currents of water or air.

correction strip: An irregular strip or area of land lying between contour strips.

corrective action: Cleanup of hazardous waste contamination at non-Superfund sites. See also *Resource Conservation and Recovery Act (RCRA)*.

correlation (soil): See *soil correlation*.

correlation (statistics): An expression indicating the degree of association or mutual relationship between the value of two attributes, not necessarily a casual or dependent relationship.

corridor: An area of variable width between two points. In highway

work, corridors are defined areas where the needs for improvement are studied.

corridor study (roads): The study of corridor locations; social, economic, and environmental considerations; and alternatives for an area.

corrosion: The solution of rocks and other materials by chemical action.

corrugation irrigation: A partial surface flooding method of irrigation, normally used with drilled crops, where water is applied in small graded channels or furrows so spaced that an adequate lateral spread is obtained by the time the desired amount of water has entered the soil.

cost allocation: The process of apportioning cost among the various purposes served by a measure or work of improvement. Various costs include:

alternate costs: The cost of providing the same or equivalent benefits from the most likely economically feasible alternative source available in the area to be served.

joint cost: The difference between the cost of a multiple purpose development as a whole and the total of the separable costs for all project purposes.

separable cost: The difference between the cost of a multiple purpose development and the cost of the development with the purpose omitted.

specific cost: That cost incurred solely for a single purpose, for example, a pipeline to carry municipal water.

cost-sharing: Monetary assistance from a federal, state, or local agency to a landowner for installation of soil and water conservation structures or other measures, such as terraces.

cotyledon: The first leaf or leaves in a seed; in some plants remaining within the seed, in others emerging upon germination.

count, range: A census of the animals using a grazing area, usually including a determination of the respective ownership.

count, tree: A simple, rapid method of timber survey in which dependence is placed on counting the number of trees without reference to their diameter and heights.

counter-cyclical payment: Counter-cyclical payments are available to eligible commodities under the 2002 Farm Act whenever the effective commodity price is less than the target price. The effective price is equal to the sum of 1) the higher of the national average farm price for the marketing year, or the commodity national loan rate and 2) the direct payment rate for the commodity. The payment amount for a farmer equals the product of the payment rate, the payment acres, and the payment yield. Payments are considered counter-cyclical since they vary inversely with market prices.

cover: Vegetation or other material providing protection; (fish) a variety of items including undercut banks, trees, roots, and rocks in the water where fish seek necessary protection or security; (forestry) low growing shrubs, vines, and herbaceous plants under the trees; (ground and soils) any vegetation producing a protecting mat on or just above the soil surface; (stream) generally trees, large shrubs, grasses, and forbs that shade and otherwise protect the stream from erosion, temperature elevation, or sloughing of banks; (vegetation) all plants of all sizes and species found on an area, irrespective of whether they have forage or other value; (wildlife) plants or objects used by wild animals for nesting, rearing of young, resting, escape from predators, or protection from adverse environmental conditions.

coverage, stereoscopic: Aerial photographs taken with sufficient overlap to permit stereoscopic examination in the overlap area, usually 60 percent in line of flight and 30 percent with adjoining flights.

cover crop: A close growing crop grown primarily for the purpose of protecting and improving soil between periods of regular crop production or between trees and vines in orchards and vineyards.

cover material (engineering): A backfill, free of organic material, used to cover compacted waste in a sanitary landfill; usually earth.

cover, percent: The area covered by the combined aerial parts of plants and mulch expressed as a percent of the total area.

cow month: The grazing needed to maintain a mature cow in good condition for 30 days.

cradle (engineering): A supporting structure shaped to fit the conduit it supports.

creep (soil): Slow mass movement of soil and soil material down relatively steep slopes, primarily under the influence of gravity but facilitated by saturation with water and by alternate freezing and thawing.

creep feeding: Supplemental feeding of suckling livestock in such a manner that the feed is not available to the mothers or other mature livestock.

crepuscular: Active in twilight at dawn or dusk; including many species of birds, mammals, and insects.

crest: The top of a dam, dike, spillway, or weir, frequently restricted to the overflow portion; the summit of a wave or peak of a flood.

crest-stage gage: Instrument designed to delineate the peak stage of a flood, usually at remote or other partial recording stations.

crest structure: Portion of spillway between the inlet channel and the chute, tunnel or conduit, which does not contain gates.

crest width (top thickness): The thickness or width of a dam at the level of the top of dam (excluding corbels or parapets). In general, the term thickness is used for gravity and arch dams, and width is used for other dams.

crib dam: A barrier of timber forming bays or cells that are filled with stone or other heavy material. See *rock fill dam*,

criterion: The level of a compound or material set by a governmental agency to be protective of human health, wildlife health, and/or the environment.

critical area: A severely eroded sediment producing area that requires special management to establish and maintain vegetation in order to stabilize soil conditions.

critical depth (hydraulics): Depth of flow in a channel of specified dimensions at which specific energy is a minimum for a given discharge.

critical habitat: The area of land, water, and airspace required for normal needs and survival of a plant or animal species.

critical height: The maximum height at which a vertical or sloped bank of soil will stand unsupported under a given set of conditions.

critical reach: The point in the receiving stream below a discharge point at which the lowest dissolved oxygen level is reached and recovery begins.

critical slope (hydraulics): that slope that will sustain a given discharge at uniform, critical depth in a given channel; (soils) See *angle of repose.*

critical wildlife habitat: Part or all of a specific place occupied by a wildlife species or a population of such species and recognized as being essential for the maintenance of the population.

critical winter range: Forested habitat, usually stands of mature or old-growth conifers, which provides deer and elk with resources critical to survival during severe winters.

critical velocity: Velocity at which a given discharge changes from tranquil to rapid flow; that velocity in open channels for which the specific energy (sum of the depth and velocity head) is a minimum for a given discharge.

crop irrigation requirement: Quantity of water, exclusive of effective precipitation, that is needed for crop production.

cropland: Land used primarily for the production of adapted, cultivated, close growing fruit or nut crops for harvest, alone or in association with sod crops.

cropping pattern: The acreage distribution of different crops in any one year in a given farm area such as a county, water agency, or farm. Thus, a change in a cropping pattern from one year to the next can occur by changing the relative acreage of existing crops, and/or by introducing new crops, and/or by cropping existing crops.

crop requirement: The amount of nutrients needed per acre, regardless of their origin, to grow a specified yield of a crop plant.

crop residue: The portion of a plant or crop left in the field after harvest.

crop residue management: Use of that portion of the plant or crop left in the field after harvest for protection or improvement of the soil.

crop root zone: The soil depth from which a mature crop extracts most of the water needed for evapotranspiration. The crop root zone is equal to effective rooting depth and is expressed as a depth in inches or feet. This soil depth may be considered as the rooting depth of a subsequent crop, when accounting for soil moisture storage in efficiency calculations.

crop rotation: The growing of different crops in recurring succession on the same land.

crop subsidy: Price support paid by the government to farmers.

crop tree: An individual tree which,

because of species, form, and condition, is selected for and is most likely to be present in the final harvestable crop, usually for sawlog purposes. See *weed tree, wolf tree*.

crop water requirement: Crop consumptive use plus the water required to provide the leaching requirements.

cross-drain culvert: A culvert used to carry ditch water from one side of the road to the other.

crosshairs: A set of wires or etched lines placed on a reticle held in the focal plane of a telescope; used as index marks for pointing of the telescope such as in a transit or level when pointings and readings must be made on a rod.

cross hatching (cartography): A method of depicting different areas on an illustration, map, or photo with ruled or screen-type patterns; not to be confused with hachures.

cross section: A horizontal grid system laid out on the ground for determining contours, quantities or earthwork, etc., by means of elevations of the grid points.

crotch injury (horticulture): The damage caused to a plant by low temperatures; it may involve three distinct groups of plant tissues-sapwood, cambium, and bark.

crotovina: A former animal burrow in one soil horizon that has been filled with organic matter or material from another horizon; also spelled krotovina.

crown (forestry): The upper part of a tree, including the branches and foliage.

crown class: All trees in a stand with tops or crowns occupying a similar position in the canopy or crown cover. **Crown classes usually distinguished are:**

dominant: Trees with crowns extending above the general level of the forest canopy and receiving full light from above and partly from the side; larger than the average trees in the stand and with crowns well developed but possibly somewhat crowded on the sides.

co dominant: Trees with crowns forming the general upper level of the forest canopy with the dominants receiving full light from above but comparatively little from the sides; usually with medium sized crowns more or less crowded on the sides.

intermediate: Trees with crowns below but still extending into the general level of the forest canopy, receiving a little direct light from above but none from the sides; usually with small crowns and stem diameter; considerably crowded on the sides.

overtopped: Trees with crowns entirely below the general forest canopy and receiving no direct light either from above or from the sides.

crown cover: The canopy formed by the crowns of all the trees in a forest.

crude oil: Raw petroleum as it comes from the earth in a liquid state; consists predominately of hydrocarbons.

cruise (forestry): A survey of forest land to locate and estimate the timber by volume, species, size classes, products, grades, and other characteristics. Also, the estimate obtained in such a survey.

crumb structure: See *soil structure type.*

crust: A dry surface layer on soils that is much more compact, hard, and brittle than the material immediately beneath it.

cryic: A soil temperature regime that has mean annual soil temperatures of more than 0 degrees C but less than 8 degrees C, more than 5 degrees C difference between mean summer and mean winter soil temperatures at 50 cm, and cold summer temperatures.

cryptogam: A plant reproducing by spores and not by flowers or seeds (mosses, lichens, and ferns) in any of the groups Tallophytes, Bryophytes, and Pteridophytes.

crystalline rocks: Rocks (igneous or metamorphic) consisting wholly of crystals or fragments of crystals.

cull (forestry): Any item of production, such as trees, logs, or lumber, sorted out for rejection or relegation because it does not meet specifications, such as poor form, limbyness, rot, or other defect. Used also with reference to inferior nursery seedlings.

cullet: Clean, color-sorted, crushed glass that is used in glass-making to speed up the melting of silica sand.

culm: The jointed stem of various grasses, usually hollow.

cultivar: An assemblage of cultivated plants that is clearly distinguished by any characters (morphological, physiological, cytological, chemical, or others) and when reproduced, sexually or asexually, retains its distinguishing characters; derived from cultivated variety; cultivar and variety are equivalents.

cultivation: Shallow tillage operations performed to create soil conditions conducive to improved aeration, infiltration, and water conservation, or to control weeds.

cultural eutrophication: Acceleration by man of the natural process of enrichment (aging) of bodies of water.

culture: Cultivation of organisms in a medium containing necessary nutrients.

cumulative impact: The environmental impact that results from actions, which when added to others of the past, present, and the foreseeable future, will have a total effect.

cumulative infiltration: Summation of the depth of water absorbed by a soil in a specified elapsed time in reference to the time of initial water application.

cumulonimbus: See *cloud*.

cumulus: See *cloud*.

current meter (hydraulics): An instrument used for measuring the velocity of flowing water. The velocity of the water is proportional to the revolutions per unit time of the propeller, vane, or wheel of the meter.

custom work: Specific farm operations performed under agreement between the farmer and the contractor; for example, custom harvesting of grain, spraying and picking fruit, and shearing sheep. The contractor furnishes labor, equipment, and material to complete the operation.

cut: Portion of land surface or area from which earth has been removed or will be removed by excavation; the depth below original ground surface to excavated surface.

cut and fill: Process of earth moving by excavating part of an area and using the excavated material for adjacent embankments or fill areas.

cutback irrigation: Water applied at a faster rate at the beginning of the irrigation period and then reduced or cutback to a lesser rate, usually one half the initial rate or that amount to balance with the intake rate.

cutback stream: The furrow stream resulting after the initial furrow stream has been reduced; approximately equal to the intake rate of the soils. The initial size flow is usually applied about one-third of the application period. The initial stream is about 160 percent of the cutback stream.

cut, final: Last cut or line of excavation made on a specific mined area.

cuticle: The thickened, waxy, surface layer of such plant organs as leaves, fruits, and shoots.

cutoff: Wall, collar, or other structure, such as a trench, filled with relatively impervious material intended to reduce seepage of water through porous strata; in river hydraulics, the new and shorter channel formed either naturally or artificially when a stream cuts through the neck of a band.

cutoff drain: See *interceptor drain*.

cut over forest: A forest in which most or all of the merchantable timber has been cut.

cutting cycle: The planned interval between major cutting operations in a managed woodland tract.

cyclone: A large-scale, atmospheric circulation system in which, in the northern hemisphere, the winds rotate counter clockwise.

cyclone collector: A device used to collect large size particulates from polluted air by centrifugal force. Because of its simplicity and effectiveness, the cyclone collector is widely used in feed mills,

sawmills, and other manufacturing operations that generate dust and particulates.

Cylindrical map projection: See *map projection*.

D

daily design capacity: The number of people that a recreation area or facility is designed to accommodate, including turnover, on an average Sunday during the normal heavy use season.

daily turnover: The number of times a specific outdoor recreation can normally be expected to be used by various individuals or groups in one day.

dam: A barrier to confine or raise water for storage or diversion, to create a hydraulic head, to prevent gully erosion, or for retention of soil, rock, or other debris.

dam failure: Catastrophic type of failure characterized by the sudden, rapid, and uncontrolled release of impounded water. It is recognized that there are lesser degrees of failure and that any malfunction or abnormality outside the design assumptions and parameters which adversely affect

a dam's primary function of impounding water could be considered a failure. Such lesser degrees of failure can progressively lead to or heighten the risk of a catastrophic failure. They are, however, normally amenable to corrective action.

dam foundation: The excavated surface or undisturbed material upon which a dam is placed.

dano biostabilizer system: An aerobic, thermophilic composting process in which optimum conditions of moisture, air, and temperature are maintained in a single, slowly revolving cylinder that retains the compostable solid waste for one to five days. The material is later windrowed.

Darcy's Law: A volume of water passing through a porous medium in unit time is proportional to the cross sectional area and to the difference in hydraulic head and inversely proportional to the thickness of the medium. The proportionality constant is called the hydraulic conductivity.

data-acquisition system: The collection of devices and media that measures physical variables and records them prior to input to the data processing system.

data bank: A well-defined collection of data, usually of the same general type, which can be accessed by a computer; also called data base.

data processing: Application of procedures, mechanical, electrical, computational, or other, whereby data are changed from one form into another.

dating (direct): Determining the age of a particular object by the study of the object itself; (radioactive) determining the age of rocks and other materials by the analysis of the constant rate of breakdown of radioactive materials.

datum (general): Any numerical or geometric quantity or set of such quantities that may serve as a reference or base for other quantities; (geodetic) a reference surface consisting of five quantities: the latitude and longitude of an initial point, the azimuth of a line from this point, and two constants necessary to define the reference spheroid; forms the basis for the computation of horizontal control surveys in which the curvature of the earth is considered; also called horizontal control datum, horizontal datum, horizontal geodetic datum; (leveling) a level surface to which elevations are referred, usually, but not always, mean sea level; also called vertical datum, vertical control.

day camping: An experience in the out of doors, under trained leadership, requiring that the camper is absent from home only during daylight hours.

daylighting: The surface mining procedures and excavation processes used to expose underground mine works for partial or complete removal of the remaining mineral underlying the surface.

dead capacity (dead storage): The reservoir capacity from which stored water cannot be evacuated by gravity.

dead end: The end of a water main which is not connected to other parts of the distribution system.

debris: The loose material arising from the disintegration of rocks and vegetative material; transportable by streams, ice, or floods.

debris basin: Detention structure constructed to retain soil material and detriment transported by runoff; structures designed to collect solids from livestock feedlot runoff.

debris dam: A barrier built across a stream channel to retain rock, sand, gravel, silt, or other material.

debris fan: Sloping mass of boulders, cobbles, gravel, sand, silt and clay formed by debris flows at the mouth of a tributary.

debris flow: Flash flood consisting of a mixture of rocks and sediment containing less than 40 percent water, by volume; forms a debris fan.

debris guard: Screen or grate at the intake of a channel, drainage, or pump structure for the purpose of stopping debris.

decay: The disintegration of organic materials into simpler forms, or into their original elements, by action of bacteria, fungi, or other micro-organisms. See *compost*.

decibel: The unit of measuring the intensity of sound. Zero on the decibel scale is the slightest sound that can be heard by humans rustling leaves, breathing. The Scale: eardrum ruptures (140 decibels jet taking off); deafening (100 decibels thunder, car horn at three feet, loud motorcycle, loud power lawn mower); very loud (80 decibels portable sander, food blender; continued exposure brings about loss of hearing, impossible to use phone); loud (60 decibels city playground, average restaurant or living room); faint (20 decibels courtroom or classroom, private office, a whisper at five feet).

deciduous plant: A plant that sheds all its leaves every year at a certain season.

declination: The difference in base direction lines between true north and magnetic north expressed as an angle read in degrees; also referred to as deviation.

decomposer: An organism, usually a bacterium or a fungus, that breaks down the bodies or parts of dead plants and animals into simpler compounds.

decomposition: The breakdown of organic waste materials by bacteria. Aerobic process refers to one using oxygen breathing bacteria, while anaerobic refers to a process using bacteria which breathe an inorganic oxidant. Total decomposition occurs spontaneously in the open (dumps and landfills) or

can be harnessed in waste treatment equipment to work under controlled conditions. See *biodegradable, compost*.

decreaser plant species (range): Plant species of the original vegetation that will generally decrease in relative amount with continued overuse. This reaction is not universal for a particular species but will vary due to kind of grazing animal, season of use, range site, and other environmental influences. Commonly termed decreasers.

deep percolation: Water that percolates below the root zone and cannot be used by plants.

deepwell disposal: Transfer of liquid wastewater to underground strata; usually limited to biological or chemically stable wastes.

deferred grazing: Discontinuance of livestock grazing on an area for a specified period of time during the growing season to promote plant reproduction, establishment of new plants, or restoration of vigor by old plants.

deferred rotation grazing: A systematic rotation of deferred grazing.

definition (photography): Degree of clarity and sharpness of an image; a subjective measure of density.

deflation: The force of wind erosion, e.g., blowouts.

deflection: Upstream or downstream movement of a dam or dike.

deflocculate: To separate the individual components of compound articles by chemical and/or physical means; to cause the particles of the disperse phase of a colloidal system to become suspended in the dispersion medium.

deformation of rocks: Any change in the original form or volume of rock masses produced by tectonic forces; folding, faulting, and solid flow are common modes of deformation.

degasification: A water treatment that removes dissolved gases from the water.

degradation: To wear down by erosion, especially through stream action.

degradation products: Compounds resulting from transformation of an organic substance through chemical, photochemical, and/or biochemical reactions.

degree of grazing: The degree of utilization of selected plant species in a designated area at the time of measurement.

degree of use (range): The portion of the current year's forage production that is consumed and/or destroyed by grazing animals; may refer either to a single species or to the vegetation as a whole.

deleterious substance: Any substance that, if added to water, would degrade or alter the quality of the water so that it becomes deleterious to fish or fish habitat, or becomes unsuitable for human consumption or any other purpose for which it is legally licensed (such as irrigation and livestock watering).

delineation: The process of drawing or plotting features on a map with lines and symbols.

delivery box (irrigation): Structure diverting water from a canal to a farm unit, often including measuring devices.

delta: An alluvial deposit formed where a stream or river drops its sediment load on entering a body of more quiet water; formed largely beneath the water surface and in an area often resembling the shape of the Greek letter Delta, with the point of entry of the stream at one corner.

demand: The quantity of any particular commodity that will be purchased on a market or groups of related markets at a given price or series of prices.

demand scheduling: Method of irrigation scheduling whereby water is delivered to users as needed and which may vary in flow rate, frequency and duration. Considered a flexible form of scheduling.

demineralization: A treatment process that removes dissolved minerals from water.

demography: The statistical study of human vital statistics and population dynamics.

demolition waste: Building materials and rubble resulting from construction, remodeling, repair, and demolition operations.

demonstration area: An area of land with definite boundaries and of sufficient size on which demonstrational work in soil and water conservation and land use was done by and between the Soil Conservation Service (SCS) and cooperating landowners and owners and operators; project areas were designated by name and number by SCS soon after its creation in 1935.

dendritic: Channel pattern of streams with tributaries that branch to form a tree-like pattern.

dendrology: The identification and systematic classification of trees and shrubs.

denitrification: The chemical or biochemical reduction of nitrate or nitrite to gaseous nitrogen, either as molecular nitrogen or as an oxide of nitrogen.

dense non-aqueous phase liquid (DNAPL): Liquid contaminants that are relatively insoluble and heavier than water; also known as sinkers because they will sink to the bottom of an aquifer, where they become especially difficult to detect and clean up.

densitometer: An instrument for the measurement of optical density of a material, generally of a photographic image.

density: In biology, the number of organisms per unit at a given time; in physical sciences, the ratio of the weight of an object to its volume; for example, in a sanitary landfill, the combined weight of solid wastes and soil cover divided by the combined volume of solid wastes and soil cover.

density slicing (remote sensing): A general class of electronic or digital techniques used to assign image points or data vectors to particular classes based on the density or level of the response in a single image or channel; classification by thresholds; also called level slicing.

density stratification: The arrangement of water masses into separate, distinct horizontal layers as a result of differences in density; may be caused by differences in temperature or dissolved and suspended solids. See *thermal stratification*.

departure (plane surveying): The orthographic projection of a line on an east–west axis of reference; the difference of the meridian distances or longitudes of the ends of the line. It is east or positive, and sometimes termed the easting, for a line whose azimuth or bearing is in the northeast or southeast quadrant; it is west or negative, and sometimes termed the westing, for a line whose azimuth or bearing is in the southwest or northwest quadrant, also called longitude difference; (navigation) the distance between two meridians at any given parallel of latitude, expressed in linear units, usually nautical miles; the distance to the east or west made good by a craft in proceeding from one point to another.

depletion curve (hydraulics): A graphical representation of water depletion from storage stream channels, surface soil, and groundwater. A depletion curve can be drawn for base flow, direct runoff, or total flow.

deposit: Material left in a new position by a natural transporting agent, such as water, wind, ice, or gravity, or by the activity of man.

depositing substrates: Bottom areas where solids are being actively deposited. These often occur in the vicinity of effluent discharges. See *sludge deposits*.

deposition: The accumulation of material dropped because of a slackening movement of the transporting agent (water or wind).

deposition velocity: The deposition rate divided by the ambient concentration of a specific air pollutant.

depreciation: The loss in trading value resulting from a period of use or ownership.

depression storage: Water stored in surface depressions and therefore not available for producing surface runoff.

depth-area-duration analysis: Determination of the maximum amounts of precipitation within various durations over areas of various sizes; used in the prediction of flood events.

depth, effective soil: The depth of soil material that plant roots can penetrate readily to obtain water and plant nutrients; the depth to a layer that differs sufficiently from the overlying material in physical or chemical properties to prevent or seriously retard the growth of roots.

depth-integrating sampler: Device designed to collect a water sample from streams and rivers that is characteristic of the average suspended sediment load in transport.

depth of field: The distance between the points nearest to and farthest from a camera that are in focus.

dermal toxicity: The ability of a pesticide chemical to poison an animal or human by skin absorption.

desalinization: Removal of salts from saline soils, usually by leaching; the conversion of salt water to sweet water. Also spelled desalination.

desert: An area of land that has an arid, hot to cool climate with vegetation that is sparse and usually shrubby.

desert soils (obsolete): A zonal great soil group consisting of soils with a very thin, light-colored surface horizon that may be vesicular and are ordinarily underlain by calcareous material formed in arid regions under sparse shrub vegetation. See *soil classification*.

desertification: When soil erosion is so severe that plants and animals can no longer exist.

desiccant: A chemical agent used to remove moisture from a material or object.

desiccation: The drying out of material.

design capacity: The number of people that a recreation area or facility is designed to accommodate at any one time.

design frequency: The time (days) between irrigations when crops have the highest consumptive use. See *irrigation frequency*.

design runoff rate (irrigation): Maximum runoff rate expected over a given period of time.

design water level: The maximum water elevation, including the flood surcharge, that a dam is designed to be able to withstand.

design wind: The most severe wind that is reasonbly possible at a particular reservoir for generating wind setup and runup. The determination will generally include the results of meteorologic studies which combine wind velocity, duration, direction, and seasonal distribution characteristics in a realistic manner.

designated floodway: The channel of a water course and those portions of the adjoining flood plain required to provide for the passage of a selected flood with a small increase in flood stage above that of natural conditions.

designated frequency flood:

Refers to the probability that a flood will occur in a given year. A 100-year flood is often considered in the design of diversion dams and for diversion-during-construction requirements. Service spillways, stilling basins, and some outlet works components may also be designed to pass certain level of floods designated by a return period. The return period should be thought as the chance that such a flood will be equaled or exceeded in any one year. For example, the 100-year flood is the flow level with a 0.01 annual exceedance probability, or there is 1 chance in 100 that this flood flow level will be equaled or exceeded in any given year.

desilting area: An area of grass, shrubs, or other vegetation used for inducing deposition of silt and other debris from flowing water; located above a stock tank, pond, field, or other area needing protection from sediment accumulation. See *filter strip*.

desorption: The release or removal of an adsorbed material from the surface of a solid adsorbent.

destratification: Vertical mixing within a lake or reservoir to totally or partially eliminate separate layers of temperature, plant, or animal life.

destructive distillation: The airless heating of organic matter that results in the evolution of volatile substances and produces a solid char consisting of fixed carbon and ash. See *lantz process*.

detachment: The removal of transportable fragments of soil material from a soil mass by an eroding agent, usually falling raindrops, running water, or wind. Through

detachment, soil particles or aggregates are made ready for transport soil erosion.

detect: To determine the presence of a compound.

detection limit: The concentration below which a particular analytical method cannot determine, with a high degree of certainty, a concentration.

detector (radiation): A device providing an electrical output that is a useful measure of incident radiation; broadly divisible into two groups: thermal, sensitive to temperature changes, and photodetectors, sensitive to changes in photon flux incident on the detector.

detention dam: A dam constructed for the purpose of temporary storage of streamflow or surface runoff and for releasing the stored water at controlled rates.

detention storage (irrigation): Water temporarily stored on the soil surface while enroute to streams; most leave the area as runoff, but some may leave as infiltration.

detergent: Synthetic washing agent that lowers the surface tension of water, emulsifies oil, and holds dirt in suspension; thus used for laundry or other cleaning purposes.

detention time: The theoretical calculated time required for a small amount of water to pass through a tank at a given rate of flow; the actual time that a small amount of water is in a settling basin, flocculating basin, or rapid-mix chamber; in storage reservoirs, the length of time water will be held before being used.

detonation: Practically instantaneous decomposition or combustion of an unstable compound, with tremendous increase in volume.

detrimental soil disturbance: Changes caused by forest practices in the physical, chemical, or biological properties of the soil, including the organic forest floor and the mineral soil extending from the surface to the depth at which the unweathered parent material is encountered. Such changes may result in a loss of productive growing site, reduced site productivity, or adverse impacts on resource values.

detrital: Clastic; rock and minerals occurring in sedimentary rocks that were derived from pre existing igneous, sedimentary, or metamorphic rocks.

detritus: Matter worn from rocks by mechanical means; generally, alluvial deposits.

development plan (recreation): A detailed construction plan including drawings and specifications.

deviation (surveying): The angular difference between magnetic and compass headings; also called magnetic deviation.

deviation, standard (statistics): A measure of the average variation of a series of observations or items of a population about their mean. In normally distributed sets of moderate size the interval of the mean plus or minus the standard deviation includes about two thirds of the items.

dew: Moisture in the air that condenses on solid surfaces when the air is saturated with water vapor.

dewatering: The removal of water by filtration, centrifugation, pressing, open air drying, or other methods. Dewatering makes sewage sludge suitable for disposal by burning or landfilling. The term is also applied when removing water from pulp.

dew point: The temperature at which a known quantity of moisture in the atmosphere condenses into rainfall.

diadromous: Fish that migrate from freshwater to saltwater or the reverse; a generic term that includes anadromous, catadromous, and amphidromous fish.

diagnostic horizons (As used in the Soil Classification System of the National Cooperative Soil Survey in the United States): Combinations of specific soil characteristics that are indicative of certain classes of soils. Those which occur at the soil surface are called epipedons, those below the surface, diagnostic subsurface horizons.

    agric horizon: A mineral soil horizon in which clay, silt, and humus derived from an overlying cultivated and fertilized layer have accumulated. The wormholes and illuvial clay, silt, and humus occur as horizontal lamellae or fibers or as coating on ped surfaces or in wormholes.

    albic horizon: A mineral soil horizon from which clay and free iron oxides have been removed or in which the oxides have been segregated to the extent that the color of the horizon is determined primarily by the color of the primary sand and silt particles rather than by coatings on these particles.

anthropic epipedon: A surface layer of mineral soil that has the same requirements as the mollic epipedon with respect to color, thickness, organic carbon content, consistence, and base saturation, but that has more than 250 ppm of P205 soluble in one percent citric acid, or is dry more than 10 months (cumulative) during the period when not irrigated. The anthropic epipedon forms under long, continued cultivation and fertilization.

aquic horizon: A mineral soil horizon in which clay, silt, and humus derived from an overlying cultivated and fertilized layer have accumulated. The wormholes and illuvial clay, silt, and humus occupy at least five percent of the horizon by volume. The illuvial clay and humus occur as horizontal lamellae or fibers, or as coating on ped surfaces or in wormholes.

argillic horizon: A mineral soil horizon that is characterized by the illuvial accumulation of layer lattice silicate clays. The argillic horizon has a certain minimum thickness depending on the thickness of the solum, a minimum quantity of clay in comparison with an overlying eluvial horizon depending on the clay content of the eluvial horizon, and usually has coatings of oriented clay on the surface of pores or peds or bridging sand grains.

calcic horizon: A mineral soil horizon of secondary carbonate enrichment that is more than 15 cm (six inches) thick, has a calci-

um carbonate equivalent of more than 15 percent, and has at least five percent more calcium carbonate equivalent than the underlying C horizon.

cambic horizon: A mineral soil horizon that has a texture of loamy very fine sand or finer, has soil structure rather than rock structure, contains some weatherable minerals, and is characterized by the alteration or removal of mineral material as indicated by mottling or gray colors, stronger chromas or redder hues than in underlying horizons, or the removal of carbonates. The cambic horizon lacks cementation or induration and has too few evidences of illuviation to meet the requirements of the argillic or spodic horizon.

duripan: A subsurface horizon that is cemented by silica.

fragipan: A natural subsurface horizon with high bulk density relative to the solum above, seemingly cemented when dry but showing a moderate to weak brittleness when moist. The layer is low in organic matter, mottled, slowly or very slowly permeable to water, and usually shows occasional or frequent bleached cracks forming polygons. It may be found in profiles or either cultivated or virgin soils but not in calcareous material.

gypsic horizon: A mineral soil horizon of secondary calcium sulfate enrichment that is more than 15 cm thick, has at least five percent more gypsum than the C horizon, and in which the product of the thickness in centimeters and in percent calcium sulfate is equal to or greater than 150 percent cm.

histic epipedon: A thin organic soil horizon that is saturated with water at some period of the year unless artificially drained and that is at or near the surface of a mineral soil. The histic epipedon has a maximum thickness depending on the kind of materials in the horizon and the lower limit of organic carbon is the upper limit for the mollic epipedon.

mollic epipedons: A surface horizon of mineral soil that is dark colored and relatively thick, contains at least 0.58 percent organic carbon, is not massive and hard or very hard when dry, has a base saturation of more than 50 percent when measured at ph 7, has less than 250 ppm of P205 soluble in 1 percent citric acid, and is dominantly saturated with bivalent cations.

natric horizon: A mineral soil horizon that satisfied the requirements of an argillic horizon, but that also has prismatic columnar, or blocky structure and a subhorizon within 40 cm of the upper boundary, has the sodium adsorbtion ration (SAR) of less than or equal to 13 or an exchangeable sodium percentage (ESP) of less than or equal to 15.

ochric epipedon: A surface horizon of mineral soil that is too light in color, too high in chroma, too low in organic carbon, or too thin to be a plaggen, mollic, umbric, anthropic, or histic epipedon, or that is both hard and massive when dry.

oxic horizon: A mineral soil horizon that is at least 30 cm (12 inches) thick and characterized by the virtual absence of weatherable primary minerals or 2:1 lattice clays, the presence of 1:1 lattice clays and highly insoluble minerals such as quartz sand, the presence of hydrated oxides of iron and aluminum, the absence of water dispersible clay, and the presence of low cation exchange capacity and small amounts of exchangeable bases.

petrocalcic horizon: A continuous, indurated calcic horizon that is cemented by calcium carbonate and, in some places, with magnesium carbonate. It cannot be penetrated with a spade or auger when dry, dry fragments do not slake in water, and it is impenetrable to roots.

petrogypsic horizon: A continuous, strongly cemented, massive gypsic horizon that is cemented by calcium sulfate. It can be chipped with a spade when dry. Dry fragments do not slake in water and it is impenetrable to roots.

placic horizon: A black to dark reddish mineral soil horizon that is usually thin but that may range from 1 mm to 25 mm in thickness. The placic horizon is commonly cemented with iron and is slowly permeable or impenetrable to water and roots.

plaggen epipedon: A man made surface horizon more than 50 cm thick that is formed by long continued manuring and mixing.

salic horizon: A mineral soil horizon of enrichment with secondary salts more soluble in cold water than gypsum. A salic horizon is 15 cm or more in thickness, contains at least two percent salt, and the product of the thickness in centimeters and percent salt by weight is 60 percent cm or more.

sombric horizon: A subsurface mineral horizon that is darker in color than the overlying horizon but that lacks the properties of a spodic horizon. Common in cool, moist soils of high altitude in tropical regions.

spodic horizons: A mineral soil horizon that is characterized by the illuvial accumulation of amorphous materials composed of aluminum and organic carbon with or without iron. The spodic horizon has a certain minimum thickness, and a minimum quantity of extractable carbon plus iron plus aluminum in relation to its content of clay.

sulfuric horizon: A mineral or organic soil horizon that has both a pH less than 3.5 (1:1 in water) and jarosite mottles (the color of fresh straw that has a hue of 2.5Y or yellower and chroma of six or more).

umbric epipedon: A surface layer of mineral soil that has the same requirements as the mollic epipedon with respect to color, thickness, organic carbon content, consistence, structure, and P205 content, but that has a base saturation of less than 50 percent when measured at pH 7.

diameter breast high (DBH): The diameter of a tree 4.5 feet above ground level.

diaphragm-type earthfill: An embankment dam which is constructed mostly of pervious material and having a diaphragm of impermeable material which forms a water barrier. The

diaphragm which forms the water barrier may consist of earth, Portland cement concrete, bituminous concrete, or other material, and may occupy a position within the embankment or on the upstream face.

diapositive (photogrammetry): A positive photograph on a transparent medium, usually glass; generally used to refer to a transparent positive on a glass plate used in a plotting instrument, a projector, or a comparator; image is right-reading when viewed through its base.

diatomaceous earth (diatomite): A fine-grained siliceous material accumulated from the shells of diatoms; used in waste-water treatment to filter solids from sewage effluent and also as a base in dusting or powder pesticides.

diatoms: Single-celled, colonial, or filamentous algae with siliceous cell walls constructed of two overlapping parts.

diazo: A reproduction process with lines in the image usually developed by gaseous ammonia; prints are made only from a transparent or translucent original; also called blueline, blackline, or ozalid.

dibber: A dibble.

dibble: A tool for opening holes for planting seeds or small seedlings; also called planting bar, spud, or planting iron.

dichloro-diphenyl-trichloro-ethane (DDT): The first modern chlorinated hydrocarbon insecticide; because of its 15-year halflife and ability to bioaccumulate in food chains, it has been banned for registration and sale for almost all uses in the United States.

dieback: A condition in woody plants in which the ends or the branches die, often progressively backward, due to disease, insect injury, winter injury, or excessive or insufficient moisture.

dieldrin: An organochlorine insecticide no longer registered for use in the United States. Also a degradation product of the insecticide aldrin.

differential head (unbalanced head): The condition in which the water pressure on the upstream and downstream sides of an object differ.

differential settlement: Settlement of different magnitude occurring within a soil mass over a short horizontal distance; may cause cracking of soil mass and supported structures.

differentiation (horticulture): Any change of shape, texture, or structure associated with growth.

diffuse light: Light that does not reach the subject from a single direction; sunlight which has been scattered by the atmosphere or clouds.

diffusion: The even mixing of one compound throughout another.

digester: In a wastewater treatment plant, a closed tank that decreases the volume of solids and stabilizes raw sludge by bacterial action.

digestion: The anaerobic breakdown of organic matter in water solution or suspension into simpler or more biologically stable compounds or both; organic matter may be decomposed to soluble organic acids or alcohols and subsequently converted to such gases as methane and carbon dioxide; also called aerobic digestion.

digital computer: Type of electronic computer that performs arithmetical operations upon discrete numbers in a defined sequence.

digital data: Data which is in the form of ones and zeros.

digital image (remote sensing): Image having numeric values representing gray tones; each numeric represents a different gray tone.

digitize: To computerize (automate) mapped data by tracing it with a cursor (mouse) on a tablet equipped with an electronic grid for use in a GIS system.

digitizer: To translate an analogue measurement of data into a numerical description expressed in digits in a scale of notion.

dike (engineering): an embankment to confine or control water, especially one built along the banks of a river to prevent overflow of lowlands; a levee; (geology) a tabular body of igneous rock that cuts across the structure of adjacent rocks or cuts massive rocks.

dilution: Reduction of the concentration of a substance in air or water.

dilution ratio (waste management): The ratio of the volume of water in a stream to the volume of incoming waste; the capacity of a stream to assimilate waste is reflected in the dilution ration.

dinitroanalines: A family of soil applied herbicides absorbed mainly by shoots and roots, moving very little within the plant and inhibiting cell division resulting in curtailment of the lateral root formation commercial names include Treflan, Surflan, Basalin, Prowl, Balan, and Cobex. See *herbicide*.

dimictic: Lakes and reservoirs that freeze over and normally go through two stratifications and two mixing cycles a year.

dioecious (botany): Plants having staminate (male) flowers on one plant and pistillate (female) flowers on another plant.

dip (mining): The angle at which a plane, usually a rock bedding plane, is inclined fro m the horizontal, measured perpendicular to the strike. See *angle of dip strike*.

diphenyl ethers: A family of herbicides that have contact activity and also inhibit photosynthesis; broadleaf weeds are affected more than grasses; commercial names include Modown, Blazer, and Goal. See *herbicide*.

direct runoff: Water that flows over the ground surface or through the ground directly into streams, rivers, and lakes.

direct toxicity: Toxicity that has an effect on organisms themselves instead of having an effect by actual alteration of their habitat or interference with their food supply. See *acute toxicity, chronic toxicity, indirect toxicity*.

discharge (hydraulics): Rate of flow, specifically fluid flow; a volume of fluid passing a point per unit time, commonly expressed as cubic feet per second, million gallons per day, gallons per minute, or cubic meters per second.

discharge capacity: The maximum amount of water that can safely released from a given waterway.

discharge coefficient (hydraulics): The ratio of actual rate of flow to the theoretical rate of flow through orifices, weirs, or other hydraulic structures.

discharge curve (irrigation): Rating curve showing the relation between stage and rate of flow of a stream; curve showing the relation of discharge of a pump and the speed, power, and head. See *capacity curve pump*.

discharge formula (hydraulics): A formula to calculate rate of flow of fluid in a conduit or through an opening. For steady flow discharge, $Q = AV$, where Q is rate of flow, A is cross-sectional area, and V is mean velocity. Common units are cubic feet per second, square feet, and feet per second, respectively. To calculate the mean velocity, V, for uniform flow in pipes or open channels, see *Manning's formula*.

discharge period: The period of time during which effluent is discharged.

discharge point: A location at which effluent is released into a receiving stream.

discounting: Determining the present value of future income or payments.

discount rate: The rate at which current generation discount future income or payments.

disintegration: The reduction of rock to smaller pieces mainly by mechanical means; also used to include chemical changes.

disperse: To break up compound particles, such as aggregates, into the individual component particles; to distribute or suspend fine particles, such as clay, in or throughout a dispersion medium, such as water.

dispersion: The act of dispersing; to separate, spread, scatter. That which is dispersed could be open textured and porous. On the other hand, colloidal particles may be dispersed and held in suspension in a fluid state as a gel and to move with the mass as a mud flow.

dispersion medium: The portion of a colloidal system in which the disperse phase is distributed.

dispersion ratio: The ratio of silt plus clay remaining in suspension after limited shaking and settling, using specific procedure, to the total silt plus clay as determined by mechanical analysis. The greater this ratio, the more easily the soil can be dispersed.

dispersion, soil: The breaking down of soil aggregates into individual particles, resulting in single grain structure. Ease of dispersion is an important factor influencing the erodibility of soils. Generally speaking, the more easily dispersed the soil, the more erodible it is.

dispersive clay: A soil that has a high percentage of sodium in the pore water salts and is subject to rapid colloidal erosion from concentrated flow through cracks or openings in the soil.

displacement (cartography): The horizontal shift of the plotted positions of a topographic feature from its true position, caused by required adherence to prescribed line weights and symbol sizes; any shift in the position of an image on a photograph that does not alter the perspective characteristics of the photograph (i.e., shift due to tilt of the photograph, scale change in the photograph, and relief of the objects photographed).

display: An output device that produces a visible representation of a data set for visual access; usually the primary hardware component is a cathode ray tube.

disposal: The transference of unwanted material, such as wastes, into new hands, a new place, or a new form. Types include:

ocean: The deposition of waste into an ocean or estuarine body of water.

on site: The utilization of methods or processes to eliminate or reduce the volume or weight of solid waste.

waste: The orderly process of discarding useless or unwanted material.

disposal field: Area used for spreading liquid effluent for separation of wastes from water, degradation of impurities, and improvement of drainage waters. Also called infiltration field.

dissolved constituent: Operationally defined as a constituent that passes through a 0.45-micrometer filter.

dissolved oxygen (DO): The amount of gaseous oxygen (O) dissolved in a liquid usually water.

dissolved solids: The total amount of dissolved material, organic and inorganic, contained in water or wastes. Excessive dissolved solids make water unpalatable for drinking and unsuitable for industrial uses.

distillation: The removal of impurities from liquids by boiling. The steam, condensed back into liquid, is almost pure water; the pollutants remain in the concentrated residue.

distortion: Lens aberrations affecting the positions of images from their true relative positions; also called lens distortion.

distributary: Smaller conduit taking water from a canal for delivery to farms; any system of secondary conduits; river channel flowing away from the main stream and not rejoining it, as contrasted to a tributary.

distribution efficiency (irrigation): Measure of the uniformity of irrigation water distribution over a field.

distribution system (irrigation): System of ditches and their appurtenances which convey irrigation water from the main canal to the farm units; any system that distributes water within a farm.

disturbed area (mining): Area were vegetation, topsoil, overburden is removed, or where topsoil, spoil, and processed waste is placed.

ditch: Generally, a long narrow excavation. Constructed open channel for conducting water.

diurnal: An event, process, or specific change that occurs every day; usually associated with changes from day to night; pertaining to those organisms that are active during day time. See *nocturnal*.

diversion: A process which, having return flow and consumptive use elements, turns water from a given

path. Removal of water from its natural channel for human use. Use of part of a stream flow as a water supply. Channel constructed across the slope for the purpose of intercepting surface runoff, changing the accustomed course of all or part of a stream. A structural conveyance (or ditch) constructed across a slope to intercept runoff flowing down a hillside, and divert it to some convenient discharge point.

diversion channel (canal or tunnel): A waterway used to divert water from its natural course. The term generally applies to a temporary arrangement (e.g., to bypass water around a damsite during construction). Channel is normally used instead of canal when the waterway is short. Occasionally the term is applied to a permanent arrangement (diversion canal, diversion tunnel, diversion aqueducts).

diversion dam: A barrier built to divert part or all of the water from a stream into a different course.

diversion inlet: A conduit or tunnel upstream from an intake structure. Diversion inlet may be integral with the outlet works or be part of a separate conveyance structure that will only be used during construction.

diversion terrace: Diversions, which differ from terraces in that they consist of individually designed channels across a hillside; may be used to protect bottomland from hillside runoff or may be needed above a terrace system for protection against runoff from an unterraced area; may also divert water out of active gullies, protect farm buildings from runoff, reduce the number of waterways, and sometimes used in connection with stripcropping to shorten the length of slope so that the strips can effectively control erosion. See *terrace*.

diversity: The variety of species within a given association of organisms. Areas of high diversity are characterized by a great variety of species; usually relatively few individuals represent any one species. Areas with low diversity are characterized by a few species; often relatively large numbers of individuals represent each species.

divert: To direct a flow away from its natural course.

divide: A ridge or high area of land that separates one drainage basin from another.

division box (irrigation): A structure used to divide and direct the flow of water between two or more irrigation ditches.

domestic water use (residential water use): Water for household purposes, such as drinking, food preparation, bathing, washing clothes and dishes, flushing toilets, and water lawns and gardens.

dominant (ecology): Species which by their activity, behavior, or number have considerable influence or control upon the conditions of existence of associated species; a species which "controls" its habitat and food web. See *predominant*.

dormancy: The condition of a plant or seed in which life functions are virtually at a standstill.

dose: A specific concentration of an air pollutant for a specific period of time to which an object is exposed.

dose: A specific concentration of an air pollutant for a specific period of time to which an object is exposed.

dosimeter: An instrument used to measure the amount of radiation a person has received; also spelled dosemeter.

double working (horticulture): The regrafting, at a somewhat higher point on a woody plant, of an already grafted plant; commonly used to produce dwarfing for growing in smaller space and for easier care.

downstream face: The inclined surface of a dam away from the reservoir.

draft: The act of drawing or removing water from a reservoir.

drain (n.): A buried pipe or other conduit (closed drain); ditch (open drain) for carrying off surplus surface water or groundwater.

drain (v.): To provide channels, such as open ditches or closed drains, so that excess water can be removed by surface flow or by internal flow; to lose water (from the soil) by percolation.

drainage: The removal of excess surface water or groundwater from land by means of surface or subsurface drains; soil characteristics that affect natural drainage.

drain area (surface): That area, measured in a horizontal plane, enclosed by a topographic divide from which direct surface runoff from precipitation normally drains by gravity into a stream above the specified point of measurement;

(sub-surface) That area of a reservoir contributing oil or gas to a well; poor descriptive term because it suggests gravity rather than pressure as the agent of movement; inexact because any such area is affected by the thickness, porosity, permability and pressure.

drainage basin: The area of land that drains water, sediment, and dissolved materials to a common outlet at some point along a stream channel.

drainage blanket: A layer of pervious material placed directly over the foundation material to facilitate drainage of the foundation and/or embankment.

drainage coefficient: Design rate at which water is to be removed from a drainage area.

drainage curtain: A line of vertical wells or boreholes to facilitate drainage of the foundation and abutments and to reduce water pressure (also called drainage wells or relief wells).

drainage curves (irrigation): Design curves giving prescribed rates of surface runoff for different levels of crop production, and which may vary according to size of drainage area.

drainage district: A special purpose district created under state law to finance, construct, operate, and maintain a drainage system involving a group of land holdings.

drainage field ditch: A shallow graded ditch for collecting excess water within a field, usually constructed with flat side slopes of ease of crossing.

drainage layer: A layer of pervious material in an earthfill dam to relieve pore pressures or to facili-

tate drainage of the fill.

drainage, soil: As a natural condition of the soil, soil drainage refers to the frequency and duration of periods when the soil is free of saturation; for example, in well drained soils the water is removed readily but not rapidly; in poorly drained soils the root zone is waterlogged for long periods unless artificially drained, and the roots of ordinary crop plants cannot get enough oxygen; in excessively drained soils the water is removed so completely that most crop plants suffer from lack of water. Strictly speaking, excessively drained soils are a result of excessive runoff due to steep slopes or low available waterholding capacity due to small amounts of silt and clay in the soil material.

drainage system: Collection of surface and/or subsurface drains, together with structures and pumps, used to remove surface or groundwater.

drainage well (irrigation): vertical opening to a permeable substation into which surface and subsurface water is channeled.

draw: A small valley or gully.

drawdown: Lowering of the water surface (in open channel flow), water table, or piezometric surface (in groundwater flow) resulting from a withdrawal of water.

dredge spoils: Material removed from a water body by dredging for subsequent storage and/or disposal.

dredging: A method for deepening streams, swamps, or waters by scraping and removing solids from the bottom.

drift (mining): A deep mine entry

driven directly into a horizontal or near horizontal mineral seam or vein when it outcrops or is exposed at the ground surface. See *adit, shaft*; (aerial photography) The lateraklshaft or displacement of an aircraft from its course, due to the action of wind or other causes; photography obtained under this condition proves successive photographs whose edges are parallel but sidestepped.

drift fence: A fence without closure used to influence animal movement.

drift, glacial: See *glacial drift*.

drift organisms: Benthic organisms temporarily suspended in the water and carried downstream by the current.

drill seeding: Planting seed with a drill in relatively narrow rows, generally less than a foot apart. See *broadcast seeding*.

drip irrigation: See *irrigation, drip*.

driveway (range): A strip of land specially designated for the controlled movement of livestock.

drop inlet spillway: Overfall structure in which the water drops through a vertical riser connected to a discharge conduit.

drops: Structures to reduce or control water velocity within an irrigation ditch or canal by lowering the water abruptly from one level to a lower level; often used as a check as well.

drop spillway: Overfall structure in which the water drops over a vertical wall onto an apron at a lower elevation.

drop structure: A structure for dropping water to a lower level and dissipating its surplus energy; a fall. A drop may be vertical or inclined.

drought: A continued period of lack of moisture, so serious that crops fail to develop and mature properly.

drumlin: A ridge or oval hill with a smooth summit composed of material deposited by a glacier.

drying-off: The process of reducing moisture to induce dormancy or a rest period in plants.

dryland farming: The practice of crop production in low rainfall areas without irrigation.

dry well: A deep hole, covered, and usually lined or filled with rocks, that holds drainage water until it soaks into the ground.

dry weight (soils): The weight of the solid soil particles after all the water has been vaporized by heating to 105 degrees centigrade.

duckfoot: An implement with horizontally spreading, V shaped tillage blades or sweeps which are normally adjusted to provide shallow cultivation without turning over the surface soil or burying surface crop residues.

duff: The more or less firm organic layer on top of mineral soil, consisting of fallen vegetative matter in the process of decomposition, including everything from pure humus below to the litter on the surface; a general, nonspecific term.

dugout pond: An excavated pond as contrasted with a pond formed by constructing a dam.

dummy: A preliminary drawing or layout made up to show the size, shape, style, and content of a book, booklet, or pamphlet.

dump: An open land site where waste materials are burned, left to decompose, rust, or simply remain. In most localities, dumps are being phased out because of problems such as water pollution, creation of unsanitary conditions, and general unsightliness. Some dumps are left burning as waste is accumulated. This practice does not lend itself to control and, therefore, very little of the waste is actually consumed by fire. The burning also generates obnoxious smoke, fumes, and ash particles. See *sanitary landfill*.

dumping: An indiscriminate method of disposing of solid waste.

dumpy level: A leveling instrument that has its telescope permanently attached to the leveling base, either rigidly or by a hinge that can be manipulated by a micrometer screw.

dune: A mound or ridge of sand piled up by wind.

duplicating: A lithography process by which a press plate is made directly form an original and not a negative; plates are paper or plastic.

duration curve (hydraulics): A graphical representation of the number of times given flows are equaled or exceeded during a certain period of record.

duripan: See *diagnostic horizons*.

dust: Particles over 1 micron in size produced by the physical breakdown of organic and inorganic substances.

dustfall jar: An open mouthed container for collecting particulate pollutants which settle because of gravitational forces.

dust, fugitive: Particulate matter not emitted from a duct or stack that becomes airborne due to the forces of wind or mining operations, or both.

dust mulch: A loose, finely granular or powdery condition on the surface of the soil, usually produced by shallow cultivation when the soil is dry.

dwarf plants: Clonal varieties or strains of plants that grow to a lesser height than is normal for their kind.

dwarfing understocks: Species or clonal varieties of trees that by their nature restrict the growth of scions grafted to them.

dynamic compaction: A method of compacting soil by dropping a heavy weight onto loose soil.

dynamic equilibrium: Condition achieved when the average sand load transported by flowing water is in balance with the sand load being supplied by tributaries.

dynamic head (irrigation): The total of the following factors: a) the total static head, including suction lift; b) friction head in the discharge pipeline; c) head losses in fittings, elbows, and valves; and d) pressure required to operate lateral lines.

dynamic sampling: Any form of forest sampling designed to discover significant changes with time, particularly seral changes or increments. Continuous forest inventory is a form of dynamic sampling.

dystrophic lakes: Shallow lakes with brown water, high organic matter content, low nutrient availability, poor bottom fauna, and high oxygen demand; oxygen is continually depleted and pH is usually low. In lake aging, the age between a eutrophic lake and a swamp.

E

earth dam: An embankment dam in which more than 50 percent of the total volume is formed of compacted earth material generally smaller than three-inch size. Seepage through the dam is controlled by the designed use of upstream blankets and/or internal cores constructed using compacted soil of very low permeability.

earthquake: A sudden motion or trembling in the earth caused by the abrupt release of accumulated stress along a fault.

earthwork: Any one or combination of the operations involved in altering or movement of earth.

easement: A limited right over land owned by someone else. An easement may be for a certain number of years or be perpetual in duration. An affirmative easement gives the owner of the easement the right to use the land for a stated purpose. A negative easement is an agreement with a private property owner to limit the development of his land in specific ways.

ebb tide: That period of tide between a high water and the succeeding low water; falling tide.

ecofallow: A system to control weeds and conserve soil moisture during fallow periods with a min-imum disturbance of crop residues and soil; herbicides and/or sweep tillage are used to control weeds between harvesting of one crop and the planting of the next.

ecological balance: A state of dynamic equilibrium within a community of organisms in which genetic, species and ecosystem diversity remain relatively stable, subject to gradual changes through natural succession.

ecological classification: An approach to categorizing and delineating, at different levels of resolution, areas of land and water having similar characteristic combinations of the physical environment (such as climate, geomorphic processes, geology, soil and hydrologic function), biological communities (plants, animals, microorganisms and potential natural communities) and the human dimension (such as social, economic, cultural and infrastructure).

ecological factor: Any part or condition of the environment that influences the life of one or more organisms. See *biotic factor.*

ecological niche: See *niche.*

ecological processes: A complex mix of interactions among animals, plants, and their environment that ensures maintenance of an ecosystem's full range of biodiversity. Examples include population and predator-prey dynamics, pollination and seed dispersal, nutrient cycling, migration and dispersal.

ecological studies: Studies of biological communities and habitat characteristics to evaluate the effects of physical and chemical characteristics of water and hydrologic conditions on aquatic biota and to determine how biological and habitat characteristics differ among environmental settings in NAWQA Study Units.

ecological units: Areas of land with similar biological, geological, and climatic environments.

ecology: The study of interrelationships or organisms to one another and to their environment.

econometrics: The application of quantitative analysis to economic theory that has been formulated in mathematical terms.

economic base: The economic characteristics that contribute to the region's income, growth, economic trends, and cycles.

economic growth: An increase in a nation's or an area's capacity to produce and the actual production of such goods and services.

economic poisons: Chemicals used to control insects, rodents, plant diseases, weeds, and other vectors; also chemicals used to defoliate economic crops.

ecoregion: A territory defined by a combination of biological, social, and geographic criteria, rather than geopolitical considerations; generally, a system of related, interconnected ecosystems.

ecospecies: A biological group comprising organisms fully fertile among themselves but only weakly fertile with member of allied groups.

ecosphere: The mantle of earth and troposphere inhabited by living organisms.

ecosystem: A community, including all the component organisms, together with the environment, forming an interacting system.

ecosystem approach: A way of looking at socio-economic and environmental information based on the boundaries of ecosystems like watersheds, rather than on geopolitical boundaries.

ecosystem degradation: Ecosystems are degraded when recovery to original conditions is unlikely under normal circumstances (without management). Degraded ecosystems can be distinguished by those that can be restored, rehabilitated, or reclaimed. All ecosystems found today within the Region have experienced some form of anthropogenic disturbance resulting in degradation in different degrees. This degradation may have resulted from fragmentation, fire suppression, invasive species invasions, and/or over-grazing by deer, among other things.

ecosystem integrity: Ecological processes that are essential for ecosystems to function in a defined and predictable manner.

ecosystem management: The integration of ecological, social, and economic objectives for natural resource planning and management.

ecosystem productivity: The ability of an ecosystem to produce, grow or yield products - whether trees, shrubs or other organisms.

ecosystem service: A benefit or service provided free by an ecosystem or by the environment, such as clean water, flood mitigation, or groundwater recharge.

ecotone: A transition line or strip of vegetation between two communities, having characteristics of both kinds of neighboring vegetation as well as characteristics of its own.

ecotype: A locally adapted population of a species which has a distinctive limit of tolerance to environmental factors. See *biotype*.

edaphic factor: A condition or characteristic of the soil (chemical, physical, or biological) which influences organisms.

edatope: Refers to a specific combination of soil moisture regime and soil nutrient regime.

eddy: Circular current of water moving against the main current.

edge (wildlife): The transitional zone where one cover type ends and another begins.

effective force: The force transmitted through a soil or rock mass by intergranular pressures.

effective porosity: The ratio of the volume of a soil or rock mass that can be drained by gravity to the total volume of the mass.

effective precipitation: That portion of total precipitation that becomes available for plant growth. It does not include precipitation lost to deep percolation below the root zone or to surface runoff.

effective size: The maximum diameter of the smallest 10 percent of the particles of a sediment; the average diameter of irregular shaped particles.

effective soil depth: See *depth, effective soil.*

effluent: Solid, liquid, or gas wastes which enter the environment as a by product of man oriented processes; the discharge or outflow of water from ground or sub surface storage.

effluent limitation: The maximum amount of a specific substance or characteristic that can be present in effluent discharge without violating water quality standards in receiving waters.

effluent seepage: Diffuse discharge onto the ground of liquids that have percolated through solid waste or another medium; they contain dissolved or suspended materials.

ejector: A device used to disperse a chemical solution into water being treated.

elasticity of demand: The percentage change in the demand for a good due to a percentage change in price.

electrical conductivity: Conductivity of electricity through water or an extract of soil; can be used to estimate the soluble salts in solution.

electrical resistance blocks (irrigation): Small blocks with a pair of electrodes set in absorbent material, plaster of Paris, or gypsum, used to estimate soil moisture content of surrounding soil as a function of the electrical resistance between the electrodes.

electrostatic precipitator: An apparatus that removes particles from a stream of air through an electric field and collects the charged particulates on electrodes.

elevated ditch: Earth fill, constructed to specifications similar to those for earth fill dams, to provide normal grade as a substitute for flumes or siphons. Also raised ditch.

elevation: The variation in the height of the earth's surface; the measure of vertical distance from a known datum plane which on most maps is mean sea level.

electrolysis: Chemical decomposition of certain substances by an electric current passing through a substance.

electromagnetic spectrum: The ordered array of known electromagnetic radiations, extending from the shortest cosmic rays, through gamma rays, X-rays, ultra-violet radiation, visible radiation, infrared radiation, and including microwave and all other wavelengths, of radio energy.

elutriation: Separation of solid waste into heavy and light fractions by washing.

eluvial horizon: A soil horizon formed by the process of eluviation. See *eluviation, illuvial horizon.*

eluviation: The removal of soil material in suspension (or in solution) from a layer or layers of a soil. (Usually, the loss of material in solution is described by the term "leaching".) See *illuviation, leaching.*

embankment: An artificial deposit of material that is raised above the natural surface of the land and used to contain divert, or store water; support roads or railways; or for other similar purposes.

emergency episode (pollution):

An air pollution incident in a given area caused by a concentration of atmospheric pollution reacting with meteorological conditions that results in a significant increase in illnesses or deaths.

emergency spillway: A spillway used to carry runoff exceeding a given design flood.

emergent vegetation: Herbaceous wetland vegetation that is erect and rooted.

emergent wetland: Wetlands dominated by erect, rooted, herbaceous plants.

emigration: The movement of an organism out of a locality, usually without the probability of returning.

eminent domain: The right of a government to acquire private property for public use or benefit on payment of just compensation.

emission: A substance released into the air.

emission factor: Statistical average of the amount of a specific pollutant emitted from each type of polluting source in relation to a unit quality of material handled, processed, or burned.

emission inventory: The amount of each primary air pollutant released daily into a community's atmosphere.

emission rates: The rate at which the average automobile is expected to emit the various air pollutants.

emission standard: The maximum amount of pollutant permitted to be discharged from a single polluting source.

emissivity: The amount of energy given off by an object relative to the amount given off by a black body at the same temperature; normally expressed as a positive number between 0 and 1.

emittance: The emittance of a material refers to its ability to release absorbed heat. Scientists use a number between 0 and 1, or 0 and 100 percent, to express emittance. With the exception of metals, most construction materials have emittances above 0.85 (85 percent).

emulsion: A suspension of either light-sensitive silver salts, diazos, or photopolymers, in a colloidal medium that is used for coating films, plates, and papers.

enclosure: An area fenced to confine animals.

end moraine (terminal moraine): Ridge of sediment piled at the front edge of a glacier.

endangered species (native): A species of native fish, wildlife, or plants found by the Secretary of Interior to be threatened with extinction because its habitat is threatened with destruction, drastic modification, or severe curtailment, or because of over-exploitation, disease, predation or other factors; its survival requires assistance.

endemic species: An organism or species that is restricted to a relatively small geographic area or to an unusual or rare type of habitat.

endemic species: An organism or species that is restricted to a relatively small geographic area or to an unusual or rare type of habitat.

endocrine system: The collection of ductless glands in animals that secrete hormones, which influ-ence growth, gender and sexual maturity.

energy: The capacity to produce head or do work.

energy balance: An energy balance is a detailed accounting of all energy flowing into and out of a volume or surface. Examples of energy flows include convection, evaporation, heat stored or conducted, and heat generated in a volume (such as anthropogenic heat in a city). Energy balances of urban and rural areas can illustrate the cooling effects of trees and vegetation on evaporation and heat storage rates.

energy gradient: Change in energy per unit length in direction of flow or motion.

energy source: The primary source that provides the power that is converted to electricity through chemical, mechanical, or other means. Energy sources include coal, petroleum and petroleum products, gas, water, uranium, wind, sunlight, geothermal, and other sources.

enhancement (remote sensing): Data filtering and other processes that improve the visual quality of the pictorially presented data or which visually accentuate a characteristic of the data; e.g., edge enhancement, noise reduction.

enrichment: The addition of nutrients such as nitrogen and phosphorus and carbon compounds, into a lake or waterway to the point that the trophic state is greatly increased because of the stimulation of the growth of algae and other aquatic plants.

Entisols: See *soil classification*.

entrain: To trap bubbles in water

either mechanically through turbulence or chemically through a reaction.

entrainment: Mobilization, by flowing water, of sediment or organic debris from the bed or banks of a stream channel.

entrance head: The head required to cause flow into a conduit or other structure, including both entrance loss and velocity head.

enumeration: In a forest, the counting of one or more species, generally above a specific size limit, and their classification by size, condition, etc.

environment: The sum total of all the external conditions that may act upon an organism or community to influence its development or existence.

environmental assessment: A concise, public document that briefly provides sufficient evidence and analysis for determining whether to prepare a more complete environmental impact statement or a finding of no significant impact.

environmental damage costs: Costs incurred by society as a result pf pollution; benefits of pollution abatement are measured by the reduction of damage costs.

environmental education: Educational programs and activities that create greater understanding of environmental problem-solving and decision-making; involves teaching the ecological principles and relationships through which the solutions to environmental problems may be found.

environmental evaluation: That part of the planning process of federal agencies that inventories

and estimates the potential effects on the human environment of alternative solutions to resource problems; determines the need for an environmental assessment or an environmental impact statement, and aids in the consideration of alternatives and identification of available resources.

environmental framework: Natural and human-related features of the land and hydrologic system, such as geology, land use, and habitat, that provide a unifying framework for making comparative assessments of the factors that govern water-quality conditions within and among study units.

environmental impact statement: A document prepared by a federal or state agency or a private firm detailing the environmental impact of a proposed law, a construction project, or other major action that may significantly affect the quality of the environment. Statements are required by the National Environmental Policy Act and various state environmental laws.

environmental quality: The state of man's habitat created by the management, conservation, preservation, creation, restoration, or improvement of the quality of certain national and cultural resources and ecological systems involving related land and water resources.

Environmental Quality Incentives Program (EQIP): EQIP was established by the 1996 Farm Act as a new program to consolidate and better target the functions of the Agricultural Conservation Program, Water Quality Incentives Program, Great Plains Conservation Program, and Colorado River Basin Salinity Program. The objective of EQIP, like its predecessor programs, is to encourage farmers and ranchers to adopt practices that reduce environmental and resource problems through five- to 10-year contracts. The program provides education, technical assistance and financial assistance, targeted to watersheds, regions, or areas of special environmental sensitivity identified as priority areas. The 1996 Farm Act called for half of EQIP funds to be devoted to conservation practices related to livestock production and for maximized environmental benefits per dollar expended. EQIP is designed to consider all sources of conservation funding from CRP, Wetland Reserve Program, other Federal programs, State or local programs, and nongovernmental partners. Proposed projects with greater funding from these sources receive more favorable scoring for EQIP funding. EQIP is run by Natural Resources Conservation Service and funded through Commodity Credit Corporation.

environmental sample: A water sample collected from an aquifer or stream for the purpose of chemical, physical, or biological characterization of the sampled resource.

environmental setting: Land area characterized by a unique combination of natural and human-related factors, such as row-crop cultivation or glacial-till soils.

eolian soil material: Soil material accumulated through wind action. The most extensive areas in the United States are silty deposits (loess), but large areas of sandy deposits also occur.

ephemeral data: Data that help to characterize the conditions under which remote sensing data were collected; may be used to calibrate the sensor data prior to the analysis; includes such information as the positioning and spectral stability of sensors, sun angle, platform attitude, ect.

ephemeral creek: A creek or stream that flows briefly only in direct response to precipitation and whose channel is above the water table.

ephemeral stream: A stream or portion of a stream that flows only in direct response to precipitation, and receives little or no water from springs or no long continued supply from snow or other sources, and its channel is at all times above the water table.

epicenter: Focal point on the earth's surface directly above the origin of a seismic disturbance. Point on the Earth's surface vertically above the earthquake focus or hypocenter.

epidemiology: Study of causes of disease or toxic effects in human populations.

epilimnion: A stream or portion of a stream that flows only in direct response to precipitation, and receives little or no water from springs or no longer continued supply from snow or other sources, and its channel is at all the time above the water table. See *intermittent stream.*

epipedon: See *diagnostic horizons.*

epiphyte: A plant that grows on another plant, but which obtains its nutrients from the atmosphere.

equal-area map projection: See *intermittent stream.*

equilibrium: The condition in which a population or community is maintained with only minor fluctuations in composition over an extended period of time. Sometimes called dynamic equilibrium; a dynamic interaction of two opposing chemical or physical processes occurring at equal rates.

erode: To wear away or remove the land surface by wind, water, or other agents.

erodible: Susceptible to erosion.

erodibility index (EI): The natural erosion potential of a soil divided by the soil's tolerance level.

erosion: The wearing away of the land surface by running water, wind, ice, or other geological agents, including such processes as gravitational creep; detachment and movement of soil or rock fragments by water, wind, ice, or gravity. The following terms are used to describe different types of water erosion:

accelerated erosion: Erosion much more rapid than normal, natural, or geologic erosion, primarily as a result of the influence of the activities of man or, in some cases, of other animals or natural catastrophies that expose base surfaces, for example, fires.

geological erosion: The normal or natural erosion caused by geological processes acting over long geologic periods and resulting in the wearing away of

mountains, the building up of floodplains, coastal plains, etc. Also called natural erosion.

gross: A measure of the potential for soil to be dislodged and moved from its place of origin; it is not necessarily the amount of soil that actually reaches a stream or lake, but is the amount of soul that can be calculated from water and wind equations.

gully erosion: The erosion process whereby water accumulates in narrow channels and, over short periods, removes the soil from this narrow area to considerable depths, ranging from one to two feet to as much as 75 to 100 feet.

natural erosion: Wearing away of the earth's surface by water, ice, or other natural agents under natural environmental conditions of climate, vegetation, etc., undisturbed by man. Also called geological erosion.

normal erosion: The gradual erosion of land used by man which does not greatly exceed natural erosion.

overfall: Erosion caused by water flowing over an overfall.

rill erosion: An erosion process in which numerous small channels only several inches deep are formed; occurs mainly on recently cultivated soils. See *rill.*

sheet erosion: The removal of a fairly uniform layer of soil from the land surface by runoff water.

shore: Removal of soil, sand or rock from the land adjacent to a body of water due to wave action.

splash erosion: The spattering of small soil particles caused by the impact of raindrops on wet soils. The loosened and spattered particles may or may not be subsequently removed by surface runoff.

streambank: Scouring of material and cutting of channel beds by running water.

streambed: Scouring of material and cutting of channel beds by running water.

undercutting: Removal of material at the base of a steep slope, overfall, or cliff by falling water, a stream, wind erosion, or wave action; removal steepens the slope or produces an overhanging cliff.

erosion index: An interaction term of kinetic energy times maximum 30 minute rainfall intensity that reflects the nutrients in adequate amounts and in proper balance for the growth of specified plants when other growth factors, such as light, moisture, temperature and the physical condition of the soil resource, are favorable.

erosion classes (soil survey): A grouping of erosion conditions based on the degree of erosion or on characteristic patterns; applied to accelerated erosion, not to normal, natural, or geological erosion.

erosive: Refers to wind or water having sufficient velocity to cause erosion. Not to be confused with erodible as a quality of soil.

erratic: Boulder transported by a glacier and left behind when the ice melted.

escapement: Unharvested spawning stocks that return to the streams.

escarpment: A steep face or a ridge of high land; the escarpment of a mountain range is generally on that side nearest the sea.

escherichia coli (E. coli): One of the species of bacteria in the coliform group, its presence is considered indicative of fresh fecal contamination.

esker: A narrow ridge of gravelly or sandy drift deposited by a stream in association with glacier ice.

espalier: A method of training plants to grow flat against a wall or trellis in a desired shape or form.

essential element (plant nutrition): A chemical element required for the normal growth of plants.

estimate: In mensuration, an approximate determination of the volume and quality of standing timber; also called cruise.

estuarine: Pertaining to a river.

estuary: That portion of a costal stream influenced by the tide of the body of water into which it flows, for example a bay or mouth of a river, where the tide meets the river current; an area where fresh and marine waters mix.

ethologist: A person who studies animal behavior.

ethology: The study of animal behavior.

euphotic zone: The lighted region of a body of water that extends vertically from the water surface to the depth at which photosynthesis fails to occur because of insufficient light penetration.

eutrophication: A means of aging of lakes whereby aquatic plants are abundant and waters are deficient in oxygen. The process is usually accelerated by enrichment of waters with surface runoff containing nitrogen and phosphorus.

eutrophic lakes: Lakes that are rich in nutrients and organic materials, therefore, highly productive. These lakes are often shallow and seasonally deficient of oxygen in the hypolimnion. See *oligotrophic lakes*.

evaporite minerals (deposits): Minerals or deposits of minerals formed by evaporation of water containing salts. These deposits are common in arid climates.

evaporation: The process by which a liquid is changed to a vapor or gas.

evaporation ponds: Shallow ponds in which sewage sludge is placed to dry and then removed for further treatment and/or disposal.

evaporative emissions: Evaporative emissions are from fuel evaporating from vehicle carburetors or fuel systems. Evaporative emissions can occur while vehicles are refueling, operating, or even when vehicles are parked.

evaporities: Sediments deposited from an aqueous (water) solution as a result of extensive or local evaporation of a solvent, such as salts in Great Salt Lake.

evapotranspiration: The combined loss of water from a given area and during a specific period of time, by evaporation from the soil surface and by transpiration from plants.

even aged: A stand of trees in which only small differences in age occur between the individuals.

evergreen: Perennial plants that are never entirely without green foliage.

evolution: The development of organisms or cultures from simple and homogenous to complex and heterogeneous forms.

excessive precipitation: Standard

US Weather Bureau term for "rainfall in which the rate of fall is greater than certain adopted limits, chosen with regard to the normal precipitation (excluding snow) of a given place or area." Not the same as excess rainfall.

excess rainfall: Direct runoff at the place where it originates.

exchange capacity: The capacity to exchange ions as measured by the quantity of exchangeable ions in a soil or rock.

exchangeable nutrient: A plant nutrient that is held by the adsorption complex of the soil and is easily exchanged with the anion or cation of neutral salt solutions.

exclosure: An area fenced to exclude animals.

exclusion of livestock: Excluding all livestock from a designated area for the purpose of protecting or establishing forage or woody plants and for controlling erosion.

exhaust emissions: The air pollutants emitted from the exhaust of the internal combustion engine, namely carbon monoxide, nitrogen oxides, and hydrocarbons.

exhaustion: The process leading to or the state in which the exploitation of a resource has ceased as a consequence of the net social benefits of a resource use being nonpositive.

exotic: An organism or species that is not native to the region in which it is found.

expansion: The increase in volume of a soil mass.

exploration: See *mining*.

exposure: Direction of slope with respect to points of a compass.

exposure time: The time during which a light-sensitive material is subjected to the action of light.

exploratory sampling: Forest sampling to determine such basic ecological or economic data as composition and condition, constitution and stocking; generally for introducing management into forests.

extensional landscape: The landscape beyond the boundaries of a property.

external economies: Favorable externalities.

external diseconomies: Adverse externalities.

externalities: Effects on one or more persons resulting from an action by a different person or firm.

extraction well: A discharge well used to remove groundwater or air.

extrapolate: Effects on one or more persons resulting from an action by a different person or firm.

eye: In meteorology, usually the "eye of the storm" (hurricane, typhoon): that is, the roughly circular area of a comparatively light winds and fail weather found at the center of a severe tropical cyclone. The winds are generally ten knots or less; no rain occurs; sometimes blue sky may be seen. Eye diameters vary from four miles to more than forty miles.

eye wall: The cloudy mass surrounding the eye of a tropical cyclone or hurricane in which winds reach high intensity.

eyrie: The nest of a bird on a cliff or mountaintop; applies especially to a bird of prey.

F

face planting: Frontal planting to taller groups of plants or structures.

factor, filter (photography): The amount that film exposure must be increased to offset the reduction in light resulting from the use of a filter. A filter factor of two means that the normal exposure must be doubled.

facultative: Capable of adaptive response to varying environment.

Fairfield Hardy digester: A machine that decomposes garbage, sewage sludge, industrial, and other organic wastes by a controlled continuous aerobic thermophilic process.

fair market value: That value that would induce a willing seller to sell and a willing buyer to buy, usually applied to real estate in cases where the right of eminent domain is being exercised.

falldown effect: A decline in timber supply or harvest level associated with the transition from harvesting the original stock of natural mature timber over one rotation to harvesting at a non declining level (typically equal to the annual increment) after conversion to a forest with a balanced age class structure.

fall overturn: A physical phenomenon that may take place in a body of water during early autumn. The sequence of events leading to fall overturn include: 1) cooling of surface waters; 2) density change in surface waters producing convection currents from top to bottom; 3) circulation of the total water volume by wind action; and 4) vertical temperature equality. The overturn results in a uniformity of the physical and chemical properties of the entire water mass. See *spring overturn*.

fallow: Allowing cropland to lie idle, either tilled or untilled, during the whole or greater portion of the growing season.

false color: See *color infrared film*.

family (soil): See *soil classification*.

family farm: A farm business in which the operating family does most of the work, most of the managing, and takes the risks.

fan: An accumulation of debris brought down by a stream on a steep gradient and debouching on a gently sloping plain in the shape of a fan, forming a section of a very low cone.

fanglomerate: Heterogeneous materials that were originally deposited in an alluvial fan but since deposition have been cemented into solid rock.

farm: Any place from which $1,000 or more of agricultural products were sold, or normally would have been sold, during the census year.

farmability: The ease of efficiently farming a field or terrace system; can also refer to field size, shape, and topography as well as terracing or conservation systems.

farm forestry: The practice of forestry on farm or ranch lands generally integrated with other farm or ranch operations.

farmland: Land used for agricultural purposes. Types, as defined in the United States include:

prime: Land that has the best combination of physical and chemical characteristics for producing food, feed, fiber, and oilseed crops, and is also available for these uses; includes cropland, pastureland, rangeland, forestlands, but not urbanized land or water; it has the soil quality, growing season, and moisture supply needed to produce sustained high yields of crops economically when treated and managed, including water management, according to modern agricultural methods.

unique: Land other than prime farmland that is used for the production of specific high value food and fiber crops; such as citrus, nuts, olives, cranberries, fruits and vegetables, ect.; has the special combination of soil quality, location, growing season, and moisture supply needed to produce sustained high quality and or high yields of a specialty crop economically when treated and managed according to modern agricultural methods.

additional farmland of statewide importance: Land in addition to prime and unique farmland that is of statewide importance for the production of food, fiber, feed, forage, and oilseed crops; criteria for defining and delineating these lands are to be determined by the appropriate state agency or agencies; generally these lands include those that are nearly prime farmland and that economically produce high yields or crops when treated and managed according to acceptable farming methods; some may produce as high a yield as prime farmlands if conditions are favorable; in some states these lands may include tracts of land that have been designated for agriculture by state laws.

additional farmland of local importance: Land not identified as having national or statewide importance, but important locally for the production of food, fiber, forage, and oilseed crops; identified by local agencies and may include land that has been designated for agriculture by local ordinances.

Farmland Protection Program (FPP): Established in the 1996 Farm Act, FPP provides funding to State, local, or tribal entities with existing farmland protection programs to purchase conservation easements or other interests in order to keep agricultural land in farming. The goal of the program, run by Natural Resources Conservation Service, is to protect between 170,000 and 340,000 acres of farmland. Priority is given to applications for perpetual easements, although a minimum of 30 years is required.

farming contract: An agreement to deliver specific goods and serviced at a later time.

farm management: The organization and administration of farm resources, including land, labor, crops, livestock, and equipment.

farm manager: A salaried person who operates land for others and is paid a salary and/or commission for his services.

farm operator: A person who operates a farm either by performing the labor himself or directly supervising it.

farm pond: A water impoundment made by constructing a dam or embankment or by excavating a pit or "dug out." See *tank, earth.*

farm sprinkler system: See *field sprinkler system.*

farm tenancy: The leasing or renting of farm land together with improvements and sometimes equipment by non owners for the purposes of occupying and operating.

fastigate: A narrow, erect habit of plant growth due to closely associated vertical branches.

fault: A fracture or fracture zone of the earth along which there has been displacement of one side with respect to the other.

fault-line scarp: A steep slope produced along and old fault ling by differential weathering and erosion, rather than by fault movement. See *fault scarp, scarp.*

fault scarp: A cliff formed by a fault, unusually modified by erosion unless the fault is very recent. See *fault-line scarp, scarp.*

fauna: The animal life of a region.

feature: In pattern recognition, one of the measurements of a pattern of mathematical transformation of such measurements; in remote sensing, often the reflectance measurement in one channel of the sensor; the number of features associated with a pattern defines its dimensionality.

fecal bacteria: Microscopic single-celled organisms (primarily fecal coliforms and fecal streptococci) found in the wastes of warm-blooded animals. Their presence in water is used to assess the sanitary quality of water for body-contact recreation or for consumption. Their presence indicates contamination by the wastes of warm-blooded animals and the possible presence of pathogenic (disease producing) organisms.

fecal coliform: A group of bacteria normally present in large numbers in the intestinal tracts of humans and other warm-blooded animals.

fecal streptococcus: A group of bacteria normally present in large numbers in the intestinal tracts of warm blooded animals other than humans. By assessing the ratio of coliforms to streptococci in a water sample, a rough estimate can be made of the relative contribution of fecal contamination from the two mentioned possible sources.

Federal Agriculture Improvement and Reform Act of 1996 (1996 Act): The omnibus food and agriculture legislation (Farm Act) signed into law on April 4, 1996, that provided a seven-year framework (1996 to 2002) for the

Secretary of Agriculture to administer various agricultural and food programs. The 1996 Act redesigned income support and supply management programs for producers of wheat, corn, grain sorghum, barley, oats, rice, and upland cotton. Production flexibility contract payments were made available under Title I of the 1996 Act (see *Agricultural Market Transition Act*). Acreage reduction programs were suspended. Federal milk marketing orders were revised and consolidated under the Act. Program changes were also made for sugar and peanuts. Trade programs were targeted and environmental programs were consolidated and extended in the 1996 Act.

feed: Harvested forage, such as hay, fodder, or grain; grain products; and other foodstuffs processed for feeding livestock.

feedlot: A relative small, confined land area on which a large concentration of livestock is raised.

fee fishing: A facility where impounded water is used for planting, rearing, and harvesting of fish; the user pays a fee to take fish.

fee simple title: A title on which the owner owns all rights, entire property, with unconditional power of disposition during his life.

feldspar: Group of light-colored minerals often found as crystals in intrusive igneous rocks. The most common rock-forming mineral.

feral: Escaped from cultivation or domestication and existing in the wild.

ferritic: See *soil mineralogy classes for family groupings.*

fertigation: The use of irrigation water as a vehicle for spreading fertilizer on the land.

fertility (soil): The quality of a soil that enables it to provide nutrients in adequate amounts and in proper balance for the growth of specified plants when other growth factors, such as light, moisture, temperature and the physical condition of the soil resource, are favorable.

fertilizer: Any organic or inorganic material of natural or synthetic origin that is added to a soil to supply elements essential to plant growth. **Types include:**

acid-forming: A fertilizer capable of increasing the residual acidity and eventually decreasing the pH of the soil following application.

bulk-blend: Two or more granular fertilizers of similar size mixed together to form a compound fertilizer; also called blended fertilizer.

chemical: A manufactured fertilizer product containing a substantial amount of one or more of the primary nutrients unless otherwise noted; the manufacturing process usually involves chemical reactions but may consist of refining or physically processing naturally occurring materials, such as potassium salts or sodium.

coated: Granular fertilizer that has been coated with a think layer of some substance, such as clay, to prevent caking or to control dissolution rate.

conditioned: Fertilizer treated with an additive to improve physical condition or prevent caking; the conditioning agent may be applied as a coating or incorporated into the product.

granular: A fertilizer processed to achieve uniform size, stability, and shape, sized between an upper and lower limit or between two screen sizes, usually within the range of one to four millimeters, often more closely sized.

liquid: A fertilizer wholly or partically in solution that can be handled as a fluid; includes clear liquids, liquid containing solids in suspension, and (usually) anhydrous ammonia; however, anhydrous ammonia sometimes is referred to as a gaseous fertilizer even though it is applied as a liquid.

nongranular: Fertilizer containing fine particles, usually with some upper limit, such as three millimeters, but now lower limit.

prilled: A type of granular fertilizer of near spherical form made by solidification of free-falling droplets in air or other fluid medium.

solution: Aqueous liquid fertilizer free from solids.

straight: Fertilizer containing only one nutrient, for example, urea or super phosphate.

suspension: A liquid (fluid) fertilizer containing solids held in suspension, for example, by the addition of a small amount of clay; the solids may be water-soluble materials in a saturated solution, or they may be insoluble or both.

fertilizer analysis: The percentage composition of fertilizer, expressed in terms of nitrogen, phosphoric acid, and potash. For example, a fertilizer with a 6 12 6 analysis contains 6 percent nitrogen (N), 12 percent

available phosphoric acid (P_205), and six percent water soluble potash (K_20). Minor elements may also be included. Recent analysis expresses the percentages in terms of the elemental fertilizer (nitrogen, phosphorus, potassium).

fertilizer formula: The quantity and grade of the crude stock materials used in making a fertilizer mixture; for example, one formula for a fertilizer with an analysis of 5 10 5 could be 625 pounds of 16 percent nitrate of soda, 1,111 pounds of 18 percent superphosphate, 200 pounds of 50 percent muriate of potash, and 64 pounds of filler per ton.

fertilizer grade: The guaranteed minimum analysis, in percent, of the major plant nutrient elements contained in a fertilizer material or in a mixed fertilizer.

fertilizer unit: One percent, or 20 pounds, of a ton of fertilizer.

fertilizer value: A monetary value assigned to a quantity of organic wastes representing the cost of obtaining the same plant nutrients in their commercial form and in the amounts found in the waste.

fetch: The straight line distance across a body of water subject to wind forces. The distance which wind passes over water. The fetch is one of the factors used in calculating wave heights in a reservoir. The area in which waves are generated by a wind having a fairly constant direction and speed.

fibers (as used in the Soil Classification System of the National Cooperative Soil Survey in the United States):

Fragments or pieces of plant tissue larger than 0.15 millimeter (0.006 inches) but exclusive of fragments of wood that are larger than 20 millimeters (0.8 inches) in cross section and so undecomposed that they cannot be crushed and shredded with the hands.

fibric materials: See *organic soil materials*.

fibrous root system: A plant root system having a large number of small, finely divided, widely spreading roots but no large individual roots. Typified by grass root system. See *taproot system*.

fiducial mark(s): (surveying) An index line or point; a line or point used as a basis of reference; (photogrammetry) index markers, usually four in number, rigidly connected to the camera lens through the camera body that form images on the negative defining and principal point of a photograph; also, markers in any instrument that define the axes whose intersection fixes the principal point of a photograph and fulfills the requirements of interior orientation.

field capacity: The amount of water retained in a soil or in solid wastes after it has been saturated and has drained freely. In soils also called field moisture capacity (obsolete in technical work) and is usually expressed as a percentage of the oven dry weight of the soil. In waste management also called moisture holding capacity.

field crops: General grain, hay, root, and fiber crops. See *vegetable crop, fruit crop*.

field-of-view (remote sensing): The solid angle through which an instrument is sensitive to radiation.

field planting (forestry): The establishment of woody plants on land essentially free of trees, including woody plantings for the protection of critical slopes, stabilization of spoil banks and sand dunes, production of wood crops, and recreation.

field sheet: An aerial photo on which soil survey, ground control surveys, or other data is placed in the field; a plane-table or other sheet used to record field data as it is gathered.

field sprinkler system: A system of enclosed conduits carrying irrigation water under pressure to orifices designed to distribute the water over a given area; designed for either an individual unit or movement from field to field.

field stripcropping: A system of stripcropping in which crops are grown in parallel strips laid out across the general slope but which do not follow the contour. Strips of grass or close growing crops are alternated with strips of cultivated crops.

field test: An experiment conducted under field conditions. Ordinarily, less subject to control than a formal experiment and maybe less precise. Also called field trial.

field tile: Short lengths of clay pipe that are installed as subsurface drains.

field trip: An excursion away from the normal base of operations to a place or some special significance so that the resources unavailable at the normal base of operations may be seen and interpreted.

filamentous algae: Aggregations of one celled plants that grow in long strings or mats in water and are either attached or free floating; tend to plug canals, weirs, and other structures; also provide habitat for invertebrate animals.

fill (geology): Any sediment deposited by any agent so as to fill or partly fill a channel, valley, sink, or other depression; (solid wastes) a site on which solid waste is disposed of using sanitary landfilling techniques; and (construction) a site on which earth is moved to raise elevation.

filter (remote sensing): Any mechanism that modifies optical electrical, or digital signals in accordance with specified criteria; often a filter is a means of extracting a particular subset of data from a larger set containing irrelevant data; an optical filter passes only desired optical wavelengths of energy; a digital filter is an arithmetic procedure that operates on a digitized data stream in much the same way as an electric filter operates on a continuous electrical signal; its purpose is generally to eliminate irrelevant data or noise.

filter cloth: Synthetic fabrics used as a filter, usually beneath rock riprap or between materials with significant differences in size; to prevent movement of fine material through coarser material.

filter collector: A mechanical apparatus for removing particulate matter from the atmosphere.

filter strip: Strip of permanent vegetation above farm ponds, diversion terraces, and other structures to retard flow of runoff water, causing deposition of transported material, and thereby reducing

sediment flow. See *desilting area.*

final cut: The last cut or line of excavation made when mining a specific property or area.

finding of no significant impact: In the United States, a document used by federal agencies that explains why an action not otherwise excluded will not have a significant effect on the human environment and an environmental impact statement therefore will not be prepared; shall include an environmental assessment or a summary of it and shall note related environmental documents.

fine: See *particle size classes for family groupings.*

fine loamy: See *particle size classes for family groupings.*

fines: Minute particulates.

fine sand: A soil separate. See *soil separates.* A soil textural class. See *soil texture.*

fine sandy loam: See *soil texture.*

fine silty: See *particle size classes for family groupings.*

fine texture: Consisting of or containing large quantities of the fine fractions, particularly silt and clay. Includes sandy clay, silty clay, and clay textural classes. See *soil texture.*

finger drains: A series of parallel drains of narrow width (instead of a continuous drainage blanket) draining to the downstream toe of the embankment dam.

fingerling: A small fish no longer than a finger; especially a young fish.

finished grade: The elevation or surface of the earth after all earthwork has been completed (also finish grade). The final grade required by specifications.

fire blight: A disease of apples, pears, hawthorns, pyracantha, and related members of the rose family that results in death of twigs and branches due to bacherial infection tips of shoots turn black and die back, even to main limbs.

firebreak (forestry): A space cleared of flammable material to stop or check creeping or running fires. It also serves as a line from which to work and to facilitate the movement of men and equipment in fire suppression. Designated roads also serve as firebreaks

fireclay: A sedimentary clay containing only small amounts of fluxing impurities. It is high in hydrous aluminum silicates and is, therefore, capable of withstanding high temperatures.

fire control line (forestry): The line used either directly to stop the advance of a fire or the line from which to backfire.

fire hazard (forestry): The risk or danger of loss or damage from burning due to the presence and type of inflammable material together with conditions favorable to burning and probable source of fire origin.

fire suppression: Fire suppression is an issue facing many ecosystems today. Fire is important in determining natural characteristics, such as habitat structure and composition. Absence of fire in an area can result in profound changes to community characteristics and often leads to reduced species diversity. For instance, fire absence in prairies and oak savannas can lead to woody vegetation encroachment and severe invasion of non-native grasses which can eliminate many prairie plants and associated fauna.

firm: The consistence of a moist soil that offers distinctly noticeable resistance to crushing but can be crushed with moderate pressure between the thumb and forefinger. See *consistence*.

fisheries: A place where large numbers of fish are caught.

fishery: The aquatic region in which a certain species of fish lives.

fisheries–sensitive zones: Side and back channels, valley wall ponds, swamps, seasonally flooded depressions, lake littoral zones and estuaries that are seasonally occupied by over- wintering anadramous fish.

fish kills: Refers to large numbers of fish being killed, usually because there is not enough oxygen in the water or because of a chemical spill.

fishing waters: Waters used for angling or for commercial fishing.

fishpond: A small body of water managed for fish.

fish screen: A porous barrier placed across the inlet or outlet of a pond to prevent the passage of fish.

fishway: A passageway designed to enable fish to ascend a dam, cataract, or velocity barrier. Also called fish ladder.

fissile: A property of splitting easily along closely spaced, parallel planes.

fixation: The process or processes in a soil in which certain chemical elements essential for plant growth are converted from a soluble or exchangeable form to a much less soluble or to a nonexchangeable form, for example, phosphate fixation. See *nitrogen fixation*.

fixed carbon: The ash free carbonaceous material that remains after volatile matter is driven off during the proximate analysis of a dry solid waste sample.

fixed costs: Costs that are largely determined in advance of the year's operation and subject to little or no control on the part of the farmer or businessman, for example, rent of land or buildings, payment of taxes, interest on borrowed money, and upkeep of buildings, fences, and drains; costs not affected by the amount of use.

fixed phosphorus: Soluble phosphorus that has become attached to the solid phase of the soil in forms highly unavailable to crops; unavailable phosphorus; phosphorus in other than readily or moderately available forms.

flaggy: An adjective incorporated into the soil textural class designations of horizons when the soil mass contains between 15 and 90 percent by volume of flagstones. See *flagstone as defined under coarse fragments.*

flagstone: See *coarse fragments.*

flashboard: Plank generally held horizontally in vertical slots on the crest of a dam or check structure to control the upstream water level.

flashflood: A flood which follows within a few hours of heavy or excessive rainfall. A flood of short duration with a relatively high peak rate of flow, usually resulting from a high intensity rainfall over a small area.

flat planting: A planting method in which seed is planted on a flat surface in contrast to ridge or furrow planting.

flatirons: Triangular-shaped land-

forms along mountain ranges formed by erosion of steeply inclined rock layers or hogbacks.

flight altitude: The vertical distance above a given datum, usually mean sea level, of an aircraft in flight.

flight line: A line drawn on a map or chart to represent the track over which an aircraft is to fly.

flight map: A map on which are indicated the proposed lines of flight and/or positions of exposure stations; flight data are plotted on the best available map of the area; generally used for planning purposes.

fling: Refers to a near field long period pulse from a strong ground motion resulting in a unidirectional ground heave after rupture. Great kinetic energy may be associated with a fling and is important in near field records.

flip bucket: An energy dissipator located at the downstream end of a spillway and shaped so that water flowing at a high velocity is deflected upwards in a trajectory away from the foundation of the spillway.

floc (waste management): Clumped solids or precipitates formed in sewage by chemical activity.

flocculate: To aggregate or clump together individual, tiny soil particles, especially fine clay, into small clumps or granules.

flocculation: The process by which suspended colloidal or very fine particles are assembled into larger masses or floccules which eventually settle out of suspension.

flood: An overflow or inundation that comes from a river or other body of water and causes or threatens damage.

flood abatement: See *flood control.*

flood, annual: The highest mean daily flow or the maximum flood period during each year of record.

flood control: Methods or facilities for reducing flood flows.

flood control project: A structural system installed for protection of land and improvements from floods by the construction of dikes, river embankments, channels, or dams.

floodgate: A gate placed in a channel or closed conduit to keep out floodwater or tidal backwater.

flood irrigation: The application of irrigation water where the entire surface of the soil is covered by a sheet of water, called "controlled flooding" when water is impounded or the flow directed by border dikes, ridges, or ditches.

flood peak: The highest value of the stage or discharge attained by a flood, thus, peak stage or peak discharge.

floodplain: Nearly level land situated on either side of a channel which is subject to overflow flooding.

floodplain management: A comprehensive program for the wise use of developed floodplains for protection or preservation to keep them in the natural state; includes measures to protect, preserve, or otherwise manage floodplains by both structural and nonstructural mean.

flood prevention: Methods or structural measures used to prevent floods; generally means flood control.

flood routing: A procedure whereby the time and magnitude of a flood wave at a point on a stream is determined from known or assumed data at upstream points.

flood stage: The stage at which overflow of the natural banks of a stream begins to cause damage in the reach in which the elevation is measured.

floodwater retarding structure: A structure providing for temporary storage of floodwater and for its controlled release.

floodway: A channel, either natural, excavated, or bounded by dikes and levees, used to carry excessive flood flows to reduce flooding. Sometimes considered to be the transitional area between the active channel and the floodplain.

floor–area ration: A channel, either natural, excavated, or bounded by dikes and levees, used to carry excessive flood flows to reduce flooding. Sometimes considered to be the transitional area between the active channel and the floodplain.

flora: The sum total of the kinds of plants in an area at one time.

flow: Volume of water that passes a given point within a given period of time.

flow augmentation: The release of water stored in a reservoir or other impoundment to increase the natural flow of a stream.

flow channel: The portion of a flow net bounded by two adjacent flow lines.

flow line: The path that a particle of water follows in its course of seepage under laminar flow conditions.

flow path: An underground route for ground–water movement, extending from a recharge (intake) zone to a discharge (output) zone such as a shallow stream.

flow slide: The failure of a sloped

bank of soil in which the movement of the soil mass does not take place along a well-defined surface of sliding.

flue dust: Solid particles, smaller than 100 microns, carried in the products of combustion.

flue gas scrubber: A type of equipment that removes fly ash and other objectionable materials from flue gas by the use of sprays, wet baffles, or other means that require water as the primary separation mechanism, also called flue gas washer.

fluidized bed: A reaction chamber in which finely divided solid reactants are suspended by a stream of gas or liquid from below; the reactants flow and mix freely, the entire surface area of the particles is exposed for reaction, and a high rate of heat exchange is obtained.

flume: An open conduit on a prepared grade, trestle, or bridge for the purpose of carrying water across creeks, gullies, ravines, or other obstructions. It may also apply to an entire canal that is elevated above natural ground for its entire length. Sometimes used in reference to calibrated devices used to measure the flow of water in open conduits. See *Venturi flume*.

fluorides: Gaseous and particulate pollutants containing fluorine matter.

flushing: Feeding female animals a concentrate feed shortly before and during the breeding period for the purpose of stimulating ovulation.

fluvial: Of or pertaining to rivers; growing or living in streams or ponds; produced by river action, as a fluvial plain.

fluvial deposit: A sedimentary deposit consisting of material transported by suspension or laid down by a river or stream.

fluvial processes: All processes and events by which the configuration of a stream channel is changed; especially processes by which sediment is transferred along the stream channel by the force of flowing water.

fluvioglacial: Pertaining to streams flowing from glaciers or to the deposits made by such streams.

flux: The rate of movement of liquid, particles, or energy over a given surface area.

fly ash: Particulate pollutants exhausted into the atmosphere; a by-product of coal-fired powerplants which reacts with water and the free lime in cement while generating only half the heat of an equal amount of cement.

flyway: A broad, generalized migration route of birds.

focal length: The distance between the center, vertex, or rear mode of a lens (or the vertext of a nirror) and the point at which the image of an infinitely distant object comes into critical focus; must be preceded by an adjective, such as equivalent or calibrated, to have a precise meaning.

focal plane: The plane (perpendicular to the axis of the lens) in which images of points in the object field of a camera lens are focused.

focus: To make the camera adjustments necessary to have the focal plane of the lens and film or ground-glass coincide; the point at which the rays from a point source of light reunite and cross after passing through a camera lens; in practice, the plane in which a sharp image of any scene is formed.

fodder: The dried, cured plants of tall, coarse grain crops, such as corn and soybeans, including the grain, stems, and leaves; grain parts not snapped off or threshed. See *stover, hay.*

fog: Condensation of water vapor in the air.

fogging: Pesticide application in which material in a solution is atomized by mechanical or other physical means creating very small particles and giving the appearance of fog or smoke.

fold (geology): A bend or flexure in a layer or layers of rock.

foliar diagnosis: Estimation of the plant nutrient status of a plant or the plant nutrient requirements of the soil for producing a crop through chemical analyses or color manifestations of plant leaves or by both methods.

foliar fertilization: Application of soluble fertilizer in the form of spray on the foliage of plants.

fomite: An inanimate object that can harbor or transmit pathogenic organisms.

food chain: A series of plant or animal species in a community, each of which is related to the next as a source of food.

food cycle: All the interconnecting food chains in a community; also called food web.

food web: Complex of interacting organisms, accounting for feeding relations, production, consumption, decomposition, and energy flow.

forage: All browse and herbaceous food that is available to livestock or game animals, used for grazing or harvested for feeding.

forage fish: Small fish which breed prolifically and serve as food for predatory fish.

forage production: The weight of forage that is produced within a designated period of time on a given area. The weight may be expressed as either green, air dry, or oven dry. The term may also be modified as to time of production such as annual, current year's, or seasonal forage production.

forb: A herbaceous plant which is not a grass, sedge, or rush.

ford: A place where a road crosses a stream under water.

foresight (surveying): An observation of the distance and direction to the next instrument station.

foreshore: That part of the shore between the ordinary high-and low-watermarks and generally crossed by the tide each day.

forest: A plant association predominantly of trees and other woody vegetation.

forest association: The community described by a group of dominant plant (tree) species occurring together, such as spruce-fir or northern hardwoods.

forest cover: Forest stands or cover types consisting of a plant community made up of trees and other woody vegetation, growing more or less closely together.

forest ecology: The relationships between forest organisms and their environment.

forest fire: Any wildfire or prescribed fire that is burning in forest, grass, alpine or tundra vegetation types.

forest floor: Layers of fresh leaf and needle litter, moderately decomposed organic matter, and humus or well-decomposed organic residue.

forest health: A forest condition that is naturally resilient to damage; characterized by biodiversity, it contains sustained habitat for timber, fish, wildlife, and humans, and meets present and future resource management objectives.

forest hydrology: The study of hydrologic processes as influenced by forest associated vegetation.

forest influences: The effects of forests on soil, water supply, climate, and environment.

forest management: The practical application of scientific, economic and social principles to the administration and working of a forest for specified objectives. Particularly, that branch of forestry concerned with the overall administrative, economic, legal and social aspects and with the essentially scientific and technical aspects, especially silviculture, protection and forest regulation.

forest range: See *grazable woodland.*

forested land: Land dominated by trees.

forested wetlands: Wetlands dominated by trees.

formal garden: A symmetrically arranged garden; in contrast to an informal garden.

formation (geology): Any assembly of rocks that have some characteristic in common, whether of origin, age, or composition.

FORTRAN: Acronym for FORmula

TRANslation coding used on digital computers. It is a problem oriented, high level program language for scientific and mathematic use. The source program is combination of algebraic and English statements of a standard but readable form.

fossil fuels: Fuels derived from the remains of ancient plant and animal life; coal, oil, and natural gas.

fouling: The impedance to the flow of gas or heat that results when material accumulates in gas passages or on head absorbing surfaces in a incinerator.

foundation planting: The planting of shrubs, ground covers, forbs, and sometimes low-growing trees near the foundation of a building.

fracture: A manner of breaking or appearance of a mineral when broken that is distinctive for certain minerals, as conchoidal fracture.

fragile area: Areas that, due to steepness, soil type, exposure, and cover, are especially subject to soil erosion and rapid deterioration; same as critical area.

fragipan: See *diagnostic horizons.*

fragmental: See *particle size classes for family groupings.*

frame: Any individual member of a continuous series of photographs or images; also called exposure.

framework plan: A statement describing the objectives or goals of a program and the general methods to be followed in working toward these goals. Frequently issued as one of the first reports in a comprehensive planning program; also called policies plan.

freeboard (hydraulics): Vertical distance between the maximum water surface elevation anticipated in design and the top of retaining banks or structures provided to prevent overtopping because of unforeseen conditions.

free flow (hydraulics): Flow through or over a structure not affected by submergence or backwater.

freeflowing stream: A stream or a portion of a stream that is unmodified by the works of man or, if modified, still retains its natural scenic qualities and recreational opportunities.

free flowing weir: A weir which in use has the tailwater lower than the crest of the weir. See *submerged weir.*

free swimming: Actively moving about in water or capable of moving about in water. See *sessile.*

freezeout: Deeply frozen over for long periods of time.

freezing nucleus: Any particle which, when present within a mass of super-cooled water, will initiate growth of an ice crystal about itself; thus, special forms of ice nuclei that nucleate the liquid phase, while the other type sublimation nuclei, nucleate the vapor phase in starting the growth of an ice crystal.

frequency: A statistical expression of the presence or absence of individuals of a species in a series of subsamples, that is, the ratio between the number of sample areas that contains a species and the total number of sample areas.

frequency analysis (hydrology): A method used to predict the frequency that a hydrologic event of a given magnitude may be equaled or exceeded.

frequency curve: A graphical representation of the frequency of occurrence of specific events.

fresh mulch: The primary layer of bulky, coarse, largely undecayed herbage residuum.

freshwater: Refers to water from rivers, lakes, reservoirs, underground streams, and other sources. Water is continually lifted from the oceans by evaporation and then returned to the land as ice, snow, or rain. Ice and snow melt from mountains to release freshwater to our rivers, streams, lakes, and to resupply underground streams.

freshwater chronic criteria: The highest concentration of a contaminant that freshwater aquatic organisms can be exposed to for an extended period of time (four days) without adverse effects.

friable: The ease of crumbling of soils. See *consistency.*

friction head: Energy required to overcome friction due to fluid movement with respect to the walls of the conduit or containing medium.

friction slope: The energy loss per unit of length of conduit due to friction.

frigid: See *soil temperature classes for family groupings.*

fringe water: Water occurring in the capillary fringe.

front (meteorology): A line of separation between cold and warm air masses.

fossil fuels: Fossil fuels are the nation's principal source of electricity. The popularity of these fuels is largely due to their low costs. Fossil fuels come in three major forms—coal, oil, and natural gas. Because fossil fuels are a finite resource and cannot be replenished once they are extracted and burned, they are not considered renewable.

frost cracks: Bark fissures in trees that results from sudden drops in temperature, especially on immature tissue, also called bark splitting.

frost heave: The raising of a surface due to the accumulation of ice in the underlying soil.

frost line: The lowest level that frost will reach in the soil.

frost pockets: A low area or depression at the base of a slope where frost collects.

fruit crop: Tree fruits and berries for local markets, home consumption, and distant markets.

fruitful: Producing fruits but not necessarily seeds.

fruiticose: Many small branches, bush-like.

fruiting body: The reproductive part of a fungus that contains or bears spores. Also known as a conk.

fry: Fish at and immediately after hatching.

full pool: Volume of water in a reservoir at normal water surface. The reservoir level that would be attained when the reservoir is fully utilized for all project purposes, including flood control.

fully permanent sprinkler system: An irrigation system usually composed of buried enclosed conduits carrying water under pressure to fixed orifices to distribute water over a given area.

fully portable sprinkler system: A system of enclosed conduits lying on the ground surface carrying water under pressure to orifices to distribute water over a given area.

Usually made with convenient couplers to disconnect conduit in short lengths for ease of moving from one setting to another. Water may be supplied by either a portable or fixed pumping plant.

fumes: Particulate or gaseous emissions formed from the chemical reactions of condensation of cooling vapors.

fumigation: The controlled or natural exposure of vegetation to phytotoxic pollutants.

functional plan: A plan for one, element or closely related elements of a comprehensive plan, for example, transportation, recreation, and open spaces. Such plans, of necessity, should be closely related to the land use plan. Plans that fall short of considering all elements of a comprehensive plan may be considered as functional plans. Thus, resource conservation and development plans and watershed project plans are considered functional plans.

fungi: Simple plants that lack a photosynthetic pigment. The individual cells have a nucleus surrounded by a membrane, and they may be linked together in long filaments called hyphae, which may grow together to form a visible body. Simpler fungi are involved in the stabilization of solid waste and sewage.

fungicide: Chemical pesticides that kill fungi or prevent them from causing diseases on plants of economic importance.

furbearer: A mammal sought for its fur.

furrow: A natural or man-made

narrow depression in the earth's surface. A narrow trenchlike plowed depression in the earth surface to keep surface water away from the slopes of cuts.

furrow dams: Small earth dams used to impound water in furrows. See *lister*.

furrow irrigation: A partial surface flooding method of irrigation normally used with clean tilled crops where water is applied in furrows or rows of sufficient capacity to contain the designed irrigation stream.

furrow stream: The size of water flow released into the furrow; size of stream is adjusted to prevent erosion, limited in amount to capacity of furrow, and as needed for intake rates of soil involved.

G

gabion: A rectangular or cylindrical wire mesh cage filled with rock and used as a protecting apron, revetment, etc., against erosion.

gage or gauge: Device for registering precipitation, water level, discharge, velocity, pressure, temperature, etc.

gage height (hydraulics): The height of the water surface above some arbitrary datum, such as the bottom of the channel. See *stage*.

gaging station: A selected section of a stream channel equipped with a gage, recorder, or other facilities for determining stream discharge.

gall: An abnormal growth of cellulose plant tissue about the eggs or larva of an insect parasite.

game animal: An animal sought for its fur, flesh, or trophy value, or one so defined by law.

game fish: Those species of fish considered to possess sporting qualities on fishing tackle, such as salmon, trout, black bass, striped bass, etc.; usually more sensitive to environmental changes than rough fish.

game management: The art of producing sustained annual crops of wild game animals.

game refuge: An area designated for the protection of game animals within which hunting and fishing is either prohibited or strictly controlled.

Gamma ray: Waves of radiant nuclear energy, of low ionizing capacity but highly penetrating.

garbage: Animal and vegetable waste resulting from the handling, storage, sale, preparation, cooking, and serving of foods.

gas barrier: Any device or material

used to divert the flow of gases produced in a sanitary landfill or by other land disposal techniques.

gaseous supersaturation: Condition of higher levels of dissolved gases in water due to entrainment, pressure increases, or heating.

gasification: Conversion of solid material such as coal into a gas for use as a fuel.

gasohol: A mixture of gasoline and alcohol; generally in the United States a mixture of 10 percent ethanol and 90 percent unleaded gasoline; used as a substitute for gasoline.

gate (irrigation): Structure or device for controlling the rate of water flow into or from a canal, ditch, or pipe.

gated pipe: Portable pipe with small gates installed along one side for distributing water to corrugations or furrows.

gel: A jellylike material formed by the coagulation of a colloidal suspension or sol.

generalization (cartography): Smoothing the character of features without destroying their visible shape; increases as map scale decreases.

general land office survey: The method of subdividing the public lands of the United States in accordance with regulations imposed by federal and state laws and carried out by the General Land Surveying Service of the Bureau of Land Management, US Department of Interior.

general plan: See *comprehensive plan*.

genetic diversity: Variation among and within species that is attributable to differences in hereditary material.

genetically improved seed and/or vegetative propagules: Seed or propagule that originate from a tree breeding program and that have been specifically designed to improve some attribute of seeds, seedlings, or vegetative propagules selection.

genotype: The genetic constitution of an individual or group.

genus: A category of closely related organisms; below the family and above a species in scope. See *species*.

geochemistry: All parts of geology that involve chemical changes; the study of 1) the relative and absolute abundances of the elements and the atomic species (isotypes) in the earth, and 2) the distribution and migration of the individual elements in the various parts of the earth (the atmosphere, hydrosphere, lithosphere, etc.) and in minerals and rocks.

geocoding: Geographic referencing or coding of location of data items.

geode: A hollow nodule that may be lined with inwardly pointing crystals.

geodesy: The science that deals with the determination of the size and figure of the earth (geoid) by such direct measurements as triangulation, leveling, and gravimetric observations; which determines the external gravitational field or the earth and, to a limited degree, the internal structure.

geographic information system: An information system that can input, manipulate, and analyze geographically referenced data to support the decision-making processes of an organization.

geography: The science dealing with the distribution and interaction of phenomena on the earth's surface.

geoid: The equipotential surface in the gravity field of the earth which coincides with the undisturbed mean sea level extended continuously through the continents; the direction of gravity is perpendicular to the geoid at every point; the geoid is the surface of reference for astronomical observations and for geodetic leveling.

geologic resources: Those elements of the earth's crust such as soils, sediments, rocks, and minerals, including petroleum and natural gas, that are not included in the definitions of ground and surface water resources.

geological erosion: See *erosion*.

geology: The study of the composition structure, and history of the earth.

geomorphic: Of or relating to the form or shape of the earth.

geomorphology: That branch of both physiography and geology that deals with the form of the earth, the general configuration of its surface, and the changes that take place in the evolution of land forms.

geo-referenced data (geospatial): Mapped data tied to real-world geographic coordinates such as latitude and longitude.

geothermal: Relating to the Earth's internal heat; commonly applied to springs or vents discharging hot water or steam.

germination: The initiation of growth by the embryo and development of a young plant from seed.

girdling: The encircling of the trunk of a tree with a continuous series of cuts deep enough to kill the tree.

girdling root: A root that grows around another root or a stem, thus tending to strangle the plant.

glacial drift: Rock debris transported by glaciers and deposited either directly from the ice or from the meltwater. The debris may or may not be heterogenous.

glacial moraine: A mass of loose rock, soil, and earth deposited by the edge of a glacier.

glacial strations: Lines carved into rock by overriding ice, showing the direction of glacial movement.

glacial till: See *till*.

glaciofluvial deposits: Material moved by glaciers and subsequently sorted and deposited by streams flowing from the melting ice. The deposits are stratified and may occur in the form of outwash plains, deltas, kames, eskers, and kame terraces. See *glacial drift, till*.

glade: An open space surrounded by forest.

global positioning systems (GPS): Space-based radio positioning systems that provide 24-hour, three-dimensional position, velocity, and time information to suitably equipped users anywhere on or near the surface of the Earth.

global warming: Global warming is the gradual rise of the Earth's surface temperature. Global warming is believed to be caused by the greenhouse effect and is responsible for changes in global climate patterns and an increase in the near-surface temperature of the Earth. Global warming has occurred in the distant past as the result of natural influences, but the term is most often used to refer to the warming predicted to occur as a result of increased emissions of greenhouse gases.

gneiss: Metamorphic rock that displays distinct banding of light and dark mineral layers.

goods (economics): All physical objects and those personal and other services used by people.

gooseneck: A portion of a water service connection between the distribution system water main and a meter. Sometimes called a pigtail.

gore (surveying): An irregularly shaped tract of land, generally triangular, left between two adjoining surveyed tracts because of inaccuracies in the boundary surveys or as a remnant of a systematic survey; (soils engineering) the frequency distribution of the various sized grains that constitute a sediment, soil, or other material.

graben: Down-dropped block of rock bounded on both sides by faults.

grab sample: A single sample collected at a particular time and place that represents the composition of the water, air, or soil only at that time and place.

gradation (geology): The bringing of a surface or a stream bed to grade, to running water; (soils engineering) the frequency distribution of the various sized grains that constitute a sediment, soil, or other material.

grade: The slope of a road, channel, or natural ground; the finished surface of a canal bed, roadbed, top of embankment, or bottom of excavation; any surface prepared

for the support of construction like paving or laying a conduit. To finish the surface of a canal bed, roadbed, top of embankment, or bottom of excavation.

graded stream: A stream in which, over a period of years, the slope is delicately adjusted to provide, with available discharge and with prevailing channel characteristics, just the velocity required for transportation of the load (of sediment) supplied from the drainage basin. The graded profile is a slope of transportation. It is a phenomenon in which the element of time has a restricted connotation. Works of man are limited to his experience and of design and construction.

graded terrace: See *terrace*.

grade stabilization structure: A structure for the purpose of stabilizing the grade of a gully or other watercourse, thereby preventing further head cutting or lowering of the channel grade.

gradient: Change of elevation, velocity, pressure, or other characteristics per unit length; slope.

gradually varied flow (hydraulics): Non-uniform flow in which depth of flow changes gradually through a reach; e.g. normal natural valley and channel flow; can be either steady or unsteady flow.

graduation: In geology, the bringing of a surface or a stream bed to grade, to running water; in soils engineering, the frequency distribution of the various sized grains that constitute a sediment, soil, or other material.

graftage: Implanting a scion from one plant into a growing plant, called a stock, so that their cambium layers contact each other; thus enabling the scion to derive water and nutrients from the stock, eventually resulting in a union of the two parts.

graft union: The point of union between the two parts of a graft, the stock and the scion.

grain (photography): One of the discrete silver particles resulting from the development of an exposed light-sensitive material; the random distribution of these particles in an area of uniform exposure gives rise to the appearance known as graininess.

granite: Light-colored, coarse-grained intrusive igneous rock with quartz and feldspar as dominant minerals and typically peppered with mica and hornblende.

granitic: General term for all light-colored, granite-like igneous rocks.

granodiorite: Coarse-grained intrusive igneous rock with less quartz and more feldspar than true granite and typically darker.

grain, wood: The direction, size, arrangement, appearance, or quality of the fibers in wood.

granular structure: See *soil structure*.

graphic scale: A graduated line by means of which distances on the map or chart may be measured in terms of ground distances; also called bar scale.

grass: A member of the botanical family Gramineae, characterized by bladelike leaves arranged on the culm or stem in two ranks.

grass barriers: Strips of grass for snow management or wind erosion control.

grassed waterway: A natural or constructed waterway, usually broad and shallow, covered with erosion resistant grasses, used to conduct surface water from cropland.

grassland: Land on which the existing plant cover is dominated by grasses. See *prairie*.

Grassland Reserve Program (GRP): This newly established program will assist owners, through long-term contracts or easements, in restoring grassland and conserving virgin grassland. Up to two million acres of restored, improved, or natural grassland, rangeland, and pasture, including prairie, can be enrolled. Tracts must be at least 40 contiguous acres, subject to waivers. Eligible grassland can be enrolled under 10- to 30-year contracts or under 30-year or permanent easements.

grasslike plants: A plant that resembles a true grass, for example, sedges and rushes, but is taxonomically different.

grassroots conservation organization: Any group of concerned citizens who act together to address a conservation need.

gravel: A mass of pebbles. See *coarse fragments*.

gravel envelope: Selected aggregate placed around the screened pipe section of well casing or a subsurface drain to facilitate the entry of water into the well or drain.

gravel filter: Graded sand and gravel aggregate placed around a drain or well screen to prevent the movement of fine materials from the aquifer into the drain or well.

gravelly: An adjective incorporated into the soil textural class designations of horizons when the soil mass contains between 15 and 90 percent pebbles by volume; used to describe soils or lands. See *pebble as defined under coarse fragments.*

gravitational water: Water that moves into, through, or out of the soil under the influence of gravity.

gravity dam: Dam that depends on its weight to resist overturning.

gravity irrigation: Irrigation in which the water is not pumped but flows and is distributed by gravity, includes sprinkler systems when gravity furnishes the desired head.

gravity potential: The work per unit quanitity of pure water that has to be done to overcome the earth's gravitational force; it is negative if the reference point is above a free water surface and positive if the reference point is below a free water surface; the gravity and matric potential are equal and opposite in sign when the reference point is above a free water surface.

gravity sprinkler irrigation: See *irrigation, gravity-sprinkler.*

graybody (remote sensing): An energy absorber/radiator that has a spectral radiant exitance curve of the same functional form as an ideal blackbody radiation curve, but reduced by a constant factor for every wavelength, equivalently, a graybody has an emissivity which is less than 1.0 and the same at all wavelengths.

gray scale: A monochrome strip of shades ranging from white to black with intermediate shades of gray.

gray water: Domestic wastewater

composed of wash water from kitchen, bathroom, and laundry sinks, tubs, and washers.

grazable woodland: Forest land on which the understory includes, as an integral part of the forest plant community, plants that can be grazed without significantly impairing other forest values.

grazing: The eating of any kind of standing vegetation by domestic livestock or wild animals.

grazing capacity: The maximum stocking rate possible without inducing damage to vegetation or related resources.

grazing, deferred rotation: A discontinuance of grazing on various parts of a range in succeeding years, allowing each part to rest successively during the growing season to permit seed production, establishment of seeding, or restoration of plant vigor.

grazing distribution: Dispersion of livestock grazing within a management unit or area.

grazing land: Land used regularly for grazing. The term is not confined to land suitable only for grazing. Cropland and pasture used in connection with a system of farm crop rotation are usually not included.

grazing period: See *grazing season.*

grazing permit: A document authorizing the use of public or other lands for grazing purposes under specified conditions, issued to the livestock operator by the agency administering the lands.

grazing preference: In the administration of public grazing lands, the basis upon which permits and licenses are issued for grazing use.

grazing season: The portion of the year that livestock graze or are permitted to graze on a given range or pasture. Sometimes called grazing period.

grazing system: The manipulation of grazing animals to accomplish a desired result.

grazing unit: Any division of the range or pasture used to facilitate administration or the handling of livestock.

great group: See *soil classification.*

greenbelt: A strip of land kept in its natural or relatively undeveloped state or in agricultural use and which serves to break up the continuous pattern of urban development, frequently planned around the periphery of urban settlements.

Green box policies: Domestic or trade policies that are deemed to be minimally trade distorting and that are excluded from domestic support reduction commitments in the Uruguay Round Agreement on Agriculture. Examples are domestic policies dealing with research, extension, inspection and grading, environmental and conservation programs, disaster relief, crop insurance, domestic food assistance, food security stocks, structural adjustment programs, and direct payments not linked to production. Trade measures or policies, such as export market promotion, are also exempt (but not export subsidies or foreign food aid).

greenhouse effect: The absorption of light wave energy by the earth's surface and its release as heat into the air. Thus, a passage of light occurs but the heat mass is retained like glass does in a greenhouse.

Greenhouse gases (GHG): Gases in the Earth's atmosphere that produce the greenhouse effect. Changes in the concentration of certain greenhouse gases, due to human activity such as fossil fuel burning, increase the risk of global climate change. Greenhouse gases include water vapor, carbon dioxide, methane, nitrous oxide, halogenated fluorocarbons, ozone, perfluorinated carbons, and hydrofluorocarbons.

green manure crop: Any crop grown for the purpose of being turned under while green or soon after maturity for soil improvement.

green power: Electricity that is generated from eligible renewable energy sources and is purchased voluntarily by consumers, including both residential and non-residential consumers.

green roofs: Green roofs are rooftops planted with vegetation. Intensive green roofs have thick layers of soil (six to 12 inches, or more) that can support a broad variety of plant or even tree species. Extensive roofs are simpler green roofs with a soil layer of six inches or less to support turf, grass, or other ground cover.

green tree retention: The reservation of live trees of a specific species and size from harvesting, to achieve a site-specific objective.

grid: Two sets of parallel lines intersecting at right angles and forming squares; the grid is superimposed on maps, charts, and other similar representations of the earth's surface in an accurate and consistent manner to permit identification of ground locations with respect to other locations and the computation of direction and distance to other points; also called reference grid.

grid data: A type of GIS data consisting a rows and columns of square 'cells' or pixels, generally used for analysis purposes; each cell will have a value or classification assigned to it .

grid ticks: Ticks emanating from the neat line of a map or chart in their correct declination, indicating overlapping or secondary grids; ticks on interior grid lines, subdividing the grid interval into smaller units for ease of referencing. See *tick mark*.

gross crop value: This value is the sum of annual receipts from sale of crops produced. Production of crops, such as pasture and hay which normally are consumed on the farm by livestock, shall be converted to cash market values and included with crop sales. Total market value of all crop production from irrigated lands before deducting costs of production. Unit prices represent the weighted average prices received by farmers for the part of the crop that is sold. Production and price information are obtained from reports of farmers, project-operating personnel, local agricultural specialists, and State-Federal agricultural statisticians.

gross duty of water (irrigation): The irrigation water diverted at the intake of a canal system, usually expressed in depth on the

irrigable area under the system; diversion requirement. See *net duty of water*.

gross national product (GNP): The monetary value of the total output of goods and services within a country in a given period of time, usually a year. Its value does not include allowances for depreciation or the consumption of capital goods.

ground control (remote sensing): A point or system of points on the earth's surface whose position has been established by ground survey(s), referenced to the celestial sphere, the geoid, a given ellipsoid of reference, or an assumed origin; also called field control.

ground cover: Grasses or other plants grown to keep soil from being blown or washed away.

ground truth (remote sensing): Term coined for data/information obtained on surface/subsurface features to aid in interpretation of remotely sensed data; a vague, misleading term suggesting that the truth may be found on the ground. See *reference data*.

groundwater: Phreatic water or subsurface water in the zone of saturation.

groundwater runoff: That part of the groundwater that is discharged into a stream channel as spring or seepage water.

groundwater under the direct influence (UDI) of surface water: Any water beneath the surface of the ground with: 1) significant occurence of insects or other microorganisms, algae, or large-diameter pathogens; 2) significant and relatively rapid shifts in water characteristics such as turbidity, temperature, conductivity, or pH which closely correlate to climatological or surface water conditions. Direct influence is determined for individual sources in accordance with criteria established by a state.

Groundwater Disinfection Rule: A 1996 amendment of the Safe Drinking Water Act requiring EPA to promulgate national primary drinking water regulations requiring disinfection as for all public water systems, including surface waters and groundwater systems.

grout: A cementing or sealing mixture of cement and water to which sand, sawdust, or other fillers may be added.

grouting: Filling the area between pieces of rock, brick, etc., with mortar or concrete.

grove: A small group of trees, usually without understory, planted or natural.

growing season: The period and/or number of days between the last freeze in the spring and the first frost in the fall for the freeze threshold temperature of the crop or other designated temperature threshold.

growing stock (forestry): The sum, by number or volume, of all the trees in a forest or a specified part of it.

growth form: The characteristic shape or appearance of an organism.

growth regulator: A substance that, when applied to plants in small amounts, inhibits, stimulates, or otherwise modifies the growth process.

guest ranch: A rural area operated as a working or simulated ranch that provides vacation living accommodations for a fee.

guided interpretive services: An interpretive tour, hike, or walk that is led by a guide.

guild: A group of organisms, not necessarily taxonomically related, that are ecologically similar in characteristics such as diet, behavior, or microhabitat preference, or with respect to their ecological role in general.

gully: A channel or miniature valley cut by concentrated runoff but through which water commonly flows only during and immediately after heavy rains or during the melting of snow; may be dendritic or branching or it may be linear, rather long, narrow, and of uniform width. The distinction between gully and rill is one of depth. A gully is sufficiently deep that it would not be obliterated by normal tillage operations, whereas a rill is of lesser depth and would be smoothed by ordinary farm tillage. See *erosion, rill*.

gully erosion: See *erosion*.

gully control plantings: The planting of forage, legume, or woody plant seeds, seedlings, cuttings, or transplants in gullies to establish or re establish a vegetative cover adequate to control runoff and erosion and incidentally produce useful products.

guying (horticulture): Using rope, wire, cable, etc. to support or steady a tree or other object.

H

habitat: The environment in which the life needs of a plant or animal organism, population, or community are supplied.

habitat fragmentation: Habitat fragmentation is a serious problem with potentially devastating effects for biological diversity. The issue of fragmentation has been identified recently as one of the most pressing issues in wildlife management and the conservation of biodiversity. Habitat fragmentation refers to a phenomenon where habitats are broken up into small, isolated pieces which results in new landscapes being developed that differ substantially from the previous landscape. The shape, size, proximity, and contrast of each new landscape piece determines how the fragmented habitat affects wildlife. For instance, the splintering of wetlands, prairies, and forests into small isolated "pieces" makes it difficult for isolated populations of plants and animals to move from one "piece" to another, thus impacting their ability to breed with one another. Problems associated with isolated populations of plants and animals have been described by researchers in conservation biology and island biogeography. Isolated groups often have trouble maintaining the genetic integrity and variability needed for their continued evolutionary viability and prospects for long-term survival (if they cannot move to or be reached by other populations of their species). Such situations occur if there are no corridors of appropriate habitat for the species to move through. This is the situation for many forest interior species in fragmented forest landscapes throughout the Midwest.

habitat indicator: A physical attribute of the environment measured to characterize conditions necessary to support an organism, population, or community in the absence of pollutants; e.g. salinity of estuarine waters or substrate type in streams or lakes.

habitat management: Management of the forest to create environments which provide habitats (food, shelter) to meet the needs of particular organisms.

habitat niche: See *niche.*

hachures: A method of portraying relief by short, wedge-shaped marks radiating from high elevations and following the direction of slope to the lowland.

half life: The period of time during which one-half of the atoms of a radioactive element or isotope will disintegrate.

half shrub: A perennial plant with a woody base whose annually produced stems die back each year.

halftone: Any photomechanical printing surface or the impression therefrom in which detail and tone values are represented by a series of evenly spaced dots of varying size and shape, varying in direct proportion to the intensity of the tones they represent.

halophyte: A plant adapted to existence in a saline environment, such as greasewood (Sarcobatus), saltgrass (Distichlis), and the saltbushes (Atriplex spp.).

hand level: A hand-held instrument for approximate leveling; consists of a sighting tube with a split field of view; a horizontal crosshair in one-half of the field bisects the image of a spirit level in the other half when the instrument is held level; often identified by designer's name, such as Locke hand level, Abney level.

hardiness: The adaptation of a plant or other organisms to the rigors of a climate, particularly to the occurrence of freezing, although conditions of moisture, extreme heat, etc. may influence the ability of a plant to survive.

hardness: See *consistence, Moh's scale of hardness.*

hardpan: A hardened soil layer in the lower A or in the B horizon caused by cementation of soil particles with organic matter or with materials such as silica, sesquioxides, or calcium carbonate. The hardness does not change appreciably with changes in the moisture content, and pieces of the hard layer do not slake in water. See *caliche, duripan, ortstein.*

hard pinch (horticulture): Pruning by removal of more of the shoot than with a soft pinch, the cut being made in harder wood at the second or third node below the growing tip. See *soft pinch.*

hard seed: See *seed.*

hardware: The physical components of a data processing system, including the central processor, data carriers, and remote terminals. See *software.*

hard water: Alkaline water containing dissolved salts that interfere with some industrial processes and prevent soap from sudsing.

hardwoods: A term applied to one of the botanical group of trees that have broad leaves, in contrast to the conifers; also wood produced by trees of this group regardless of texture.

hardy (horticulture): Capable of living over winter without artificial protection.

harvestable fish: A fish that is of sufficient size to be of value to the fisherman for food.

harvestable surplus: The number of wild animals which may be taken from a discrete population without reducing the capability of that population to restore itself, within one generation, or within one year, whichever is longer, to the population level existing before the surplus was harvested.

harvest cutting (forestry): The removal of a crop or stand of financially or physically mature trees as a final cut in even aged management or the removal of mature trees in uneven age management. One of the major objectives is to encourage regeneration.

harvest forecast: The flow of potential timber harvests over time. A harvest forecast is usually a measure of the maximum timber supply that can be realized, over time, for a specified land base and set of management assumptions.

harvest pattern: The spatial distribution of cutblocks and reserve areas across the forested landscape.

harvest rate: The rate at which timber is harvested, commonly expressed as an allowable annual cut (AAC).

haul road (mining): Road from a mine pit to loading dock, tipple ramp, or preparation plant used for transporting mined material by truck.

hay: The dried stems and leafy parts of plants cut and harvested by man, such as alfalfa, clovers, other forage legumes, and the finer stemmed, leafy grasses. See *fodder, stover*.

hayland: Land used primarily for the production of hay from long term stands of adapted forage plants.

hazardous substance: A broad term that includes all substances that can be harmful to people or the environment.

hazardous waste: Waste materials which by their nature are inherently dangerous to handle or dispose of, such as old explosives, radioactive materials, some chemicals, and some biological wastes; usually produced in industrial operations or in institutions. See *waste*.

haze: Fine particles of dust or liquid dispersed in an atmosphere, thereby rendering it a characteristic opalescent appearance that nullifies all colors.

head: The height of water above any plane of reference; the kinetic or potential energy possessed by each unit weight of a liquid, expressed as the vertical height through which a unit weight would have to fall to release the average energy possessed; used in various compound terms such as pressure head, velocity head, and lost head; the internal pressure expressed in "feet" or pounds per square inch of an enclosed conduit.

head capacity curve: See *capacity curve*.

head ditch: An open ditch used to convey and distribute water in a field for surface irrigation.

head gate: Water control structure; the gate at the entrance to a conduit.

heading back (horticulture): Pruning the tips of a plant so to encourage a bushier shape.

head loss: Energy loss due to friction eddies, changes in velocity, or direction of flow. See *friction head*.

head of the hollow fill: The placement of overburden material from adjacent contour or mountain top mines in compacted layers in narrow, steep-sided hollows so that surface drainage is possible.

headwater: The source of a stream; the water upstream from a structure or point on a stream.

headworks: The diversion structures at the head of a conduit.

heap: The soil carried above the sides of a body or bucket.

heartwood: The inner core or layers of a woody stem, made up wholly of nonliving cells, and usually differentiated from the outer enveloping layer (sapwood) by its darker color.

heat island effect: The collection of warm air in the center of a city; as the air disperses, it cools and sinks at the extremities; in time, cooler air from the edges of the city flows into the center to repeat a self-contained circulatory pattern.

heating season: The coldest months of the year when buildings are heated.

heave: The upward movement of land surfaces or structures due to subsurface expansion of soil or rock, or vertical faulting of rock. Upward movement of soil caused by expansion or displacement resulting from phenomena such as moisture absorption, removal of overburden, driving of piles, frost action, and loading of an adjacent area.

heaving: The partial lifting of plants out of the ground, frequently breaking their roots, as a result of freezing and thawing of the surface soil during the winter.

heavy media separation: Separation of solid wastes into heavy and light fractions in a fluid medium whose density lies between theirs.

heavy metals: Metals present in municipal and industrial wastes that pose long term environmental hazards; they include boron, cadmium, cobalt, chromium, copper, mercury, nickel, lead, and zinc.

heavy soil: various fine textured soils.

hectare: A metric unit of land measure; equals to 10,000 square meters or 2.471 acres. See *metric system*.

hedge: Plants growing close to each other in a row to form a continuous mass of foliage, either trimmed or allowed to grow naturally.

hedged: A term used to describe the appearance of browse plants that have been browsed so as to appear artificially clipped.

hedgerow: A barrier of bushes, shrubs, or small trees growing close together in a line.

heel in: To store young trees and other plants in a temporary trench, covering the roots with soil, to keep them from drying out before they are permanently planted.

helitack: Initial attack on wildfires involving the use of helicopters and trained crews, deployed as a complete unit.

hemic materials: See *organic soil materials*.

herb: Any flowering plant except those developing persistent woody bases and stems above ground.

herbaceous: A vascular plant that does not develop woody tissue.

herbage: The sum total of all herbaceous plants.

herbicide: A chemical substance used for killing plants, especially weeds. See *amides, benzoics, dinitroanalines, diphenyl ethers, phenoxys, and traizines*.

herbicide, contact: A herbicide designed to kill on contact by killing foliage.

herbicide, non-selective: A herbicide that destroys or prevents all plant growth.

herbicide, post-emergence: A herbicide designed to be applied after the crop is above ground.

herbicide, pre-emergence: A herbicide designed to be applied before the crop emerges through the soil surface.

herbivore: A plant eating animal.

herd: A group of animals, especially cattle or big game, collectively considered as a unit in grazing practices.

heterogeneous: Differing in kind; having unlike qualities; possessed of different characteristics; opposed to homogeneous.

heterogeneous waste: Differing in kind; having unlike qualities; possessed of different characteristics; opposed to homogeneous.

heterophylous: Bearing foliage of leaves of more than one form on the same plant or stem.

heterotroph: An organism that feeds on organic materials.

heterotrophic: Pertaining to organisms that are dependent on organic material for food. See *autotrophic*.

hibernation: A state of resting associated with reduced respiration and other body functions. Applies to some animals, especially in winter.

highly erodible land (HEL): Soils with an erodibility index (EI) equal to or greater than eight are defined as HEL. An EI of eight indicates that without any cover or conservation practices, the soil will erode at a rate eight times the soil tolerance level. Fields containing at least one-third or 50 acres (whichever is less) of HEL are designated as highly erodible for the purpose of Highly-Erodible Land Conservation Provisions.

Highly Erodible Land Conservation (Compliance and Sodbuster): First established in 1985, this provision requires that farm program participants with highly erodible cropland develop and implement an approved conservation plan for their land to maintain program eligibility. Conservation compliance pertains to farming existing cropland but is commonly known as the Sodbuster

provision when applied to newly planted cropland. Natural Resources Conservation Service certifies technical compliance, and USDA's Farm Services Agency administers changes in farm program benefits.

highwall: The unexcavated face of exposed overburden and mineral in a surface mine or the face or bank on the uphill side of a contour strip mining excavation.

highway erosion control: The prevention and control of erosion in ditches, at cross drains, and on fills and road banks within a highway right of way; includes vegetative practices and structural practices.

histic epipedon: See *diagnostic horizons*.

histosols: See *soil classification*.

hi volume sampler: A filtering apparatus for measuring and analyzing suspended particular pollutants.

hogback: A sharp crested ridge formed by a hard rock ledge.

holding pond: A pond or reservoir usually made of earth built to store polluted runoff.

holding tank: A prefabricated structure of concrete or steel or like materials constructed to store liquid manure from animals.

hollow gravity dam (cellular gravity dam): A dam which has the outward appearance of a gravity dam but is of hollow construction. A dam constructed of concrete and/or masonry on the outside but having a hollow interior and relying on its weight for stability.

holophytic: Obtaining food after the manner of a green plant.

holozoic: Obtaining food after the

manner of most animals by ingesting complex organic matter.

homogeneous: Of the same kind or nature; consisting of similar parts or of elements of a like nature; opposed to heterogeneous.

homogeneous earthfill dam: An embankment dam construction throughout of more or less uniform earth materials, except for possible inclusion of internal drains or blanket drains. Used to differentiate it from a zoned earthfill dam. An embankment type dam constructed of only one type of material.

homogeneous waste: A body of waste material made up of similar parts or of elements of a like nature; opposed to heterogeneous.

homologous: The condition where an image of a given object point or series of such points is common to two or more projections having different perspective centers.

homothermous: Having the same temperature throughout.

hood inlet: Entrance to a closed conduit that has been shaped to induce full flow at minimum water surface elevation.

horizon: See *soil horizon*.

hornblende: Black blade-like mineral common in igneous and metamorphic rocks.

horticultural variety: A plant variety or cultivar originating as a result of controlled fertilization, selective breeding of progeny or hybridization. See *cultivar*.

horticulture: The art and science of growing fruits, vegetables, and ornamental plants.

host: An organism that supplies the life needs of another organism of a different species.

hotspot (remote sensing): The destruction of fine image detail on a portion of a wide-angle aerial photograph; caused by the absence of shadows and by halation near the prolongation of a line from the sun through the exposure station; also called sunspot.

hue: One of the three variables of color, caused by light of certain wavelengths and changes with the wavelength. See *Munsell color system, chroma, value*.

hulled seed: Any seed normally covered by a hull, that is, by bracts or other coating, from which the hull has been removed.

human environment: The natural and physical environment and the relationship of people with that environment.

humic mulch: Decayed and fragmented residuum of fresh mulch.

humid: Regions or climates where moisture, when distributed normally throughout the year, should not be a limiting factor in the production of most crops. The lower limit of precipitation under cool climates may be as little as 20 inches (0.508 meters) annually. In hot climates it may be as much as 60 inches (1.524 memters). Natural vegetation is generally forest. See *subhumid*.

humidity, absolute: The actual quantity or mass of water vapor present in a given volume of air, generally expressed in grams per cubic foot or in grams per cubic meter.

humidity, critical: The humidity above which a fertilizer material absorbs water.

humidity, relative: The ratio of the

actual amount of water vapor present in the portion of the atmosphere under consideration to the quantity that would be there if it were saturated.

humus: That more or less stable fraction of the soil organic matter remaining after the major portion or added plant and animal residues have decomposed, usually amorphous and dark colored; includes the F and H layers in undisturbed forest soils. See *soil organic matter; soil horizons, 01 and 02*.

humus layer: The top portion of the soil which owes its characteristic features to the humus contained in it.

hunting area: A tract of land or land and water managed for the production and harvest of wildlife.

hurricane: A severe tropical cyclone with winds exceeding 75 miles per hour.

husklage: Forage material that falls behind the harvesting combine of corn, consisting of cob, husks, and grain.

hybrid: A plant resulting from a cross between parents of different species, subspecies, or cultivar.

hybrid, F1: The first filial generation of hybrids produced by crossing dissimilar plant parents.

hydration: The chemical combination of water with another substance.

hydraulic conductivity: See *permeability*.

hydraulic fill dam: A dam composed of earth material pumped into place with water; generally the fines are washed toward the center for greater imperviousness.

hydraulic grade line: In a closed conduit, a line joining the elevations to which water could stand in risers or vertical pipes connected to the conduit at their lower end and open at their upper end. In open channel flow, the hydraulic grade line is the free water surface.

hydraulic gradient: The slope of the hydraulic grade line; the slope of the free surface of water flowing in an open channel.

hydraulic jump: Sudden turbulent rise in water level from a flow stage below critical depth to flow stage above critical depth, during which the velocity passes from supercritical to subcritical.

hydraulic mining: See *mining*.

hydraulic radius: The cross sectional area of a stream divided by its wetted perimeter. The "r" in Manning's formula. See *Manning's formula*.

hydraulics: A branch of science that deals with practical applications (as the transmission of energy or effects of flow) of water or other fluid in motion.

hydric: Characterized by, or thriving in, an abundance of moisture.

hydrocarbons: Compounds containing hydrogen and carbon that are subdivided into alicyclic, aliphatic, and aromatic groups based on their chemical activity and atomic structure.

hydroelectric plant: An electric power plant in which energy of falling water is converted into electricity by turning a turbine generator.

hydrogen sulfide (H_2S): A poisonous gas with the odor of rotten eggs that is produced from the reduction of sulfates in and the putrefaction of a sulfur containing organic material.

hydrogeologic conditions: Conditions stemming from the interaction of groundwater and the surrounding soil and rock.

hydrogeological cycle: The natural process recycling water from the atmosphere down to (and through) the earth and back to the atmosphere again.

hydrogeologist: A person who studies and works with groundwater.

hydrogeology: The geology of groundwater, with particular emphasis on the chemistry and movement of water.

hydrograph: A graph showing variation in stage (depth) or discharge of a stream of water over a period of time.

hydrographic chart: A nautical chart showing depths of water, nature of the bottom, contours of bottom and coastline, and tides and currents in a given sea or sea and land area; also called nautical chart.

hydrologic cycle: The circuit of water movement from the atmosphere to the earth and return to the atmosphere through various stages or processes, as precipitation, interception, runoff, infiltration, percolation, storage, evaporation, and transpiration.

hydrologic model: Mathematical formulations that simulate hydrologic phenomenon considered as processes or as systems.

hydrologic soil groups: Classification of soils by their reference to intake rate of infiltration of water, which is influenced by texture, organic matter content, stability of the soil aggregates, and soil horizon development.

hydrology: The science dealing with the properties, distribution, and circulation of water and snow.

hydrolysis: The reaction of a salt with water to produce a basic or acidic solution.

hydrometeorology: The science of the application of meteorology to hydrologic problems.

hydrophilic: Having a strong affinity (liking) for water.

hydrophobic: Having a strong aversion (dislike) for water.

hydrophyte: A plant that grows in water or in wet or saturated soils. See *xerophyte, mesophyte.*

hydroseeding: Dissemination of seed, hydraulically in a water medium. Mulch, lime, and fertilizer can be incorporated into the sprayed mixture.

hydrosphere: The water layer of the earth, including oceans, seas, and lakes.

hydrostatic pressure: The force per unit area exerted by a liquid at rest.

hydrous mica: A hydrous aluminum silicate clay mineral with a 2:1 lattice structure and containing a considerable amount of potassium that serves as an additional bonding between the crystal units, resulting in particles larger than normal in montmorillonite. It has a smaller cation exchange capacity than montmorillonite. Sometimes referred to as illite or mica. See *clay mineral; montmorillonite.*

hydroxide: A compound of an element with the radical or ion OH negative, as sodium hydroxide, NaOH.

hygrometer: An instrument for measuring the relative humidity of the air.

hygrophyte: Hydrophyte; plants extremely sensitive to dry air, growing only in habitats where relative humidity is always high. See *hydrophyte, mesophyte, xerophyte.*

hygroscopic: Absorption of moisture from the atmosphere.

hygroscopic water: Water so tightly held by the attraction of soil particles that it cannot be removed except as a vapor by raising the temperature above the boiling point of water. It is unavailable to plants.

hyperconcentrated flow: Moving mixture of sediment and water between 40 and 80 percent water by volume.

hyperthermic: A soil temperature regime that has mean annual soil temperatures of 22 degrees C or more and more than 5 degrees C difference between mean summer and mean winter soil temperatures at 50 cm (2.15 in). See *isohyperthermic.*

hypocenter: The point or focus within the earth which is the center of an earthquake and the origin of its elastic waves. The location within the Earth where the sudden release of energy is initiated. The focus of an earthquake.

hypolimnetic: Pertaining to the lower, colder portion of a lake or reservoir which is separated from the upper, warmer portion (epilimnion) by the thermocline.

hypolimnion: The region of a body of water that extends from the thermocline to the bottom and is essentially removed from major surface influences. See *epilimnion.*

hyporheic zone: Groundwater habitats created by the movement of river water from the active channel to areas to the side and beneath the active channel. Uniquely adapted organisms that can provide food for fish live in the groundwater habitat.

hypoxia: A condition where there isn't enough oxygen in the water. This forces fish to either swim away or die and can suffocate plants living in the water. Hypoxia occurs when there are too many nutrients in the water.

hypsography: The science or art of describing elevations of land surfaces with reference to a datum, usually sea level; that part of topography dealing with relief or elevation of terrain.

I

ice nucleus: Any particle that serves as a nucleus in the formation of ice crystals in the atmosphere.

ichthyology: The scientific study of fish.

igneous rocks: Rock formed by solidification from a molten or partially molten state; primary rock.

illite: See *hydrous mica*.

illitic: See *soil mineralogy classes for family groupings*.

illuvial horizon: A soil layer or horizon in which material carried from an overlying layer has been precipitated from solution or deposited from suspension. The layer of accumulation. See *eluvial horizon*.

illuviation: The process of deposition of soil material removed from one horizon to another in the soil, usually from an upper to a lower horizon in the soil profile. See *eluviation*.

image (cartography): The permanent record of the likeness of any natural or man-made features, objects, and activities reproduced on photographic materials. This image can be acquired through the sensing of visual or any other segment of the electromagnetic spectrum by sensors, such as panchromatic infrared, and high resolution radar.

image processing system: Any optical, electro-optical, or electronic system that is capable of manipulating photographic or digital images and extracting information from them.

imagery: The products of image-forming instruments; analogous to photography.

immature: Trees or stands that have grown past the regeneration stage, but are not yet mature.

immiscibility: The inability of two or more substances or liquids to readily dissolve into one another, such as soil and water.

impact assessment: A study of the potential future effects of resource development on other resources and on social, economic and/or environmental conditions.

impermeable: Not easily penetrated. The property of a material or soil that does not allow, or allows only with great difficulty, the movement or passage of water.

impervious soil: A soil through which water, air, or roots cannot penetrate. No soil is impervious to water and air all the time.

implementation plan: A document of the steps to be taken to attain environmental quality standards within a specified time, required by various laws.

implementation plan: A document of the steps to be taken to attain environmental quality standards within a specified time, required by various laws.

impoundment: Generally, an artificial collection or storage of water, as a reservoir, pit, dugout, or sump. See *reservoir*.

improvement cutting, intermediate (forestry): A cutting made in an immature stand to harvest a useable product and to improve the stand's composition and character by removing undesirable species and trees of poor form and condition. See *thinning; harvest cutting*.

incentive payments: Payments to producers in an amount or at a rate necessary to encourage producers to adopt one or more land management practices.

Inceptisols: See *soil classification*.

incineration: The controlled process by which solids, liquid, or gaseous combustible wastes are burned and changed into gases; the residue produced contained little or no combustible material.

incinerator: A plant designed to reduce waste volume by combustion. Incinerators consist of refuse handling and storage facilities, furnaces, combustion chambers, subsidence chambers, residue handling and removal facilities, and chimneys.

incised stream: A stream that has cut its channel into the bed of the valley through degradation.

income producing recreation: Providing recreation opportunities planned and developed as a suitable use of land and water resources primarily to produce income.

increaser plant species (range):

Plant species of the original plant community that generally increases in relative amount, at least for a time, under continued use; not universal for particular species, but will vary due to range site, kind of grazing animal, season of use, and other environmental influences. Commonly termed increasers.

increment (forestry): The increase in diameter, basal area, height, volume, quality, or value of a tree or stand during a given period.

increment borer: An auger like instrument with a hollow bit and an extractor, used mainly to extract thin radial cylinders of wood (increment cores) from trees having annual growth rings to determine increment (growth) and age: also to determine the depth of preservative penetration in wood preservation processes.

index number: Expression of the relationship of a given situation with that of a base-period value of 100; used to express the rate or degree change, especially in prices or production.

indicator (biology): An organism, species, or community that shows the presence of certain environmental conditions; (chemistry) a substance that by means of a color change, identifies the endpoint of a titration.

indicator bacteria: Nonpathogenic bacteria whose presence in water indicate the possibility of pathogenic species in the water.

indicator plant: Any plant that, by its presence, its frequency, or its vigor indicates any particular property of the site particularly but not exclusively of the soil.

indicator sites: Stream sampling sites located at outlets of drainage basins with relatively homogeneous land use and physiographic conditions; most indicator-site basins have drainage areas ranging from 20 to 200 square miles.

indicator species: Any organism that by its presence or absence, its frequency, or its vigor indicates a particular property of its surrounding environment; for example, a particular plant may indicate a soil type or the presence or absence of an air or water pollutant.

indigenous: Born, growing, or produced naturally in a region or country; native.

indirect effects: Changes resulting from the production, utilization, and disposition of intermediate goods and services.

indirect toxicity: Toxicity that affects organisms by interfering with their food supply or modifying their habitat instead of directly acting on the organisms themselves. see *direct toxicity*.

individual sewage disposal system: A single system of sewage treatment tanks and disposal facilities serving only a single lot.

indore process: An anaerobic composting method that originated in India; organic wastes are placed in alternate layers with human or animal exreta in a pit or pile; piles are turned twice in six months and drainage is used to keep the compost moist.

induced effects: Changes resulting from consumer spending from direct and indirect activities.

indurate: Applied to rocks hardened by heat, pressure, or cementation.

indurated (soil): Soil material cemented into a hard mass that will not soften on wetting. See *hardpan, consistence*.

industrial park: A tract of land, the control and administration of which are vest in a single body, suitable for industrial use because of location, topography, proper zoning, availability of utilities, and accessibility to transportation.

industrial waste: Those waste materials generally discarded from industrial operations or derived from manufacturing processes. See *waste*.

industrial waste dam: An embankment dam, usually built in stages, to create storage for the disposal of waste products from an industrial process. The waste products are conveyed as fine material suspended in water to the reservoir impounded by the embankment. The embankment may be built of conventional materials but sometimes incorporates suitable waste products.

inert gas: A gas that does not react with other substances under ordinary conditions; also called noble or rare gas.

inertial separators: Air pollution control equipment that uses the principle of inertia to remove particulate matter from a stream of air or gas.

infestation: Surface attack, as of an insect, disease, or weed.

infiltration: The gradual downward flow of water from the surface through soil to groundwater and water table reservoirs.

infiltration gallery: A horizontal conduit for intercepting and collecting groundwater by gravity flow. A subsurface groundwater collection system, typically shallow in depth, constructed with open-jointed or perforated pipes that discharge collected water into a water-tight chamber. From this chamber the water is pumped to treatment facilities and into a distribution system. Infiltration galleries are usually located close to streams or ponds and may be under the direct influence of surface water. A horizontal well or subsurface drain that intercepts underflow in permeable materials or infiltration of surface water.

infiltration index: The rate of infiltration calculated from records of rainfall and runoff. There are several different indices, each average rainfall intensity for a given storm, above which the mass of rainfall equals the mass of runoff.

infiltration rate: A soil characteristic determining or describing the maximum rate at which water can enter the soil under specified conditions, including the presence of an excess of water.

infiltration velocity: The actual rate at which water is entering the soil at any given time. It may be less than the maximum (the infiltration rate) because of a limited supply of water (rainfall or irrigation).

infiltrometer: A device for measuring the rate of entry of fluid into a porous body, for example, water into soil.

inflow: Entry of extraneous rain water into a sewer system from sources other than infiltration, such as basement drains, manholes, storm

drains, and street washing.

influent water: Water that flows into sink holes, open cavities, and porous materials and disappears into the ground.

information repository: A set of information, technical reports, and reference documents regarding a Superfund site; it usually is located in a public building that is convenient for local residents, such as a public school, city hall, or public library.

infrared: Energy waves in the 0.7 to 100 micrometer wavelength region of the electromagnetic spectrum; invisible to the eye, infrared rays are detected by their thermal and photographic effects; wavelengths are longer than those of visible light and shorter than those of radio waves; often broken down in the near infrared (0.7-1.3 um), middle infrared (1.3-3.0 um), and far infrared (7.0-15.0 um); far infrared is sometimes referred to as thermal or emissive infrared.

infrastructure: The services and facilities that are an integral part of the life of an urban community; includes transport facilities and communications, power, shopping facilities, housing, schools, and recreational facilities.

initial attack: The action taken to halt the spread or potential spread of a fire by the first fire fighting force to arrive at the fire.

initial stocking rate (range): The stocking rate determined at the inception of a management program planned to allow proper grazing of the key species. The rate is a reflection of range site and condition, season and system of use, kind and class of grazing animal, management objectives, grazing experience, and other related factors.

initial storage: That portion of precipitation required to satisfy interception by vegetation, the wetting of the soil surface, and depression storage.

inlet (hydraulics): A surface connection to a closed drain; a structure at the diversion end of a conduit; the upstream end of any structure through which water may flow.

inoculation: The process of introducing pure or mixed cultures of microorganisms into natural or artificial culture media.

inoculum: Microorganisms placed in a culture medium, soil, compost, etc.

inoperable lands: Lands that are unsuited for timber production now and in the foreseeable future by virtue of their: elevation; topography; inaccessible location; low value of timber; small size of timber stands; steep or unstable soils that cannot be harvested without serious and irreversible damage to the soil or water resources; or designation as parks, wilderness areas, or other uses incompatible with timber production.

inorganic: All chemical compounds in nature, except the compounds of carbon, but including the carbonates.

inorganic compounds: Molecules that consist of chemical combinations of two or more elements that are not carbon, hydrogen, oxygen, or nitrogen.

inorganic silts: Silts formed from parent material of a mineral nature.

iIn-plant waste: Waste generated in the manufacturing process that might be recovered through internal recycling or through a salvage dealer.

insecticide: A substance or mixture of substances intended to destroy or repel insects.

inset (cartography): A portion of a map or chart covering an isolated island, or ground of islands, which is enclosed by border lines and positioned within the open water area of a nearby sheet, eliminating the necessity for publishing a separate map sheet; a representation of a small area at a larger scale (e.g., town-plan inset) or of a large area at a smaller scale (e.g., orientation inset)

in situ: In place; rocks, soil, and fossils that are situated in the place where they were originally formed or deposited.

in situ flushing: Introduction of large volumes of water, at times supplemented with cleaning compounds, into soil, waste, or groundwater to flush hazardous contaminants from a site.

in situ oxidation: Technology that oxidizes contaminants dissolved in groundwater, converting them into insoluble compounds.

in situ processing (mining): Activities conducted on the surface or underground in connection with in-place distillation, retorting, leaching, or other chemical or physical processing of coal.

in situ stripping: Treatment system that removes or "strips" volatile organic compounds from contaminated ground or surface water by forcing an airstream through the water and causing the compounds to evaporate.

in situ vitrification: Technology that treats contaminated soil in place at extremely high temperatures, at or more than 3000 degrees F.

instantaneous discharge: The volume of water that passes a point at a particular instant of time.

instantaneous field of view (remote sensing): When expressed in degrees or radians, the smallest plane angle over which an instrument is sensitive to radiation; when expressed in linear or area units such as meters or hectares, it is an altitude-dependent measure of the ground resolution of the scanner, in which case it is also called "instantaneous viewing area." See *field of view*.

instar: A stage in the life cycle of an insect or other anthropod between two successive molts.

institutional factors: The collective actions of people in the control, liberation, or expansion of individual actions, for example, government organizations, laws, education, and customs.

institutional waste: Waste material originating in schools, hospitals, research institutions, and public buildings. The materials include packaging materials, certain hazardous wastes, food wastes, disposable products, etc. See *waste*.

instream flow requirements: Amount of water flowing through a defined stream channel needed to sustain instream values, e.g. flows designated for fish and wildlife.

instream uses: Water uses that can

be carried out without removing the water from its source, as in navigation and recreation.

intake: The headworks of a conduit; the place of diversion; entry of water into soil. See *infiltration*.

intake rate: The rate of entry of water into soil. See *infiltration rate*.

integrated pest management: A system in which pests are managed by biological, cultural, and/or chemical means.

integrated resource use: A decision making process whereby all resources are identified, assessed and compared before land use or resource management decisions are made. The decisions themselves, whether to approve a plan or carry out an action on the ground, may be either multiple or single use in a given area. The application of integrated resource management results in a regional mosaic of land uses and resource priorities which reflect the optimal allocation and scheduling of resource uses.

intensive cropping: Maximum use of the land by means of frequent succession of harvested crops.

intensive recreation: Activities that are or can be enjoyed in a limited amount of space and along with relatively high concentration of participants or spectators.

interaction: Mutual or reciprocal action or influence between organisms, between organisms and environment, or between environmental factors.

interception (hydraulics): The process by which precipitation is caught and held by foliage, twigs, and branches of trees, shrubs, and other vegetation. Often used for "interception loss" or the amount of water evaporated from the precipitation intercepted.

interception channel: A channel excavated at the top of earth cuts, at the foot of slopes, or at other critical places to intercept surface flow; a catch drain; also called interception ditch.

interceptor drain: Surface or subsurface drain, or a combination of both, designed and installed to intercept flowing water.

interface: The common boundary between two substances such as a water and a solid, water and a gas, or two liquids such as water and oil.

interferometer (remote sensing): An apparatus used to produce and measure interference from two or more coherent wave trains from the same source; used to measure wavelengths, to measure angular width of sources, to determine the angular position of sources (as in satellite tracking), and for many other purposes.

interflow: That portion of rainfall that infiltrates into the soil and moves laterally through the upper soil horizons until intercepted by a stream channel or until it returns to the surface at some point downslope from its point of infiltration.

intermediate scale map: See *map*.

intermittent grazing: Alternate grazing and resting of a pasture or range for variable periods of time. See *rotation grazing*.

intermittent stream: A stream or portion of a stream that flows only in direct response to precipitation.

It receives little or no water from springs and no long continued supply from melting snow or other sources. It is dry for a large part of the year, ordinarily more than three months.

internal erosion: The formation of voids within soil or soft rock caused by the mechanical or chemical removal of material by seepage.

internal soil drainage: The downward movement of water through the soil profile. The rate of movement is determined by the texture, structure, and other characteristics of the soil profile and underlying layers and by the height of the water table, either permanent or perched. Relative terms for expressing internal drainage are none, very slow, medium, rapid, and very rapid.

internal vibration: A method of consolidating soil in which vibrators are used within a thoroughly wetted soil mass to consolidate the soil to the desired density.

internode: That part of a plant stem between two nodes or joints.

interplanting: In cropland, the planting of several crops together on the same land, for example, the planting of beans with corn; in orchards, the planting of farm crops among the trees, especially while the trees are too small to occupy the land completely; in woodland, the planting of young trees among existing trees or brushy growth.

interpretation: An educational activity that aims to reveal meaning and relationships through the use of original objects, by first hand experience, and by illustrative media rather than simply to communicate factual information.

interseeding: Seeding into an established vegetation.

interspersion (wildlife): The distribution of heterogenous cover types and plant species in a limited area.

interstate waters: Waters legally defined as rivers, lakes, and other waters that flow across or form a part of state or international boundaries; and coastal waters—whose scope has been defined to include ocean waters seaward to the territorial limits and waters along the coast that are influenced by tide.

interstices: The pore space or voids in soil and rock.

interstitial flow: Portion of surface water that infiltrates the streambed and moves through pores in subsurface.

interstock: In grafting, the name given to the piece that occupies the position between the root and the top in a double-worked tree.

intertidal: Area of the shore between mean high water and mean low water.

intolerant organisms: Organisms that are not adaptable to human alterations to the environment and thus decline in numbers where human alterations occur. See *tolerant species.*

introduced species: See *exotic.*

intrusive: Denoting igneous rocks in a molten state which have evaded other rock formations and cooled below the surface of the earth.

inundate: To cover with impounded waters or floodwaters.

invader plant species: Plant species that were absent in undisturbed portions of the original plant community and will invade under dis-

turbance or continued overuse. Commonly termed invaders.

invasion: The migration and establishment of organisms from one area to another area.

inventorying: Gathering data needed for analyses and evaluation of the status or condition of a specific universe or area of concern. See *resource inventory.*

inventory, management volume: An enumeration of such pertinent data as volume or basal area and increment and mortality of stands made to assess silvicultural opportunities.

inventory survey: A survey for the purpose of collecting and correlating engineering data of a particular type, or types, over a given area; may be recovered on a base map.

inversion: The state of the atmosphere in which a layer of cold air is trapped near the earth's surface by an overlaying layer of warm air; may cause serious air pollution problems.

invert: Lowest part of the internal cross-section of a lined channel or conduit.

invertebrates: Animals without an internal skeletal structure, for example, insects, mollusks, crayfish. See *vertebrate.*

inverted siphon: Pipeline with end sections above the middle section, used for crossing under a highway or depression. The term is common but inappropriate as no siphon action is involved.

iodometric method: A chemical method for measuring the quantity of oxidants in the air based on the release of iodine from solutions of potassium iodide. ion: An atom or group of atoms which has become electrically charged either by loss or by gain of one or more electrons.

ion: An atom or group of atoms that has become electrically charged through the addition or reduction of extranuclear electrons.

ionization: The process by which atoms are electrically charged through the addition or reduction of extranuclear electrons.

irradiance: The measure of radiant flux incident on a surface; it has the dimensions of energy per unit time (e.g., watts).

irrigable lands: Lands having soil, topographic, drainage, and climatic conditions favorable for irrigation and located in a position where a water supply is or can be made available.

irrigation: Application of water to lands for agricultural purposes. Different systems include:

center pivot: Automated sprinkler irrigation achieved by automatically rotating the sprinkler pipe or boom, supplying water to the sprinkler heads or nozzles, as a radius from the center of the field to be irrigated. Water is delivered to the center or pivot point of the system. The pipe is supported above the crop by towers at fixed spacings and propelled by pneumatic, mechanical, hydraulic, or electric power on wheels or skids in fixed circular paths at uniform angular speeds. Water is applied at a uniform rate by progressive increase of nozzle size from the pivot to the end of the line. The depth of water applied is determined by the rate of travel of the system. Single units are ordinarily about 1,250 to 1,300 feet long and irrigate approximately a 130 acre circular area.

drip: A planned irrigation system where all necessary facilities have been installed for the efficient application of water directly to the root zone of plants by means of applicators (orrices, emitters, porous tubing, perforated pipe, etc.) operated under low pressure. The applicators may be placed on or below the surface of the ground.

furrow: A partial surface flooding method of irrigation normally used with clean-tilled crops where water is appled in furrows or rows of sufficient capacity to contain the designed irrigation stream.

gravity: Irrigation in which the water is not pumped but flows and is distributed by gravity.

gravity sprinkler: A sprinkler irrigation system in which gravity furnishes the desired head.

rotation irrigation: A system by which irrigators receive an allotted quanitity of water, not a continuous rate, but at stated intervals; for example, a number of irrigators receiving water from a lateral may agree to rotate the water, each taking the entire flow in turn for a limited period.

sprinkler: A planned irrigation system where all necessary facilities have been installed for the efficient application of water for irrigation by means of perforated pipe or nozzles operated under pressure.

subirrigation: Applying irrigation water below the ground surface either by raising the water table within or near the root zone or by using a buried perforated or porous pipe system that discharges directly into the root zone.

supplemental: Irrigation to insure increased crop production in areas where rainfall normally supplies most of the moisture needed.

surface: Irrigation where the soil surface is used as a conduit, as in furrow and border irrigation as opposed to sprinkler irrigation or subirrigation.

irrigation application efficiency: Percentage of irrigation water applied to an area that is stored in the soil for crop use.

irrigation canal: A permanent irrigation canal constructed to convey water from the source of supply to one or more farms.

irrigation district: In the United States, a cooperative, self-governing public corporation set up as a subdivision of the state, with definite geographic boundaries, organized to obtain and distribute water for irrigation of lands within the district; created under authority of the state legislature with the consent of a designated fraction of the landowners or citizens and has taxing power.

irrigation frequency: Time interval between irrigations.

irrigation lateral: A branch of a main canal conveying water to a farm ditch; sometimes used in reference to farm ditches.

irrigation period: The number of hours or days that it takes to apply one irrigation to a given design area during the peak consumptive use period of the crop being irrigated.

irrigation pit: A small storage reservoir constructed to regulate or store the supply of water

available to the irrigator.

irrigation return flow: The part of irrigation applied to the surface that is not consumed by evapotranspiration or uptake by plants and that migrates to an aquifer or surface-water body.

irrigation system tailwater recovery: A water runoff collection and storage system to provide a constant quantity of water back to the initial system or to another field. Water is applied to the rows at the same rate for the entire irrigation period. Advance time should equal irrigation recession time as nearly as possible. Recession time is usually one-fourth of the entire irrigation period.

irrigation structure: Any structure or device necessary for the proper conveyance, control, measurement, or application of irrigation water.

irrigation water management: The use and management of irrigation water where the quantity of water used for each irrigation is determined by the waterholding capacity of the soil and the need of the crop, and where the water is applied at a rate and in such a manner that the crop can use it efficiently and significant erosion does not occur.

irrigation water requirement: Quantity of water, exclusive of effective precipitation, that is required for crop production.

isotope: Elemental variation with the same atomic number as the element itself, but with a different atomic weight because of a different number of neutrons.

J

jetting: A method of compacting soil using a hose or other device, with a high velocity stream of water, worked down through the depth of soil placed. Drilling with high pressure water or air jets.

jetty: A structure built of piles, rocks, or other material extending into a stream or into the sea to induce scouring or bank building, or for protection.

joint: A fracture or parting that abruptly interrupts the physical continuity of a rock mass.

Joule: A unit of energy or work; equivalent to one watt per second, 0.737 foot-pounds, or 0.238 calories.

junk: Unprocessed waste materials suitable for reuse or recycling.

juvenile: Growth and structural characteristics of young plants that are not found in older plants or the same type; young fish older than one year but not capable of reproduction.

K

kame: A conical hill or short irregular ridge of gravel or sand deposited in contact with glacier ice.

kaolin: A rock consisting of clay minerals of the kaolinite group.

kaolinite: Hydrous aluminum silicate clay mineral of the 1:1 crystal lattice group, that is, consisting of one silicon tetrahedral layer and one aluminum oxide hydroxide octahedral layer; the 1:1 group or family of aluminosilicates.

kaolinitic: See *soil mineralogy classes for family groupings*.

karst: A geologic formation of irregular limestone deposits with sinks, underground streams, and caverns.

key grazing area: That portion of a pasture or grazing unit that, because of its nature, location, and the pattern of grazing use, will indicate the grazing use of the entire area.

key management species: Forage species whose use serves as an indicator of the degree of use of associated species; species on which management of a specific unit is based.

keystone species: A species that plays an important ecological role in determining the overall structure and dynamic relationships within a biotic community. A keystone species presence is essential to the integrity and stability of a particular ecosystem.

key terrace: Staked terrace line that is selected as a reference in laying out other terraces.

key utilization species: Species whose use indicates the degree of

use of key grazing areas.

K factor: See *universal soil loss equation.*

kill: Dutch term for stream or creek.

kilowatt-hour: A unit of work or energy equal to that expended by one kilowatt in one hour.

knifing: A means to incorporate slurry or liquid manures into the soil; the waste is injected just behind a thin, knifelike tool that opens a narrow slit in the soil.

Kraft paper: A comparatively coarse paper particularly noted for its strength; its unbleached grades are used primarily as a wrapper or packaging material; a paper made primarily from wood pulp produced by the sulfate pulping process.

krotovina: See *crotovina.*

L

laccolith: Igneous intrusion that squeezes between sedimentary layers and domes the overlying layers.

lacustrine: Pertaining to a lake.

lacustrine deposit: Material deposited in lake water and later exposed either by lowering of the water level or by the elevation of the land.

lagging: In tunneling, planking placed against the dirt or rock walls and ceiling, outside the ribs.

lagoon: In geology, a shallow sound, channel, pond, or lake connected with the sea; in sewage treatment,

a reservoir or pond built to contain water and animal wastes until they can be decomposed either by aerobic or anaerobic action.

lagtime (flood irrigation): The period between the time that the irrigation stream is turned off at the upper end of an irrigated area and the time that water disappears from the surface at the point or points of application; (hydrology). See *watershed lag.*

laminar flow (hydraulics): Flow in which there are no cross currents or eddies and where the fluid particles move in approximately parallel directions.

lamination: A layering or bedding less than one centimeter thick in sedimentary rocks.

land: The total natural and cultural environment within which production takes place; a broader term than soil. In addition to soil, its attributes include other physical conditions, such as mineral deposits, climate, and water supply; location in relation to centers of commerce, populations, and other land; the size of the individual tracts or holdings; and existing plant cover, works of improvement, and the like. Some use the term loosely in other senses: as defined above but without the economic or cultural criteria; especially in the expression "natural land"; as a synonym for "soil"; for the solid surface of the earth; and also for earthy surface formations, especially in the geomorphological expression "land form."

land adequately protected: Land on which conservation practices and management systems necessary to arrest or prevent deterioration and maintain the productive capability of the resource base have been installed in accordance with established guidelines.

land capability: The suitability of land for use without permanent damage. Land capability, as ordinarily used in the United States, is an expression of the effect of physical land conditions, including climate, on the total suitability for use without damage for crops that require regular tillage, for grazing, for woodland, and for wildlife. Land capability involves consideration of 1) the risks of land damage from erosion and other causes, and 2) the difficulties in land use owing to physical land characteristics, including climate.

land capability class: One of the eight classes of land in the land capability classification of the U.S. Soil Conservation Service; distinguished according to the risk of land damage or the difficulty of land use; They include:

Class I: Soils that have few limitations restricting their use.

Class II: Soils that have some limitations, reducing the choice of plants or requiring moderate conservation practices.

Class III: Soils that have severe limitations that reduce the choice of plants or require special conservation practices, or both.

Class IV: Soils that have very severe limitations that restrict the choice of plants, require very careful management or both.

Land generally not suitable for cultivation (without major treatment).

Class V: Soils that have little more no erosion hazard, but that have other limitations, impractical to remove, that limit their use largely to pasture, range, woodland, or wildlife food and cover.

Class VI: Soils that have severe limitations that make them generally unsuited for cultivation and limit their use largely to pasture or range, woodland, or wildlife food and cover.

Class VII: Soils that have very severe limitations that make them unsuited to cultivation and that restricts their use largely to grazing, woodland, or wildlife.

Class VIII: Soils and landforms that preclude their use for commercial plant production and restrict their use to recreation, wildlife, water supply, or aesthetic purposes.

land capability classification: A grouping of kinds of soil into special units, subclasses, and classes according to their capability for intensive use and the treatments required for sustained use, prepared by the Natural Resources Conservation Service, USDA.

land capability map: A map showing land capability units, subclasses, and classes or a soil survey map colored to show land capability classes.

land capability subclass: Groups of capability units within classes of the land capability classification that have the same kinds of dominant limitations for agricultural use as a result of soil and climate. Some soils are subject to erosion if they are not protected, while others are naturally wet and must be drained if crops are to be grown. Some soils are shallow or droughty or have other soil deficiencies. Still other soils occur in areas where climate limits their use. The four kinds of limitations recognized at the subclass level are: risks of erosion, designated by the symbol (e); wetness, drainage, or overflow (w); other root zone limitations (s); and climatic limitations (c). The subclass provides the map user information about both the degree and kind of limitation. Capability class I has no subclasses.

land capability unit: A group of soils that are nearly alike in suitability for plant growth and

responses to the same kinds of soils management. Capability units provide more specific and detailed information for application to specific fields on a farm or ranch than the subclass of the land capability classification.

land classification: The arrangement of land units into various categories based on the properties of the land or its suitability for some particular purpose. land disturbing activity: Any land change which may result in soil erosion from water or wind and the movement of sediments into state waters or onto lands in the state including, but not limited to, tilling, clearing, grading, excavating, transporting, and filling of land, other than federal lands, except that the term shall not include such minor land disturbing activities as home gardens and individual landscaping, repairs, and maintenance work.

land-disturbing activity: In the United States, any land change that may result in soil erosion from water or wind and the movement of sediments into state waters or into lands in the state including, but not limited to, tilling, clearing, grading, excavating, transporting, and filling of land, other than federal lands, except that the term shall not include such minor land-disturbing activities as home gardens and individual landscaping, repairs, and maintenance work.

landfill: An open area where trash is buried. Facility in which solid waste from municipal and/or industrial sources is disposed; sanitary landfills are those that are operated in accordance with environmental protection standards.

landform: A discernible natural landscape, such as a floodplain, stream terrace, plateau, or valley.

Land-Grant Institutions: Originally, land-grant colleges and university were educational institutions that arose from or met the mission of the Land-Grant College Act of 1862, also known as the Morrill Act of 1862. The legislation provided funding for institutions of higher learning in each state. Each state received 30,000 acres of federal land per congressional representative. The land was intended for sale to provide an endowment for at least one college where the leading object was learning related to agriculture and the mechanical arts. The original act was supplemented through the years to provide additional funding for the land grant institutions.

land leveling: The process of shaping the land surface for better movement of water and machinery over the land. Also called land forming, land shaping, or land grading.

land, marginal: Land that returns barely enough to meet expenses in a specific use.

land reclamation: Making land capable of more intensive use by changing its general character, as by drainage of excessively wet land; irrigation of arid or semiarid land; or recovery of submerged land from seas, lakes, and rivers. Large scale reclamation projects usually are carried out through collective effort. Simple improve- ments, such as cleaning of stumps or stones from land, should not be referred to as land reclamation.

land reconstruction (abandoned mined land): Restoring land and water areas adversely affected by past mining practices and increasing the productivity of the areas for a beneficial use; (currently mined land) Restoring currently mined land to an acceptable form and for a planned use.

land resource area: An area of land reasonably alike in its relationship to agriculture with emphasis on combinations and/or intensities of problems in soil and water conservation; ordinarily larger than a land resource unit and smaller than a land resource region. land resource region: A generalized grouping of land resource areas reflecting regional relationships to agriculture with emphasis on soil and water conservation.

land resource region: A generalized grouping of land resource areas reflecting relationship to agriculture with emphasis on soil and water conservation.

land resource unit: A subdivision of a land resource area with emphasis on a specialized type of agriculture, intensities, or problems in soil and water conservation.

land resting: Temporary discontinuous of cultivation of a piece of land. See *fallow*.

land rights: Any interest acquired in or permission obtained to use land, buildings, structures, or other improvements; includes the acquisition of land by fee title or certain designated rights to the use of land by perpetual easement; also includes the costs of modifying utilities, roads, and other improvements.

Landsat: An unmanned, earth-orbiting satellite of the National Aeronautics and Space Administration that transmits images to earth receiving stations; designed primarily for collection of earth resources data; Landsat satellites contain two sensor systems: a return beam vidicon system and a four-band multispectral system; formerly called ERTS; Landsat-1 (ERTS-1), launched June 1972, ceased functioning January 1978; Landsat-2, launched January 1975, used intermittently after December 1979; Landsat-3, launched January 1978.

Landsat-MSS: A four-band optical-mechanical multispectral scanner. Band 4 = 0.5-0.6 um (green), band 5 = 0.6-0.7 um (red), band 6 = 0.7-0.8 um (IR) and band 7 = 0.8-1.1 um (IR).

landscape: All the natural features, such as fields, hills, forests, and water that distinguish one part of the earth's surface from another part; usually that portion of land or territory which the eye can comprehend in a single view, including all of its natural characteristics.

landscape architecture: The art of arranging land, and the objects upon it, for human use and beauty.

landscape construction: The alteration of existing ground conditions together with construction and development of ground features, including minor structures.

landscape design: A creative environmental problem solving process to organize external space and attain the optimum balance of natural factors and human needs.

landscape garden: An area

designed and built to contain the natural and manmade elements for everyone to enjoy.

landscape level: A watershed, or series of interacting watersheds or other natural biophysical (ecological) units, within the larger Land and Resource Management Planning areas. This term is used for conservation planning and is not associated with visual landscape management and viewscape management.

landslide: A mass of material that has slipped downhill under the influence of gravity, frequently occurring when the material is saturated with water; rapid movement down slope of a mass of soil, rock, or debris.

land, submarginal: Land that does not return enough to pay costs of operation in a specific use.

land, supermarginal: Land that returns a profit after all expenses are paid.

land tenure: The holding of land and the rights that go with such holding, including all forms of holding from fee simple title embracing all possible rights within the general limitations imposed by the government, to the various forms of tenancy or holding of land owned by another.

land use: The primary or primary and secondary use(s) of land, such as cropland, woodland, pastureland, etc. See *multiple use*.

land use plan: The key element of a comprehensive plan; describes the recommended location and intensity of development for public and private land uses such as residential, commercial, industrial, recreational, and agricultural.

land use planning: The process of inventorying and assessing the status, potentials, and limitations of a particular geographic area and its resources, interacting with the populations associated and/or concerned with the area to determine their needs, wants, and aspirations for the future.

land use study: A network of existing shallow wells in an area having a relatively uniform land use. These studies are a subset of the Study-Unit Survey and have the goal of relating the quality of shallow groundwater to land use.

land voiding: The process of damaging land by gully action causing this land to be unproductive for agricultural uses; that area actually within a gully; usually has value only for wildlife and recreation uses.

lantz process: A destructive distillation technique in which the combustible components of solid waste are converted into combustible gases, charcoal, and a variety of distillates.

large scale map: See *map*.

large water system: A water system that services more than 50,000 customers.

larva: The immature form of an animal, chiefly insects, that must pass through metamorphosis before reaching the adult form.

laser induced fluorescence: A method for measuring the relative amount of soil and/or groundwater with an in-situ sensor.

latent: Not in an actively growing condition and ordinarily not able to resume growth when environmental conditions become favorable, though capable of doing so when subjected to some unusual stimulus. See *dormancy*.

latent image (photography): An invisible image produced by the physical or chemical effect of light upon matter (usually silver halide or halides), which can be rendered visible by the subsequent process of photographic development.

lateral: Secondary or side channel, ditch, or conduit; sometimes called branch line or drain, spur, lateral ditch, or group lateral.

lateral earth pressure: The horizontal pressure acting on a structural member due to the earth in place behind it; the amount of pressure depends on the type of soil, the amount of compaction, degree of saturation, and the resistance of the structure to the pressure.

lateral moraine: Ridge-like pile of sediment along the side of a glacier.

latitude: Angular measurement in degrees north or south of the equator. Lines denoting latitude are also called parallels. (One minute of arc of meridian is one nautical mile.)

laundering weir: Sedimention basin overflow weir.

lava: Fluid, molten igneous rock erupted on the earth's surface.

law of diminishing returns: When other factors in production do not change, successive increases in the input of one factor will not yield proportionate increases in product; for example, fertilizer can be used so heavily that additional applications will give little or no increase in yield.

law of supply and demand: The quantity of a commodity that will be produced or offered for sale (supply) varies directly with the price. The quantity of a commodity that potential buyers are willing to take (demand) varies inversely with the price. The greater the amount of a given product offered for sale on a given market at a given time, the lower the price per unit at which the entire amount can be sold.

law of the minimum: See *Liebig's law, limiting factor.*

law of tolerance: See *Shelford's law, limiting factor.*

LD50: Term commonly used in pesticide work to designate the lethal dosage of toxic ingredient required to kill 50 percent of a group of test animals; toxicity values are either acute oral or acute dermal LD50 expressed as milligrams of active ingredient per kilogram of body weight.

leach: To remove components from the soil by the action of water trickling through.

leachates: Liquids that have percolated through a soil and that contain substances in solution or suspension.

leached layer: A soil layer from which the soluble materials ($CaCO_3$ and $MgCO$ and material more soluble) have been dissolved and washed away by percolating water.

leached soil: A soil from which most of the soluble materials ($CaCO_3$ and $MgCO_3$ and more soluble materials) have been removed from the entire profile or have been removed from one part of the profile and have accumulated in another part.

leaching: The removal from the soil in solution of the more soluble materials by percolating waters.

leaching field: The area used for disposal of liquid through a non-water-tight artificial structure, conduit, or porous material by downward or lateral drainage, or both, into the surrounding permeable soil.

leaching requirement: The amount of excess irrigation water passing through the root zone to reduce the salt concentration in the soil for reclamation purposes; the fraction of excess water from irrigation or rainfall passing through the soil to prevent salt accumulation in the root zone and sustain production; also called leaching fraction.

lead agency: In the United States, the agency or agencies preparing or having taken primary responsibility for preparing an environmental impact statement.

leader: The main stem or trunk that forms the apex of a tree.

leaf curl: The rolling back of leaf edges as a result of damage caused by disease, insects, or environmental factors.

leaf mold: A substance formed by decayed and partially decayed leaves, found on the surface of some forested areas, or produced by composting leaves.

leaf spot: A term for fungus and bacterial diseases that cause distinct discolored spots on plant foliage, thus weakening the plant's ability to produce food.

leave trees: All trees, regardless of species, age, or size, remaining on a harvested area as a result of a predetermined silviculture prescription to address a possible range of silviculture or resource needs.

legend: A list, usually shown as marginal information on a map or mosaic, giving an explanation of or identifying symbols used in the map.

leggy: A condition of plants with little foliage at the base, usually caused by excessive shade.

legume: A member of the pulse family, one of the most important and widely distributed plant families. The fruit is a pod that opens along two sutures when ripe. Leaves are alternate, have stipules, and are usually compound. Includes many valuable food and forage species, such as peas, beans, peanuts, clovers, alfalfas, sweet clovers, lespedezas, vetches, and kudzu. Practically all legumes are nitrogen fixing plants.

legume inoculation: The addition of nitrogen fixing bacteria to legume seed or to the soil in which the seed is to be planted.

length of run: Distance water must run in furrows or between borders over the surface of a field from one head ditch to another, or to the end of the field.

lens: A disk of optical glass, or plastic, or a combination of two or more such disks, by which rays of light may be made to converge or to diverge; such disks have two surfaces, which may both be spherical, one plane and one spherical, or various other combinations, cylindrical, paraboloid, or hyperboloid.

lentic: Pertaining to standing (nonflowing) waters such as lakes, ponds, and swamps. See *lotic*.

lesion: Abnormal change in the structure of an organ or tissue due to injury or disease.

lethal concentration, median (MC50): A standard for toxicity in which the concentration of a substance within another medium will kill 50 percent of a specific type of animal. See *LD50*.

levee: See *dike*.

leveling (surveying): The operations of measuring vertical distances, directly or indirectly, to determine elevations; (photogrammetry) in absolute orientation, the operation of bringing the model datum parallel to a reference plane, usually the tabletop of the stereoplotting instrument, also called horizontalizing the model, leveling the model. See *land leveling*.

level terrace: See *terrace*.

L factor: See *universal soil loss equation*.

liability: Under Superfund, a party responsible for the presence of hazardous waste at a site is also legally responsible for acting and paying to reduce or eliminate the risks posed by the site.

Liebig's law: The growth and reproduction of an organism is dependent on the nutrient substance (such as oxygen, carbon dioxide, calcium, and others) that is available in minimum quantity. See *limiting factor*.

life cycle: The stages passed through from the fertilized egg to death of a mature plant or animal.

life form: Characteristic form or appearance of a species at maturity; such as tree, shrub, herb, etc.

lift: In a sanitary landfill, a compacted layer of solid wastes and the top layer of cover material.

light non-aqueous phase liquid (LNAPL): Liquid contaminants that are relatively insoluble and lighter than water; also known as floaters because they will float on top of an aquifer.

light soil: A coarse textured soil with a low drawbar pull and, hence, easy to cultivate. See *coarse texture, soil texture.*

lignin: The noncarbohydrate, organic structural constituent of woody fibers in plant tissues that, along with cellulouse, encrusts the cell walls and cements the cells together, providing strength.

lime: From the strictly chemical standpoint, refers to only one compound, calcium oxide (Ca0); however, the term is commonly used in agriculture to include a great variety of materials that are usually composed of the oxide, hydroxide, or carbonate of calcium or of calcium and magnesium; used to furnish calcium and magnesium as essential elements for the growth of plants and to neutralize soil acidity. The most commonly used forms of agricultural lime are ground limestone (carbonates), hydrated lime (hydroxides), burnt lime (oxides), marl, and oyster shells.

lime (calcium) requirement: The amount of agricultural limestone, or the equivalent of other specified liming material, required per acre to a soil depth of six inches (or on two million pounds of soil) to raise the pH of the soil to a desired value under field conditions.

lime concretion: An aggregate of precipitated calcium carbonate or

other material cemented by precipitated calcium carbonate.

limestone: A sedimentary rock composed of calcium carbonate, $CaCO_3$. There are many impure varieties.

liming: The application of lime to land, primarily to reduce soil acidity and supply calcium for plant growth. Dolomitic limestone supplies both calcium and magnesium. May also improve soil structure, organic matter content, and nitrogen content of the soil by encouraging the growth of legumes and soil microorganisms. Liming an acid soil to a pH value of about 6.5 is desirable for maintaining a high degree of availability of most of the nutrient elements required by plants.

limiting factor: A factor whose absence, or excessive concentration, exerts some restraining influence upon a population through incompatibility with species requirements or tolerance. See *Liebig's law, Shelford's law.*

limiting nutrient: Any nutrient limiting plant growth. See *nutrients.*

limnetic zone: The open water region of a lake, especially in areas too deep to support rooted aquatic plants; supports plankton and fish as the principal plants and animals. See *littoral zone.*

limnic materials (As used in the Soil Classification System of the National Cooperative Soil Survey in the United States): Includes both organic and inorganic materials either 1) deposited in water by precipitation or action of aquatic organisms, such as algae or diatoms, or 2) derived from underwater and floating aquatic plants subsequently modified by aquatic animals. Examples are marl, diatomaceous earth, and coprogenous earth (sedimentary peat).

limnology: The study of the biological, chemical, geographical, and physical features of fresh waters.

limnological conditions: Conditions on freshwater lakes.

linear programming: A mathematical method of systematically budgeting enterprises to efficiently use available resources.

line intercept method: The sampling of vegetation by recording the plants intercepted by a measured line set close to the ground or by vertical projection from the line. In regeneration assessments, this method is termed linear regeneration sampling.

line plot survey: A survey employing plots as sampling units. Plots of specified size are laid out, usually at regular intervals along parallel survey lines.

line printer: A computer system output device that produces a line-by-line printed record of the data it receives, usually in discrete symbols such as letters and numbers.

lining (hydraulics): A protective covering over all or part of the perimeter of a reservoir or a conduit to prevent seepage losses, withstand pressure, resist erosion, reduce friction, or otherwise improve conditions of flow.

lining-out stock: All plant material coming from propagating houses, beds, or frames, and young material of suitable size to plant in nursery rows.

liquefication: The sudden large decrease of the shearing resistance of a cohesionless soil, caused by a collapse of the structure from shock or other type of strain and associated with a sudden but temporary increase in the pore fluid pressure; a temporary transformation of the material into a fluid mass.

liquid petroleum gas (LPG): A mixture of gaseous hydrocarbons, principally propane and butane, which can be liquefied under moderate pressure at normal temperatures.

liquid fertilizers: A fluid in which the plant nutrients are in true solution.

liquid waste: A general term denoting pollutants such as soap, chemicals, or other substances in liquid form.

lister: A double plow, the shares of which throw the soil in opposite directions, leaving the field with a series of alternate ridges and furrows. Row crops may be seeded in the bottoms of the furrows or on top of the ridge as they are opened up. When no seed is planted, the operation is sometimes referred to as blank listing.

lithic contact (As used in the Soil Classification System of the National Cooperative Soil Survey in the United States): A boundary between soil and continuous, coherent underlying material which has a hardness of three or more (Mohs scale). When moist, the underlying material cannot be dug with a spade and chunks will not disperse in water with 15 hours shaking. Example, basalt.

lithification: The process of converting a sedimentary deposit into an indurated rock.

lithography: A planographic method of printing based on the chemical repulsion between grease and water to separate the printing from nonprinting areas.

lithology: The study of rocks based on the megascopic examination of samples.

litter (forestry): A surface layer of loose organic debris in forests, consisting of freshly fallen or slightly decomposed organic materials; (waste) that highly visible portion of solid waste that is generated by the consumer and is carelessly discarded outside of the regular disposal systems; accounts for about two percent of the total solid waste volume.

littoral: Off or pertaining to a shore, especially a seashore; more specifically, the zone of the seafloor lying between tide levels.

littoral zone: The zone or strip of land along the shoreline between the high and low water marks. That portion of a body of fresh water extending from the shoreline lakeward to the limit of occupancy of rooted plants.

livestock: Domestic animals produced or kept primarily for farm, ranch, or market purposes, including beef and dairy cattle, hogs, sheep, goats, and horses.

livestock pond: An impoundment, the principal purpose of which is to supply water to livestock; includes reservoirs, pits, and tanks.

load: The quantity (i.e., mass) of a material that enters a water body over a given time interval.

loading (waste management): Addition of organic wastes to soils at such a rate as to benefit plant growth and help to meet fertility requirements of a particular soil; the quantity of waste added would not tax the soils ability to degrade and assimilate the waste nor contribute to environmental degradation.

loading schedule (waste management): A timetable indicating an agreed-upon load of material to a water body for a given time interval.

loam: A soil textural class. See *soil texture.*

loamy: Intermediate in texture and properties between fine textured and coarse textured soils; includes all textural classes with the words "loamy" or "loam" as a part of the class name, such as clay loam or loamy sand. See *soil texture; or particle size classes for family groupings for its use in the Soil Classification System of the National Cooperative Soil Survey in the United States.*

loamy coarse sand: See *soil texture.*

loamy fine sand: See *soil texture.*

loamy sand: See *soil texture.*

loamy skeletal: See *particle size classes for family groupings.*

loamy very fine sand: See *soil texture.*

loess: Material transported and deposited by wind and consisting of predominantly silt sized particles.

loessial: Medium-textured materials (usually silt or very fine sand) transported and deposited by wind action. These materials may be deposited in depths ranging from less than one foot to well over 100 feet.

log boom: A floating structure used to protect the face of a dam by deflecting floating material and waves away from the dam. A device used to prevent floating debris from obstructing spillways and intakes. A chain of logs, drums, or pontoons secured end to end and floating on the surface of a reservoir so as to divert floating debris, trash, and logs.

longitude: The angle at the pole between the meridian of the place and some standard meridian. For American maps, the standard meridian is the one passing through Greenwich, England.

long-term cleanup: A response action that eliminates or reduces a release or threatened release of hazardous substances that is a serious but not an immediate danger to people or the environment. This action, also known as a Remedial Action (RA), may take years to complete.

long term costs: See *fixed costs*.

long-term monitoring: Data collection over a period of years or decades to assess changes in selected hydrologic conditions.

look angle (radar): The direction of the look, or direction in which the antenna is pointing when transmitting and receiving from a particular cell.

loose: A soil consistency term. See *consistence*.

loose rock dam: A dam built of rock without the use of mortar; a rubble dam. See *rock fill dam*.

loose yards: Measurement of soil or rock after it has been loosened by digging or blasting.

lopping: Chopping branches, tops and small trees after felling into lengths such that the resultant slash will lie close to the ground.

losing stream: A stream or reach that contributes water to a zone of saturation.

lotic: Pertaining to flowing waters such as streams and rivers. See *lentic*.

low oblique: An oblique photograph that does not show the horizon line.

low strength: Refers to the relative value of shear strength.

luminanace (photometry): A measure of the intrinsic luminous intensity emitted by a source in a given direction; the illuminance produced by light from a source upon a unit surface area oriented normal to the line of sight at any distance fro the source, divided by the solid angle subtended by the source at the receiving surface.

lysimeter: A device to measure the quantity or rate of water movement through or from a block of soil, usually undisturbed and in situ, or to collect such percolated water for quality analysis.

macrocategory soil erosion: Soil erosion beyond the farm boundary, extending to national and international factors. See *microcategory soil erosion*.

macroclimate: The climate representative of relatively large area.

macrohabitat: An extensive habitat presenting considerable variation of the environment, containing a variety of ecological niches and supporting a large number and variety of complex flora and fauna.

macronutrient: A chemical element necessary in large amounts (usually greater than 1 part per million) for the growth of plants; usually applied artificially in fertilizer or liming materials. "Macro" refers to quantity and not the essentiality of the element. See micronutrient.

macroorganisms: Those organisms retained on a US standard sieve no. 30 (openings of 0.589 mm); those organisms visible to the unaided eye. See *microorganisms*.

macrophyte: Any plant that can be seen with the unaided eye, such as aquatic mosses, ferns, liverworts, or rooted plants.

made land: Areas filled with earth and trash, with less than 50 percent earthy material in the control section, or with a cover of earthy material less than 20 inches thick. Not soil. A miscellaneous land type.

magma: Molten or fluid rock material from which igneous rock is derived.

main channel: The deepest or central part of the bed of a stream, containing the main current.

main channel pool: Reach of a stream or river with a low bed elevation, relative to rapids or riffles.

mainstream: The main course of a stream where the current is the strongest.

major federal action: In the United States, actions with effects that may be major and that are potentially subject to federal control and responsibility.

Malthusian theory of population: That theory, asserted by Thomas Malthus, that man could increase his subsistence only arithmetically, whereas population tended to increase geometically. Thus population always tended toward the limit set by subsistence and was contained within that limit by the operation of positive and preventive checks, such as famine, pestilence, war, and premature mortality.

managed forest land: Forest land that is being managed under a forest management plan utilizing the science of forestry.

management plan: A program of action designed to reach a given set of objectives.

Manning's formula (hydraulics): A formula used to predict the velocity of water in an open channel or pipeline:

$$V= (1.486 \ r^{\ 2/3}S^{1/2}) \ /n$$

where V is the mean velocity of flow in feet per second; r is the hydraulic radius in feet; s is the slope of the energy gradient or, for assumed uniform flow, the slope of the channel in feet per foot; and n is the roughness coefficient or retardance factor of the channel lining.

manometer: An instrument that measures fluid pressure by fluid displacement; can be a differential or U tube manometer.

mantle: A thick layer of rock deep within the earth that separates the earth's crust above from the earth's core below.

manure: The excreta of animals, with or without the admixture of bedding or litter, in varying stages of decomposition.

manure, collectable: Manure accumulating in animal confinements that may be brought together and transported elsewhere; compared to manure voided at random in pastures and rangeland.

manure, liquid: A suspension of livestock manure in water, in which the concentration of manure solids is low enough so the flow characteristics of the mixture are more like those of Newtonian fluids than plastic fluids; animal wastes or manure having a total solids content of less than eight percent, wet-weight basis.

manure, slurry: Animal manures or wastes with a total solids content ranging from eight to 20 percent, wet weight basis.

manure, solid: An animal manure or wastes having a total solid content greater than 20 percent, wet-weight basis.

manure bunker: A structure with an impervious flood and side walls to contain manure and bedding until it may be recycled.

manure tank: A storage unit in which accumulations of manure are collected before subsequent handling or disposal.

man-year equivalent: The amount of labor supplied by an able-bodied man in one year or its equivalent.

map: To prepare a map or engage in a mapping operation; a graphic representation, usually on a plane surface and at an established scale, of natural and artificial features on the surface of a part or the whole of the earth or other planetary body; the features are positioned as accurately as possible, usually relative to a coordinate reference system; also a graphic representation of a part or the whole of the celestial sphere.

map, intermediate scale: A map normally of a scale from 1:200,000 to 1:500,000.

map, large scale: A map that shows only the horizontal position of features with sufficient accuracy for purposes of measurement; the drainage and cultural features of a portion of the earth's surface.

map, planimetric: A map which shows only the horizontal position of features with sufficient accuracy for purposes of measurement; the drainage and cultural features of a portion of the earth's surface.

map, plastic relief: A topographic map printed on plastic and molded into a three-dimensional form; the plastic medium is formed by heat and vacuum over a terrain model to achieve the three-dimensional representation.

map, small scale: A map having a scale of 1:600,000 or smaller.

map, topographic: A representation of the physical features of a portion of the earth's surface as a plane surface, on which terrain relief is shown by a system of lines, each representing a constant elevation above a datum or reference plane.

map, grid: Two sets of parallel lines at right angles, drawn on a plane surface and used as a rectangular coordinate system (a reference system) for plotting position, measuring areas, and scaling distance and direction in surveying and mapping; may or may not be based on a map projection.

mapping unit: See *soil mapping unit.*

map projection: An orderly system of lines on a plane representing a corresponding system of imaginary lines on an adopted terrestrial or celestial datum surface; also the mathematical concept for such a system. For maps of the earth, a projection consists of latitude and meridians of longitude, or of a grid based on such parallels and meridians.

Aitoff equal-area: A Lambert

equal-area azimuthal projection of a hemisphere converted into a map projection of the entire sphere; a projection bounded by an ellipse in which the line representing the equator (major axis) is double the length of the line representing the central meridian (minor axis).

Alber conical equal-area: An equal-area projection of the conical type, on which the meridians are straight lines that meet in a common point beyond the limits of the map, and the parallels are concentric circles whose center is at the point of intersection of the meridians; meridians and parallels intersect at right angles and the arcs or longitude along any given parallel are of equal length; the parallels are spaced to retain the condition of equal area; on two selected parallels, the arcs of longitude are represented in their true length; between the selected parallels, the scale along the meridians will be a trifle too large, and beyond them, too small.

conformal: A map projection on which the shape of any small area of the surface mapped is preserved unchanged; sometimes termed orthomorphic map, meaning right-shape, but this is misleading because if the area mapped is large, only the shape of each small section will be preserved. The exact condition of a conformal map projection is that the scale of any point be the same in all directions; the scale may change from point to point, but at each point it will be independent of the azimuth. Among the more important conformal map projections are the Mercator, the stenographic, the Mercator transverse, and the Lambert conformal; the latter two being used in the state coordinate systems.

conic: A map projection produced by projecting the geographic meridians and parallels onto a cone that is tangent to (or intersects) the surface of a sphere, and then developing the cone into a plane; there are several methods of passing from the sphere to the cone, most of which are analytical in character, and do not admit of graphical construction, for example, the Lambert conformal conic map projection.

cylindrical: A map projection produced by projecting the geographic meridians and parallels onto a cylinder that is tangent to (or intersects) the surface of a sphere, and then developing the cylinder into a plane.

equal–area: A map projection on which a constant ratio of areas is preserved; that is, any given part of the map bears the same relation to the area on the sphere which it represents as the whole map bears to the entire area represented.

Lambert conformal conic: A conformal map projection of the so-called conic type on which all geographic meridians are represented by straight lines that meet in a common point outside the limits of the map; the geographic parallels are represented by a series of arcs of circles having this common point for a center; meridians and parallels intersect at right angles, and angles on the earth are correctly represented on the projection.

Mercator: A conformal map projection of the cylindrical type; the equator is represented by a straight line true to scale; the geographic meridians are represented by parallel straight lines perpendicular to the line representing the equator, and spaced according to their distance apart at the equator; the geographic parallels are represented by a second system of straight lines perpendicular to the family of lines representing the meridians, and therefore parallel with the equator.

Mercator equal–area: The sinusoidal map projection.

Mercator transverse: A map projection of the cylindrical type being, in principle, equivalent to the regular Mercator map projection turned (transversed) 90 degrees in azimuth; the central meridian is represented by a straight line, corresponding to the line that represents the equator on the regular Mercator map projection; neither the geographic meridians, except the central meridian, nor the geodetic parallels, except the equator (if shown), are represented by a straight line; it is a conformal projection and is the base used in the state plane-coordinate systems for the grids of those zones whose greater dimension is in a north-south direction.

orthographic: A map projection produced by straight parallel lines through points on the sphere and perpendicular to the plane of the projection; corresponds to a perspective projection with the point of projection at an infinite distance from the sphere.

polyconic: A map projection having the central geographic meridian represented by a straight line, along which the spacing for lines representing the geographic parallels is proportional to the distances apart of the parallels; the parallels are represented by arcs of circles that are not concentric, but whose centers lie on the line representing the central meridian, and whose radii are determined by the lengths of the elements of cones that are tangent along the parallels; all meridians, except the central one, are curved; this projection is neither conformal nor equal-area.

sinusoidal: A map projection employing the equator as the standard parallel, and showing all geographic parallels as truly spaced parallel straight lines, along which exact scale is preserved; an equal-area projection; also called the Mercator equal-area map projection.

transverse polyconic: A polyconic map projection that is turned (transversed) 90 degrees in azimuth by substituting for the central meridian, a great circle perpendicular to the geographic meridian to provide control axis for the projection, along which axis will lie the centers of the circular arcs representing lines of tangency of cones with the surfaces of the sphere.

map scale: A ratio of the units measured on the ground to each unit measured on the map; (small scale = little detail, large area, small value of ratio such as 1:250,000); (large scale = much detail, small area, large value of ratio such as 1:24,000).

marble: A metamorphosed form of limestone or dolomite in which the grains are recrystallized.

margin: The point at which the value of the added output just equals the value of the unit of input that produced it; the point of maximum net return.

marina: A water based facility used for storage, service, launching, operation, or maintenance of watercraft.

marine: Pertaining to the sea.

marking trees: Selection and indication, usually by blaze or paint spot, of trees to be cut or retained in a cutting operation.

marl: An earthy, unconsolidated deposit formed in freshwater lakes, consisting chiefly of calcium carbonate mixed with clay or other impurities in varying proportions.

marsh: A periodically wet or continually flooded area where the surface is not deeply submerged; covered dominantly with sedges, cattails, rushes, or other hydrophytic plants. Subclasses include freshwater and saltwater marshes. A miscellaneous land type. See *swamp*.

marsh, tidal: A low, flat area traversed by interlacing channels and tidal sloughs and periodically inundated by high tides; vegetation usually consists of salt tolerant plants.

masonry dam: A dam built of rock and mortar.

mass diagram: A graphical representation of cumulative quantities, such as the integral of a time flow curve; an integral curve; each point on the curve is the sum of all preceding quantities considered. The diagram is used extensively in water storage analyses.

massive head buttress dam: A buttress dam in which the buttress is greatly enlarged on the upstream side to span the gap between buttresses.

mast: Plant fruit, such as acorns, beechnuts, walnuts, and conifer seeds, in a collective sense, especially when used as food by animals.

master plan: In early state legislation on planning, this term was often defined and considered synonymous with comprehensive plan; more recently, used to modify a functional element of a comprehensive plan such as a master highway plan or master recreation plan.

matching: The act by which detail or information on the edge, or overlap area, of a map or chart is compared, adjusted, and corrected to agree with the existing overlapping chart.

material balance (waste management): An accounting of the weights of materials entering and leaving a processing unit, such as an incinerator, usually on an hourly basis.

matric potential: The work per unit quantity of pure water that has to be done to overcome the attractive forces of water molecules and the attraction of water to solid surfaces; the matric potential is negative above a water table and zero below a free water table.

matrix (geology): Natural material in which larger particles are embedded.

mattress (engineering): A blanket of brush, poles, or other material interwoven or otherwise lashed together and weighted with rock, concrete blocks, or otherwise held in place, to cover an area subject to scour.

meadow: An area of natural or planted vegetation dominated by grasses and grasslike plants used primarily for hay production.

mean (statistics): The average of a group of items obtained by adding together all items and dividing by the total number of items used.

mean depth (hydraulics): Average depth; crosssectional area of a stream or channel divided by its surface or top width.

meander: The turn of a stream, either live or cut off.

mean discharge: The arithmetic mean of individual daily mean discharges during a specific period, usually daily, monthly, or annually.

mean velocity: Average velocity, obtained by dividing the flow rate (discharge) by the cross sectional area for that given cross section.

measuring weir: A shaped notch through which water flows are measured. Common shapes are rectangular, trapezoidal, and triangular.

mechanical analysis: See *particle size analysis, particle size distribution*.

mechanical practices: Soil and water conservation practices that primarily change the surface of the land or that store, convey, regulate, or dispose of runoff water without excessive erosion.

mechanical turbulence: The erratic movement of air or water influenced by local obstructions.

median: The value of the middle item when items are arrayed according to size.

median lethal concentration (MC50): A standard for toxicity in which the concentration of a substance within another medium will kill 50 percent of a specific type of animal.

medium scale: Aerial photographs with a representative fraction of 1:12,000 to 1:30,000; maps with a representative fraction (scale) of 1:100,000 to 1:1,000,000.

medium texture: Intermediate between fine and coarse textured soils, containing moderate amounts of sand, silt, and clay. Includes the following textural classes: very fine sandy loam, loam, silt loam, and silt. See *soil textures.*

megascopic: Large enough to be distinguished by the naked eye or without the aid of a microscope.

megawatt: 1,000 kilowatts or one million watts. See *watt.*

mellow soil: A very soft, very friable, porous soil without any tendency toward hardness or harshness.

membrane barrier: Thin layer of material impermeable to the flow of gas or water.

Mercator map projection: See *map projection.*

Mercator equal-area map projection: See *map projection.*

Mercator transverse map projection: See *map projection.*

meridian: A true north and south line.

meromictic lakes: Lakes in which dissolved substances create a gradient of density differences with depth; preventing complete mixing or circulation of water masses.

meromixis: A condition of permanent stratification of water masses in lakes.

mesa: Table land, flat in nature, moderately elevated, and well drained.

mesic: See *soil temperature classes for family groupings.*

mesophyte: A plant that grows under intermediate moisture conditions.

mesotrophic: Reservoirs and lakes which contain moderate quantities of nutrients and are moderately productive in terms of aquatic animal and plant life.

metabolism: The sum of all chemical processes occurring within an organism; includes both synthesis (anabolism) and breakdown (catabolism) of organic compounds.

metadata: Data about data; if the data is the equivalent of a word in the dictionary, the metadata is the definition and history of the word.

metalimnion: Middle layer of a thermally stratified lake or reservoir with a rapid temperature decrease with depth.

metamorphic rock: Rock derived from pre existing rocks but that differ from them in physical, chemical, and mineralogical properties as a result of natural geological processes, principally heat and pressure, originating within the earth. The pre existing rocks may have been igneous, sedimentary, or another form of metamorphic rock.

metamorphosis: Transformation of an animal from one distinctive life history stage to another in its postembryonic development; e.g., larva of an insect to a pupa. See *life cycle.*

methane (CH₄): An odorless, colorless, and asphyxiating gas that can explode under certain circumstances; can be produced by solid waste undergoing anaerobic decomposition.

method detection limit: The minimum concentration of a substance that can be accurately identified and measured with present laboratory technologies.

metric system: A decimal system of weights and measure based on the gram and meter. See tables (pages *xi*) for common units used in the system and conversion factors.

metrogon lens: The trade name of a wide-angle lens for aerial cameras used in mapping, charting, and reconnaissance photography.

mho: The unit of electrical conductance; the reciprocal of ohm.

mica: Group of minerals that form thin, platy flakes, typically with shiny surfaces, especially common in metamorphic rocks.

micaceous: See *soil mineralogy classes for family groupings.*

microcategory soil erosion: Soil erosion on the individual farm level. See *macrocategory soil erosion.*

microclimate: The climatic condition of a small area resulting from the modification of the general climatic conditions by local differences in elevation or exposure; the sequence of atmospheric changes within a very small region.

microdensitometer: A special form of densitometer for reading densities in very small areas; used for studying astronomical images spectroscopic records, and for measuring image edge gradients and graininess in films.

microfauna: Protozoa and smaller nematodes.

microflora: Bacteria, including actinomycetes, viruses, and fungi.

micronutrient: A chemical element necessary in only extremely small amounts (less than one part per million) for the growth of plants. "Micro" refers to the amount used rather than to its essentiality. Examples are boron, chlorine, copper, iron, manganese, and zinc. See *macronutrient.*

microorganisms: Those organisms retained on a US standard sieve no. 100 (openings of 0.149 mm); those minute organisms invisible or only barely visible to the unaided eye. See *macroorganisms.*

micropropagation: The reproduction of new plants with only a few cells; also called meristem culture, mericloning, tissue culture, test tube plants, single cell culture, anther culture, embryo culture.

microrelief: Small scale local differences in topography, including mounds, swales, or pits that are only a few feet in diameter and with elevation differences of up to six feet.

microsite: A small area which exhibits localized characteristics different from the surrounding area. For example, the microsites created by a rock outcrop with thin soils, or the shaded and cooled areas created on a site by the presence of slash.

microsystem irrigation: Method of precisely applying irrigation water to the immediate root zone of the target plant at very low rates.

microwave: A very short electromagnetic wave; any wave between one meter and one millimeter in wavelength or 300 gigahertz to 0.3 gigahertz in frequency; the portion of the electromagnetic spectrum in the millimeter and centimeter wavelengths, bounded on the short wavelength sides by the far infrared (at one mm) and on the long wavelength side by very high-frequency radio waves. Passive systems operating at these wavelengths sometimes are called microwave systems; active systems are called radar, although the literal definition of radar, although the literal definition of radar requires a distance-measuring capability not always included in active systems. The exact limits of the microwave region are not defined.

midden: In archeology, waste materials marking the site of a prehistoric dwelling, usually kitchen midden.

migrate: To move (usually periodically) from one area to another for feeding or breeding.

migration pathways: The routes a contaminant may move around in the environment (e.g., soil, groundwater, surface water, air).

megmatite: Rock composed of a complex mixture of metamorphic rock and igneous granitic rock.

military crest: A ridge that interrupts the view between a valley and a hilltop.

milled refuse: Solid waste that has been mechanically reduced in size.

mine drainage: Water pumped or flowing from a mine.

mine dumps: Areas covered with overburden and other waste materials from ore and coal mines, quarries, smelters, usually with little or no vegetative cover. A miscellaneous land type.

mine tailings dam: An industrial waste dam in which the waste materials come from mining operations or mineral processing.

mined land: Land with new surface characteristics due to the removal of mineable commodity.

mineral: A natural inorganic substance that possess a definite chemical composition and definite physical and chemical properties.

mineralization: The conversion of an element from an organic form to an inorganic state as a result of microbial decomposition.

mineral soil: A soil consisting predominantly of, and having its properties determined predominantly by, mineral matter, usually containing less than 20 percent organic matter but sometimes containing an organic surface layer up to 30 centimeters thick. See *organic soil*.

miner's inch: The rate of discharge through an orifice one inch square under a specified head. An old term used in the western United States, now seldom used except where irrigation or mining water rights are so specified. The equivalent flow in cubic feet per second is fixed by state statute. One miner's inch is equivalent to 0.025 cubic foot per second in Arizona, California, Montana, and Oregon; 0.020 cubic foot per second in Idaho, Kansas, Nebraska, New Mexico, North and South Dakota, and Utah; 0.026 cubic foot per second in Colorado; and 0.028 cubic foot per second in British Columbia.

mine wash: Water deposited accumulations of sandy, silty, or clayey material recently eroded in mining operations.

minimum flow: Negotiated lowest flow in a regulated stream that will sustain an aquatic population of agreed-upon levels. Flow may vary seasonally. Lowest flow in a specified period of time.

minimum operating level: The lowest level to which the reservoir is drawn down under normal operating conditions.

minimum tillage: That amount of tillage required to create the proper soil condition for seed germination and plant establishment.

mining: The process of obtaining useful minerals from the earth's crust; includes both underground excavations and surface workings.

mining, area: Surface mining that is performed on level to gently rolling topography.

mining, auger: A mining method in which holes are drilled into the side of an exposed mineral seam and the mineral transported along an auger bit to the surface.

mining, contour surface: The removal of overburden in steep or mountainous areas and mining from a mineral seam that outcrops or approaches the surface at about the same elevation.

mining, hydraulic: Mining by washing sand and dirt away with water, leaving the desired mineral.

mining, open-pit: Mining of metalliferous ores by surface mining methods.

mining, surface: Mining method in which the overlying materials are removed to expose the mineral seam for extraction.

mining, underground: Mining method in which the minerals are extracted without removing the overlying materials.

mining by-products: Any of the spoils, tailings, and slag resulting from mining and processing of minerals.

mining operation: All of the premises, facilities, railroad loops, roads, and equipment used in the process of extracting and removing a mineral commodity from a designated surface mine or in determining the location, quality, and quantity of a natural mineral deposit.

mini-park: A relatively small, intensely developed area for recreation in a highly populated community or neighborhood.

minor element: See *micronutrient*.

miscellaneous area: A mapping unit for areas of land that have little or no natural soil, that are too nearly inaccessible for orderly examination, or that occur where, for other reasons, it is not feasible to classify the soil. Examples are alluvial land, badlands, made land, marsh, mine dump, rock land, rough broken land, rubble land, scoria land, swamp, urban land. See *individual definitions*. Formerly called miscellaneous land type.

mitigation (wildlife): The reduction or elimination of damages to fish and wildlife resources.

mixed: See *soil mineralogy classes for family groupings*.

mixed fertilizers: Two or more fertilizer materials mixed, or granulated together into individual pellets; includes dry mixed powders, granulates (bulk blends), granulated mixtures, and clear liquid mixed fertilizers, suspensions, and slurries.

mixed forest: A forest composed of two or more species of trees. In practice, usually a forest in which at least 20 percent are trees of other than the dominant species. See *pure forest*.

mixing depth: An area in which rising air from the earth's surface mixes with the atmosphere above it until a layer equal or warmer in temperature is reached.

mixing layer: The atmosphere's mixing layer is the near-surface area where air is well mixed from turbulence caused by the interaction of the Earth's surface and atmosphere. The mixing layer is usually located at the base of a temperature inversion.

mode (statistics): The most frequent or most common value, provided that a sufficiently large number of items are available to give a smooth distribution.

moderately coarse texture: Intermediate between coarse and medium texture and consisiting predominantly of coarse particles. In soil textural classification it includes all the sandy loams except the very fine sandy loam. See *course texture*.

moderately fine texture: Intermediate between fine and medium texture and consisting predominantly of intermediate size (soil) particles or relatively small amounts of fine or coarse particles. In soil textural classification it includes clay loam, sandy clay loam, and silty clay loam. See *fine texture*.

modified block cut: A modified block cut method of surface mining in which the backfill consists

of the spoil from the succeeding blocks rather than from the spoil producing block.

Mohs' scale of hardness: Relative hardness of minerals ranging from a rating of one for the softest (talc) to 10 for the hardest (diamond). Calcite has a hardness of three and can be scratched with a copper coin.

moisture equivalent (soil): An empirical measure of the power of different soils to hold moisture; the percentage of water retained by soil when submitted to a pressure of 1,000 times the pull of gravity; closely approximates field capacity in fine textured soils.

moisture penetration: See *water penetration*.

moisture tension: See *water tension*.

moisture volume percentage: The ratio of the volume of water in a soil to the total bulk volume of the soil.

moisture weight percentage: The moisture content expressed as a percentage of the oven dry weight of soil.

molded pulp products: Contoured fiber products molded from pulp for such uses as egg packaging, trays for fresh meat or produce, plates, and protective packaging.

molecule: The smallest part of a substance that can exist separately and still retain its chemical properties and characteristic composition; the smallest combination of atoms that will form a given chemical compound.

mole drain: Unlined drain formed by pulling a bullet shaped cylinder through the soil.

mollic epipedon: See *diagnostic horizons.*

mollisols: See *soil classification.*

molt: To cast or shed periodically the outer body covering which permits an increase in size; especially characteristic of invertebrates. See *instar.*

monitoring: The process of checking, observing, or keeping track of something for a specified period of time or at specified intervals. See *multiresource, resource monitoring.*

monoculture: Raising crops of a single species, generally even aged.

monocyclic aromatic hydrocarbons: Single-ring aromatic compounds. Constituents of lead-free gasoline; also used in the manufacture of monomers and plasticizers in polymers.

monolithic: Of or pertaining to a structure formed from a single mass of stone.

monomictic: Lakes and reservoirs which are relatively deep, do not freeze over, and undergo a single stratification and mixing cycle during the year. These lakes and reservoirs usually become destratified during the mixing cycle, usually in the fall. Warm-water lakes which turn over annually, usually in winter, and where the temperature never falls below four degrees C.

montmorillonite: An aluminosilicate clay mineral with 2:1 expanding crystal lattice, that is, with two silicon tetrahedral layers enclosing an aluminum octahedral layer. Considerable expansion may be caused along the C axis by water moving between silica layers of contiguous units.

montmorillonitic: See *soil mineralogy classes for family groupings.*

moraine: An accumulation of drift, with an initial topographic expression of its own, built within a glaciated region chiefly by the direct action of glacial ice. Examples are ground, lateral, recessional, and terminal moraines.

morning glory spillway: A circular or glory hole form of a drop inlet spillway. Usually free standing in the reservoir and so called because of its resemblance to the morning glory flower.

mosaic: An assemblage of overlapping aerial photographs whose edges have been matched to form a continuous photographic representation of an area.

mosaic, controlled: A mosaic that is assembled to ground control in which photos are placed that have been ratioed and/or rectified as necessary to fit the control, providing an accurate base for measurement.

mosaic, uncontrolled: A mosaic composed of uncorrected photos, assembled so that detail matches as best as possible with no regard to ground control or correct relative orientation.

most probable number: An estimate, based on certain probability formulas, of the most probable number of coliform organisms in a water sample.

motile: See *free swimming, sessile.*

mottled (soils): Soil horizons irregularly marked with spots of color. A common cause of mottling is impeded drainage, although there are other causes, such as soil development from an unevenly weathered rock. The weathering of different kinds of minerals may cause mottling.

mound system: A septic tank effluent disposal system in which a mound of soil is built up and effluent distributed in the mound about 3.3 feet (one m) above the normal soil surface.

mountain top removal: A mining method in which 100 percent of the overburden covering a mineral deposit is removed in order to recover 100 percent of the mineral. Excess spoil material is hauled to a nearby hollow to create valley fill.

mouth: The place where a stream discharges to a larger stream, a lake, or the sea.

movable dam: A movable barrier that may be opened in whole or in part, permitting control of the flow of water through or over the dam.

muck: Highly decomposed organic material in which the original plant parts are not recognizable. Contains more mineral matter and is usually darker than peat. See *muck soil, peat, peat soil, organic soil materials.*

muck soil: An organic soil in which the organic matter is well decomposed (US usage); a soil containing 20 to 50 percent organic matter.

mud: Generally, any soil containing enough water to make it soft. A mixture of soil and water in a fluid or weakly solid state.

mudflat: A mud-covered, gently sloping tract of land alternately covered and left bare by water. The muddy, nearly level bed of a dry lake.

mudstone: Fine-grained sedimentary rock formed from hardened clay and silt that lacks the thin layers typical of shale.

mulch: A natural or artificial layer of plant residue or other materials, such as sand or paper, on the soil surface.

mulch tillage: Soil tillage that employs plant residues or other materials to cover the ground surface.

multiband system (remote sensing): A system for simultaneously observing the same (small) target with several filtered bands, through which data can be recorded; usually applied to cameras, may be used for scanning radiometers that use dispersant optics to split wavelength bands apart for viewing by several filtered detectors.

multichannel: Scanning systems capable of observing and recording several channels of data simultaneously, preferably through the same aperture.

multiple use: Harmonious use of land for more than one purpose; i.e., grazing of livestock, wildlife production, recreation, watershed and timber production. Not necessarily the combination of uses that will yield the highest economic return or greatest unit output.

multiplex: A name applied to anaglyphic double-projection steroplotters with the following characteristics: a) the steromodel is projected from diapositives reduced from an aerial negative according to a fixed ratio, b) the projection system illuminates the entire diapositive format area, and

c) the stereomodel is measured and drawn by observation of a floating mark.

multipliers: (economics) A measurement, expressed as a mathematical relationship of the total effects, including indirect and induced effects, in the economy from direct outputs of a specific activity; (plant science) plant species that multiply rapidly.

multiresource inventorying: The act of collecting a combination of natural and related resources data for analysis of the state or condition of the resource and for determining the relationship among resources.

multiresource monitoring: The act of continued or periodic collecting a combination of natural and related resource data previously inventoried for analysis and for detection of change and trends in the status and condition of the resources and for determining changes in the relationship among resources.

multispectral: Remote sensing in two or more spectral bands, such as visible and infrared.

multispectral scanner (MSS): A line-scanning sensor that uses an oscillating or rotating mirror, a wavelength-selective dispersive mechanism, and an array of detectors to measure simultaneously the energy available in several wavelength bands, often in several spectral regions; the movement of the platform usually provides for the along-track progression of the scanner.

mutitemporal: Of or pertaining to more than one time or period, as multitemporal analysis, indicating studies (usually of the same area or object) carried out at specified time intervals.

mungo: The waste of milled wool that is combined with other fibers to make a low-quality cloth.

municipal solid waste: Garbage that is disposed of in a sanitary or municipal solid waste landfill.

Munsell color system: A color designation system that specifies the relative degrees of the three simple variables of color: hue, value, and chroma. For example: 10YR 614 is a color (of soil) with hue 10YR, value 6, and chroma 4. These notations can be translated into several different systems of color names as desired. See *chroma, hue, value.*

mutagenic: Causing alteration in the DNA (genes or chromosomes) of an organism.

mutation: An abrupt change in heredity producing new individuals differing from parents.

mycorrhiza: The association of a fungus found in the soil with the roots of certain plants; in some cases beneficial to the higher plant, also spelled mycorhiza.

N

nadir: The point on the celestial sphere vertically below the observer, or 180 degrees from the zenith; the point on the ground vertically beneath the perspective center of the camera lens.

nanoplankton: Very minute plankton not retained in a plankton net equipped with no. 25 silk bolting cloth (mesh, 0.03 to 0.04 mm).

nappe: The sheet or curtain of water overflowing a weir.

national economic development: One of the two main objectives of planning for water and related land resources by governmental agencies whose activities involve planning and development of water resources; reflects increases in the nation's productive output, an output which is partly reflected in a national product and income accounting framework to measure the continuing flow of goods and services into direct consumption or investment.

national forest: A federal reservation, generally forest, range, or wildland, which is administered by the Forest Service, US Department of Agriculture, under a program of multiple use and sustained yield for timber production, range, wildlife, watershed, and outdoor recreation purposes.

national monument: An area owned by the federal government and administered by the National Park Service, US Department of Interior, for the purpose of preserving and making available to the public a resource of archaeological, scientific, or aesthetic interest.

national park: An area of unusual scenic or historic interest owned by the federal government and administered by the National Park Service, US Department of the Interior, to conserve the scenery, the flora and fauna, and any natural and historical objects within its boundaries for public enjoyment in perpetuity.

native grazing land: Grazing land used primarily for production of native forage plants maintained or manipulated primarily through grazing management. Native grazing lands include rangeland, grazable woodland, and native pasture, individually or collectively.

native pasture: Land on which the climax (natural potential) plant community is forest, but which is used and managed primarily for the production of native species for forage.

native species: A species that is a part of an area's original fauna or flora.

natric horizon: See *diagnostic horizons.*

natural area: A site or area in its natural state, undisturbed by man's activities; an area set aside indefinitely to preserve a representative unit of a major forest, range, or wetland type primarily for the purposes of science, research, or education.

natural boundary: The visible high water mark of any lake, stream, or other body of water where the presence and action of the water are so common and usual and so long continued in all ordinary years as to mark upon the soil of the bed of the lake, river stream, or other body of water a character distinct from that of the banks, both in vegetation and in the nature of the soil itself.

natural disturbance event: Any natural event that significantly alters the structure, composition, or dynamics of a natural community: e.g., floods, fires, and storms.

natural erosion: See *erosion.*

natural floodway: The channel of a water course and those portions of the adjoining flood plain which are reasonably required to carry a selected probability flood.

natural form: The general plant shape that develops when outside influences, such as crowding, pruning, dwarfing, etc., are absent.

natural gas: A mixture of the low molecular weight paraffin series hydrocarbons methane, ethane, propane, and butane with small amounts of higher hydrocarbons; also frequently containing small or large proportions of nitrogen, carbon dioxide, hydrogen sulfide, and occasionally small proportions of helium.

natural grassland: See *prairie.*

naturalized plant: A plant introduced from other areas which has become established in and more or less adapted to a given region by long continued growth there.

natural potential vegetation: See *climax.*

natural range barrier: A river, rock face, dense timber or any other naturally occurring feature that stops or significantly impedes livestock movement to and from an adjacent area.

natural regeneration: The renewal of a forest stand by natural seeding, sprouting, suckering, or layering seeds may be deposited by wind, birds or mammals.

natural resources: Naturally occurring resources needed by an organism, population, or ecosystem, which, by their increasing availability up to an optimal or sufficient level, allow an increasing rate of energy conversion.

natural resources, nonrenewable: natural resources that do not naturally replenish themselves within the limits of human time.

natural resources, renewable: Natural resources that continuously can be replenished in the course of natural events within the limits of human time.

natural revegetation: Natural re establishment of plants; propagation of new plants over an area by natural processes.

natural scenic area: Area with exceptional scenery, fauna or flora, and geological or mineral interest, with or without minimum development for access.

natural selection: The natural process inferred to take place when organisms best adapted to their environment survive relative to the extirpation of those organisms less well adapted.

nature center: A facility or outdoor area where an audience comes together with the land to observe, learn about, and enjoy the complexities of nature.

nature trail: A marked pathway or trail through a natural area, usually designed for foot travel in such a way that individuals or small groups can study the flora and fauna of the area.

nauplius: Free-swimming microscopic larval stage characteristic of many crustaceans, barnacles, etc.

nautical Chart: See *hydrographic chart*.

navigable waters: Traditionally, waters sufficiently deep and wide for navigation by all, or specified vessels; such waters in the United States come under federal jurisdiction and are protected by certain provisions of the Clean Water Act.

navigation channel: An artificially maintained waterway that ensures a minimum water depth to allow unimpeded passage for a variety of vessels.

near infrared: The preferred term for the shorter wavelengths in infrared region extending from about 0.7 micrometers (visible red), to around two or three micrometers (varying with the author). The longer wavelength end grades into the middle infrared; The term emphasizes the radiation reflected from plant materials, which peaks around

0.85 micrometers; also called solar infrared, as it is only available for used during daylight hours.

neatlines: The lines that bound the body of a map, usually parallels and meridians; also called sheet lines.

neighborhood: A primary informal group consisting of all persons who live in local proximity; often considered to be the locality served by an elementary school or neighborhood convenience shopping center.

negative: A photographic image on film, plate, or paper, in which the subject tones to which the emulsion is sensitive are reversed or complementary.

nekton: Macroscopic organisms swimming actively in water, such as fish. See *plankton*.

nematocide: A chemical agent which is destructive to nematodes.

nephelometric: Method of measuring turbidity in a water sample by passing light through the sample and measuring the amount of the light that is deflected.

neritic zone: Relatively shallow water zone which extends from the high tide mark to the edge of the continental shelf.

net benefit (economics): The net gain from goods and services that improve the welfare of the community as a whole; the results of all public and private gains and losses.

net duty of water: The amount of water delivered to the land to produce a crop, measured as the point of delivery to the field. See *gross duty of water*.

net primary reduction: The new increase in plant biomass within a specified area and time interval.

netting: A concept in which all emissions sources in the same area that owned or controlled by a single company are treated as one large source, thereby allowing flexibility in controlling individual sources in order to meet a single emissions standard.

neuston: Organisms resting or swimming on the water surface.

neutralization: The addition of an alkaline material to an acid material to raise the pH and overcome an acid condition, or the addition of an acid material to an alkaline material to lower the pH.

neutral soil: A soil in which the surface layer, at least to normal plow depth, is neither acid nor alkaline in reaction. For most practical purposes, soil with a pH ranging from 6.6 through 7.3. See *acid soil; alkaline soil; pH; reaction, soil.*

neutron probe: Probe, with radioactive source, that measures soil water content through reflection of scattered neutrons by hydrogen atoms in soil water.

niche: A habitat that supplies the factors necessary for the existence of an organism or species.

nimbostratus: See *cloud.*

nitrate (NO$_3$): The most highly oxidized phase in the nitrogen cycle, which normally reaches important concentrations in the final stages of biologic oxidation.

nitrate reduction: The chemical or biochemical reduction of nitrates to the nitrite form.

nitric oxide (NO): A gas formed in great part from atmospheric nitrogen and oxygen when combustion takes place under high temperature and pressure; while not itself a pollutant, converts to nitrogen dioxide which is a major constituent of photochemical smog.

nitrification: The biological oxidation of ammonium to nitrite and the further oxidation of nitrite to nitrate.

nitrite: An intermediate stage in the nitrogen cycle, may occur in water as a result of the biological decomposition of proteinaceous materials.

nitrogen: The gaseous, essential element for plant growth, composing 78 percent of the atmosphere, which is quite inert and unavailable to most plants in its natural form.

nitrogen assimilation: The incorporation of nitrogen compounds into cell substances by living organisms.

nitrogen cycle: The sequence of biochemical changes undergone by nitrogen, wherein it is used by a living organism, liberated upon the death and decomposition of the organism, and converted to its original state of oxidation.

nitrogen dioxide (NO$_2$): A gas resulting from the internal combustion engine and other sources. It is important as an air pollutant due to its role in smog formation.

nitrogen fixation: The conversion of elemental nitrogen (N$_2$) to organic combinations or to forms readily useable in biological processes.

nitrogen fixing plant: A plant that can assimilate and fix the free nitrogen of the atmosphere with the aid of bacteria living in the root nodules. Legumes with the associated rhizobium bacteria in the root nodules are the most important nitrogen fixing plants.

nitrogen oxide (NO$_x$): The result of photochemical reactions of nitric oxide in ambient air; major component of photochemical smog. Product of combustion from transportation and stationary sources and a major contributor to the formation of ozone in the troposphere and to acid deposition.

nitrogenous wastes: Wastes of animal or plants that contain significant concentrations of nitrogen.

nitrophenols: Synthetic organopesticides containing carbon, hydrogen, nitrogen, and oxygen.

noble metal: Chemically inactive metal such as gold; does not corrode easily.

nocturnal: Active primarily during the night.

node: A joint on a stem, at which a bud, leaf, or flower stalk is attached.

nodule: A structure developed on the roots of most legumes and some other plants in response to the stimulus of root nodule bacteria. Legumes bearing these nodules are nitrogen fixing plants, utilizing atmospheric nitrogen instead of depending on nitrogen compounds in the soil; (geology) Rounded, hard concretions that can be separated intact from the geologic formation in which they occur.

noise: Any sound or combination of sounds that has an unpleasant or undesired effect on the auditory senses, the level or intensity of which is measurable. See *decibel.*

noise pollution: The persistent intrusion of noise into the environment at a level that may be injurious to human health.

non-conventional pollutant: Any

pollutant not statutorily listed or which is poorly understood by the scientific community.

nonforested wetlands: Wetlands dominated by shrubs or emergent vegetation.

nonpoint pollution: Pollution whose sources cannot be pinpointed; can best be controlled by proper soil, water, and land management practices. See *pollution, point source.*

nonpoint source: A diffused form of water quality degradation produced by erosion of land that causes sedimentation of streams, eutrophication from nutrients and pesticides used in agricultural and silvicultural practices, and acid rain resulting from burning fuels that contain sulfur.

nonpoint source contaminant: A substance that pollutes or degrades water that comes from lawn or cropland runoff, the atmosphere, roadways, and other diffuse sources.

nonpoint source water pollution: Water contamination that originates from a broad area (such as leaching of agricultural chemicals from crop land) and enters the water resource diffusely over a large area.

non-potable: Water that is unsafe or unpalatable to drink because it contains pollutants, contaminants, minerals, or infective agents.

nonproject actions: Technical and/or financial assistance provided to an individual group or local unit of government by the US Soil Conservation Service, primarily through a cooperative agreement with a local conservation district; may include consultations, engineering, and other assistance that land owners usually cannot accomplish themselves.

nonrenewable natural resources: Natural resources that, once used, cannot be replaced.

non-road emissions: Pollutants emitted by combustion engines on farm and construction equipment, gasoline-powered lawn and garden equipment, and power boats and outboard motors.

nonsaline alkali soil: See *sodic soil.*

nonselective herbicide: Kills or significantly retards growth of most higher plant species.

nonsoil: A substance not defined as soil in soil taxonomy; a substance on which land plants usually do not grow; for example, bare rock, highly acid material, etc.

non-spatial attribute: Information related to an items that has no geographic information associated with it (e.g. the cost of a land parcel).

nonstructural measures (water resources): Any means of alleviating flood losses by the means of land treatment.

nonuniform flow (hydraulics): Flow in which the mean velocity or cross sectional area vary at successive channel cross-sections. If the velocity at a given cross section is constant with time, it is referred to as steady nonuniform flow. If the velocity changes with time at each cross section, it is known as unsteady nonuniform flow.

normal: A mean or average value established from a series of observations for purposes of comparison, for example, normal precipitation, normal temperature, normal flow.

normal depth: Depth of flow in an open conduit during uniform flow for the given conditions. See *uniform flow.*

normal erosion: See *erosion.*

normal forest: A standard with which to compare an actual forest to bring out its deficiencies for sustained yield management; a forest with normal increment, normal age and size classes, normal composition, and normal stocking.

notch: The opening in a dam or spillway for the passage of water. See *weir notch.*

notice of intent: A brief statement inviting public reaction to the decision by the responsible federal official to prepare an environmental impact statement for a major federal action.

no-tillage: A method of planting crops that involves no seedbed preparation other than opening the soil for the purpose of placing the seed at the intended depth; usually involves opening a small slit or punching a hole into the soil; usually no cultivation during crop production; chemical weed control is normally used; also called slot planting or zero tillage.

noxious species: A plant that is undesirable because it conflicts, restricts, or otherwise causes problems under the management objectives. Not to be confused with species declared noxious by laws.

nuclear energy: Energy released as particulate or electromagnetic radiation and heat during reactions of atomic nuclei.

nuclear fission: The splitting of a heavy nucleus into two approximately equal parts, which are radioactive nuclei of lighter elements, accompanied by the release of a large amount of energy and generally one or more neutrons.

nuclear fusion: The combining of atomic nuclei of very light elements by collision at high speed to form new and heavier elements, resulting in release of large amounts of energy.

nuclear reactor: A device in which a fission chain reaction can be initiated, maintained, and controlled.

nuclear winter: Prediction by some scientists that smoke and debris rising from massive fires of a nuclear war could block sunlight for weeks or months, cooling the earth's surface and producing climate changes that could, for example, negatively affect world agricultural and weather patterns.

nucleating agent: In cloud physics, any substance that serves to accelerate the nucleation of cloud particles; nucleating agents may themselves be nuclei (silver iodide, salt, sulfur dioxide, dust) or they may enhance the nucleation environment (dry ice, propane spray).

nucleation: Any process by which the phase change of a substance to a more condensed state (condensation, sublimation, freezing,) is initiated at certain loci, nublei, within the less condensed state.

nuclide: An atom characterized by the number of protons, neturons, and energy in the nucleus.

nurse crop: See *companion crop.*

nurse log: A larger and decomposing fallen log which acts as a germination substrate for tree species establishing in the understorey. Such logs provide moisture, nutrients and

often some degree of elevation above other potentially competing vegetation on the forest floor.

nurse tree: A tree that protects or fosters the growth of another in youth.

nursery: A place where plants, such as trees, shrubs, vines, and grasses, are propagated for transplanting or for use as stocks for grafting; a planting of young trees or other plants, the young plants being called nursery stock or planting stock.

nutria: Animals with reddish brown and black fur, webbed feet, orange front teeth that stick out, and long tails. Nutria live throughout Louisiana in coastal swamps, brackish marshes, ponds, streams, rivers, and lakes. They eat plants and grass and can grow up to four feet long.

nutrient management: Determining the additional nutrients the soil needs for crop growth, and applying animal manure, compost, or commercial fertilizer in forms, amounts, and ways that foster crop yields and farm profitability, while reducing nutrient loss to the environment.

nutrient pollution: Contamination of water resources by excessive inputs of nutrients. In surface waters, excess algal production is a major concern.

nutrients: Elements, or compounds, essential as raw materials for organism growth and development, such as carbon, oxygen, nitrogen, phosphorus, etc.; the dissolved solids and gases of the water of an area.

nutritive ratio: The ratio or proportion between digestible protein and digestible non nitrogeneous nutrients (carbohydrates and fats) in a livestock feed.

nymph: An immature developmental form characteristic of the preadult stage in insects that do not have a pupal stage, such as mayflies and stoneflies. See *larva*.

O

observation well: Hole bored to a desired depth below the ground surface, used for observing the water table or piezometric level.

occurrence and distribution assessment: Characterization of the broad-scale spatial and temporal distributions of water-quality conditions in relation to major contaminant sources and background conditions for surface water and groundwater.

ocean thermal energy conversion: Electricity generation by making use of the temperature difference (some 40 degrees F) between the top and the bottom layers of the ocean to convert a fluid to vapor, which in turn powers a turbine generator.

ochric epipedon: See *diagnostic horizons*.

odd area (wildlife): A small area of land, such as a bare knob, fence corner, sink hole, blow out, borrow pit, or an irregularly shaped area, that may be best used to produce wildlife habitat.

odor threshold: The minimum odor of a water or air sample that can just be detected after successive dilutions with odorless water. Also called threshold odor.

offal: Intestines and discarded parts including paunch manure, of slaughtered animals.

official map: An ordinance that designates the location of future streets, parks, and drainage ways and regulates the construction of buildings or other improvements in future street right of ways, street widenings, or street extensions. The official map must be legally registered. After it has been adopted and registered, the governmental unit is relieved of compensating the property owner for any buildings or improvements subsequently constructed in the designated areas, although the governmental unit must compensate the landowner for the land at the time of its acquisition.

off-site damage costs: Costs incurred by society as a result of erosion; such costs are external to producer decision-making.

off-site facility: A hazardous waste treatment, storage or disposal area that is located away from the generating site.

offstream use: Water withdrawn from surface or groundwater sources for use at another place.

oil and gas waste: Gas and oil drilling muds, oil production brines, and other waste associated with exploration for, development and production of crude oil or natural gas.

oil desulfurization: Widely used precombustion method for reducing sulfur dioxide emissions from oil-burning power plants. The oil is treated with hydrogen, which removes some of the sulfur by forming hydrogen sulfide gas.

oil fingerprinting: A method that identifies sources of oil and allows spills to be traced to their source.

open dump: An uncovered site used for disposal of waste without environmental controls.

oil spill: An accidental or intentional discharge of oil which reaches bodies of water. Can be controlled by chemical dispersion, combustion, mechanical containment, and/or adsorption. Spills from tanks and pipelines can also occur away from water bodies, contaminating the soil, getting into sewer systems and threatening underground water sources.

ogee: Profile of a weir, overflow dam, or spillway shaped as a compound reverse curve (letter "S") with the crest being a convex

curve and the outfall section being a concave curve.

ohm: The unit of electrical resistance, equal to the resistance of a circuit in which an electromotive force of one volt maintains a current of one ampere.

oil shale: A sedimentary rock containing solid organic matter fro which oil can be obtained when the rock is heated to a high temperature.

old fields: Areas formerly cultivated or grazed, where woody vegetation has begun to invade.

oligotrophic lakes: Deep lakes that have a low supply of nutrients; thus they support very little organic production. Dissolved oxygen is present at or near saturation throughout the lake during all seasons of the year. See *eutrophic lakes*.

omnivore: A organism that eats both animal and vegetable substances; an animal that can be on any level of the food chain. See *herbivore, carnivore*.

omnivorous: Eating both animal and vegetable substances; an animal that can be on any level of the food chain. See *herbivorous, carnivorous*.

open drain: Natural watercourse or constructed open channel that conveys drainage water.

open pit mines: Mining facilities where the ratio of overburden to mineral small. See *mining*.

open pit mining: See *mining*.

open range: An extensive grazing area on which the movement of livestock is unrestricted.

open space: A relatively undeveloped green or wooded area provided usually within an urban development to minimize feelings of congested living.

operational plans: The administrative and legislative actions taken by an agency to carry out the decisions that were made in a comprehensive plan. Such actions might include a capital improvements program, intergovernmental coordinating committees, land development regulations, and construction codes.

operational waste (irrigation): The water wasted through spillways or otherwise discarded from an irrigation system after having been diverted into it.

opportunity cost: The return to the best alternative use by employing a unit of resource in a given manner.

opportunity time: The time that surface water is available for infiltration, relative to the length of an irrigation run

optical density: The amount of opacity of a translucent object.

optical-mechanical scanner: A system using a rotating mirror and a detector, in conjunction with lenses and prisms, to record reflected and/or emitted electromagnetic energy in a scanning mode along a flight path.

optimum tillage: A combination of tillage operations designed to maximize growth of crop plants.

orbital wave (hydraulics): A wave, such as an ocean wave, where the water particles move in a closed transverse and do not translate.

orchard: A group of crop trees usually arranged in a symmetrical pattern.

order (soils): A class in classification

schemes. See *soil classification*.

organic chemicals/compounds: Naturally occuring (animal or plant-produced or synthetic) substances containing mainly carbon, hydrogen, nitrogen, and oxygen.

organic content: Synonymous with volatile solids, except for small traces of some inorganic materials, such as calcium carbonate, that lose weight at temperatures used in determining volatile solids.

organic farming: Crop production system that avoids or largely excludes the use of synthetically compounded fertilizers, pesticides, growth regulators, and livestock feed additives; to the maximum extent feasible, organic farming systems rely upon crop rotations, crop residues, animal manures, legumes, green manures, off-farm organic wastes, mechanical cultivation, mineral-bearing rocks, and aspects of biological pest control maintain soil productivity and tilth, to supply plant nutrients, and to control insects, weeds, and other pests

organic detritus: Any loose organic material in streams (such as leaves, bark, or twigs) removed and transported by mechanical means, such as disintegration or abrasion.

organic fertilizer: By product from the processing of animals or vegetable substances that contain sufficient plant nutrients to be of value as fertilizers.

organic gardening: A system of farming or home gardening that utilizes organic wastes and composts to the exclusion of chemical fertilizers.

organic matter: See *soil organic matter*.

organic soil: A soil that contains a high percentage (greater than 20 or 30 percent) of organic matter throughout the solum.

organic soil materials (As used in the Soil Classification System of the National Cooperative Soil Survey in the United States): Saturated with water for prolonged periods unless artificially drained and having more than 30 percent organic matter if the mineral fraction is more than 50 percent clay, or more than 20 percent organic matter if the mineral fraction has no clay; never saturated with water for more than a few days and having more than 34 percent organic matter. See *soil classification, Histosols*. Kinds of organic materials include:

fibric materials: The least decomposed of all the organic soil materials, containing very high amounts of fiber that are well preserved and readily identifiable as to botanical origin. These materials have a bulk density of less than 6-1/4 pounds per cubic foot and a fiber content (unrubbed) that exceeds two thirds of the organic volume, more than four tenths after rubbing. When saturated, the maximum water content of the material ranges from 850 to 3,000 percent on an oven dry basis.

hemic materials: Intermediate in degree of decomposition between the less decomposed fibric and the more decomposed sapric materials. These materials have a bulk density of 6-1/4 to 12-1/2 pounds per cubic foot, and fiber content (unrubbed) is between one third and two thirds of the organic volume, more than one tenth after rubbing. When

saturated, the maximum water content of the material ranges from 450 to 850 percent on an oven dry basis.

sapric materials: The most highly decomposed of the organic materials, having the highest bulk density, least amount of plant fiber, and lowest water content at saturation. These materials have a bulk density of more than 12-1/2 pounds per cubic foot and fiber content (unrubbed) of less than one third the organic volume. When saturated, the maximum water content of the material averages less than 450 percent on an oven dry basis.

organism: Any living thing.

organochlorine compound: Synthetic organic compounds containing chlorine. As generally used, term refers to compounds containing mostly or exclusively carbon, hydrogen, and chlorine. Examples include organochlorine insecticides, polychlorinated biphenyls, and some solvents containing chlorine.

organochlorine insecticide: A class of organic insecticides containing a high percentage of chlorine. Includes dichlorodiphenylethanes (such as DDT), chlorinated cyclodienes (such as chlordane), and chlorinated benzenes (such as lindane). Most organochlorine insecticides were banned because of their carcinogenicity, tendency to bioaccumulate, and toxicity to wildlife.

organonitrogen herbicides: A group of herbicides consisting of a nitrogen ring with associated functional groups and including such classes as triazines and acetanilides. Examples include atrazine, cyanazine, alachlor, and metolachlor.

organophosphate insecticides: A class of insecticides derived from phosphoric acid. They tend to have high acute toxicity to vertebrates. Although readily metabolized by vertebrates, some metabolic products are more toxic than the parent compound.

organophosphates: A group of pesticide chemicals that contain phosphorus, such as a malathion and parathion, that are formulated as insecticides; they are short lived and normally do not reach environmentally toxic concentrations; some of these chemicals are initially, extremely toxic and can be environmentally dangerous.

organophosphorus insecticides: Insecticides derived from phosphoric acid and are generally the most toxic of all pesticides to vertebrate animals.

organophyllic: A substance that easily combines with organic compounds.

organotins: Chemical compounds used in anti-foulant paints to protect the hulls of boats and ships, buoys, and pilings from marine organisms such as barnacles.

orifice plate (irrigation): A known size orifice in a metal plate installed across a furrow to measure furrow stream flows.

ornamental: A plant grown for the beauty of its form, foliage, flowers, or fruit, rather than for food, fiber, or other uses.

orogenic: Of or pertaining to mountain building.

orographic cloud: A cloud whose form and extent is determined by the distributing effects of orography, mountains, upon the passing flow of air; because these clouds are linked with the form of the terrestrial relief, they generally move very slowly, if at all, although the winds at the same level may be very strong.

orphan banks: Abandoned surface mines, operated prior to the enactment of comprehensive reclamation laws, that require additional reclamation.

orphan lands: Disturbed surfaces resulting from mine operations that were inadequately reclaimed by the operator and for which the operator no longer has any fixed responsibilities; usually refers to lands mined previous to the passage of comprehensive reclamation laws.

orstein: An indurated layer in the B horizon of Podzols in which the cementing material consists of illuviated sesquioxides (mostly iron) and organic matter. See *hardpan*.

orthographic map projection: See *map projection*.

osmoregulation: The adjustment in the osmotic concentration of solutes in body fluids to environmental conditions, for example, when salmon migrate from salt to freshwater.

osmosis: The tendency of a fluid to pass through a semipermeable membrane, as the wall of a living cell, into a solution of higher concentration, so as to equalize concentrations on both sides of the membrane.

osmotic potential: The work per unit quantity of pure water that has to be done to overcome the effect of ions in the soil solutions; unlike the matric potential, it has little effect on movement of water in soils; its major effect is on uptake of water by plant roots.

outcrop: The surface exposure of bedrock or strata.

outdoor air supply: Air brought into a building from outside.

outdoor education: A structured educational activity performed outdoors.

outdoor laboratory: An outdoor area, usually on or near school-grounds, used to integrate the principles of conservation/environmental education into specific subject matter areas, reinforcing classroom learning through authentic experiences that will result in knowledge and appreciation of the way the natural world works and the dependence of all living things on it.

outdoor recreation: The use of soil, water, and natural resources, their aesthetic values and productivity, in accordance with the suitability of these resources for providing outdoor leisure time activities to serve the needs of the people.

outfall: Point where water flows from a conduit, stream, or drain.

outlet: Point of water disposal from a stream, river, lake, tidewater, or artificial drain.

outlet channel: A waterway constructed or altered primarily to carry water from man made structures, such as terraces, tile lines, and diversions.

outslope: The exposed area sloping away from a bench cut section.

outwash: See *glaciofluvial deposit.*

outwash plain: The plain formed by deposits from a stream or river originating from the melting of glacial ice that are distributed over a considerable area; generally coarser, heavier material is deposited nearer the ice and finer material carried further away.

oven-dry weigh: The weight of a substance after it has been dried in an oven at 105 degrees C, to equilibrium.

overburden: The earth, rock, and other materials that lie above a mineral deposit.

overdraft: The pumping of water from a groundwater basin or aquifer in excess of the supply flowing into the basin; results in a depletion or "mining" of the groundwater in the basin.

overfall: Abrupt change in stream channel elevation; the part of a dam or weir over which the water flows.

overfall dam: A dam constructed to allow water to overflow its crest.

overfire air: Air forced into the top of an incinerator or boiler to fan the flames.

overflow standpipe: A standpipe located in a dam or other structure at an elevation that allows removal of excess water, preventing overflow.

overgrazed range: A range that has lost its productive potential because of overgrazing.

overgrazing: Grazing so heavy that it impairs future forage production and causes deterioration through damage to plants or soil, or both.

overhaul: Transportation of excavated material beyond a specified haul limit, usually expressed in cubic yard stations (one cubic yard hauled 100 feet).

overland flow: Water that travels over the ground surface to a point of concentration where turbulent flow occurs; also called surface runoff. See *runoff.*

overlap: The amount by which one photograph includes the same area as covered by another, customarily expressed as a percentage; that area of a map or chart that overlaps the same geographical area on an adjoining map or chart. An area included within two surveys of record, which by record are described as having one or more common boundary lines with no inclusion of identical parts.

overlay: A printing or drawing on a transparent or translucent medium at the same scale as a map, chart, or other graphic, to show details not appearing, or requiring special emphasis, on the original; (lithography) additional data, or a pattern, printed after the other features.

overpopulation: A population density that exceeds the capacity of the environment to supply the health requirements of the individual organism.

overseeding: A population density that exceeds the capacity of the environment to supply the health requirements of the individual organism.

overstocked (forestry): A condition in a stand or forest indicating more trees than normal or that full stocking would require.

overstocking: Placing a number of animals on a given area that will result in overuse at the end of the planned grazing period.

overstory: The portion of the trees in a forest stand forming the upper crown cover. See *understory.*

overtopped: Trees with crowns entirely below the general level of the crown cover receiving little or no direct light from above or from the sides.

overturn: The period of mixing (turnover), by top to bottom circulation, of previously stratified water masses. This phenomenon may occur in spring and/or fall; the result is a uniformity of physical and chemical properties of the water at all depths. See *thermal stratification, spring overturn, fall overturn.*

overuse: Excessive use of the current year's growth, resulting in range deterioration or overgrazing, if continued.

own-root plants: Plants that have been grown from own cuttings or layerings, thus producing their own roots; in contrast to graftage.

oxic horizon: See *diagnostic horizons.*

oxidant: The ability of some oxygen containing compounds to oxidize other compounds. Specific examples include ozone, peroxyacetyl nitrates, and nitrogen dioxide.

oxidation: Combination with oxygen; addition of oxygen or other atom or group; removal of hydrogen or other atom or group.

oxidation ditch: A shaped ditch, usually oval, with a revolving drum-like aerator which circulates the liquid within it and supplies air to it, to reduce the organic material by aerobic action.

oxidation pond: A man made lake or pond in which organic wastes are reduced by bacterial action.

Often oxygen is bubbled through the pond to speed the process.

oxidation-reduction potential: The electric potential required to transfer electrons from one compound or element (the oxidant) to another compound (the reductant); used as a qualitative measure of the state of oxidation in water treatment systems.

oxidizing agent: A substance capable of accepting electrons from another substance and, thereby, being reduced.

Oxisols: See *soil classification.*

oxygen debt: A temporary phenomenon that occurs in an organism when available oxygen is inadequate to supply the respiratory demand. During such a period the metabolic processes result in the accumulation of breakdown products that are not oxidized until sufficient oxygen becomes available.

oxygen demand: The oxygen required by all the biological and chemical processes that occur within a pond.

oxygen deficit: The difference between observed oxygen concentration and the amount that would theoretically be present at 100 percent saturation for existing conditions of temperature and pressure.

ozonation/ozonator: Application of ozone to water for disinfection or for taste and odor control. The ozonator is the device that does this.

ozone (O_3): A pungent, colorless, toxic gas; one component of photochemical smog.

ozone depletion: Destruction of the stratospheric ozone layer which shields the earth from ultraviolet radiation harmful to

life. This destruction of ozone is caused by the breakdown of certain chlorine and/or bromine containing compounds (chlorofluorocarbons or halons), which break down when they reach the stratosphere and then catalytically destroy ozone molecules.

ozone hole: A thinning break in the stratospheric ozone layer. Designation of amount of such depletion as an "ozone hole" is made when the detected amount of depletion exceeds fifty percent. Seasonal ozone holes have been observed over both the Antarctic and Arctic regions, part of Canada, and the extreme northeastern United States.

ozone layer: A region of the upper atmosphere (around 18 miles or 30 kilometers altitude) where the ultraviolet component of sunshine generate ozone; the ozone layer shields the surface of the earth from harmful radiation.

P

package plant: A prefabricated or pre-built waste water treatment plant.

packaging materials: Any of a variety of papers, cardboard, metals, wood, paperboard, and plastics used in the manufacture of containers for foods and household and industrial products.

packed bed scrubber: An air pollution control device in which emissions pass through alkaline water to neutralize hydrogen chloride gas.

packed tower: A pollution control device that forces dirty air through a tower packed with crushed rock or wood chips while liquid is sprayed over the packing material. The pollutants in the air stream either dissolve or chemically react with the liquid.

palatability: Plant characteristics or conditions that stimulate a selective response by animals.

palatable water: Water, at a desirable temperature, that is free from objectionable tastes, odors, colors, and turbidity.

paleoflood: Paleoflood peak discharges are estimated using geology, fluvial, geomorphology, and stratigraphic records. Geologic information is used to determine flood depths, carbon 14 dating techniques are typically used to determine the time frame when these depths were reached, and hydraulic models, such as step backwater techniques, are used to determine the associated flow given the depth. These floods are used to extend gage records. Floods that have happened approximately 200 to 10,000 years ago can be estimated.

paleoflood data: Paleoflood data include two broad categories: fluvial geomorphic evidence and botanical evidence. Paleoflood data are distinguished from both historical and systematic (conventional) flood data by lack of human observation, regardless of the time of occurrence.

paleoflood hydrology: The study of past or ancient floods which occurred prior to the time of human observation or direct measurement by modern hydrologic procedures. The study of the movements of water and sediment in channels before the time of continuous hydrologic records or direct measurements.

paleosol: A buried soil, particularly one developed during interglacial periods and subsequently covered by younger materials.

palustrine: Pertaining to marsh.

pan: Horizon or layer in soil that is strongly compacted, indurated, or very high in clay content. See caliche, claypan, duripan, fragipan, hardpan, orstein.

pan evaporation: Evaporative water losses from a standardized pan. Pan evaporation is sometimes used to estimate crop evapotranspiration and assist in irrigation scheduling.

pan, pressure or induced: A subsurface horizon or soil layer having a high bulk density and a lower total porosity than the soil directly above or below it as a result of pressure applied by normal tillage operations or by other artificial means, frequently referred to as plow, pan, plowsole, tillage pan, or traffic pan.

paper: In a general sense, all kinds of matted or felted sheets of fiber formed on a fine screen from a water suspension. More specifically, paper is one of two broad subdivisions (the other being paperboard) of the general term paper. Paper, usually lighter in basis weight, thinner, and more flexible than paperboard, is used largely for printing, writing, wrapping, and sanitary purposes.

paperboard: Relatively heavier in basis weight, thicker, and more rigid than paper. There are three broad classes of paper board: (1) container board, (2) boxboard, and (3) special types such as automobile board, building board, and tube board.

paperstock: A general term used to designate waste papers that have been sorted or segregated at the source into various recognized grades. It is a principle ingredient in the manufacture of certain types of paperboard.

paralithic contact (As used in the Soil Classification System of the National Cooperative Soil Survey in the United States): A boundary between soil and continuous coherent underlying material that has a hardness of less than three (Mohs scale). When moist, the underlying material can be dug with a spade and chunks will disperse in water with 15 hours shaking. Example, shale. See *lithic contact.*

parallax: The apparent displacement of the position of a body, with respect to a reference point or system, caused by a shift in the point of observation; the apparent displacement between objects on the earth's surface due to their difference in elevations.

parallel (cartography): A circle on the surface of the earth, parallel to the plane of the equator and connecting all points of equal latitude, or a circle parallel to the primary great circle of a sphere or spheroid; also, a closed curve approximately such a circle.

parameter: Units of information, supplied where required, to provide additional definition or data.

paraquat: A standard herbicide used to kill various types of crops, including marijuana. Causes lung damage if smoke from the crop is inhaled.

parasite: An organism that lives on or in a host organism during all or part of its existence. Nourishment is obtained at the expense of the host.

parent material (soils): The unconsolidated, more or less chemically weathered mineral or organic matter from which the solum of soils has developed by pedogenic processes. The C-horizon may or may not consist of materials similar to those from which the A- and B-horizons developed.

parity: Measure of the degree of comparison between farm produce prices or farm incomes and nonfarm prices or nonfarm incomes.

parity price: Price per bushel (or pound or bale) that would be necessary for a bushel today to buy the same quantity of goods (from a standard list) that a bushel would have bought in the 1910 to 1914 base period at prices prevailing then; oversimplified, it is the price per bushel of wheat that farmers would need today to buy a suit of clothes with the same number of bushels that it took in 1910 to 1914.

parity ratio: The ratio of the index of prices received by farmers to the parity index. park: An area dedicated to recreation use and generally characterized by its natural, historic, and landscape features. It is used for both passive and active forms of recreation and may be designed to serve the residents of a neighborhood, community, county, state, region, or nation.

park: An area dedicated to recreational used and generally characterized by its natural, historic and landscape features. It is used for both passive and active forms of recreation and may be designed to serve the residents of a neighborhood, community, county, state, region, or nation.

Parshall measuring flume: See *Venturi flume.*

partial-duration series: A statistical grouping or graph involving all rates or volumes for a period of record that are greater than some selected minimum. In contrast, an annual series is a graph or tabulation in which only the maximum value for each year is included.

particle displacement: The difference between the initial position of a soil particle and any later temporary position during shaking.

particle count: Results of a microscopic examination of treated water with a special "particle counter" that classifies suspended particles by number and size.

particle size: The effective diameter of a particle measured by sedimentation, sieving, or micrometric methods.

particle size analysis: Determination of the amounts of different particle sizes in a soil sample, usually by sedimentation, sieving, micrometry, or combinations of these methods.

particle size classes for family groupings: (As used in the Soil Classification System of the National Cooperative Soil Survey in the United States): Various particle size classes are applied to arbitrary control sections that vary according to the depth of the soil, presence or absence of argillic horizons, depth to paralithic or lithic contacts, fragipans, duripans, and petrocalcic horizons. No single set of particle size classes is appropriate as a family grouping for all kinds of soil. The classification tabulated below provides a choice of either seven or eleven particle size classes. This choice permits relatively fine distinctions in soils if texture is important and broader groupings if texture is not susceptible to precise measurement or if the use of narrowly defined classes produces undesirable groupings.

fragmental: Stones, cobbles, gravel, and coarse sand, with fines too few to fill interstices larger than one millimeter.

sandy skeletal: More than 35 percent, by volume, coarser than two millimeters, with enough fines to fill interstices larger than one millimeter; fraction less than two millimeters is as defined for particle size class five.

loamy skeletal: More than 35 percent, by volume, coarser than two millimeters, with enough fines to fill interstices larger than one millimeter; fraction less than two millimeters is as defined for particle size class siz.

clayey skeletal: More than 35 percent, by volume, coarser than two millimeters, with enough fines to fill interstices larger than one millimeter; fraction less than two millimeters is as defined for particle size class seven.

sandy: Sands, except very fine sand, and loamy sands, except loamy very fine sand.

loamy or coarse loamy: With less than 18 percent clay and more than 15 percent coarser than very fine sand (including coarse fragments up to 7.5 centimeters).

fine loamy: With more than 18 percent clay but less than 35 percent clay and more than 15 percent coarser than very fine

sand (including coarse fragments up to 7.5 centimeters).

coarse silty: With less than 18 percent clay and less than 15 percent coarser than very fine sand (including coarse fragments up to 7.5 centimeters).

fine silty: With more than 18 percent clay and less than 35 percent clay and less than 15 percent coarser than very fine sand (including coarse fragments up to 7.5 centimeters).

clayey or fine: With more than 35 percent clay but less than 60 percent clay.

very fine: With more than 60 percent clay.

particle size distribution: The amount of the various soil separates in a soil sample, usually expressed as weight percentages. See *soil texture, particle size classes for family groupings.*

particulate matter: Solid particles, such as ash, that are released from combustion process in exhaust gases.

particulate organic matter: Particles of living or dead organic matter that are suspended in water.

particulates: Finely divided solid or liquid particles in the air or in an emission. Particulates include dust, smoke, fumes, mist, spray, and fog.

partition coefficient: Measure of the sorption phenomenon, whereby a pesticide is divided between the soil and water phase; also referred to as adsorption partition coefficient.

part-owner-operators: Those who operate land which they own and rent additional land from others.

part-owner-operators-landlords:

Those who operate a portion of the land they own and rent out some land.

parts per million: A means of expressing concentration, usually by weigh, as one portion of a substance in 999,999 portions of a second substance; for example, one pound of lime in 999,999 pounds of water; one part per million equals one milligram per liter.

passive earth pressure: The maximum value of earth pressure. This condition exists when a soil mass is compressed sufficiently to cause its internal shearing resistance along a potential failure surface to be completely mobilized.

passive treatment walls: Technology in which a chemical reaction takes place when contaminated groundwater comes in contact with a barrier such as limestone or a wall containing iron filings.

pasture: An area devoted to the production of forage, introduced or native, and harvested by grazing.

pasture improvement: Any practice of grazing, mowing, fertilizing, liming, seeding, scattering droppings, contour furrowing, or other methods of management designed to improve vegetation for grazing purposes.

pasture management: The application of practices to keep pasture plants growing actively over as long a period as possible so that they will provide palatable feed of high nutritive value; to encourage the growth of desirable grasses and legumes while crowding out weeds, brush, and inferior grasses.

pasture planting: Establishing adapted herbaceous species on land to be treated and grazed as tame pasture.

pasture planting: Establishing adapted herbacious species on land to be treated and grazed as tame pasture.

pasture, tame: Grazing lands, planted to primarily introduced or domesticated native forage species, that receive periodic renovation and/or cultural treatments such as tillage, fertilization, mowing, weed control, and irrigation. Not in rotation with crops.

patch: In landscape ecology, a particular unit with identifiable boundaries which differs from its surroundings in one or more ways. These can be a function of vegetative composition, structure, age or some combination of the three.

pathogen: An organism capable of producing disease.

pattern: In a photo image, the regularity and characteristic placement of tones or textures; some descriptive adjectives for patterns are regular, irregular, random, concentric, radial, and rectangular; the relations between any more-or-less independent parameters of a response; for example, the pattern in the frequency domain of the response from an object.

pattern recognition: The automated process through which unidentified patterns can be classified into a limited number of discrete classes through comparison with other class-defining patterns or characteristics.

payment acres: Equal to 85 percent of the base acres for calculating direct and counter-cyclical payments under the provisions of the 2002 Farm Act.

PCB: See *polychlorinated biphenyls.*

peak discharge: See *flood peak.*

peak use rate: Maximum periodic rate of consumptive use (evapotranspiration) of water by plants.

peat: Unconsolidated soil material consisting largely of undecomposed or only slightly decomposed organic matter accumulated under conditions of excessive moisture. See *organic soil materials.*

peat soil: An organic soil in which the organic matter is not yet decomposed or is slightly decomposed (US usage); an organic soil containing more than 50 percent organic matter. See *peat, muck, muck soil.*

pebble: See *coarse fragments.*

pecuniary externalities: Changes in income of persons or firms resulting from direct outputs of an action by a different person or firm.

ped: A unit of soil structure, such as an aggregate, crumb, prism, block, or granule, formed by natural processes. See *clod.*

pediment: A gently inclined erosion surface of low relief, typically developed in arid or semiarid regions at the foot of a receding mountain slope. The pediment may be bare or mantled by a thin layer of alluvium in transit to the adjoining basin.

pedogenic: Having to do with the factors and processes of soil formation.

pedon (As used in the Soil Classification System of the National Cooperative Soil Survey in the United States): The smallest volume that can be

called "a soil." It has three dimensions. It extends downward to the depth of plant roots or to the lower limit of the genetic soil horizons. Its lateral cross section is roughly hexagonal and ranges from one to ten square meters in size depending on the variability in the horizons.

pelagic: Living in the water column, well above the bottom and some distance from land, as do oceanic fish or birds.

pelagic zone: The open sea, away from the shore; comparable with the limnetic zone of lakes.

percent moisture content (solid waste): The percent of moisture contained in solid waste; it can be calculated on a dry or wet basis, as follows:

1. Wet = 100 (water content of sample)

Dry weight of sample = water content of sample

2. Dry = 100(water content of sample)

Dry weight of sample

percent use: Grazing use of current growth, usually expressed as a percent of weight removed.

percent saturatiuon: The amount of a substance that is dissolved in a solution compared to the amount that could be dissolved in it.

perched water: Zone of unpressurized water held above the water table by impermeable rock or sediment.

perched water table: See *water table, perched.*

percolation: The downward movement of water through soil, especially the downward flow of water in saturated or nearly saturated soil at hydraulic gradients of the order of 1.0 or less.

percolation test: A measurement of the percolation of water in soil to determine the suitability of different soils for development including private sewage systems such as septic tanks and drain fields.

percolating water: Water that passes through rocks or soil under the force of gravity.

perennial plant: A plant that normally lives three or more years.

perennial stream: A stream that normally has water in its channel at all times.

pergelic: A soil temperature regime that has mean annual soil temperatures of less than 0 degrees C. Permafrost is present.

perigee: The point that is nearest to the earth in the orbit of an earth-orbiting satellite; opposite of the apogee.

periodic drift: Drift of bottom organisms at regular or predictable intervals such as diurnal, seasonal, etc. See *drift organisms, catastrophic drift.*

periphyton: Organisms that grow on underwater surfaces, including algae, bacteria, fungi, protozoa, and other organisms.

perlite: A lightweight, granular material made of a volcanic mineral treated by heat and water so that it expands like popcorn; used as or in growing media

periphyton: Microscopic organisms attached to and growing on the bottom of a waterway or on submerged objects. Also called aufwuchs.

permafrost: Permanently frozen material underlying the solum; A perennially frozen soil horizon.

permanent pasture: Grazing land occupied by perennial pasture plants or by self seeding annuals, usually both, which remains unplowed for many years. See *rotation pasture.*

permanent wilting percentage: See *wilting point.*

permeability: Capacity for transmitting a fluid. It is measured by the rate at which a fluid of standard viscosity can move through material in a given interval of time under a given hydraulic gradient.

permeability, soil: The quality of a soil horizon that enables water or air to move through it. The permeability of a soil may be limited by the presence of one nearly impermeable horizon even though the others are permeable.

permissible velocity (hydraulics): The highest velocity at which water may be carried safely in a channel or other conduit; the highest velocity that can exist through a substantial length of conduit and not cause scour of the channel; also called safe or noneroding velocity.

pest: A plant, animal, or thing that is troublesome or annoying.

pesticide: Any chemical agent used for control of specific organisms; such as insecticides, herbicides, fungicides, etc.

pest management: Determining weed, insect, disease, and other threats to crop growth, yield, and quality and what preventive or remedial actions to take against those pests (including whether to plant genetically modified varieties with pest management qualities), mindful of food and worker safety and environmental impacts.

pesticide tolerance: Legal, scientifically determined limit for the amount of residue that can be permitted in or on a harvested food or feed crop as a result of a chemical applied to control pests; usually such level are set well below the point where they are harmful to consumers.

petiole: The stalk or stem of a leaf.

petrocalcic horizon: See *diagnostic horizons*.

petroleum derivatives: Chemicals formed when gasoline breaks down in contact with groundwater.

P factor: See *universal soil loss equation*.

pH: A numerical measure of acidity or hydrogen ion activity. Neutral is pH 7.0. All pH values below 7.0 are acid, and all above 7.0 are alkaline. See *reaction, soil*.

pH$_c$: The calculated pH that water would have if it were in equilibrium with calcium carbonate.

phase, soil: A subdivision of a soil taxon, usually a soil series or other unit of classification based on characteristics that affect the use and management of the soil but which do not vary sufficiently to differentiate it as a separate soil series. A variation in a property or characteristic, such as degree of slope, degree of erosion, content of stones, texture of the surface, etc. Phases of soil series are the major components of the soil-mapping units shown on detailed soil maps in the United States.

phenology: The study of the time of appearance of characteristic periodic events in the life cycles of organisms in nature and how these events are influenced by environmental factors.

phenols: The study of periodic biological phenomenon, such as flowering, seeding, etc., especially as related to climate.

phenotype: The appearance of an individual as contrasted with genetic makeup or genotype.

phenoxys: Broadleaf herbicides that cause abnormal growth by upsetting the plant's hormone balance; rapidly translocated, have both preemergence and postemergence activity, and are taken up by foliage or roots. See *herbicide*.

pheromone: A substance secreted by an insect that influences the behavior of the same or another insect species.

phosphate or potash fixation (soils): The process or processes by which these two elements are converted from a soluble or exchangeable form to a much less soluble or nonexchangeable form in a soil.

phosphates: Salts or esters of phosphoric acid.

phosphorus: An element that is essential to life but contributes to an increased trophic level of water bodies.

phosphorus cycle: The sequence of biological, chemical, and other changes undergone by phosphorus wherein it is used by living organisms, liberated upon the death and decomposition of the organism, and converted to its original state of oxidation.

phosphorus fixation: See *fixed phosphorus*.

photic zone: See *euphotic zone*.

photochemical process: The chemical alterations caused by radiant light energy acting on various gases in the atmosphere.

photochemical oxidants: Secondary pollutants formed by the action of sunlight on the oxides of nitrogen and hydrocarbons in the air; the primary contributors to photochemical smog.

photochemical smog: A combination of photochemical gases, liquids, and particles in a polluted atmosphere.

photogrammetry: (general) The science or art of obtaining reliable measurements from photographic images; (cartography) the science of preparing charts and maps from aerial photographs using stereoscopic equipment and methods; also called aerial photogrammetry; stereophotogrammetry.

photograph: A picture formed by the action of light on a base material coated with a sensitized solution that is chemically treated to fix the image points at the desired density.

photo map: A mosaic to which place names, marginal data, and other map information, usually including a grid or coordinate system, have been added.

photosynthesis: The synthesis of carbohydrates from carbon dioxide and water by chlorophyll, using light as energy with oxygen as a by product.

phototriangulation: The process for the extension of horizontal and/or vertical control whereby the measurements of angels and/or distances on overlapping photographs are related into a special solution using the perspective principles of the photographs; generally, this process involves using aerial photographs and is called aerotriangulation, aerial triangulation, or photogrammetric triangulation.

photovoltaic cells: Photovoltaic cells are designed and engineered to convert solar radiation into usable energy. They are considered a "renewable" form of energy and can be installed on rooftops in conjunction with cool roof materials.

photovoltaic conversion: Direct transformation of solar radiation into electicity.

phreatic line: The line marking the upper surface of the zone of water saturation in the soil.

phreatic surface: The free surface of water seeping at atmospheric pressure through soil or rock.

phreatophyte: A plant deriving its water from subsurface sources; commonly used to describe non-beneficial, water loving vegetation.

phthalates: A class of organic compounds containing phthalic acid esters $[C_6H_4(COOR)^2]$ and derivatives. Used as plasticizers in plastics. Also used in many other products (such as detergents, cosmetics) and industrial processes (such as defoaming agents during paper and paperboard manufacture, and dielectrics in capacitors).

physiography: A description of the surface features of the Earth, with an emphasis on the origin of landforms.

phytophagous: Plant eating.

phytoplankton: Unattached microscopic plants of plankton, subject to

movement by wave or current
action. See *plankton, zooplankton*.

planned grazing system   **193**

phytoplankton die-off: An abrupt, massive mortality of phytoplankton resulting from natural or manmade causes.

phytotoxic: Any chemical agent injurious to vegetation.

piezometer: A tube for measuring the pressure (piezometric) head or potential of a fluid.

piezometric surface: The imaginary surface to which water in a well will rise above an aquifer.

pine straw: Dead pine needles that are frequently used for a mulch.

piping: Removal of soil material through subsurface flow channels or "pipes" developed by seepage water. pit: See dugout pond.

pistil: The female part of a flower; comprised of the ovary, stigma, and style.

pistillate: A flower that has a pistil but no stamens, or a plant or variety whose flowers have this characteristic.

pit: (mining) Used in reference to a specifically describable area of open-cut mining; may be used to refer to only that part of the open-cut mining area from which coal is actively removed or may refer to entire contiguous mind area; (range) See *dugout*.

pilot tube: Device for measuring the velocity head of flowing fluid.

pitting: Making shallow pits of suitable capacity and distribution to retain water from rainfall or snowmelt on rangeland or pasture; small cavities in a surface created by corrosion, cavitation, or subatmospheric pressures.

pixel: A data element having both spatial and spectral aspects; the spatial variable define the apparent size of the resolution cell (i.e., the area on the ground represented by the data values), and the spectral variable defines the intensity of the spectral response for that cell in a particular channel; derived from "picture element."

plain: Level of gently rolling land, usually below 2,000 feet (610 m) in elevation.

planetable: A field device for plotting the lines of a survey directly from observations; consists essentially of a drawing board mounted on a tripod, with a leveling device designed as part of the board and tripod; used in combination with an alidade and stadia or Philadelphia leveling rod.

planimeter: An instrument used for measuring the area of any plane figure by passing a tracer around its perimeter or boundary line.

planimeteric map: See *map*.

plankton: Suspended, floating, or weakly swimming microscopic plants and animals in the water that provide a basis for the aquatic food chain. See *phytoplankton, zooplankton*.

plankton boom: A large quantity of plankton giving water a definite color; pond water usually appears green because the majority of plankton organisms are greenish, but plankton blooms may also appear black, yellow, red, brown, or blue-green.

planned grazing system: A system of grazing in which two or more grazing units are alternately rested in a planned sequence over a period of years. The resting period may be throughout the year or during the growing season of the key species.

planned unit development (PUD): A special zone in some zoning ordinances which permits a unit of land under control of a single developer to be used for a variety of uses and densities, subject to review and approval by the local governing body. The location of the zone is usually decided on a case by case basis.

plant analysis: Estimation of the plant-nutrient status of a plant or the plant-nutrient requirements of the soil for producing a crop through chemical analyses of plants or parts of plants.

plantation, forest: A stand of trees established by planting young trees or by sowing seed.

plant competition: The struggle among plants for the available light, moisture, and soil nutrients.

plant food: The organic compounds elaborated within the plant to nourish its cells. The term is a frequent synonym for plant nutrients, particularly in the fertilizer trade.

plant form: Each species' unique expression that is determined within a plant to nourish its cells; a frequent synonym for plant nutrients, particularly in the fertilizer trade.

plant grown substances: Chemicals that affect the rate and character of the growth of plants.

plant hybridization: To hybridize plants by crossing inbreds of special selections of plant species.

plant indicator: See *indicator*.

planting saucer: The saucer shape of the soil (man-made) surrounding the immediate area of a newly planted tree, for the purpose of water concentration; also called planting basin.

planting stock: Young plants, either nursery stock or wildings, for planting.

plant material center: A place where plants are assembled and their value and use in a conservation program is determined. This includes both domestic collections and plant introductions. Plants are assembled; their performance is evaluated; selections are made and increased for field testing; varieties are named and released; and foundation quality seed and/or stock is produced and distributed to cooperative seed growers and nurseries for commercial production and use.

plant nutrients: The elements or groups of elements taken in by a plant which are essential to its growth and used in elaboration of its food and tissues; includes nutrients obtained from fertilizer ingredients. See *essential element, macronutrients, micronutrients*.

plant residue: See crop residue, humus, litter, mor, mulch, soil organic matter.

plantsman: An individual who has amassed considerable knowledge about plant materials through identification, experimentation, etc.

plant succession: The process of vegetation development whereby an area becomes successively occupied by different plant communities of higher ecological order.

plastic relief map: See *map*.

plastics: Man made materials containing primarily carbon and hydrogen, with lesser amounts of oxygen, nitrogen, and various organic and inorganic compounds. Plastics, technically referred to as "polymers," are normally solid in their finished state, but at some stage in their manufacture, under sufficient heat and pressure, they will flow sufficiently to be molded into desired shape. Thermoplastics, such as polyethylene, polyvinyl chloride (PVC), polystyrene, and polypropylene, become soft when exposed to heat and pressure and harden when cooled. Thermosetting plastics, such as phenotic and polyester, are set to permanent shapes when heat and pressure are applied to them during forming, and reheating will not soften these materials.

plastic soil: A soil capable of being molded or deformed continuously and permanently by relatively moderate pressure. See *consistence*.

plat: A plan or map showing land lines or subdivisions usually with few, if any, other features.

plateau: A level, elevated land area, usually between 2,000 and 6,000 feet (610-1,830 m) in elevation.

platform: (remote sensing) A vehicle or object used to take remote sensing measurements, such as satellites, airplanes, balloons, kites, or rockets.

platy: See *soil structure types*.

playa: A shallow central basin of a plain where water gathers after a rain and is evaporated.

pleach: To train and interlace the tops of trees or other plants to form an archway over an alley or walkway.

plinthite: A nonindurated mixture of iron and aluminum oxides, clay, quartz, and other dilvents that commonly occurs as red soil mottles usually arranged in platy, polygonal,

or reticulate patterns. Plinthite changes irreversibly to ironstone hardpans or irregular aggregates on exposure to repeated wetting and drying.

plot plain: A map of an area with all existing objects shown to scale. See *site plan*.

plow layer: The soil ordinarily moved in tillage; equivalent to surface soil or surface layer.

plow pan: See *pan, pressure or induced*.

plow plant: Plowing and planting a crop in one operation, with no additional seedbed preparation.

plowsole: See *pan, pressure or induced*.

plume: The smoke pattern made by a visible emission from a flue, stack, or chimney.

plutonium: A heavy, fissionable, radioactive metallic element with atomic number 94; Plutonium-239 occurs in nature in trace amounts only; however, it can be produced as a by-product of the fission reaction in a uranium-fueled nuclear reactor and can be recovered for future use.

point: A feature on a map such as a nest that is a point location with no real area (acreage) involved.

point gage: Sharp point attached to graduate scale, staff, or vernier for accurate measurement of the surface elevation of water or soil.

point-of-disinfectant application: The point where disinfectant is applied and water downstream of that point is not subject to recontamination by surface water runoff.

point row: A row that forms an angle with another row instead of paralleling it to the end of the field; a row that "comes to a point," ending part way across the field instead of at the edge of the field.

point source pollution: A stationary pollution source, such as a smoke stack or discharge pipe See nonpoint pollution.

poisonous plant: A plant containing or producing substances that cause sickness, death, or a deviation from the normal state of health of animals.

pollen: The dust-like grains, containing male sex cells, produced on the anthers of flowers.

pollination: The transfer of pollen from the stamens of staminate flower to the pistil or pistillate flower.

police power: The state's inherent right to regulate an individual's conduct or property to protect the health, safety, welfare, and morals of the community.

pollutant: Any introduced substance that limits a resource use for a specific purpose.

pollution: The condition caused by the presence in the environment of substances of such character and in such quantities that the quality of the environment is impaired or rendered offensive to life. See *air pollution, water pollution.* Can be subdivided as follows:

point source: Pollution arising from a well-defined origin, such as a discharge from an industrial plant or runoff from a beef cattle feedlot.

nonpoint source: Pollution arising from an ill-defined and diffuse source, such as runoff from cultivated fields, grazing land, or urban areas.

polychlorinated biphenyls (PCB): A group of organic compounds used in the manufacture of plastics. They are toxic, persistent, and bioaccumulate in the environment and are frequently confused with a pesticide.

polyconic map projection: See *map projection.*

polycyclic aromatic hydrocarbon (PAH): A class of organic compounds with a fused-ring aromatic structure. PAHs result from incomplete combustion of organic carbon (including wood), municipal solid waste, and fossil fuels, as well as from natural or anthropogenic introduction of uncombusted coal and oil. PAHs include benzo(a)pyrene, fluoranthene, and pyrene.

polygon: A mapped feature such as a wetland with curved or straight edges and area; used in vector coverages.

polypedon (As used in the Soil Classification System of the National Cooperative Soil Survey in the United States): Two or more contiguous pedons, all of which are within the defined limits of a single soil series. In early stages of development, called a soil individual.

polyvinyl chloride (PVC): Common plastic material that is used for pipe, utensils, and household items that releases hydrochloric acid when burned.

pomology: The science of cultivating plants for their fruit.

pond, wastewater stabilization: An impoundment area for water, natural or artificial, into which untreated or partially treated wastewater is discharged and in which natural purification and stabilization processes take place under the influence of sunlight, air, and biological activity. See *lagoon*.

pools: Areas of a stream where the velocity of current is reduced. The reduced velocity provides a favorable habitat for plankton. Silts and other loose materials that settle to the bottom of pools are favorable for burrowing forms of benthos. See *riffle*.

poorly graded soil (engineering): A soil material consisting mainly of particles nearly the same size. Because there is little difference in size of the particles in poorly graded soil material, density usually can be increased only slightly by compaction.

pore space: Total space not occupied by soil particles in a bulk volume of soil, commonly expressed as a percentage.

porosity: The degree to which the total volume of a soil, sediment, or rock is permeated with pores or cavities, generally expressed as a percentage of the whole volume unoccupied by solid particles. See *air porosity, capillary porosity*.

portal: The surface entrance to an underground mine.

positive displacement pump: Pump that moves a fixed quantity of fluid with each stroke or revolution.

posted area: Property on which the owners have posted signs in clear view. Designed to prevent certain uses of land.

post emergence (crop production): Application of chemicals, fertilizers, or other materials and operations associated with crop

production after the crop has emerged through the soil surface.

potable water: Water suitable for drinking or cooking, from both health and aesthetics considerations.

potamon zone: Stream reach at lower elevations characterized by reduced flow, higher temperature, and lower dissolved oxygen levels. See *rithron zone*.

Pot-bound: The condition of a potted plant whose roots have become densely matted; also called root-bound.

potential natural plant community: See *climax*.

potentiometric surface: The surface to which water in an aquifer can rise by hydrostatic pressure.

power: The rate at which work is done or energy is transferred; measured in units of work per unit time; typical units are horsepower and watt.

prairie: A tract of level to hilly land that has a dominance of grasses and (orbs, has a scarcity of shrubs, and is treeless. The natural plant community consists of various mixtures of tall, mid, and short growing native species, also known as true prairie, mixed prairie, and shortgrass prairie, respectively.

precast concrete: A plain or reinforced concrete element cast in other than its final position in the structure.

precipitate: A solid which separates from a solution because of some chemical or physical change; the formation of such a solid.

precipitation: A general term for all

forms of falling moisture, including rain, snow, hail, sleet.

precipitators: Devices using mechanical, chemical, or electrical means for colleting particulates.

precision conservation: getting the right practices, in the right places, at the right time, and at the right scale.

predator: An animal that lives by capturing and devouring other animals.

pre emergence (crop production): Application of chemicals, fertilizers, or other materials and operations associated with crop production before the crop has emerged through the soil surface.

preemergence herbicide: Herbicide applied to bare ground after planting the crop but prior to the crop sprouting above ground to kill or significantly retard the growth of weed seedlings.

prescribed burning: The deliberate use of fire under conditions where the area to be burned is predetermined and the intensity of the fire is controlled.

prescribed rights, water: See *water rights*.

preservice training: Training given to individuals before they graduate and enter on professional duty.

pressure head: See *head*.

pressure, static: In flowing air, the total pressure minus velocity pressure, pushing equally in all directions.

pressure, total: In flowing air, the sum of the static and velocity pressures.

pressure, velocity: In flowing air, the pressure due to velocity and density of air.

prestressed concrete: Reinforced concrete in which there have been introduced internal stresses of such magnitude and distribution that the stresses resulting from loads are counteracted to a desired degree.

pretreatment: Any process used to reduce pollution of wastewater before it is introduced into a main sewer system or delivered to a treatment plant for a substantial reduction of pollution load.

prevalent level samples: Air samples taken under normal conditions (also known as ambient background samples).

prevention over mitigation or restoration: The importance of protecting existing, relatively intact biological systems cannot be overstated, for it is these systems that will ultimately provide the biota and other natural materials for future restorations.

previsual (remote sensing): Detectable before it is visible to the human eye or by remote sensing n the visible portion of the electromagnetic spectrum; plants under water stress are to some degree characterized by a breakdown in leaf structure that may affect reflectance in the infrared portion of the spectrum.

prey: An animal taken by a predator as food.

prices–paid index: The index of prices farmers pay for goods and services used for producing farm products and in family living.

prices–received index: An index of average prices received by farmers for 55 of the most important products sold.

primary air pollutants: Emissions directly evolved from an identifiable source of pollution, such as fluorides from smoke stacks.

primary effect: An effect where the stressor acts directly on the ecological component of interest, not on other parts of the ecosystem.

primary materials: Virgin or new materials used for manufacturing basic products. Examples include wood pulp, iron ore, silica sand, and bauxite.

primary productivity: The rate at which organic matter is stored by photosynthetic and chemosynthetic activity of producer organisms (autotrophs), e.g., grams per day.

primary project benefits: In water resource development, the value of products and services directly resulting from the project; net of all associated cost incurred in their realization.

primary tillage: Tillage which constitutes the major soil manipulation operation.

primary waste treatment: The first stage in wastewater treatment in which substantially all floating or settleable solids are mechanically removed by screening and sedimentation.

prime agricultural land: Land that is best suited for producing food, feed, forage, fiber, and oilseed crops, and also available for those uses; includes cropland, pastureland, rangeland, forest lands, but not urbanized land or water. It has the soil quality, growing season, and moisture supply needed to produce sustained high yields of crops economically when treated and managed, including water management, according to modern agricultural methods.

prime meridian: The meridian of longitude 0 degrees, used as the origin for measurement of longitude; the meridian of Greenwich, England, is almost universally used for this purpose.

priming: The first filling or first seasonal filling of a canal, reservoir, or other structure with water; starting the flow, as in a pump or siphon.

primitive area: See *wilderness*.

primitive campground: A campground in a natural area without the benefit of modern facilities or equipment. In some states may have a legal definition.

principal meridian: A cardinal line extending north and south along the astronomical meridian through the initial point, along which areas of land measurement are established.

prismatic soil structure: See *soil structure types*.

private development (recreation): Recreation areas established and operated by private entities.

probable maximum precipitation (PMP): An estimate of the physical upper limit to the amount of precipitation that can fall over a specific area in a given time.

probe: Small diameter rod pushed into the soil to determine depth of water penetration following irrigation or precipitation. See *neutron probe*.

process wastewater: Any water that comes into contact with any raw material, product, byproduct, or waste.

processing: Any method, system, or other treatment designed to change the physical form or chemical content of solid waste.

procumbent: A prostrate plant whose branches usually do not root.

producer (biology): An organism that can use radiant energy to synthesize organic substances from inorganic materials. See *consumers, reducers*.

production expenses: Total cash outlays for production, excluding land ownership costs, plus "non-cash" outlays, such as depreciation.

productivity: The rate at which organic matter is stored in any organism.

productivity, soil: See *soil productivity*.

profile: A vertical section of the surface of the ground, or of underlying strata, or both, along any fixed line. See *soil profile*.

profundal zone: The deep, bottom water area beyond the depth of effective light penetration. All of the lake floor beneath the hypolimnion.

program (computer science): An item-by-item series of statements in programming language, designed to solve a particular problem that has been isolated; programs and their functions are computer software.

project costs: In water resource development, the value of goods and services (land, labor, and materials) used for the establishment, maintenance, and operation of a project together with the value of any net induced adverse effects, whether or not compensated for.

projection: (geometry) The extension of lines or planes to intersect a given surface; the transfer of a point from one surface to a corresponding position on another surface by graphical or analytical methods; (surveying) the extension of a line beyond the points that determine its character and position. The transfer of a series of survey lines to a single theoretical line by a series of lines perpendicular to the theoretical line; in surveying a traverse, a series of measured short line may be projected onto a single long line, connecting, two main survey stations, and the long line is then treated as a measured line of the traverse.

proliferation: Abnormal production of plant parts beyond what is normally terminal growth; a natural method of vegetative self-propagation common to many plants; excessive plant cell division at some point, resulting in an unusual enlargement of some tissues or organs.

propagation: The increase or multiplication of plants by sexual (seeds) or asexual methods such as cuttings, grafts, layers, or meristem culture.

proper grazing use: Grazing ranges and pastures in a manner that will maintain adequate cover for soil protection and maintain or improve the quality and quantity of desirable vegetation.

proper stocking: Stocking the grazing unit to obtain proper grazing use.

prospecting: The removal of overburden, core drilling, construction of roads, or any other disturbance of the surface for the purpose of determining the location, quantity, or quality of the natural mineral deposit.

protection forest: An area wholly or partly covered with woody growth, managed primarily for its beneficial effects on soil and water conservation rather than for wood or forage production.

protoplasm: The living material in cells of plants and animals.

provenance: The geographic source or place of origin of a lot of seed (or pollen); the geographic location to which the parent plant or plants are native and within which their genetic makeup has been developed through natural selection.

provenance test: A progeny test of populations of the same species but of different provenances. Objectives may include the study of their performance under a range of site and climatic conditions, identifying the most desirable provenances for seed or seedling increase, and establishing a collection of biotypes of direct and potential plant breeding value.

pruning (forestry): The removal of live or dead branches from standing trees, usually the lower branches of young trees, and the removal of multiple leaders in plantation trees, for the improvement of the tree or its timber; the cutting away of superfluous growth, including roots, from any plant to improve its development. See *self pruning*.

public access site: A controlled area which affords the public a point of ingress to a particular facility such as a beach, river, pond, or lake.

Public Law 566 projects: Projects authorized by Watershed Protection and Flood Prevention Act (Public Law 566, 83rd U.S. Congress, as amended) that allow the US Department of Agriculture to assist sponsoring local organizations plan and carry our a program for the

development, use, and conservation of the nation's soil and water resources; the primary purpose must be flood prevention, irrigation, or drainage; other purposes such as recreation, fish and wildlife development, municipal and industrial water supply, and other soil and water management measures may also be included; projects must cover a watershed or subwatershed are of not more than 250,000 acres (10,125 ha); no structure providing more than 12,500 acre feet (15.4 million m^3) of floodwater detention capacity or more than 25,000 acre-feet (30.8 million m^3) of total capacity may be included; except for land rights, the program may provide federal cost-sharing of all installation costs ofr flood prevention, and up to 50 percent of installation costs for all other purposes, except municipal and industrial water supply.

public development (recreation): Recreation areas established and operated by a governmental unit in the public interest.

puddled soil: A dense soil dominated by massive or single grain structure, almost impervious to air and water; resulting from handling a soil when it is in a wet, plastic condition so that when it dries it becomes hard and cloddy.

puddling: The act of destroying soil structure; reducing porosity and permeability; sometimes used to reduce leakage of reservoirs and canals.

pulp: Fiber material that is produced by chemical or mechanical means, or a combination or the two, from fibrous cellulose raw material and from which, after suitable treatment, paper and paperboard are made; may include virgin wood pulp, secondary fibers, or rags.

pulping system: A system of equipment used to convert wood and other fibers into a slurry like homogeneous mixture of water and fibers which can be further processed into paper products.

pulpwood: Roundwood cut from trees and prepared primarily for manufacture into wood pulp or wood fiber; does not include chips and sawdust produced as residues of lumber and plywood operations, but does include chips manufactured from roundwood in the forest or at chipmills remote from a pulp mill.

pulverization: The crushing and grinding of material into small pieces.

pump characteristics: Speed-head-discharge-power relations for a given pump.

pump drainage: Any drainage system that uses a pump to convey the water to the outlet channel.

pumped well drain: A well sunk into an aquifer from which water is pumped to lower the water table.

pump efficiency: Ratio of the energy delivered (mass multiplied by head) by the pump to the energy input.

pumping station: A location and apparatus whereby water, sewage, or other liquids are pumped from a lower level to a higher level.

pump stand (irrigation): A vertical pipe extending above ground from a buried pipeline, generally located at the connection of the pump to the buried pipeline.

pupa: An intermediate, usually quiescent, form following the larval stage in insects, and maintained until metamorphosis to the adult stage. See *larva*.

purchase of development rights (PDR): Public agency acquisition of the rights to develop private land; acquired through compensation payments.

pure forest: A forest composed essentially of trees of one species. In practice, a forest in which at least 80 percent of the trees are of one species. Contrast with mixed forest; also called pure timber stand.

pure live seed: The product of the percentage of germination plus the hard seed and the percentage of pure seed, divided by 100.

purging: Removing stagnant air or water from sampling zone or equipment prior to sample collection.

putrefaction: The decomposition of organic matter by microorganisms and oxidation, resulting in odors.

putrescible: Organic matter capable of being decomposed by microorganisms.

pyramidal: A plant shape resembling a pyramid.

pyrite: A yellowish mineral (iron disulfide, FeS^2), generally metallic appearing; also known as fool's gold.

pyrolysis: The process of chemically decomposing an organic substance by heating it in an oxygen deficient atmosphere. High heat is usually applied to the material in a closed chamber evaporating all moisture and breaking down materials into various hydrocarbon gases and carbon like residue.

The gases may be collected with suitable equipment and used or sold. The residue may be further processed into useful materials, such as carbon, sand, and grit, or can be landfilled.

pyrotechnic generator (weather

modification): A type of silver-iodide smoke generator in which the silver iodide forms a part of the pyrotechnic fuel mixture.

Q

quadrangle: A rectangular, or nearly so, area covered by a map or plat, usually bounded by given meridians of longitude and parallels of latitude, sometimes shortened to quad; also called quadrangle map.

quadrant: A quarter of a circle or of its circumference; an arc or angle of 90 degrees.

quadrat: A small plot or sample area, frequently one square meter or one mile acre in size.

quality assurance: Evaluation of quality-control data to allow quantitative determination of the quality of chemical data collected during a study. Techniques used to collect, process, and analyze water samples are evaluated.

quarry: An open pit, mine, or excavation where stone, sand, gravel, or minerals are obtained from open faces, with or without a waste rock overburden.

quench trough: A water-filled trough into which burning residue drops from an incinerator furnace.

quicksand: Sand that is unstable because of upward pressure of water.

quiescent: The temporary cessation of development, movement, or other activity, for example, the pupal stage of a life cycle.

R

R horizon: See *soil horizon*.

raceway: Rectangular fish rearing unit that has a continuous flow of fresh water to maintain suitable oxygen, temperature, and cleanliness for intensive production.

radar: A method, system, or technique, including equipment components, for using beamed, reflected, and timed electromagnetic radiation to detect, locate, and/or track objects, to measure altitude, and to acquire a terrain image; derived from radio detection and ranging.

radiance: The accepted term for radiant flux in power units (watts) and not for flux density per solid angle (watts/cm²sr) as often found in recent publications.

radiation: The emission of fast atomic particles or rays by the nucleus of an atom; some elements are naturally radioactive whole others become radioactive after bombardment with neutron or other particles; three major forms of radiation are alpha, beta, and gamma.

radiation standards: Regulations that include exposure standards, permissible concentrations, and transportation regulations.

radioactivity: The spontaneous decomposition of an atom accompanied by the release of energy.

radiometer: An instrument for quantitatively measuring the intensity of electromagnetic radiation in some band of wavelengths in any part of the electromagnetic spectrum.

radius of influence: See *cone of depression*.

radon: A naturally occurring, colorless, odorless, radioactive gas formed by the disintegration of the element radium; damaging to human lungs when inhaled.

raindrop splash: Primary soil particles and small soil aggregates that are detached and transported with splashing water drops as a result of raindrop impact on the soil.

raindrop erosion: See *raindrop splash*.

rainfall component: That part of the flow of a channel attributed to rain falling directly on the surface of the channel.

rainfall duration: The period of time during which rainfall occurs, exceeds a given intensity, or maintains a given intensity.

rainfall excess (hydraulics): The volume of rainfall that will result in runoff.

rainfall frequency: The frequency,

usually expressed in years, at which a given rainfall intensity and duration can be expected to be equaled or exceeded.

rainfall intensity: The rate at which rain is falling at any given instant, usually expressed in inches per hour.

rain forest: A tropical woodland that has and annual rainfall of at least 100 inches (254cm) and often much more, typically restricted to certain lowland areas.

rainshadow: An area of light rainfall situated on the lee side of a range of mountains or hills.

ranch: An establishment with specific boundaries, together with its lands and improvements, used for the grazing and production of domestic livestock and/or wildlife.

random sample: A sample selected in such a manner that all possible samples of the same size have an equal and independent change of being included.

range: rangeland; and many forestlands that support an understory or periodic cover of herbaceous or shrubby plants suitable for grazing without impairing other forest values; in biology, the geographic area occupied by an organism.

range condition: The present state of the plant community on a range site in relation to the potential natural plant community for that site.

range condition class: One of a series of arbitrary categories used to classify range condition, usually expressed as either excellent, good, fair, or poor.

range condition trend: The direction of change in range condition.

range examiner: A person who

collects and compiles information pertaining to range management and who prepares grazing management plans.

range improvement: Any practice designed to improve range condition or facilitate more efficient use of range; any structure or excavation to facilitate management of range or livestock.

range inventory: An itemized list of resources of a management area such as range sites, range condition classes, range condition trends, range use, estimated proper stocking rates, physical developments, and natural conditions such as water, barriers, etc.

rangeland: Land on which the native vegetation (climax or natural potential) is predominantly grasses, grass like plants, forbs, or shrubs suitable for grazing or browsing use. Includes lands revegetated naturally or artificially to provide a forage cover that is managed like native vegetation. Rangelands include natural grasslands, savannas, shrublands, most deserts, tundra, alpine communities, coastal marshes, and wet meadows.

range line: See *township line.*

range management: A distinct discipline founded on ecological principles and dealing with the husbandry of all rangeland and range resources.

range science: The organized body of knowledge upon which the practice of range management is based.

range seeding: Establishing adapted plant species on ranges by means other than natural revegetation.

range site: A distinctive kind of rangeland that differs from other kinds of rangeland in its potential to produce native plants.

rapidly varied flow (hydraulics): Non-uniform flow in which the depth of flow changes dramatically in a short reach; for example, hydraulic jump or bore; can be either steady or unsteady.

raptor: A bird of prey.

rare species: Species identified for special management emphasis because of their uncommon occurrence within a watershed.

raster: A type of data using grid cells rather than polygons; used especially for analysis, rather than display.

rating curve: A graphic or sometimes tabular representation of performance or output under a stated series of conditions; for example, a rating curve for a flume shows volume of flow per unit time at various stages or depths of flow.

rating flume: An open conduit built in a channel to maintain a consistent regimen for the purpose of measuring the flow and developing stage-discharge relation.

ration: The amount of feed allotted to a given animal for a 24 hour day. It may be fed at one time or in portions at different times during the day.

ration, balanced: A ration that furnishes the various essential nutrients in such proportion and amounts that it will properly nourish a given animal for one day.

ratoon: A crop production sequence in which a crop is allowed to regrow or come back after harvest; typical of pineapple or sugar cane in a tropical climate.

raw sewage: Untreated domestic or commercial wastewater.

raw water: Intake water prior to any treatment or use.

reach: A specified length of a stream or channel.

reaction, soil: The degree of acidity or alkalinity of a soil, usually expressed as a pH value. Descriptive terms commonly associated with certain ranges in pH are extremely acid, less than 4.5; very strongly acid, 4.5 to 5.0; strongly acid, 5.1 to 5.5; medium acid, 5.6 to 6.0; slightly acid, 6.1 to 6.5; neutral, 6.6 to 7.3; mildly alkaline, 7.4 to 7.8; moderately alkaline, 7.9 to 8.4; strongly alkaline, 8.5 to 9.0; and very strongly alkaline, more than 9.0.

reactive: One of four categories of hazardous waste; substances capable of changing into something else in the presence of other chemicals, usually violently or producing a hazardous by-product.

reaeration: Introduction of air into the lower layers of a reservoir. As the air bubbles form and rise through the water, the oxygen dissolves into the water and replenishes the dissolved oxygen. The rising bubbles also cause the lower waters to rise to the surface where they take on oxygen from the atmosphere.

recarbonization: Process in which carbon dioxide is bubbled into water being treated to lower the pH.

receiving stream: The body of water into which effluent is discharged.

receptor: Ecological entity exposed to a stressor.

recession curve (hydraulics): See *depletion curve.*

recession time: The interval of time after the water supply is shut off for the surface water to disappear in a specified length of a run.

recharge: Process by which water is added to the zone of saturation, as recharge of an aquifer.

recharge area: A land area in which water reaches the zone of saturation from surface infiltration, e.g., where rainwater soaks through the earth to reach an aquifer.

recharge rate: The quantity of water per unit of time that replenishes or refills an aquifer.

reclamation: The process of reconverting disturbed lands to their former uses or other productive uses.

reconnaissance: A preliminary inspection or survey of a forest or range area to gain general information useful for future management.

reconnaissance survey: A preliminary inspection or survey of an area, such as a forest, range, watershed, or wildlife area, to gain general information useful for future management.

recording gage: An automatic instrument for making a graphic record of quantities or conditions, such as flow, stage, rainfall, and temperature, in relation to time.

recoverable resources: Materials that still have useful physical or chemical properties after serving a specific purpose and can, therefore, be reused or recycled for the same or other purposes.

recovery: The process of obtaining materials or energy resources from solid wastes, also called extraction, reclamation, salvage; the energy available from the heat generated when solid wastes are burned.

recreation area improvement: Establishing grasses, legumes, vines, shrubs, trees, or other plants or selectively reducing stand density and trimming woody plants to improve an area for recreation.

recreation complex: An area providing wide and varied recreation opportunities and facilities; it may be public, private, and/or commercially owned and operated.

recreation development: A created or improved outdoor area for the enjoyment of outdoor recreation.

recreation enterprise: A private outdoor recreation business operated for profit.

recreation land: Land used or usable primarily for outdoor recreation activities and facilities.

recreation layout: The planning and arrangement of facilities, programs, and apparatus within a given recreation setting requiring special consideration for its orientation, safety and utility.

recreation resource: Land and water areas and their natural attributes, with or without man made facilities, that provide opportunities for outdoor recreation.

recurrence interval: The average time interval between actual occurrences of an event at a given or greater magnitude. See *frequency.*

recycling: A resource recovery method involving the collection and treatment of a waste product for use as raw material in the manufacture of the same or a similar product, such as ground glass used in manufacture of new glass.

redd: A type of fish spawning area associated with flowing water and clean gravel. Fishes that utilize this type of spawning area include trout, salmon, some minnows, etc.

red dog (mining): A gob pile after it has burned; the material, often reddish in color, is generally used as a road-surfacing material; it usually has no harmful acid or alkaline reaction.

red tide: A visible red to orange coloration of the sea caused by the presence of a bloom of certain plankton: often the cause of major fish kills.

reduced tillage: A tillage sequence designed to reduce or eliminate secondary tillage operations.

reducers: Organisms, usually bacteria or fungi, that break down complex organic material into simpler compounds, also called decomposers. See *producers, consumers.*

reducing environment: An environment conducive to the removal of oxygen; also expressed by showing an increase in negative valence, representing the addition of electrons to an atom or ion.

reduction: The addition of hydrogen, removal of oxygen, or addition of electrons to an element or compound.

reefs: Skeleton-like ecosystems made up of colonies of limestone-producing, living animals. Coral reefs tell us about water quality and the health of an estuary.

reference data: Data about the physical state of the earth obtained from sources other than the primary remote sensing data source and used in support of remote sensing data analysis; may typically include maps and aerial photographs, topographic information, temperature measurements and other types of ancillary and emphemeral data; also called ground truth, ground data, ground-based measurements.

reflectance: A measure of the ability of a surface to reflect energy; specifically the ratio of the reflected energy to the incident energy; affected not only by the nature of the surface itself, but also by the angle of incidence and the viewing angle.

reflecting projector: An instrument used to project the image of photographs, maps, or other graphics onto a copying table; the scale of the projected image can be varied by raising or lowering the projector or, in some models, the copy board; these latter models also allow the tilting of the copy board in x- and y-directions in order to compensate for tip and tilt distortion in aerial photographs.

reflective infrared: The portion of the electromagnetic spectrum from approximately 0.72 to 3.0 micrometers; often subdivided into near infrared and middle infrared.

reforestation: Restocking an area with forest trees.

refractory: A nonmetallic substance used to line furnaces because it can endure high temperatures; normally able to resist one or more of the following destructive influences: abrasion, pressure, chemical attack, and rapid changes in temperature.

Types include:

castable: A hydraulic setting refractory, suitable for casting or being pneumatically formed into heat resistant shapes or walls.

high alumina: A refractory product containing 47.5 percent more alumina than regular refractories.

plastic: A blend of ground fireclay materials in a plastic form that is suitable for ramming into place to form monolithic linings or special shapes. It may be air setting or heat setting and is available in different qualities of heat resistance.

refuge lands: Lands in which the Service holds full interest in fee title or partial interest like an easement.

refuge wildlife: An area designated for the protection of wild animals, within which hunting and fishing is either prohibited or strictly controlled.

refuse: See *solid waste*.

refuse reclamation: The process of converting solid waste to saleable products, such as composition of organic waste as a soil conditioner.

regime (hydraulics): Applies to streams that make at least part of their boundaries from their transported load and part of their transported load from their boundaries, carrying out the process at different places and times in the stream in a balanced or alternating manner that permits unlimited growth or removal of boundaries.

regimen: The stability of a stream and its channel. A river or canal is "in regimen" if its channel has reached a stable form as the result of its flow characteristics.

registered variety: A variety (culti-

var) accepted, numbered, and registered as a recognized improved variety by the Committee on Varietal Standardization and Registration of the Crop Science Society of America.

regolith: The unconsolidated mantle of weathered rock and soil material on the earth's surface; loose earth materials above solid rock.

regrading: The movement of earth over a surface or depression to change the shape of the land surface.

regression: A statistical method for studying and expressing the change in one variable associated with and dependent on changes in another related variable or set of variables.

rehabilitation: Returning of land to farm use or to productivity in conformity with a prior land use plan, including a stable ecological state that does not constitute substantially to environmental deterioration and is consistent with surrounding aesthetic values.

reinforced concrete: Concrete containing reinforcement, including prestressing steel, and designed on the assumption that the two materials act together in resisting forces.

relative abundance: The number of organisms of a particular kind present in a sample relative to the total number of organisms in the sample.

relative ecological sustainability: Ability of an ecosystem to maintain relative ecological integrity indefinitely.

relative permeability: The permeability of a rock to gas, NAIL, or water, when any two or more are present.

relatively intact: The conservation status category indicating the least possible disruption of ecosystem processes. Natural communities are largely intact, with species and ecosystem processes occurring within their natural ranges of variation.

relatively stable: The conservation status category between vulnerable and relatively intact in which extensive areas of intact habitat remain, but local species declines and disruptions of ecological processes have occurred.

relict: A remnant or fragment of a flora that remains from a former period when it was more widely distributed.

release: Any spilling, leaking, pumping, pouring, emitting, emptying, discharging, injecting, escaping, leaching, dumping, or disposing into the environment of a hazardous or toxic chemical or extremely hazardous substance.

relief drain: A drain designed to remove water from the soil in order to lower the water table and reduce hydrostatic pressure.

relief well: Well, pit, or bore penetrating the water table to relieve hydrostatic pressure by allowing flow from the aquifer.

rem: A measurement of radiation dose to the internal tissue of man; derived from Roentgen equivalent man.

remote sensing: Any process by which a visual rendition of the earth or an object is obtained. It can be by standard photography, infrared or other special photography, heat sensing, video scanning, etc.

rendering: A process of recovering fatty substances from animal parts by heat treatment, extraction, and distillation.

renewable natural resources: Resources that can be restored and improved to produce the things man needs.

reportable erosion event: A natural or man-made disturbance to the forest land base which is causing or will likely cause substantial environmental impacts, or which is a threat to life or property.

representative sample: A portion of material or water that is as nearly identical in content and consistency as possible to that in the larger body of material or water being sampled.

reprocessing: The action of changing the condition of a secondary material.

reserve (mining): That portion of the actual identified resource material that can be economically and legally extracted at the time of determination.

reservoir: Impounded body of water or controlled lake in which water is collected or stored.

resident camping: A sustained group living experience in the natural environment under trained leadership.

residual contamination: Amount of a pollutant remaining in the environment after a natural or technological process has taken place (e.g., the level of chemical remaining in soil after it has been treated).

residual material: Unconsolidated

and partly weathered mineral materials accumulated by disintegration of consolidated rock in place.

residual saturation: Saturation level below which fluid drainage will not occur.

residual soil: A soil formed in material weathered from bedrock without transportation from the original location.

residue: Material that remains after gases, liquids, or solids have been removed. See *crop residue*.

resolution (remote sensing): The minimum distance between two adjacent features, or the minimum size of a feature, that can be detected by a photographic system or radar system; for photography, the distance is usually expressed in lines per millimeter recorded on a particular film under specific conditions; as displayed by radar, lines per millimeter; if expressed in size of objects or distances on the ground, the distance is termed ground resolution; a measure of the ability of an optical system to distinguish between signals that are spatially near or spectrally similar.

resolution, spatial: A measure of the smallest angular or linear separation between two objects, usually expressed in radians or meters; a smaller resolution parameter denotes greater resolving power.

resolution, spectral: A measure of both the discreteness of the bandwidths and the sensitivity of the sensor to distinguish between gray levels; also a function of the spectral contrast between objects in the scene and their background, of the shape of the objects, and of

the signal-to-noise ratio of the system.

resource area: See *land resource area*.

Resource Conservation and Recovery Act (RCRA): A Federal law whose primary goals are to protect human health and the environment from the potential hazards of waste disposal, conserve energy and natural resources, reduce the amount of waste generated, and ensure that wastes are managed in an environmentally sound manner. Management of solid waste (e.g., garbage), hazardous waste, and underground storage tanks holding petroleum products or certain chemicals is regulated by RCRA.

resource inventory: Collection of data for analysis of the status or condition of resources.

resource management system: A combination of conservation practices identified by the primary use of land or water that, if installed, will at a minimum protect the resource base by meeting tolerable soil losses, maintaining acceptable ecological and management levels for the selected resource use; may include conservation practices that provide for quality in the environment and quality in the standard of living.

resource monitoring: The act of continually or periodically observing resources to determine change and trends in their status and condition.

resource region: See *land resource region*.

resources: That which is, or may be, readily available as a source of supply or support; anything that can be drawn upon when needed, whether material or nonmaterial. See *natural resources.*

resources, other nonnatural: Elements of supply that are not natural or related resources; those resources that are available through social, economic, or political processes, such as labor, capital, land ownership, water allocations, laws and regulations, technical expertise.

resources, related: Elements of supply that are dependent upon and reflect man's influence on natural resources, such as pastures of introduced species, plantation forests, cultivated crops, land modified for recreation, or developed water storage sites.

resource unit: See *land resource unit.*

respiration: The complex series of chemical and physical reactions in all living organisms by which the energy and nutrients in foods are made available for use. Oxygen is used and carbon dioxide released during the process. See *metabolism.*

restoration: The process of restoring site conditions as they were before the land disturbance.

restoration ecology: The process of using ecological principles and experience to return a degraded ecological system to its former or original state.

rest rotation grazing: A form of deferred rotation grazing in which at least one grazing unit is rested from grazing for a full year.

retarding pool: The reservoir space allotted to the temporary impoundment of floodwater, its upper limit being the elevation of the crest of the emergency spillway.

retention: The amount of precipitation on a drainage area that does not escape as runoff. It is the difference between total precipitation and total runoff.

return beam vidicon (RBV): A modified vidicon television camera tube, in which the output signal is derived from the depleted electron beam reflected from the tube target; can be considered as a cross between a vidicon and an orthicon; provides the highest resolution television imagery.

return flow: That portion of the water diverted from a stream that finds its way back to the stream channel either as surface or underground flow.

reuse: The reintroduction of a commodity into the economic stream without any change.

revenue insurance: An insurance policy offered to farmers that pays indemnities based on revenue shortfalls. These programs are subsidized and reinsured by USDA's Risk Management Agency.

reverberation: The persistence of sound in an enclosed space after the sound source has stopped.

reverse osmosis: An advanced method of waste treatment that relies on a semipermeable membrane to separate water from pollutants.

revetment: Facing of stone or other material, either permanent or temporary, placed along the edge of a stream to stabilize the bank and to protect it from the erosive action of the stream.

R factor: See *universal soil loss equation.*

rhizobia: The bacteria capable of

living in symbiotic relationship with leguminous plants in nodules on the roots, the association usually being capable of fixing nitrogen (from the generic name Rhizobium).

rhizome: A horizontal underground stem, usually sending out roots and above ground shoots at the nodes.

ridge planting: A planting method in which crops are planted on ridges; usually refers to only one seed row planted on each ridge.

riffles: Fast sections of a stream where shallow water races over stones and gravel; usually support a wider variety of bottom organisms than other stream sections; also called rifts.

rill: A small, intermittent water course with steep sides, usually only a few inches deep and, hence, no obstacle to tillage operations.

rill erosion: See *erosion*.

ringelmann chart: A series of charts, numbered zero through five, that equate smoke densities, zero being clear and five completely opaque. They are occasionally used for measuring opacity of smoke from stacks and in setting emission standards.

riparian: Referring to the interface between freshwater habitats and the terrestrial landscape.

riparian habitat: Areas adjacent to rivers and streams with a differing density, diversity, and productivity of plant and animal species relative to nearby uplands.

riparian land: Land situated along the bank of a stream or other body of water.

riparian rights: The rights of an owner whose land abuts water.

They differ from state to state and often depend on whether the water is a river, lake, or ocean. See *water rights*.

riprap: Broken rock, cobbles, or boulders placed on earth surfaces, such as the face of a dam or the bank of a stream, for protection against the action of water (waves); also applied to brush or pole mattresses, or brush and stone, or other similar materials used for soil erosion control.

rithron zone: Stream reach at higher elevations characterized by rapid flow, low temperature, and high dissolved oxygen levels. See *potamon zone*.

river basin: A major water resource region. The United States has been divided in 20 river basin areas. See *drainage basin*.

river basin plan: A plan for development of water and related land resources to make the best use of such resources to meet the basin needs and make the greatest long term contribution to the economic growth and social well being of the people of the basin and the nation.

riverine: Within the active channel of a river or stream.

riverine wetlands: Generally, all the wetlands and deepwater habitats occurring within a freshwater river channel not dominated by trees, shrubs, or persistent emergents.

riverwash: Barren alluvial land, usually coarse textured, exposed along streams at low water, and subject to shifting during normal high water; a miscellaneous land type.

roadside erosion control: See *highway erosion control.*

rock fill dam: A dam composed of loose rock usually dumped in place, often with the upstream part constructed of handplaced or derrick placed rock and faced with rolled earth or with an impervious surface of concrete, timber, or steel.

rock hounding area: An area of land used for seeking unusual rocks and/or gems.

rockland: Areas containing shallow soils and rock outcrops occupying from 25 to 90 percent of the area; a miscellaneous land type.

rouging: The removal and destruction of plants considered off-type or diseased.

rookery: The breeding place of a group of birds or seals.

root hairs: Long hair-like outgrowths which occur just back of tips of plant rootlets, and through which plants take in water, nutrients, and gases essential to plant growth.

root hardy: Plants that regularly survive the winter although the tops are killed to the ground.

rooting hormone: A substance applied to plant tissue during propagation to stimulate more vigorous rooting. See *propagation.*

root nodule: A hypertrophy formed on the roots of leguminous plants, caused by symbiotic nitrogen fixing bacteria.

root pruning: A technique to stimulate the development of a branched root system to facilitate transplanting, to induce flowering or fruiting, and to control size and

to rejuvenate plants grown in containers. See *pruning.*

roots: Underground plant organs that extract water, gases, and nutrients from the soil and atmosphere; large roots mainly anchor plants. See *root hairs.*

rootstock: That part of a plant, including the roots, on which another variety has been budded or grafted. See *graftage.*

root zone: The part of the soil that is penetrated or can be penetrated by plant roots.

rotary tillage: An operation using a power driven rotary tillage tool to loosen and mix soil.

rotation deferred grazing: See *deferred rotation grazing.*

rotation forestry: The planned number of years required to establish and grow trees to a specific maturity. The age at harvest is called the rotation age.

rotation grazing: System of pasture utilization embracing short periods of heavy stocking followed by periods of rest for herbage recovery during the same season; generally used on tame pasture or cropland pasture.

rotation irrigation: A system by which each irrigator receives his allotted quantity of water, not at a continuous rate, but at stated intervals. For example, a number of irrigators receiving water from the same lateral may agree among themselves to rotate the water, each taking the entire flow in turn for a limited period.

rotation pasture: A cultivated area used as a pasture one or more years as part of crop rotation. See *permanent pasture.*

rotenone: An organic compound

extracted from the roots of derris, timbo, and cube and used as an insecticide and fish poison.

roughage: Feed with high fiber content and low total digestable nutrients, such as hay and stover.

rough broken land: Land with very steep topography and numerous intermittent drainage channels, usually covered with vegetation. Formerly a miscellaneous land type. See *badlands*.

rough fish: Those species of fish considered to be of either poor fighting quality when taken on tackle or of poor eating quality, such as carp, gar, suckers, etc. Most species in the group are more tolerant of widely changing environmental conditions than game fish.

roughness coefficient (hydraulics): A factor in velocity and discharge formulas representing the effect of channel roughness on energy losses in flowing water. Manning's "n" is a commonly used roughness coefficient.

row crop: A crop planted in rows, normally to allow cultivation between rows during the growing season.

rubber cracking method: A method for determining levels of air pollution; stretched strips of unvulcanized rubber are exposed to the air, and the average depth of cracks induced by oxidants determines the intensity of these air pollutants in the atmosphere.

rubbish: A general term for solid waste, excluding food waste and ashes, taken from residences, commercial establishments, and institutions.

rubble: Broken pieces of masonry and concrete.

rubble land: Land areas with 90 percent or more of the surface covered with stones and boulders. A miscellaneous land type.

run: The distance of gravity flow from the point of release to the end of the area to be watered.

runoff (hydraulics): That portion of the precipitation on a drainage area that is discharged from the area in stream channels. Types include surface runoff, groundwater runoff, or seepage.

runoff plots: Areas of land, usually small, arranged so the portion of rainfall or other precipitation flowing off and perhaps carrying soluble materials and soil may be measured. Usually, the flow from runoff plots includes only surface flow.

rural beautification: Creating, enhancing, and preserving natural beauty in the countryside.

rural cottage, camp, and home sites: Lands used for seasonal homes or vacation cottages; permanent campsites for groups, organizations, or clubs; or permanent home locations.

r-value: R-value or "thermal resistance value" is a measure of the resistance of a material to heat flow. The term is typically used to describe the resistance properties of insulation. The higher the R-value, the greater the insulation's resistance to heat flow.

S

sacrifice area: A relatively small area of land in a grazing unit that may still be overused after practical measures for securing uniform grazing distribution have been installed.

safe velocity (hydrolics): See *permissible velocity*.

safe water: Water that does not contain harmful bacteria, toxic materials, or chemicals, and is considered safe for drinking even if it may have taste, odor, color, and certain mineral problems.

safe yield: The rate at which water can be withdrawn from a groundwater basin (aquifer) without depleting the supply to such an extent that undesirable effects result; dependent on rate of recharge, change in water quality, and economics.

saline alkali: A soil containing sufficient exchangeable sodium to interfere with the growth of most crop plants and containing appreciable quantities of soluble salts. The exchangeable sodium percentage is greater than 15, the conductivity of the saturation extract greater than four millimhos per centimeter (25 degres C), and the pH in the saturated soil is 8.5 or less; also called saline sodic soil.

saline soil: A nonsodic soil containing sufficient soluble salts to impair its productivity but not containing excessive exchangeable sodium. This name was formerly applied to any soil containing sufficient soluble salts to interfere with plant growth, commonly greater than 3,000 parts per million.

saline seep: Area of recently developed salinity on nonirrigated land where salty groundwater moves to the surface and crop or grass production is reduced or eliminated.

saline soil: A nonsodic soil containing sufficient soluble salts to impair its productivity but not containing excessive exchangeable sodium. This name was formerly applied to any soil containing sufficient soluble salts to interfere with plant growth, commonly greater than 3,000 parts per million.

salinity: The concentration of dissolved solids or salt in water.

salinity control: The physical control, management, and use of water and related land resources in such a way as to maintain or reduce salt loading and concentrations of salt in water supplies.

salmonid: A fish of the fish family Salmonides; for example salmon, trout and chars.

salt-affected soil: Soil that has been adversely modified for the growth of most crop plants by the presence of soluble salts, exchangeable sodium, or both.

saltation: Particle movement in water or wind where particles skip or bounce along the stream bed or soil surface.

salting: Providing salt as a mineral supplement for animals; placing salt on the range in such a manner as to improve distribution of livestock.

salt marsh: Low area adjacent to the sea that is covered with salt tolerant vegetation and regularly flooded by the high tide; similar inland areas near saline springs or lakes, though not regularly flooded.

salt water intrusion: The invasion of fresh surface or groundwater by salt water. If it comes from the ocean it may be called sea-water intrusion.

salvage: The use of waste materials.

sample plot: An area of land, usually small, used for measuring or observing performance under existing or applied treatments. It may be temporary or permanent.

sample, random: A sample drawn without bias from a population in which every item has an equal chance of being drawn.

sample, representative: A sample drawn in such a way that it gives a true value for the population from which it is drawn.

sample strip: A long narrow strip used as a sampling unit in surveys.

sampling: The selection of a number of occurrences (a sample) from a larger number of occurrences (the universe), whose number may or

may not be known.

sand: A soil particle between 0.05 and 2.0 millimeters in diameter; any one of five soil separates: very coarse sand, coarse sand, medium sand, fine sand, and very fine sand. See *soil separates; a soil textural class.* See *soil texture.*

sand bearing method: A method of testing the crushing strength of drain tile in which the tile is bedded in sand according to ASTM specifications.

sand lens: Lenticular band of sand in distinctly sedimentary banded material.

sandplain grassland: Dry grassland that has resisted succession due to fire, wind, grazing, mowing, or salt spray.

sand trap (irrigation, drainage): A device, often a simple enlargement in a ditch or conduit, for arresting the heavier particles of sand and silt carried by the water. Means for removing such material may be included.

sandy: See *coarse textured, particle size classes for family groupings.*

sandy clay: A soil textural class. See *soil texture.*

sandy clay loam: A soil textural class. See *soil texture.*

sandy loam: A soil textural class. See *soil texture.*

sandy skeletal: See *particle size classes for family groupings.*

sanitary landfill: A site on which solid wastes are disposed of in a manner that protects the environment; wastes are spread in thin layers, compacted to the smallest practical volume, and covered with soil by the end of each working day. Various methods include:

area: Wastes are spread and compacted on the surface of the ground and cover material is spread and compacted over the top.

quarry: Wastes are spread and compacted in a depression; cover material is generally obtained elsewhere.

ramp: A variation of the area and quarry method in that the cover material is obtained by excavating in front of the working face. A variation of this method is known as the progressive slope method.

trench: A method in which the waste is spread and compacted over the waste to form the basic cell structure.

wet area: A method used in swampy areas where precautions are taken to avoid water pollution before proceeding with the area landfill technique.

sanitation: The control of all the factors in man's physical environment that exercise or can exercise a deleterious effect on his physical development, health, and survival.

sap: The juices of a plant, especially the water solution that circulates through the vascular tissue in woody plants.

sapwood: The light-coloured wood that appears on the outer portion of a cross-section of a tree.

sapric materials: See *organic soil materials.*

saprobic: Living on dead or decaying organic matter. See *scavenger.*

saprobicity: The sum of all metabolic processes that are the direct opposite of primary production; can be measured either by the dynamics of metabolism or analysis of community structure.

saprobien system: European system of classifying organisms according to their response to organic pollution in slow moving streams. Classifications include:

alpha mesasprobic zone: Area of active decomposition, partly aerobic, partly anaerobic, in a stream heavily polluted with organic wastes.

beta mesoaprobic zone: That reach of a stream that is moderately polluted with organic wastes.

oligosaprobic zone: That reach of a stream that is slightly polluted with organic wastes and contains the mineralized products of self purification from organic pollution, but with none of the organic pollution remaining.

polysaprobic zone: That area of a grossly polluted stream that contains the complex organic wastes that are decomposing primarily by anaerobic processes.

saprolite: A soft, clay-rich, thoroughly decomposed rock formed in place by chemical weathering of igneous or metamorphic rock. Forms in humid, tropical, or subtropical climates.

satellite: An attendant body, natural or man-made, that revolves about another body, the primary.

saturate: To fill all the voids between soil particles with liquid; to form the most concentrated solution possible under a given set of physical conditions in the presence of an excess of the substance.

saturated flow: The liquid flow of water in soils that occurs when the soil pores in the wettest part of the soil are completely filled with water and the direction of flow is from the wettest zone of higher potential to one of lower potential.

saturated soil paste: A particular mixture of soil and water; at saturation; the soil paste glistens as it reflects light, flows slightly when the container is tipped, and the paste slides freely and cleanly from a spatula.

saturated zone: The area below the water table where all open spaces are filled with water under pressure equal to or greater than that of the atmosphere.

saturation (remote sensing): Degree of intensity difference between a color and an achromatic light-source color of the same brightness; the condition of overload in a scanning senor system where the brightness level of the target is greater than the capacity of the sensor.

saturation extract: The solution removed from a soil completely filled with liquid, at less than 1/3 atmosphere.

saturation percentage: The water content of a saturated soil paste, expressed on a dry-weight percentage basis.

saturation point: In soils, that point at which a soil or an aquifer will no longer absorb any amount of water without losing an equal amount; in wildlife, the maximum density under which a species will normally live.

sausage dam: A dam composed of loose rock that has been wrapped with wire into cylindrical bundles and laid in a horizontal or vertical position.

savanna: A grassland with scattered

trees, either as individuals or clumps; often a transitional type between true grassland and forest; also savannah.

sawtimber: Trees with logs suitable in size and quality for the production of lumber.

scale: The relationship existing between map or photo distances and ground distances. May be expressed in like units as a representative fraction such as 1:20,000 which means that one unit of measurement on the map equals 20,000 of the same units on the ground, or in unlike units as one inch = one mile, or graphically by a bar scale.

scale (forestry): To estimate the content of sound wood in a log or bolt or group of logs or bolts using a given unit of measure or weight; the estimated content of a log or group of logs or bolts.

scalping: Removal of sod or other vegetation in spots or strips.

scan line (remote sensing): The segment of the imagery produced during a single sweep of the modulated light source across the recording film, or electronic signal of a single scan.

scanners (remote sensing): Any device that scans and by this means produces an image; a radar set incorporating a rotatable antenna or radiator element, motor drives, mounting, etc., for directing a searching radar beam through space and imparting target information to an indicator.

scarification: A method of seedbed preparation which consists of exposing patches of mineral soil through mechanical action.

scarify: To abrade, scratch, or modify the surface, for example, to scratch the impervious seed coat of hard seed or to break the surface of the soil with a narrow bladed implement.

scarp: A steep slope extending over a considerable distance and marking the edge of a terrace, plateau, bench, etc. See *fault scarp*.

scattering coefficient (pollution and remote sensing): The fractional rate in the movement of radiation through a scattering medium (light through smog) at which the flux density of radiation lessons by scattering in relation to the thickness of the traversed medium.

scavenger: An animal that eats animal wastes and the dead bodies of animals not killed by itself.

scene (remote sensing): Everything that occurs spatially or temporally before the sensor, including the earth's surface, the energy source, and the atmosphere that the energy passes through as it travels from its sources to the earth and from the earth to the sensor.

scene, Landsat: The ground area depicted on the three return beam vidicon (RBV) or the four multispectral scanner (MSS) images on Landsats one and two or the four datime MSS images, the one nighttime MSS image, or the four RBV subscenes on Landsat three.

scenic easement: An easement restricting development in order to protect roadside views and natural features.

scenic overlook: An opening in the vegetation along a trail or highway that affords the audience a scenic view of some resource.

scion: Any unrooted portion of a plant used for grafting or budding on to a root stalk. Shoots of woody plants from which scions are cut are termed scionwood.

scionwood: Shoots of woody plants from which scions are cut.

scope: The range of actions, alternatives, and impacts to be considered in an environmental impact statement.

scour: To abrade and wear away; used to describe the wearing away of terrace or diversion channels or stream beds.

scouring sluice: An opening in a dam controlled by a gate through which the accumulated silt, sand, and gravel may be ejected.

scrap: Discarded or rejected material or parts of material that result from manufacturing or fabricating operations and are suitable for reprocessing. Types include:

home: Scrap that never leaves the manufacturing plant and is reprocessed there. Also known as revert scrap.

obsolete: Scrap that results when material becomes worn or otherwise unusable for its original purpose.

prompt industrial: Scrap that is left over from the fabrication of iron and steel products.

screefing: Removal of herbaceous vegetation and soil organic matter to expose a soil surface for planting.

screen: A perforated plate or meshed fabric used to separate coarser from finer parts, as of sand or other particulate materials.

Types include:

rotary: An inclined, meshed cylinder that rotates on its axis and screens material placed in its upper end.

vibrating: An inclined screen that is vibrated mechanically and screens material placed on it.

screening: The use of any vegetative planting, fencing, ornamental wall of masonry, or other architectural treatment, earthen embankment, or a combination of any of these which will effectively hide from view any undesirable areas from the main traveled way.

scrubber: A device that uses a liquid filter to remove gaseous and liquid pollutants from an air stream.

seasonal grazing: Grazing restricted to a specific season.

seawater: Water that comes from the ocean and is very salty.

Secchi disk: A disk, 20 centimeters in diameter, painting black and white in alternate quadrants and used in fish culture and limnology to measure the passage of light through water.

secondary benefits: The values over and above the immediate products or services of a water resource development project. These result from activities stemming from or induced by a project.

secondary material: A material that is utilized in place of a primary or raw material in manufacturing a product.

secondary pollutants: Those pollutants that result from the chemical reactions involving primary pollutants or related atmospheric contaminants, for example, oxidants from photochemical activity.

secondary productivity: The rate at

which organic matter is stored in consumer organisms (heterotrophs). See *primary productivity, productivity.*

secondary tillage: Any tillage operation following primary tillage designed to develop a seedbed more satisfactory for planting.

secondary treatment: Waste water treatment, beyond the primary stage, in which bacteria comsume the organic parts of the wastes, such as by activated sludge or trickling filters.

secondary waste treatment: The removal of up to 90 percent of the organic material from sewage by the metabolic action of bacteria. See *waste treatment.*

second growth forest: A forest originating naturally after removal of the old stand by cutting, fire, or other cause. See *virgin forest.*

section line: In the general land office survey, each six mile square township is subdivided into 36 sections which are roughly a mile square. The lines bordering these sections are called section lines and the point at which two of these lines intersect is called a section corner.

sedentary farming: A system of farming practiced in the African Sahel to combat drought; natives take or send livestock on migration while cultivating some basic food staples during the growing season.

sediment: Solid material, both mineral and organic, that is in suspension, is being transported, or has been moved from its site of origin by air, water, gravity, or ice and has come to rest on the earth's surface either above or below sea level.

sediment discharge: The quantity

of sediment, measured in dry weight or by volume, transported through a stream cross-section in a given time. Sediment discharge consists of both suspended load and bedload.

sediment grade sizes: Measurements of sediment and soil particles that can be separated by screening. A committee on sedimentation of the National Research Council established a classification of textural grade sizes for standard use.

sediment load: See *sediment discharge*.

sediment pool: The reservoir space allotted to the accumulation of submerged sediment during the life of the structure.

sedimentary rock: Rock formed by the lithification of mechanical, chemical, or organic sediments.

sedimentation: The process or action of depositing sediment.

seed: The fertilized and ripened ovule of a seed plant that is capable, under suitable conditions, of independently developing into a plant similar to the one that produced it.

Types of seed include:

breeder seed: Seed or vegetative propagating material directly controlled by the originating, or in some cases the sponsoring plant breeder, institution, or firm, and which supplies the initial and recurring increase of foundation seed.

certified seed: The progeny of foundation or registered seed that is so handled as to maintain satisfactory genetic identity and purity and that has been approved and certified by the certifying agency.

commercial seed: A term used to designate other than recognized varieties of seed in commercial channels.

common seed: Non certified seed. It may be a named variety, but not grown under the certification program.

dormant seed: An internal condition of the chemistry or stage of development of a viable seed that prevents its germination, although good growing temperatures and moisture are provided.

firm seed: Dormant seeds, other than hard seeds, that neither germinate nor decay during the prescribed test period under the prescribed conditions. Firm ungerminated seeds may be alive or dead.

foundation seed: Seed stocks that are so handled as to most nearly maintain specific genetic identity and purity. Production must be carefully supervised by the originating agency and approved by the certifying agency and/or the agricultural experiment station.

hard seed: A physiological condition of seed in which some seeds do not absorb water or oxygen and germinate when a favorable environment is provided.

registered seed: The program of foundation seed that is so handled as to maintain satisfactory genetic identity and purity and that has been approved and certified by the certifying agency. This class of seed should be of a quality suitable for production of certified seed.

seedbed: The soil prepared by natural or artificial means to promote the germination of seed and the growth of seedlings.

seeding, direct (forestry): A method of establishing a stand of trees artificially by sowing seed. In broadcast seeding, seed is sown over the entire area. Partial seeding may be done in strips, furrow rows, trenches, or in seed spots.

seed inoculation: The process of adding microorganisms to seed, used frequently to designate the treatment of leguminous seed with symbiotic nitrogen fixing bacteria.

seedling: A young plant grown from seed.

seed purity: The percentage of the desired species in relation to the total quantity of other species, weed seed, and foreign matter.

seed protectant: A chemical applied before planting to protect seeds and seedlings from disease or insects.

seed tree: A tree that produces seed; usually superior trees left standing at the time of cutting to produce seed for reforestation.

seepage: Water escaping through or emerging from the ground along an extensive line or surface as contrasted with a spring where the water emerges from a localized spot; (percolation) the slow movement of gravitational water through the soil.

seepage bed: A trench or bed more than 36 inches wide containing at least 12 inches of clean, coarse aggregate and a system of distribution piping through which treated sewage may seep into the surrounding soil.

seepage pit: A covered pit with lining designed to permit treated sewage to seep into the surrounding soil.

seiche: Periodic oscillations in the water level of a lake or inland sea

that occur with temporary local depressions or elevations of the water level.

selective cutting (forestry): A system of cutting in which single trees, usually the largest, or small groups of such trees are removed for commercial production or to encourage reproduction under the remaining stand in the openings. See *harvest cutting, improvement cutting, clearcutting.*

selective grazing: The tendency for livestock and other grazing animals to graze certain plants in preference to others.

selective herbicide: A pesticide intended to kill only certain types of plants, especially broad leafed weeds, and not harm other plants such as farm crops or lawn grasses.

self-guided interpretive services: An interpretive activity undertaken without the physical presence of an interpreter; such activities may include walks, hikes, drives, tours, museum visits, or visitor centers; in most cases the audience follows a path or series of markers.

self mulching soil: A soil in which the surface layer becomes so well aggregated that it does not crust and seal under the impact of rain but instead serves as a surface mulch upon drying.

self-pollinated: Pollinated by the anthers of the same flower.

self pruning: The natural death and fall of branches from live trees due to causes such as light and food deficiencies, decay, insect attack, snow, and ice; also called natural pruning.

semiarid: A term applied to regions

or climates where moisture is normally greater than under arid conditions but still definitely limits the growth of most crops. Dryland farming methods or irrigation generally are required for crop production. The upper limit of average annual precipitation in the cool semiarid regions is as low as 15 inches, whereas in tropical regions it is as high as 45 or 50 inches. See *arid*.

semi-confined aquifer: An aquifer partially confined by soil layers of low permeability through which recharge and discharge can still occur.

senescence: The process of growing old; sometimes applied to lakes nearing extinction because of increases in trophic state toward the end of the cycle.

sensitive organisms: Organisms that exhibit a rapid response to environmental changes and are killed, driven out of the area, or as a group are substantially reduced in numbers when their environment is fouled; also called intolerant organisms. See *tolerant association*.

sensor (remote sensing): Any device that is sensitive to levels or changes in physical quantities (such as light intensity or temperature) and converts these phenomena into a form suitable for input into an information-gathering system; an active sensor system, such as radar, produces the energy needed to detect these phenomena; a passive sensor system, such as a multispectral scanner or an aerial photographic camera, depends upon already existing energy sources.

separates, soil: See *soil separates*.

separation: The systematic division of solid waste into designated categories. separator: Any of various kinds of apparatus for dividing a mixture into its constituent parts. Types included:

ballistic: A device that drops mixed materials having different physical characteristics onto a high speed rotary impeller; they are hurled off at different velocities and land in separate collecting bins.

inertial: A material separation device that relies on ballistic or gracity separation of materials having different physical characteristics.

magnetic: Any device that removes ferrous metals by means of magnets. septic tank: An underground tank used for the deposition of domestic wastes. Bacteria in the wastes decompose the organic matter, and the sludge settles to the bottom. The effluent flows through drains into the ground. Sludge is pumped out at regular intervals.

septic systems: Systems that carry wastewater away from our homes when we turn on a faucet or flush a toilet.

septic tank: An underground tank used for the deposition of domestic wastes. Bacteria in the wastes decompose the organic matter, and the sludge settles to the bottom. The effluent flows through drains into the ground. Sludge is pumped out at regular intervals.

septic tank absorption field: A soil absorption system for sewage disposal, consisting of a subsurface tile system laid in such a way that effluent from the septic tank is distributed with reasonable uniformity into the natural soil.

serial distribution: An arrangement of absorption trenches, seepage pits, or seepage beds so that each is forced to pond, utilizing the total effective absorption area, before liquid flows into the succeeding component.

series: See *soil classification.*

sessile: Pertaining to those organisms that are attached to a substrate and not free to move about, such as periphyton. See *free swimming.*

seston: All material, both organic and inorganic, suspended in a waterway.

set (irrigation): That part of a field irrigated at one time.

set time: That part of a field irrigated at one time until it receives a planned amount of water.

settleable solids: Solids in a liquid that can be removed by stilling the liquid.

settlement: A gradual subsidence of material. Differential settlement is the nonuniform subsidence of material from a fixed horizontal reference plane.

settling basin: An enlargement in the channel of a stream to permit the settling of debris carried in suspension.

settling chamber: Any chamber designed to reduce the velocity of the products of combustion and thus to promote the settling of fly ash from the gas stream. See *baffle chamber.*

sewage: The total organic waste and wastewater generated by residential and commercial establishments.

sewage treatment plants: Places where wastewater is treated with chemicals and bacteria to produce clean water that can be returned

to rivers and other waterways.

sewage sludge: Settled sewage solids combined with varying amounts of water and dissolved materials that is removed from sewage by screening, sedimentation, chemical precipitation, or bacterial digestion.

sewage treatment residues: Coarse screenings, grit, or sludge from wastewater treatment units.

S factor: See *universal soil loss equation.*

shaft: Vertical or near vertical mining excavation of limited area, compared with its depth; made for mineral exploration, lowering or raising men and materials, removal of ore or water, and/or ventilation in underground mining.

shale: Stratified sedimentary rock structure, generally formed by the consolidation of clay or clay-like material.

shaly: An adjective incorporated into the soil textural class designations of horizons when the soil mass contains between 15 and 90 percent by volume of shale fragments. See *shale fragment as defined under coarse fragments.*

sharecropper: Provincial term used in the southern United States to denote a person who provides labor and equipment while the landlord furnishes land, buildings, and cash expenses and finances that family until harvest.

sharp crested weir: A device for measuring water, featuring a notch cut in a relatively thin plate and having a sharp edge on the upstream side of the crest.

shear: A distortion, strain, or failure producing a change in form, usually without change in volume, in which parallel layers of a body are displaced in the direction of their line of contact. shear strength: The maximum resistance of a soil to shearing stresses.

shear strength: The maximum resistance of a soil to shearing stresses.

sheet erosion: See *erosion*.

sheet flow: Water, usually storm runoff, flowing in a thin layer over the ground surface; also called overland flow.

sheet piling: A diaphragm made of meshing or interlocking members of wood, steel, concrete, or other material, driven into the ground individually, used to form an obstruction to percolation, prevent movement of material, stabilize foundations, and build coffer dams.

Shelford's law: When one environmental factor or condition is near the limits of toleration, either minimum or maximum, one factor or condition will be the controlling one and will determine whether or not a species will be able to maintain itself. See *limiting factor*.

shellfish: An animal such as a mollusk (clams, oysters, and snails) or crustacean (crabs and shrimp) that have a shell or shell-like external skeleton.

shelterbelt: See *windbreak*.

shelterwood cutting (forestry): A system of timber harvesting in which the old crop is removed in two or more successive cuttings over a period of years; designed to establish a new crop of seedlings under the protection (overhead or side) of the old trees. The first cut may be a preparatory cutting if the stand is dense, followed by a seed cutting to encourage seeding from seed trees for regeneration. The last cut is the final removal cutting after reproduction is established.

shifting cultivation: A farming system in which land is cleared, the debris burned, and crops grown for a short period; the land is then abandoned and a new clearing made; also called slash-and-burn agriculture or swidden agriculture.

shock load: The arrival at a water treatment plant of raw water containing unusual amounts of algae, colloidal matter. color, suspended solids, turbidity, or other pollutants.

shooting preserve: An area devoted to the shooting of pen-reared game under controlled conditions.

short-circuiting: When some of the water in tanks or basins flows faster than the rest; may result in shorter contact, reaction, or settling times than calculated or presumed.

short-term cleanup: A cleanup process that addresses immediate threats to public health and the environment that typically consist of less complex or less extensive contamination problems than those which require a long-term cleanup. There are three types of short-term cleanups: emergencies (e.g., fire or explosions), time-critical actions, and non-time-critical actions. Also referred to as removal actions.

short term costs: See *variable costs*.

shrink swell potential: Susceptibility to volume change due to loss or gain in moisture content.

shrub: A woody perennial plant differing from a tree by its low stature and by generally producing several basal shoots instead of a single bole.

shrublands: Habitats dominated by various species of shrubs, often with many grasses and forbs.

sickle: An agricultural implement consisting of a curved cutting blade and handle.

sidelooking radar: An all-weather, day/night remote sensor that is particularly effecting in imaging large areas of terrain; it is an active sensor, as it generates its own energy that is transmitted and received to produce a photo-like picture of the ground; also called sidelooking airborne radar.

side-roll sprinkler: A sprinkler system that uses the lateral line pipe as an axle with wheels either at each coupler or fastened around the pipe near each coupler.

side slopes (engineering): The slope of the sides of a canal, dam, or embankment. It is customary to name the vertical distance first, as 1.5 to one meaning a vertical distance of 1.5 feet to one foot horizontally.

signal (remote sensing): The effect (e.g., pulse of electromagnetic energy) conveyed over a communication path or system, received by the sensor from the scene, and converted to another form for transmission to the processing system.

signature (remote sensing): Any characteristic or series of characteristics by which a material may be recognized; used in the sense of spectral signature, as in photographic color reflectance.

significant (statistics): A term applied to differences, correlations, etc., to indicate that they are probably not due to chance alone. Significant ordinarily indicates a probability of not less than 95 percent, while highly significant indicates a probability of not less than 99 percent.

silage: A fodder crop that has been preserved in a moist succulent condition by partial fermentation. Chief silage crops are corn, sorghums, and various legumes and grasses.

silica: Silicon dioxide (SiO_2), occurring in crystalline, amorphous, and impure forms.

siliceous: See *soil mineralogy classes for family groupings.*

siliciclastic rocks: Rocks such as shale and sandstone which are formed by the compaction and cementation of quartz-rich mineral grains.

silt: A soil separate consisting of particles between 0.05 and 0.002 millimeter in equivalent diameter. See *soil separates; soil textural class.* See *soil texture.*

siltation: The process of depositing silt. See *sedimentation.*

silt basin: See *sedimentation basin, basin.*

silt loam: A soil textural class containing a large amount of silt and small quantities of sand and clay. See *soil texture.*

silty clay: A soil textural class containing a relatively large amount of silt and clay and a small amount of sand. See *soil texture.*

silty clay loam: A soil textural class containing a relatively large amount of silt, a lesser quantity of clay, and a still smaller quantity of sand. See *soil texture.*

silver iodide: A compound of silver and iodine, the crystalline structure of which closely approximates that of ice crystals; used as ice nuclei in weather modification.

silver iodide generator: Any of several devices used to generate a smoke of silver iodide crystals for cloud seeding.

silverculture: The management or cultivation of forest trees.

single grain: Lack of soil structure in incoherent materials. See *soil structure grades.*

sink: Depression in the land surface; a negative potential area, as in a source and a sink.

sinkhole: A depression in the earth's surface caused by dissolving of underlying limestone, salt, or gypsum, drainage is through underground channels; may be enlarged by collapse of a cavern roof. See *karst.*

sinking: Controlling oil spills by using an agent to trap the oil and sink it to the bottom of the body of water where the agent and the oil are biodegraded.

sinuosity: The ratio of the channel length between two points on a channel to the straight-line distance between the same two points; a measure of meandering.

sinusoidal map projection: See *map projection.*

siphon (hydraulics): A closed conduit, a part of which rises above the hydraulic grade line, utilizing atmospheric pressure to cause the flow of water.

siphon tubes: Small curved pipes, .five inch to four inches (1.3-10.2 cm) in diameter, that deliver water over the side of a head ditch or lateral to furrows, corrugations, or borders.

site (ecology): An area considered for its ecological factors with reference to capacity to produce vegetation; the combination of biotic, climatic, and soil conditions of an area; an area sufficiently uniform in soil, climate, and natural biotic conditions to produce a particular climax vegetation.

site factors: The environmental factors that are present at a specified location.

site index (forestry): A numerical expression commonly accepted as an indicator of the quality or timber productivity of a site. It is an expression of the height age relationship of the tallest trees (dominants and co dominants) in normal stands at some designated age, such as 50 years.

site plan: A scale drawing of an area, showing existing site conditions and proposed development. See *plot plan.*

skeletal soils: Soils with greater than 35 percent, by volume, of fragments greater than two mm.

skimming: Diverting surface water by shallow overflow to avoid diverting sediment or debris carried as bedload.

slag: The product of smelting, containing mostly silicates; the substances not sought to be produced as matte or metal and having a lower specific gravity.

slash: The branches, bark, tops, cull logs, and broken or uprooted trees on the ground after logging.

slick spots: Barren areas having puddled or crusted, very smooth, nearly impervious surfaces, usually because of high salinity or alkalinity. A miscellaneous area.

slime flux: A diseased condition of trees in which secretion exudes from an old wound; also called wet wood.

slip: The downslope movement of a soil mass under wet or saturated conditions; a microlandslide that produces microrelief in soils.

slope: The degree of deviation of a surface from horizontal, measured in a numerical ratio, percent, or degrees. Expressed as a ratio or percentage, the first number is the vertical distance (rise) and the second is the horizontal distance (run), as 2:1 or 200 percent. Expressed in degrees, it is the angle of the slope from the horizontal plane with a 90 degree slope being vertical (maximum) and 45 degree being a 1:1 slope.

slope characteristics: Slopes may be characterized as concave (decrease in steepness in lower portion), uniform, or convex (increase in steepness at base). Erosion is strongly affected by shape, ranked in order of increasing erodibility from concave to uniform to convex.

slope stability: The resistance of any inclined surface, as the wall of an open pit or cut, to failure by sliding or collapsing.

slot planting: See *no tillage*.

slough: Wet or marshy area.

slow sand filtration: Passage of raw water through a bed of sand at low velocity, resulting in substantial removal of chemical and biological contaminants.

sludge: A semi fluid mixture of fine solid particles with a liquid.

sludge deposits: Accumulations of settled, usually rapidly decomposing organic material

in the aquatic system.

sludgeworms: Aquatic segmented worms (obligochaeta) that exhibit marked population increases in waters polluted with decomposable organic wastes. See *bloodworms*.

sluice: Channel serving to drain off surplus water from behind a flood gate; conduit for carrying water at high velocity; an opening in a structure for passing debris. Also, to cause water to flow at high velocities for ejecting debris.

slump test: A method of measuring the workability or, more properly, the consistency of concrete mixtures.

small–scale: Aerial photographs with a representative fraction (scale) smaller than 1:40,000; maps with a representative fraction less than 1:1,000,000.

smog: A polluted atmosphere in which products of combustion such as hydrocarbons, soot, sulfur compounds, etc., occur in detrimental concentrations for human beings and other organisms, especially during foggy weather.

smoke: Liquid or solid particles under one micron in diameter.

snag: A standing dead tree or part of a dead tree from which at least the smaller branches have fallen.

snow ablation: The disappearance of snow from the force of wind.

snow course: A course laid out and permanently marked on the drainage area of a stream, along which the snow is sampled at appropriate times to determine its depth and density for the purpose of forecasting subsequent runoff.

snow density: The water content of snow expressed as a percentage by volume. In snow surveys, the ratio of the scale reading (inches of water) to the length of the snow core, in inches.

snow fence: A fence of slat and wire or other material used in winter to intercept drifting snow, thus protecting roads, railways, and other areas from snowdrifts. Also used to impound snow where melting in place adds to soil moisture.

snowhedge: A planting of shrubs or other plants to intercept drifting snow; also called snowbreak; snowcatch.

snow management: The management of snow in such a way as to increase moisture for crop production; generally accomplished through the use of wind barriers, including grass and grass stubble barriers, but also including trees and shrubs.

snowpack: The packed snow layer resulting from continuous use by snowmobile, skiing, foot trails, or vehicular trails. Significant because of the possible injury to turf or soil warming, soil compaction, etc., in the following season.

snow sample: A core taken from the snow mantle on a snow course from which the depth and density may be determined.

snow sampler: The equipment, consisting essentially of light-weight, jointed tubes, used for taking snow samples to determine the water content of the snow-pack.

snow surveys: A set of measurements of the depth and density of snow, usually made to determine the water stored on a drainage basin in the form of snow as an aid to predicting the subsequent runoff.

social well-being: One of the four required accounts for categorizing, displaying, or accounting the beneficial and adverse effects of each alternative plan formulation for water and related land resources planning specified in the Water Resources Council's Principles and Standards and the US Department of Agriculture's Procedures; includes (at least): real income distribution among individuals, classes, and groups; life, health, and safety; education, cultural, and recreational opportunities; and emergency preparedness.

sod grasses: Stoloniferous or rhizomatous grasses that form a sod or turf.

sodic soil: A soil that contains sufficient sodium to interfere with the growth of most crop plants; a soil in which the exchangeable sodium percentage is 15 or more. Sodic soils, because of dispersion of the organic matter, have been called black alkali soils; sometimes also called nonsaline alkali soils.

sodium adsorption ratio, adjusted: The sodium adsorption ratio (SAR) of a water adjusted for the precipitation or dissolution of CA^{2+} that is expected to occur where a water reacts with alkaline earth carbonates within a soil; numerically, it is obtained by multiplying the sodium adsorption ratio by the value (1+8.4-pHc).

sod planting: A method of planting in killed sod with little or no tillage.

soft growth: Young, succulent plant

growth that is very easily injured.

soft pinch: Removal of only the terminal plant bud and tip of a growing shoot before maturation or differentiation of cells.

soft water: Any water that does not contain a significant amount of dissolved minerals such as salts of calcium or magnesium.

software: Computer programs that drive the hardware components of a data processing system; includes system monitoring programs, programming language processors, data handling utilities, and data analysis programs.

soil: The unconsolidated mineral and organic material on the immediate surface of the earth that serves as a natural medium for the growth of land plants; the unconsolidated mineral matter on the surface of the earth that has been subjected to and influenced by genetic and environmental factors of parent material, climate (including moisture and temperature effects), macro and microorganisms, and topography, all acting over a period of time and producing a product soil that differs from the material from which it is derived in many physical, chemical, biological, and morphological properties and characteristics; a kind of soil is the collection of soils that are alike in specified combinations of characteristics. Kinds of soil are given names in the system of soil classification. The terms "the soil" and "soil" are collective terms used for all soils, equivalent to the word "vegetation" for all plants.

soil absorption field: A system of absorption trenches.

soil absorption system: Any sys-

tem that utilizes the soil for subsequent absorption of the treated sewage, such as an absorption trench, seepage bed, or a seepage pit.

soil amendment: Any material, such as lime, gypsum, sawdust, or synthetic conditioner, that is worked into the soil to make it more amenable to plant growth.

soil and capability map: See *land capability map*.

soil and crop management: Deciding what crops and varieties to grow and in what sequence to utilize the soil's productive capacity, and what tillage, cultivation, and soil conservation measures to undertake to physically till and preserve the soil and conserve moisture.

soil association: A group of defined and named taxonomic soil units occurring together in an individual and characteristic pattern over a geographic region, comparable to plant associations in many ways. Sometimes called "natural land type"; a mapping unit used on reconnaissance or generalized soil maps in which two or more defined taxonomic units occurring together in a characteristic pattern are combined because the scale of the map or the purpose for which it is being made does not require delineation of the individual soils.

soil auger: A tool for boring into the soil and withdrawing a small sample for field or laboratory observation. Soil augers may be classified as those with worm type bits, unenclosed, or those with worm type bits enclosed in a hollow cylinder.

soil classification: The systematic arrangement of soils into groups or categories on the basis of their characteristics. Broad groupings are made on the basis of general characteristics; subdivisions on the basis of more detailed differences in specific properties. The categories of the system used in the United States since 1966 are briefly discussed below.

order: The category at the highest level of generalization in the soil classification system. The properties selected to distinguish the orders are reflections of the degree of horizon development and the kinds of horizons present.

suborder: This category narrows the ranges in soil moisture and temperature regimes, kinds of horizons, and composition, according to which of these is most important. Moisture and/or temperature or soil properties associated with them are used to define the suborders of the orders Alfisols, Mollisols, Oxisols, Ultisols, and Vertisols. Kinds of horizons are used for the order Aridisols, composition for the orders Histosols and Spodosols, and combinations for the orders Entisols and Inceptisols.

great group: The classes in this category contain soils that have the same kind of horizons in the same sequence and have similar moisture and temperature regimes. Exceptions to the horizon sequences are made for horizons near the surface that may get mixed or lost by erosion if plowed.

subgroup: The great groups are subdivided into subgroups that show the central properties of the great group, intergrade subgroups that show properties of more than one great group, and other subgroups for soils with atypical properties that are not characteristic of any great group.

family: Families are defined largely on the basis of physical and mineralogic properties of importance to plant growth.

series: The soil series is a group of soils having horizons similar in differentiating characteristics and arrangement in the soil profile, except for texture of the surface portion, or if genetic horizons are thin or absent, a group of soils that, within defined depth limits, is uniform in all soil characteristics diagnostic for series.

The ten orders of soil classification and their respective sub orders are as follows:

DIAGRAM AT BOTTOM OF PG   150

Alfisols: Soil with gray to brown surface horizons, medium to high supply of bases, and B horizons of illuvial clay accumulation. They form mostly under forest or savanna vegetation in climates with slight to pronounced seasonal moisture deficits.

Aqualfs: Alfisols seasonally saturated with water.

Boralfs: Alfisols that are cool or cold.

Udalfs: Alfisols in moist, warm temperate climates.

Ustalfs: Alfisols in warm climates that are intermittently dry for long periods during the year.

Xeralfs: Alfisols in warm climates that are continuously dry for long periods in the summer but moist in the winter.

Aridsols: Soils with pedogenic horizons, low in organic matter, that are never moist as long as three consecutive months. They have an ochric epipedon that is normailly soft when dry or that has distinct structure. Also, they have one or more of the following diagnostic horizons: argillic, nitric, cambic, calcic, petrocalcic, gypsies, or salic or a duripan.

Agrids: Aridsols with horizons of clay accumulation.

Orthids: Aridsols without horizons of clay accumulation.

Entisols: Soils that have no diagnostic pedogentic horizons. They may be found in virtually any climate on very recent geomorphic surfaces, either on steep slopes that are undergoing active erosion or on fans and floodplains where the recently eroded materials are deposited. They may also be on older geomorphic surfaces if the soils have been recently disturbed to such depths that the horizons have been destroyed or if the parent materials are resistant to alteration, as is quartz.

Aquents: Entisols permanently or seasonally saturated with water.

Arents: Entisols that contain recognizable fragments of pedogenic horizons that have been mixed by mechanical disturbance.

Fluvents: Entisols that form in recent loamy or clayey alluvial deposits, are usually stratified and have an organic carbon content that decreases irregularly with

depth.

Orthents: Entisols with loamy or clayey textures.

Psamments: Entisols with sandy textures.

Histosols: Soils formed from organic soil materials.

Fibrists: Histosols with largely undecomposed, fibrous organic materials.

Folists: Histosols with largely undecomposed, fibrous organic materials.

Hemists: Histosols intermediate between Fibrists and Saprists in decomposition of organic materials.

Saprists: Histosols with largely decomposed organic materials.

Inceptisols: Soils that are usually moist with pedogenic horizons of alteration of parent material but not of illuviation. Generally, the direction of soil development is not yet evident from the marks left by various soil0forming processes or the marks are too weak to classify in another order.

Andepts: Inceptisols with large amounts of amorphous or vitric pyroclastic materials.

Aquepts: Inceptisols seasonally saturated with water.

Ochrepts: Inceptisols that have thin or light-colored surface horizons with little organic matter and altered subsurface horizons.

Plaggepts: Inceptisols that have a ploggen epipedon.

Tropepts: Inceptisols that have a mean annual soil temperature of eight degrees celsius or more and less than five degrees celsius difference between mean summer and mean winter temperatures at a depth of 50 centimeters below the surface.

Mollisols: Soils with nearly black, organic-rich surface horizons and high supplies of bases. Soils that have decomposition and accumulation of relatively large amounts of organic matter in the presence of calcium. They have mollic epipedons and base saturation greater than 50 percent (NH^4OAc) in any cambic or argillic horizon. They lack the characteristics of Vertisols and must not have oxic or spodic horizons.

Albolls: Mollisols that have an albic horizon immediately below the mollic epipedon.

Aquolls: Mollisols seasonally saturated with water.

Borolls: Mollisols that are cool or cold.

Rendolls: Mollisols that have no argillic or calcic horizon but that contain material with more than 40 percent $CaCO^3$ equivalent within or immediately below the mollic epipedon.

Udolls: Mollisols in moist, warm-temperate climates.

Ustolls: Mollisols that are intermittently dry for long periods during the warm season of the year.

Xerolls: Mollisols that are continuously dry for long periods during the warm season of the year.

Oxisols: Soils with residual accumulations of inactive clays, free oxides, kaolin, and quartz. They are mostly in tropical climates.

Aquox: Oxisols that have continuous plinthite near the surface, or that are saturated with water sometime during the year if not artificially drained.

Humox: Oxisols that are moist all of most of the time and that have high organic carbon content within the upper meter.

Orthox: Oxisols that are most all or most of the time and that have a low to moderate content of organic carbon within the upper one meter or a mean annual soil temperature of 22 degrresC or more.

Torrox: Oxisols that have a torric soil moisture regime.

Ustox: Oxisols that have an ustic moisture regime and either hyperthermic or isohyperthermic soil temperature regimes or have less than 20 kilograms organic carbon in the surface cubic meter.

Spodosols: Soils with illuvial accumulations of amorphous materials in subsurface horizons. The amorphous material is organic matter and compounds of aluminum and usually iron. These soils are formed in acid, mainly coarse-textured materials in humid and mostly cool or temperate climates.

Aquods: Spodosols seasonally saturated with water.

Ferrods: Spodosols that have more than six times as much free iron (elemental) than organic carbon in the spodic horizon.

Humods: Spodosols that have accumulated organic carbon in the spodic horizon.

Orthods: Spodosols with subsurface accumulations of iron, aluminum, and organic matter.

Utisols: Soils that are low in supply of bases and have subsurface horizons of illuvial clay accumulations. They are usually moist, but during the warm season of the year some are dry part of the time. The balance between liberation of bases by weathering and removal by leaching is normally such that a permanent agriculture is impossible without fertilizers or the use of shifting cultivation.

Aquults: Ultisols seasonally saturated with water.

Humults: Ultisols with high or very high organic-matter content.

Udults: Ultisols with low organic-matter content in moist, warm climates.

Ustults: Ultisols that have low or moderate amounts of organic carbon, are brownish or reddish throughout, and have a ustic soil moisture regime.

Xerults: Ultisols with low to moderate organic-matter content, continuously dry for long periods in the summer but moist in the winter.

Vertisols: Clayey soils with high shrink-swell potential that have wide, deep cracks when dry. Most of these soils have distinct wet and dry periods throuout the year.

Torrerts: Vertisols of arid regions that have wide, deep cracks that remain open throughout the year in most years.

Uderts: Vertisols that crack open for only short periods, less than a total of three months in a year.

Userts: Vertisols that crack open for only short periods, less than a total of three months in a year.

Xererts: Vertisols of Mediterranian climates that have wide, deep cracks that open and close once each year and usually remain open continuously for more than two months.

soil complex: A mapping unit used in detailed soil surveys where two or more defined taxonomic units are so intimately intermixed geographically that it is undesirable or impractical, because of the scale being used, to separate them. A more intimate mixing of smaller areas of individual taxonomic units than that described under soil association.

soil conditioner: Any material added to a soil for the purpose of improving its physical condition.

soil conservation: Using the soil within the limits of its physical characteristics and protecting it from unalterable limitations of climate and topography.

soil conserving crops: Crops that prevent or retard erosion and maintain or replenish rather than deplete soil organic matter.

soil correlation: The process of defining, mapping, naming, and classifying the kinds of soils in a specific soil survey area, the purpose being to insure that soils are adequately defined, accurately mapped, and uniformly named in all soil surveys made in the United States. Also concerned with the standards and techniques for describing soils and with the application and development of soil classification.

soil creep: See *creep.*

soil depleting crops: Crops that under the usual management tend to deplete nutrients and organic matter in the soil and permit deterioration of soil structure.

soil erodibility: An indicator of a soil's susceptibility to raindrop impact, runoff, and other erosive processes.

soil erosion: The detachment and movement of soil from the land surface by wind or water. See *erosion*.

soil fertility: The quality of a soil that enables it to provide nutrients in adequate amounts and in proper balance for the growth of specified plants, when other growth factors, such as light, moisture, temperature, and physical condition of soil, are favorable.

soil formation factors: The variables, usually interrelated natural agencies, active in and responsible for the formation of soil. The factors are usually grouped as follows: parent material, climate, organisms, topography, and time. Many people believe that activities of man in his use and manipulation of soil become such an important influence on soil formation that he should be added as a sixth variable. Others consider man as an organism.

soil fumigation: Treatment of the soil with volatile or gaseous substances that penetrate the soil mass and kill one or more forms of soil organisms.

soil genesis: The mode of origin of the soil with special reference to the processes or soil forming factors responsible for the development of the solum or true soil from the unconsolidated parent material; a division of soil science concerned with the origin of soil.

soil granule: A cluster of soil particles behaving as a unit in soil structure. See *soil structure*.

soil horizon: A layer of soil or soil material approximately parallel to the land surface and differing from adjacent genetically related layers in physical, chemical, and biological properties or characteristics, such as color, structure, texture, consistence, kinds and numbers of organisms present, degree of acidity or alkalinity, etc.

soil improvement: The processes for, or the results of, making the soil more productive for growing plants by drainage, irrigation, addition of fertilizers and soil amendments, and other methods.

soil individual: See *polypedon. soil loss equation*: See *universal soil loss equation*.

soil loss tolerance: The maximum average annual soil loss in tons per acre per year that should be permitted on a given soil.

soil management: The sum total of all tillage operations, cropping practices, fertilizer, lime, and other treatments conducted on, or applied to, a soil for the production of plants.

soil map: A map showing the distribution of soil types or other soil mapping units in relation to the prominent physical and cultural features of the earth's surface. The following kinds of soil maps are recognized in the United States: 1) detailed, 2) detailed reconnaissance, 3) reconnaissance, 4) generalized, and 5) schematic.

soil mapping unit: A kind of soil, a combination of kinds of soil, or miscellaneous land type or types that can be shown at the scale of mapping for the defined purposes and objectives of the survey. (Combination of kinds of soil includes 1) soil association, 2) complexes, 3) undifferentiated soils, or any class or combination of classes at the family level or higher categories of the soil classification system.) Soil mapping units are the basis for the delineations of a soil survey map. A soil survey identification legend lists all mapping units for the survey of an area (any size area from a small plot to a county, a nation, or the world). Mapping units normally contain inclusions of soils outside the limits of the taxonomic name, or names, used as the name for the mapping unit. Mapping units are generally designed to reflect significant differences in use and management.

soil materials: Soil or portions of soil that have been displaced or mixed by either natural or mechanical means; unconsolidated and more or less chemically weathered mineral matter from which soils are developed by pedogenic processes; disintegrated and partly weathered rock from which soil parent materials are formed.

soil mineralogy classes for family groupings (As used in the Soil Classification System of the National Cooperative Soil Survey in the United States): The family category includes mineralogy classes for specific control sections which are similar to those used for particle size classes for family groupings. For example, the term micaceous

denotes that more than 40 percent by weight of the 0.02 to 20 millimeter fraction of the soil material within the control section is mica.

Examples of some mineralogy classes are listed below:

ferritic: For soils of any texture, the whole soil less than two millimeters in the control section contains more than 40 percent (weight) iron oxide as (Fe_2O_3) extractable by citrate dithionite.

illitic: In clayey soils, more than half by weight of the clay size fraction is composed of illite (hydrous mica) commonly with greater than three percent K_2O.

kaolinitic: In clayey soils, more than half by weight of the clay size fraction is composed of kaolinite, dickite, and nacrite with smaller amounts of other 1:1 or nonexpanding 2:1 layer minerals or gibbsite.

micaceous: See *soil mineralogy classes.*

mixed: Soils that have a combination of minerals in which no single class of mineralogy is dominant.

montmorillonitic: In clayey soils, more than half by weight of the clay size fraction is composed of montmorillonite and nontronite, or a mixture with more montmorillonite than any other single clay mineral.

silceous: In the 0.02 to two millimeter fraction within the control section of sandy, silty, and loamy soils more than 90 percent by weight of silica minerals (quartz, chalcedony, or opal) and other extremely durable minerals that are resistant to weathering.

soil moisture: The water content store in a soil; measured by volume (Mv), it is the volume of water per unit of soil, usually expressed as a percentage; measured by weight (Mw), it is the weight of water per unit oven-dry weight of the soil; Mv = Mw x bulk density of the soil.

soil monolith: A vertical section of a soil profile removed and mounted for display or study.

soil morphology: The physical constitution, particularly the structural properties, of a soil profile as exhibited by the kinds, thickness, and arrangement of the horizons in the profile, and by the texture, structure, consistency, and porosity of each horizon; the structural characteristics of the soil or any of its parts.

soil organic matter: The organic fraction of the soil that includes plant and animal residues at various stages of decomposition, cells and tissues of soil organisms, and substances synthesized by the soil population. Commonly determined as the amount of organic material contained in a soil sample passed through a two millimeter sieve.

soil permeability: See *permeability*.

soil piping: See *piping*.

soil pollution: The addition of harmful or objectionable material to soil in concentrations or in sufficient quantities to adversely affect its usefulness or quality.

soil pores: See *pore space*.

soil porosity: See *porosity, soil*.

soil probe: A tool having a hollow cylinder with a cutting edge at the lower end, used for probing into the soil and withdrawing a small sample for field or laboratory observation.

soil productivity: The capacity of a soil in its normal environment for producing a specified plant or sequence of plants under a specified system of management.

soil profile: A vertical section of the soil from the surface through all its horizons, including C horizons. See *soil horizons*.

soil, residual: Soil that has no been moved from its plan of origin.

soil separates: Mineral particles, less than 2.0 millimeters in equivalent diameter, ranging between specified size limits. The names and size limits of separates recognized by the National Cooperative Soil Survey in the United States are very coarse sand, 2.0 to 1.0 millimeters (called fine gravel prior to 1947, now fine gravel includes particles between 2.0 millimeters and about 12.5 millimeters in diameter); coarse sand, 1.0 to 0.5 millimeter; medium sand, 0.5 to 0.25 millimeter; fine sand 0.25 to 0.10 millimeter; very fine sand, 0.10 to 0.05 millimeter; silt, 0.05 to 0.002 millimeter; and clay, less than 0.002 millimeter. (Before 1937, clay included particles less than 0.005 millimeter in diameter and silt, those particles from 0.05 to 0.005 millimeter).

soil series: See *soil classification*.

soil stabilization: Chemical and/or mechanical treatment to increase or maintain the stability of a mass of soil or otherwise to improve its engineering properties.

soil structure: The combination or arrangement of primary soil particles into secondary particles, units, or peds. The secondary units are characterized and classified on the basis of size, shape, and degree of distinctness into classes, types, and grades, respectively.

soil structure classes: A grouping of soil structural units or peds on the basis of size.

soil structure grades: A grouping or classification of soil structure on the basis of inter and intra aggregate adhesion, cohesion, or stability within the profile. Four grades used are structureless, weak, moderate, and strong, depending on observable degree of aggregation.

soil structure types: A classification of soil structure based on the shape of the aggregates or peds and their arrangement in the profile. Generally the shape of soil structure types is referred to as either platy, prismatic, columnar, blocky, granular, or crumb.

soil survey: A general term for the systematic examination of soils in the field and in laboratories; their description and classification; the mapping of kinds of soil; the interpretation of soils according to their adaptability for various crops, grasses, and trees; their behavior under use or treatment for plant production or for other purposes; and their productivity under different management systems.

soil survey field sheet: An aerial photograph on which information relating to soils and other characteristics of the land surface are delineated or portrayed.

soil taxonomic unit: A unit of all

soils that fall within the defined limits of a class at any categoric level in a system of soil classification. Commonly used as a member of the lowest class in the present classification scheme and in that use is equivalent to a series.

soil temperature classes for family groupings (as used in the Soil Classification System of the National Cooperative Soil Survey in the United States): Classes are based on mean annual soil temperature and difference between mean summer and mean winter temperature. Soil temperature is determined at a depth of 50 centimeters (20 inches) or at a lithic or paralithic contact, whichever is shallower. Unless used in a higher category, soil temperature classes are used at the family level as follows: (1) Soils with 5°C (9°F) or more difference between mean summer (June, July, and August) and mean winter (December, January, and February) temperatures, and with mean annual soil temperatures as follows: less than 8°C (47°F), frigid; 8°C to 15°C (47°F to 59°F), mesic; 15°C to 22°C (59°F to 72°F), thermic; and more than 22°C (72°F), hyperthermic. (2) Soils with less than 5°C (9°F) difference between mean summer and winter soil temperatures, and with mean annual soil temperatures as follows: less than 8°C (47°F), isofrigid; 8°C to 15°C (47°F to 59°F), isomesic; 15°C to 22°C (59°F to 72°F), isothermic; & 22°C (72°ßF) or higher, isohyperthermic

soil texture: The relative proportions of the various soil separates in a soil as described by the classes of soil texture shown in figure The textural classes may be modified by the addition of suitable adjectives when coarse fragments are present in substantial amounts, for example, gravelly silt loam. (For other modifications see *coarse fragments*.) Sand, loamy sand, and sandy loam are further subdivided on the basis of the proportions of the various sand separates present. The limits of the various classes and subclasses are:

sand: Soil material that contains 85 percent or more of sand. The percentage of silt plus 1.5 times the percentage of clay shall not exceed 15.

coarse sand: 25 percent or more very coarse and coarse sand and less than 50 percent any other one grade of sand. sand: 25 percent or more very coarse, coarse, and medium sand and less than 50 percent fine or very fine sand.

fine sand: 50 percent or more fine sand, or less than 25 percent very coarse, more fine sand, or less than 25 percent very coarse, fine sand.

very fine sand: 50 percent or more very fine sand.

loamy sand: Soil material that contains, at the upper limit, 85 to 90 percent sand, and the percentage of silt plus 1.5 times the percentage of clay is not less than 15. At the lower limit, it contains not less than 70 to 85 percent sand, and the percentage of silt plus twice the percentage of clay does not exceed 30.

loamy coarse sand: 25 percent or more very coarse and coarse sand and less than 50 percent any other one grade of sand.

loamy sand: 25 percent or more very coarse, coarse, and medium sand and less than 50 percent fine or very fine sand.

loamy fine sand: 50 percent or more fine sand, or less than 25 percent very coarse, coarse, and medium sand and 50 percent very fine sand.

loamy very fine sand: 50 percent or more very fine sand.

sandy loams: Soil material that contains either 20 percent or less clay, and the percentage of silt plus twice the percentage of clay exceeds 30, and 52 percent or more sand; or less than seven percent clay, less than 50 percent silt, and between 43 and 52 percent sand.

coarse sandy loam: 25 percent or more very coarse and coarse sand and less than 50 percent any other one grade of sand.

sandy loam: 30 percent or more very coarse, coarse, and medium sand but less than 25 percent very coarse sand and less than 30 percent very fine or fine sand.

fine sandy loam: 30 percent or more fine sand and less than 30 percent very fine sand, or between 15 and 30 percent very coarse, and medium sand.

very fine sandy loam: 30 percent or more very fine sand, or more than 40 percent fine and very fine sand, at least half of which is very fine sand and less than 15 percent very coarse, coarse, and medium sand. loam: Soil material that contains seven to 27 percent clay, 28 to 50 percent silt, and less than 52 percent sand. silt loam: Soil material that contains 50 percent or more silt and 12 to 27 percent clay, or 50 to 80 percent silt and less than 12 percent clay. silt: Soil material that contains 80 percent or more silt and less than 12 percent clay.

sandy clay loam: Soil material that contains 20 to 35 percent clay, less than 28 percent silt, and 45 percent or more sand.

clay loam: Soil material that contains 27 to 40 percent clay and 20 to 45 percent sand.

silty clay loam: Soil material that contains 27 to 40 percent clay and less than 20 percent sand.

sandy clay: Soil material that contains 35 percent or more clay and 45 percent or more sand.

silty clay: Soil material that contains 40 percent or more clay and 40 percent or more silt.

clay: Soil material that contains 40 percent or more clay, less than 45 percent sand, and less than 40 percent silt.

CHART IN OLD GLOSSARY PG. 162

soil variant: A kind of soil whose properties are believed to be sufficiently different from recognized series to justify a new series name but comprising such a limited geographic area that creation of a new series is not justified.

soil water tension: The force per unit area that must be exerted to remove water from the soil.

solar angle: The angle made by the intersection of the sun's azimuth and a line through true north; varies with time of day, time of year, and geographic position on

earth's surface.

solar cell: A device that converts solar radiation to a current of electricity; also called photovoltaic cell.

solar radiation: Solar radiation is heat energy from the sun, including the infrared, visible, and ultraviolet wavelengths. For heat island mitigation purposes, solar radiation is measured by American Society for Testing and Materials Standard E 1918, which provides for in-field use of a pyrometer to measure incoming and outgoing radiation.

solid-phase extraction: A procedure to isolate specific organic compounds onto a bonded silica extraction column.

solid waste: Useless, unwanted, or discarded material with insufficient liquid content to be free flowing. See *waste*.
Types include:

agricultural: The solid waste that results from the rearing and slaughtering of animals and the processing of animal products and orchard and field crops.

commercial: Solid waste generated by stores, offices, and other activities that do not actually turn out a product.

industrial: Solid waste that results from industrial processes and manufacturing.

institutional: Solid wastes originating from educational, health care, and research facilities.

municipal: Normally, residential and commercial solid waste generated within a community.

pesticide: The residue resulting

from the manufacturing, handling, or use of chemicals for killing plant and animal pests.

residential: All solid waste that normally originates in a residential environment. Sometimes called domestic solid waste.

solid waste disposal: The ultimate disposition of refuse that cannot be salvaged or recycled.

solid waste management: The purposeful, systematic control of the generation, storage, collection, transport, separation, processing, recycling, recovery and disposal of solid wastes.

solifluction: The slow downhill flow or creep of soil and other loose materials that become saturated.

solum: The upper part of a soil profile, above the parent material, in which the processes of soil formation are active. The solum in mature soils includes the A and B-horizons. Usually the characteristics of the material in these horizons are quite unlike those of the underlying parent material. The living roots and other plant and animal life characteristic of the soil are largely confined to the solum.

solution: Formed when a solid, gas, or another liquid in contact with a liquid becomes dispersed homogeneously throughout the liquid. The substance, called a solute, is said to dissolve. The liquid is called the solvent.

sonic boom: The tremendous booming sound produced when a vehicle, usually a supersonic jet airplane, exceeds the speed of sound and the shock wave reaches the ground.

soot: Agglomerations of tar-impregnated carbon particles that form when carbonaceous material does not undergo complete combustion.

sorption: General term for the interaction (binding or association) of a solute ion or molecule with a solid.

sorting: The separation and segregation of rock fragments according to size and particles, specific gravity, and different shapes by natural processes, mainly the action of running water or wind. "Well sorted" refers to representation of one grade size; "poorly sorted" refers to representation of many grade sizes in a sample of material.

source reduction: The design, manufacture, or use of products that in some way reduces the amount of waste that must be disposed of; examples include reuse of by-products, reducing consumption, extending the useful life of a product, and minimizing materials going into production.

source rocks: The rocks from which fragments and other detached pieces have been derived to form a different rock.

spacecraft: Device, manned or unmanned, designed to be placed into an orbit about the earth or into a trajectory to another celestial body; generally considered to be maneuverable, as contrasted to satellites, which are placed in fixed orbits.

sparge or sparging: Injection of air below the water table to strip dissolved volatile organic compounds and/or oxygenate groundwater to facilitate aerobic biodegradation of organic compounds.

spatial: The location of, proximity to, or orientation of objects with respect to one another.

spatial data: Data that has a geographic relationship, or that can be mapped; may or may not be georeferenced.

spawn: In aquatic animals, to produce or deposit eggs or sperm; to produce eggs or young. Eggs of fishes and higher aquatic invertebrates.

special habitats: Wetlands, vernal pools, riparian habitat, and unfragmented rivers, forests and grasslands.

special riparian project: Restoring, protecting, or enhancing an aquatic environment in a discrete riparian corridor within a special focus area.

species: A group of organisms that resemble each other closely and that interbreed freely.

species diversity: An ecological concept that incorporates both the number of species in a particular sampling area and the evenness with which individuals are distributed among the various species.

specific energy: The energy of a stream referred to its bed, namely, depth plus velocity head of mean velocity.

specific gravity: The relative weight of a given volume of any kind of matter (volume occupied by solid phase, pore space excluded) compared with an equal volume of distilled water at a specified temperature. The average specific gravity for soil is about 2.65. See *bulk density*.

specific retention: That volume of water that is retained by adhesion against the pull of gravity, expressed in percent of the total volume of water bearing materials.

specific yield: The fraction of pore space that will yield water to wells, equaling porosity minus specific retention; the amount of water that will drain by gravity from saturated materials, usually expressed in percent of total volume of waterbearing materials; coefficient of storage.

specimen plant: In appearance, an ornamental plant that approaches the optimum form and density characteristics for the particular species and variety; in landscape usage, any plant that is displayed to its best advantage either singly or in multiple plantings; a typical or distinctly different form or density by pruning or other manipulation. See *character plant*.

spectra: Data that result from spectral scanning; measurements of the variations in spectral response over a range of wavelengths for a single, constant viewing area.

spectral band: An interval in the electromagnetic spectrum defined by two wavelengths, frequencies, or wave numbers.

spectral regions: Conveniently designated ranges of wavelengths subdividing the electromagnetic spectrum; for example, the visible region, x-ray region, infrared region, middle-infrared region.

spectral signature: The spectral characterization of an object or class of objects on the earth's surface; often used in a way that naively over-simplifies the complexity of the spectral representation problem in a natural scene.

spectroscopy: The science dealing with the production, transmission, measurement, and interpretation of electromagnetic spectra.

spiles (irrigation): Small pipes, generally straight, from one to four inches (2.5-10 cm) in diameter, used to distribute water fro a ditch into furrows, borders, or corrugations.

spillway: An open or closed channel, or both, used to convey excess water from a reservoir. It may contain gates, either manually or automatically controlled, to regulate the discharge of excess water.

spillway, emergency: A spillway to carry water safely though or around dams should the primary spillway fail to function properly or if larger runoff occurs than was assumed for the design of the primary spillway.

spirometer: An instrument that measures the flow of air in and out of the lungs.

splash erosion: See *erosion*.

spodic horizon: See *diagnostic horizons*.

Spodosols: See *soil classification*.

spoil: Soil or rock material excavated from a canal, ditch, basin, or similar construction.

spoilbank: A pile of soil, subsoil, rock, or other material excavated from a drainage ditch, pond, or other cut.

spot planting (forestry): Planting in small open areas among established groups or stands of trees.

See *interplanting*.

spreader (hydraulics): A device for distributing water uniformly in or from a channel.

spreader strip: A relatively permanent contour strip of variable width planted to a sod or erosion resistant crop, used to slow down and fan out the runoff from land above the strip.

sprig: Small plant shoot or twig; an ornament in the form of a twig or a stemmed flower.

sprigging: The planting of a portion of the stem and root of grass.

spring: Groundwater seeping out of the earth where the water table intersects the ground surface.

spring overturn: A physical phenomenon that may take place in a body of water during the early spring. The sequence of events leading to spring overturn include: 1) melting of ice cover, 2) warming of surface waters, 3) density changes in surface waters producing convection currents from top to bottom, 4) circulation of the total water volume by wind action, and 5) vertical temperature equality. The overturn results in a uniformity of the physical and chemical properties of the entire water mass. See *fall overturn, overturn*.

sprinkler irrigation: Irrigation system in which water is applied by means of perforated pipes or nozzles operated under pressure so as to form a spray pattern.

sprinkler pattern: The areal distribution of water applied either by perforated pipe, single sprinkler nozzle, or by the entire sprinkler lateral or laterals.

spur: A short side twig, often bearing flower buds, on certain fruiting trees, such as the spur-type apple trees; a tubular projection from a blossom, usually producing nectar.

square foot method: A standard technique in range surveys for determining average density and composition of range vegetation, using systematically located plots on which the herbage of each species is estimated individually in square feet of ground covered.

stability: An atmospheric condition with little or no vertical air transport.

stabilized grade: The slope of a channel at which neither erosion nor deposition occurs.

stable air: A motionless mass of air that holds, instead of dispersing, pollutants.

stack: An upright pipe that exhausts waste emissions into the atmosphere.

stack effect: Flow of air resulting from warm air rising, creating a positive pressure area at the top of a building and negative pressure area at the bottom. This effect can overpower the mechanical system and disrupt building ventilation and air circulation.

stack gas desulfurization (scrubber): Treating of stack gases to remove sulfur compounds.

staff gage: Graduated scale mounted on a plank, pier, wall, or other like object from which the water surface elevation may be read.

stage (hydraulics): The variable water surface or the water surface elevation above any chosen datum. See *gage height, gaging station.*

stagger: To plant alternately at equal

distances in a row on either side of a middle line (as in planting of hedges); to arrange over any area at equal distances without any reference to any definite line.

staging: Arrangement of major mining operations, such as clearing, grubbing, and scalping, into segments so that any one time the various phases of clearing, extraction, and reclamation can be carried on simultaneously.

stake: A tall rod or pole driven into the ground beside a whip or newly planted tree an used for support; a peg or short piece of wood driven into the ground which is used for securing guy wires; an engineering grade or reference marker.

stalklage: Forage material (residue) that remains on the soil surface following harvest of corn or grain sorghum.

stamen: The reproductive organ of the male-bearing flower, the top part of which is the anther.

stand: An aggregation of trees or other growth occupying a specific area and sufficiently uniform in composition (species), age arrangement, and condition to be distinguishable from the forest or other growth on adjoining areas; the number of plants per unit of area other than trees.

standard deviation (statistics): A measure of the average variation of a series of observations or items of a population about their mean. In normally distributed sets of moderate size, the interval of the mean, plus or minus the standard deviation, includes about two thirds of the items.

standard error of estimate (statistics): An estimate of the standard deviation of means of samples drawn from a single population, often calculated from a single set of samples.

standard of living: A minimum of necessities, comforts, or luxuries that is accepted or regarded as essential to maintaining a person, class, or race in his or its customary or proper status or circumstances.

standard of performance: An emission limitation imposed on a particular category of pollution sources, by a governmental agency. Limitations may take the form of emission standards or of requirements for specific operating procedures.

starter fertilizer: Liquid or solid fertilizer, placed near or in contact with the seed or the roots of new transplants.

state coordinate systems: The plane-rectangular coordinate systems established by the US Coast and Geodetic Survey, one for each state in the United States, for use in defining positions of geodetic stations in terms of plane-rectangular (x and y) coordinates; also called state system of plane coordinates.

state soil conservation committee, commission, or board: In the United States, the state agency established by state soil conservation district-enabling legislation to assist with the administration of the provisions of the state soil conservation districts law. The official title may vary from the above as new or amended state laws are made.

static head: Head resulting from elevation differences, for example, the difference in elevation of headwater and tailwater of a power plant.

static lift: Vertical distance between source and discharge water levels in a pump installation.

static stability: The state of the atmosphere when it is stable relative to vertical displacements; such an atmosphere tends to remain stratified, in that any air that is displaced vertically is subjected to a buoyant force that tends to restore it to its original level; also called hydrostatic stability, vertical stability, convective or convectional stability.

static water depth: The vertical distance from the centerline of the pump discharge down to the surface level of the free pool while no water is being drawn from the pool or water table.

steady flow: Flow in which the rate remains constant with time at a given cross section.

steam power plant: A power plant in which the turbines connected to the generators are driven by steam.

stemflow: Precipitation that accumulates on the leaves, branches, and stems of forest vegetation and consequently flows down the trunks to the ground.

step wedge: A strip of film or a glass plate whose transparency diminishes in graduated steps from one end to the other; often used to determine the density of a photograph; also called gray scale or step tablet.

stereo base: A line representing the distance and direction between complementary image points on a stereo pair of photos correctly oriented and adjusted for comfortable stereoscopic vision under a given stereoscope, or with the unaided eyes.

stereogram: A stereo pair of photos or drawings correctly oriented and permanently mounted for stereoscopic examination.

stereo pair: A pair of photos that overlap in area and are suitable for stereoscopic examination.

stereoscope: A binocular optical instrument for viewing two properly oriented photographs, constituting a stereo pair, to obtain a mental impression of a three dimensional effect.

stereoscopic image: The mental impression of a three-dimensional object that results from stereoscopic vision (stereo-viewing).

sterile: Incapable of bearing or characterized by lack of fruit or viable seed; bearing only stamens.

sterilization: The destruction, by chemical or physical means, of a microorganism's ability to reproduce; to render something barren.

stilling basin: An open structure or excavation at the foot of an overfall, chute, drop, or spillway to reduce the energy of the descending stream.

stilling well: Pipe, chamber, or compression having closed sides and bottom except for a comparatively small inlet, or inlets, connected to the main body of water; for attenuation of waves or surges while permitting the water level within the well to rise and fall

with the major fluctuations of the main body; used with water measuring devices to improve accuracy of measurement.

stock: The stem of a plant in which a graft is inserted; any plant from which slips or cuttings are taken.

stocking: The degree to which an area is effectively covered with living trees. Fully stocked stands contain as many trees per acre as can properly use the growing space available.

stocking rate: The actual number of animals per unit, for example, cows per acre.

stockpond: An impoundment, the principal purpose of which is to supply water to livestock; includes reservoirs, pits and tanks.

stockwater development: Development of new or improved sources of stockwater supplies, such as wells, springs, and ponds, together with storage and delivery systems.

stolon: A horizontal stem which grows along the surface of the soil and roots at the nodes.

stoma: Small openings or slits in the epidermis (outside) of leaves enabling them to breath.

stomated closures: Plant condition in which the stomata are closed for some reason.

stone line: A concentration of coarse fragments in soils. In cross section, the line may be marked only by scattered fragments or it may be a discrete layer of fragments. The fragments are more often pebbles or cobbles than stones. The line generally overlies material that was subjected to weathering, soil formation, and erosion before deposition of the overlying material. stones: See *coarse fragments*.

stones: See *coarse fragments*.

stoniness: The relative proportion of stones in or on the soil, used in classifying soils. See *coarse fragments, stony, very stony, stony land*.

stony: Containing sufficient stones to interfere with tillage but not to make intertilled crops impracticable. Stones may occupy 0.01 to 0.1 percent of the surface. Stoniness is not a part of the soil textural class. The terms "stony" and "very stony" may modify the soil textural class name in the soil type, but this is simply a brief way of designating stony phases.

stony land: Areas containing sufficient stones to make the use of machinery impractical, usually 15 to 90 percent of the surface is covered with stones. A miscellaneous land type. See *stoniness, rubbleland*.

storage (wastes): The interim containment of solid waste, in an approved manner, after generation and prior to ultimate disposal.

storage capacity: See *available water capacity*.

storage curve (hydraulics): A graphical expression of stage or elevation versus the accumulated storage or volume at this stage or elevation.

storage pit (wastes): A pit in which solid waste is held prior to processing.

storm: In general, a disturbance of the atmosphere. The term may be qualified to emphasize a particular part of the meteorological disturbance, such as windstorm, sandstorm, rainstorm or thunderstorm.

stormwater runoff: The water and associated material draining into streams, lakes, or sewers as a result of a storm.

stover: The dried, cured stems and leaves of tall, coarse grain crops, such as corn and sorghum, after the grain has been removed. See *fodder, hay*.

stratification: The process of arrangement or composition in strata or layers.

stratified random sample: A randomized sample composed of two or more sets of random samples, each drawn from a single homogeneous unit (stratum) of a heterogeneous population. (Stratification is the subdivision of a population into groups or strata, each of which is more homogeneous in respect to the variable being measured than the population as a whole).

stratify: To store seeds between layers of moist media, or to bury them to keep them fresh and moist, but not so warm as to cause germination; a treatment used to break the dormancy of cold-requiring seeds. See *hard seed*. To become layered, as when a warm layer of water overlies a cooler layer of water.

stratigraphy: The branch of geology that deals with the definition and interpretation of stratified rocks; the conditions of their formation; their character, arrangement, sequence, age, and distribution; and especially their correlation by the use of fossils and other means. The term is applied both to the sum of the characteristics listed and a study of these characteristics.

stratocumulus: See *cloud*.

stratus: See *cloud*.

stream–aquifer interactions: Relations of water flow and chemistry between streams and aquifers that are hydraulically connected.

streambank erosion control: The usual boundaries, not the flood boundaries, of a stream channel. Right and left banks are named facing downstream.

streambanks: The usual boundaries, not the flood boundaries, of a stream channel. Right and left banks are named facing downstream.

streambank stabilization: Natural geological tendency for a stream to mold its banks to conform with the channel of least resistance to flow; lining of stream banks with riprap, matting, etc., to control erosion.

streambed erosion: The movement of material, causing a lowering or widening of a stream at a given point.

stream, cold water: A stream that supports a cold water fishery, usually including trout. Optimum temperatures 50 degrees F to 60 degrees F.

stream, cool water: A stream that supports a cool water fishery, usually including smallmouth bass and/or rock bass. Spawning temperatures commonly between 60 degrees and 70 degrees F.

streamflow: A type of channel flow, applied to that part of surface runoff in a stream whether or not it is affected by diversion or regu-

lation.

stream gaging: The quantitative determination of stream flow using gages, current meters, weirs, or other measuring instruments at selected locations. See *gaging station*.

streamline: Path of a particle of fluid moving in steady irrotational flow; line tangent at a given instant to the velocity vector of a particle of fluid at every point.

stream line flow: See *laminar flow*.

stream load: Quantity of solid and dissolved material carried by a stream. See *sediment load*.

stream reach: The continuous portion of a stream channel and adjoining floodplain from one selected point to another, usually measured along the thalweg of the channel.

streamside management zone: Strip of land adjacent to a stream or river managed in a way that meets water quality and productivity goals.

stream mile: A distance of one mile along a line connecting the midpoints of the channel of a stream.

stream order: A ranking of the relative sizes of streams within a watershed based on the nature of their tributaries. The smallest unbranched tributary is called first order, the stream receiving the tributary is called second order, and so on.

stream reach: A continuous part of a stream between two specified points.

stream, warm water: A stream that supports a warm water fishery, usually including largemouth bass and sunfish. Spawning temperatures usually in excess of 70 degrees F.

street refuse: Material picked up when streets and sidewalks are swept manually and mechanically.

strike (mining): The direction or bearing of the intersection of a horizontal plane with the tilted bed. See *dip*.

stripcropping: Growing crops in a systematic arrangement of strips or bands which serve as barriers to wind and water erosion. See *buffer strips; contour strip cropping; correction strip; field stripcropping; filter strip; sod strips; spreader strip; strip sodding; contour; wind stripcropping.*

strip count: Any complete count taken on a sample strip through a nursery bed or a stand; also called strip enumeration.

strip grazing: A system whereby animals are confined to a small area of pasture for a short period of time, usually one to two days.

strip mining: A process in which rock and top soil strata overlying ore or fuel deposits are scraped away by mechanical shovels. Also known as surface mining.

stripping ratio (mining): The ratio of the volume of spoil or wastes to the volume of ore or mineral material.

strip survey: A survey of one or more sample strips in a forest, these commonly being based on regularly spaced, open traverses (whence termed a linear survey) along which recording of data is continuous; a survey employing continuous narrow strips as sampling units. Strips 0.5, one, or two chains wide are run across the area to be surveyed; also called strip cruise.

strip tillage: Tillage operations for seedbed preparation that are limited to a strip not to exceed 1/3 of the distance between rows; the area between is left untilled with a protective cover of crop residue on the surface for erosion control. Planting and tillage are accomplished in the same operation.

structural measures (water resources): Dams, levees, diversions, channels, or other constructed devices used to modify floods in a way that reduces food damage to land, people, or property.

stubble: The basal portion of plants remaining after the top portion has been harvested; also, the portion of the plants, principally grasses, remaining after grazing is completed.

stubble crops: Crops that develop from the stubble of the previous season; crops sowed on grain stubble after harvest for turning under the following spring.

stubble mulch: The stubble of crops or crop residues left essentially in place on the land as a surface cover during fallow and the growing of a succeeding crop.

stumpage: The value of uncut timber; the standing timber.

stylolites: Thin seams, more or less planar in gross plan but intricately irregular in detail, abundantly developed in limestones, dolomites, and marble. Columns and pits on one side fit into their counterparts on the other so that the trace in cross section is a complicated series of zigzags of microscopic to several inches amplitude.

subcritical flow (hydraulics): Flow where the depth of flow is greater than critical and where the velocity is less than the critical velocity.

subdivision: The division or redivision of a lot, tract, or parcel of land into two or more areas either by platting or metes and bounds description.

subdivision regulations: An ordinance based on the police power of government to protect the public health, safety, and general welfare. It establishes standards for the subdivision and the development of land, generally including location and width of streets, size and shape of lots, provision of water and sewage disposal facilities, surface water drainage, control of erosion, preservation of floodplains, provision of public land for schools and recreation, and other related items. It does not include land use regulations. It is one of the major methods for implementation of the comprehensive plan.

subgrade: The soil prepared and compacted to support a structure or a pavement system.

subgrade modulus (engineering): The resistance of soil material to unit area displacement under load, expressed in pounds per square inch.

subgroup: See *soil classification*.

subhumid: Regions or climates where moisture is normally less than under humid conditions but still sufficient for the production of many agricultural crops without irrigation or dryland farming. Natural vegetation is mostly tall grasses. Annual rainfall varies from 20 inches in cool regions to as much as 60 inches in hot areas. See *humid*.

subirrigation: Applying irrigation water below the ground surface either by raising the water table within or near the root zone, or by using a buried perforated or porous pipe system that discharges directly into the root zone.

sublethal dose: The fumigation of a toxicant not capable of causing cellular necrosis.

sublimation: The process by which a solid is changed into a gas, or gas into a solid, without passing through the liquid stage.

sublimation nucleus: Any particle upon which an ice crystal may grow by the process of sublimation; also called deposition nucleus.

sublittoral zone: The part of the shore from the lowest water level to the lower boundary of plant growth; transition zone from the littoral to profundal bottom.

submerged aquatic vegetation: Vegetation that lives at or below the water surface; an important habitat for young fish and other aquatic organisms.

submerged discharge: Discharge from an outlet or measuring device below or partially below a free water surface.

submerged flow: Flow across any critical depth measuring structure where discharge is interfered with by the depth of the downstream water.

submerged weir: A weir which, in use, has the tailwater level higher than the weir crest. See *free flowing* *weir.*

suborder: See *soil classification.*

subsidence: A downward movement of the ground surface caused by solution and collapse of underlying soluble deposits, rearrangements of particles upon removal of coal, or reduction of fluid pressures within an aquifer or petroleum reservoir; the movement of an aerial compound to a lower level, for example, the transport of ozone from the stratosphere to the atmosphere by winds.

subsistence farm: A low-income farm where the emphasis is on production for use by the operator and his family.

subsoil: The B horizons of soils with distinct profiles. In soils with weak profile development, the subsoil can be defined as the soil below the plowed soil (or its equivalent of surface soil), in which roots normally grow. Although a common term, it cannot be defined accurately. It has been carried over from early days when "soil" was conceived only as the plowed soil and that under it as the "subsoil."

subsoiling: The tillage of subsurface soil, without inversion, for the purpose of breaking up dense layers that restrict water movement and root penetration.

substrate: In biology, the base of substance upon which an organism is growing; in chemistry, a substance undergoing oxidation; in hydrology, the bottom material of a waterway.

substrate size: The diameter of streambed particles such as clay, silt, sand, gravel, cobble and boulders.

substratum: Any layer lying beneath the soil solum, either conforming (C or R) or unconforming.

subsurface absorption area: The area in which the liquid from a treatment tank seeps into the soil. It includes the following:

> **tile field:** A subsurface absorption area in which open jointed or perforated piping is laid in covered trenches or excavations.

> **seepage bed:** A subsurface absorption area where open jointed or perforated piping is placed on a gravel bed and then covered with earth.

> **deep wide trenches:** A tile field where the trenches are deeper and wider than three feet.

subsurface drain: A shallow drain installed in an irrigated field to intercept the rising ground-water level and maintain the water table at an acceptable depth below the land surface.

subsurface irrigation: See *subirrigation.*

subsurface tillage: Tillage with specialized equipment which loosens and prepares a seedbed but does not invert the surface residual mulch. See *mulch tillage.*

subwatershed: A watershed subdivision of unspecified size that forms a convenient natural unit. See *watershed.*

succession: The progressive development of vegetation toward its highest ecological expression, the climax; replacement of one plant community by another.

suckers: A side shoot from the roots of a plant; the side growth arising from a bud.

suction lift (irrigation): The difference in elevation between the water source and the pump.

sulfer cycle: The sequence of biochemical changes undergone by sulfur, wherein it is used upon the death and decomposition of the organism, and converted to its original state of oxidation.

sulfur dioxide (S02): A heavy pungent, colorless gas formed primarily by combustion of coal, oil, and other sulfur bearing compounds, but also produced in chemical plants while processing metals and burning trash.

sulfation rate: The measure of the cumulative effect of sulfur oxides on a reactive surface of known area.

summer fallow: The tillage of uncropped land during the summer in order to control weeds. and store moisture in the soil for the growth of a later crop.

summer kill: Complete or partial kill of a fish population in ponds or lakes during the warm months; variously produced by excessively warm water, by a depletion of dissolved oxygen, and by the release of toxic substances from a decaying algal bloom, or by a combination of these factors. See *winter kill*.

sump: Pit, tank, or reservoir in which water is collected, stored, or withdrawn.

sunscald: The destruction of tissue caused when radiant heat from the sun strikes a frozen plant or freshly exposed plant parts.

sun synchronous: An earth satellite orbit in which the orbital plane is near polar and the altitude such

that the satellite passes over all places on earth having the same latitude twice daily at the same local sun time.

supercritical flow (hydraulics): Flow where the depth of the flow is less than critical and where the velocity exceeds critical velocity.

supersaturation: A condition in which a solution has more solute dissolved than is normally possible under the existing conditions.

supersonic: Designating vibrations or waves with frequencies higher than those audible to the human ear (exceeding 20,000 per second); designating a speed greater than the speed of sound (1,087 feet per second or 738 miles per hour).

supervised classification (remote sensing): A computer-implemented process through which each measure vector is assigned to a class according to a specified decision rule, where the possible classes have been defined on the basis of representative training samples of known identify. See *unsupervised classification*.

supplemental feeding: Supplying concentrates or harvested feed to correct deficiencies of the range diet. Often erroneously used to mean emergency feeding.

supplemental irrigation: Irrigation to insure or increase crop production in areas where rainfall normally supplies most of the moisture needed.

supplemental pasture: Additional pasture for use in adverse weather, usually annual forage crops for dry periods or winter. See *temporary* *pasture.*

suppressed weir: A measuring weir with the sides of the notch flush with the walls of the channel. Also called a full width weir.

supralittoral zone: That portion of the seashore adjacent to the tidal or spray zone; also called a full-width weir.

surface cracking (wastes): Discontinuities that develop in the cover material at a sanitary landfill due to the surface drying or settlement of the solid waste; may result in the exposure of solid waste, entrance or egress of vectors, intrusion of water, and venting of decomposition gases.

surface compaction: Increasing the dry density of surface soil by applying a dynamic load.

surface drains: A channel to remove surface water from the land.

surface dump: A land site where solid waste is disposed of in a manner that does not protect the environment.

surface irrigation: Irrigation where the soil surface is used as a conduit, as in furrow and border irrigation as opposed to sprinkler irrigation or subirrigation.

surface layer (soils): The uppermost part of the soil ordinarily moved in tillage or its equivalent in uncultivated soils, ranging in depth from about five to eight inches (12.7-20.3 cm); frequently designated as the plow layer, the Ap layer, or the Ap horizon.

surface mining: See *mining.*

surface profile (hydraulics): The longitudinal profile assumed by the surface of a stream flowing in an open channel; the hydraulic grade line.

surface roughness: Surface roughness is used in the context of heat island mitigation to refer to the presence of buildings, trees, and other irregular land topography in an urban area.

surface runoff: See *overland flow, runoff.*

surface soil: The uppermost part of the soil ordinarily moved in tillage or its equivalent in uncultivated soils, ranging in depth from about five to eight inches. Frequently designated as the plow layer, the Ap layer, or the Ap horizon.

surface storage: Sum of detention and channel storage, representing, at any given moment, the total water en route to an outlet from an area or watershed.

surface water: All water whose surface is exposed to the atmosphere.

surfactant: A material that facilitates and accentuates the emulsifying, dispersing, spreading, wetting, and other surface-modifying properties of herbicide formulation.

surveillance system: A monitoring system to determine environmental quality or the compliance of a given activity to a standard; used to identify episodes of high pollution concentration in time to take preventive action.

suspended load: Solids or sediments suspended in a fluid by the upward components of turbulent currents or by colloidal suspension.

suspended sediment: The very fine soil particle that remain in suspension in water for a considerable period of time; maintained in suspension by the upward components of turbulent currents or may be fine enough to form a colloidal suspension.

suspended solid: Any solid substance present in water in an undissolved state, usually contributing directly to turbidity.

sustained yield: The yield that a forest can produce continuously at a given intensity of management. It implies a balance at the earliest practical time between increment (growth) and harvesting.

swamp: An area saturated with water throughout much of the year but with the surface of the soil usually not deeply submerged; usually characterized by tree or shrub vegetation. Formerly a miscellaneous land type. See *marsh*.

swash marks: The wavy lines of fine sand or bits of debris left on the beach at the upward limit of the rush of water following the breaking of a wave.

swidden agriculture: See *shifting cultivation*.

swill: Semiliquid waste material consisting of food scraps and free liquids.

symbiosis: Two organisms of different species living in close association, one or both of which may benefit and neither is harmed.

syncline: A fold of rock bed that is convex downward. See *anticline*.

synecology: A subdivision of ecology that deals with the study of groups of organisms associated as a unit.

synergism: The simultaneous actions of two or more agencies

that, together, have a greater total effect than the sum of their individual effects, for example, the action of certain combinations of toxicants. See *antagonism*.

synoptic view: The ability to see or otherwise measure widely dispersed areas at the same time and under the same conditions; for example, the overall view of a large portion of the earth's surface that can be obtained from satellite altitudes.

synoptic sites: Sites sampled during a short-term investigation of specific water-quality conditions during selected seasonal or hydrologic conditions to provide improved spatial resolution for critical water-quality conditions.

synthesis: The production of a substance by the union of elements or simpler chemical compounds.

synthetic natural gas: A manufactured gaseous fuel generally produced from naphtha or coal; contains 95 to 98 percent methane and has an energy content of 980 to 1,035 Btus (36.9-39 megajoules) per standard cubic foot, about the same as that of natural gas.

synthetic variety: Advanced generation projenies of a number of clones or lines (or of hybrids among them) obtained by open pollination.

systematic sample: A sample consisting of sampling units selected in conformity with some regular pattern (e.g., the sample formed from every 20th two chain strip of forest, or from every 10th tree in every fifth row).

systemic pesticide: A pesticide chemical that is carried to other parts of a plant or animal after it is injected or taken up from the soil or body surface.

T

tacking: The process of binding mulch fibers together by the addition of a sprayed chemical compound.

taiga: Coniferous forests found in the northern hemisphere.

tailings: In agriculture, only forage material that falls behind the harvesting combine of milo; in mining, second grade or waste material derived when raw material is screened or processed.

tailwater: In hydraulics, water, in a river or channel, immediately downstream from a structure; in irrigation, water that reaches the lower end of a field.

talus: Fragments of rock and other soil material accumulated by gravity at the foot of cliffs or steep slopes.

tank, earth: A structure for impounding water, formed by an excavation and an earthen dam across a drainage.

tape sampler: A mechanical device that determines the density of fine particles in the atmosphere.

taproot system: A plant root system dominated by a single large "taproot," normally growing straight down, from which most or all of the smaller roots spread out laterally. See *fibrous root system*.

tar sands: Sedimentary rocks that contain viscous, heavy petroleum that cannot be recovered by conventional methods of petroleum production.

taxadjunct: Soils that are unclassified at the series level but allowed to go under the name of a defined series. They are so like the soils of the defined series in morphology, composition, and behavior that little or nothing is gained by adding a new series.

taxon (plural taxa): Any identifiable group of taxonomically related organisms.

taxonomy: The science of classification; laws and principles governing the classifying of objects; classification, especially of animals and plants, into taxonomic units, such as species, genus, family, and order.

technical externalities (economics): The changes in income of persons or firms due to production efficiency functions resulting from improved technology from the action of a different person or firm.

temperature inversion: An air layer in which temperature increases with altitude; characterized by static stability.

temporary pasture: A pasture designed to provide grazing for only a short period, usually consisting of annual plants. See *supplemental pasture*.

tender plant: A plant that cannot withstand frost; a plant that cannot withstand the usual degree of winter cold in a particular climatic zone.

tendril: A slender, spiraling outgrowth; a modified leaf, stem, or stipule of a climbing plant that coils around anything it can grasp.

tensiometer: Instrument used for measuring the suction or negative pressure of soil water.

terrace: An embankment or combination of an embankment and channel constructed across a slope to control erosion by diverting or storing surface runoff instead of permitting it to flow uninterrupted down the slope. Terraces or terrace systems may be classified by their alignment, gradient, outlet, and cross section. Alignment may be parallel or non parallel. Gradient may be level, uniformly graded, or variably graded. Grade is often incorporated to permit paral-

leling the terraces. Outlets may be soil infiltration only, vegetated waterways, tile outlets, or combinations thereof. Cross section may be narrow base, broad base, bench, steep backslope, flat channel, or channel; a level, usually narrow plain bordering a river, lake, or sea. Rivers sometimes are bordered by terraces at different levels.

terrace interval: The distance, measured either vertically or horizontally, between corresponding points on two adjacent terraces.

terrace outlet channel: Channel, usually having a vegetative cover, into which the flow from one or more terraces is discharged and conveyed from the field.

terrace system: A series of terraces occupying a slope and discharging runoff into one or more outlet channels.

territory (wildlife): The defended part of an animal's range.

tertiary-treated sewage: The third phase of treating sewage that removes nitrogen and phosphorus before it is discharged.

tertiary waste treatment: Wastewater treatment beyond the secondary or biological stage that includes removal of nutrients such as phosphorus and nitrogen, and a high percentage of suspended solids; also known as advanced waste treatment.

texture: See *soil texture*.

thalwag: In a flowing stream, the line following the deepest part of the channel; the line following the lowest part of a valley whether under water or not.

thermal band: A general term for

middle–infrared wavelengths that are transmitted through the atmosphere window at eight to 13 micrometers; occasionally used for the windows around three to six micrometers.

thermal pollution: A term describing the act of changing the natural temperatures of bodies of water by dumping warmer water into them.

thermal power plant: Any electric power plant that operates by generating heat and converting the heat to electricity.

thermal stratification: The layering of water masses owing to different densities in response to temperature; the condition of a body of water in which the successive horizontal layers have different temperatures, each layer more or less sharply differentiated from the adjacent ones. See *overturn*.

thermal turbulence: Air mixing caused by convection.

thermic: See *soil temperature classes for family groupings*.

thermocline: The transition zone between the warm epilimnion and cold hypolimnion of stratified bodies of water; temperature change equals or exceeds 1 degrees C for each meter of depth. See *thermal stratification*.

thinning (forestry): A cutting made in immature tree stands to provide adequate growing space and accelerate diameter growth but also, by suitable selection, to improve the average form of the remaining trees.

thin–wood pruning: The removal of thin, crowded, shaded, and unproductive branches of a tree or shrub, such as suckers and water sprouts.

thiocarbamates: Soil-applied herbicides that restrict plant growth as they inhibit cell division and cell elongation, uptake may be through seed, shoots, or roots; shoots are more affected than roots.

threatened species: Any species that is likely to become endangered within the foreseeable future through all or a significant portion of its range.

threshold: The maximum or minimum duration or intensity of a stimulus that is required to produce a response in an organism; also called the critical level.

threshold dose: The minimum concentration of an air pollutant that can cause injury.

threshold velocity: The minimum velocity at which wind will begin moving particles of sand or other soil material.

throughfall: Precipitation falling unhindered though and dripping from the crowns of forest vegetation.

tick mark: A small cross or other symbol used on maps to define the intersection of survey or land lines.

tides: The rise and fall of ocean waters produced by the gravitational pull of the moon and the sun.

tidal marsh: Low, flat marshlands traversed by interlaced channels and tidal sloughs and subject to tidal inundation; normally, the only vegetation present is salt tolerant bushes and grasses.

tide gate: A swinging gate on the outside of a drainage conduit from a diked field that excludes water at high tide and permits drainage at low tide.

tight soil: A compact, relatively impervious and tenacious soil, or subsoil, which may or may not be plastic.

tile, drain: Pipe made of burned clay, concrete, or similar material, in short lengths, usually laid with open joints to collect and carry excess water from the soil.

tile drainage: Land drainage by means of a series of tile lines laid at a specified depth and grade.

till: Unstratified glacial drift deposited directly by the ice and consisting of clay, sand, gravel, and boulders intermingled in any proportion; to plow and prepare for seeding; to seed or cultivate the soil.

tillage: The operation of implements through the soil to prepare seedbeds and root beds.

tillage pan: See *pan, pressure or induced*.

tiller: An erect or semi erect branch arising from a bud in the axils of leaves at the base of a plant. Wheat along with other annual and perennial grasses increase in circumference by tillers.

till plant: Seedbed preparation for row crops by scalping the area of the old crop row and pushing soil and residue aside, leaving a protective cover of crop residue on and mixed in the surface layer between the crop rows. Seedbed preparation and planting are completed in the same operation.

tilth: The physical condition of soil as related to its ease of tillage, fitness as a seedbed, and impedance to seedling emergence and root penetration.

tilting gate (hydraulics): A hinged gate, counterbalanced by weights,

that automatically opens or closes with a change in head.

timber: Trees, whether standing, fallen, living, dead, limbed, bucked or peeled.

time of concentration: Time required for water to flow from the most remote point of a watershed, in a hydraulic sense, to the outlet.

tip layering: The practice of bending the tips of plant branches to the ground and covering them with soil so that they take root. See *propagation*.

tipple: A surface structure at a mine for preparation and loading the mineral.

tissue study: The assessment of concentrations and distributions of trace elements and certain organic contaminants in tissues of aquatic organisms.

titration: The determination of the volume of a solution needed to react with a known volume of sample, usually involving the progressive addition of the solution to the sample until the sample has reacted fully.

threatened species: A plant or animal that is likely to become endangered if not protected.

toe (engineering): Terminal edge or edges of a structure; (mining) The point of contact between the base of an embankment or spoil and the foundation surface; usually the outer portion of the spoil bank where it contacts the original ground surface.

toe drain: Interceptor drain located near the downstream toe of a structure.

toe wall: Downstream wall of a

structure.

tolerance: The relative ability of a species to survive a deficiency of an essential growth requirement, such as moisture, light or nutrient supply, or an overabundance of a site factor such as excessive water, toxic salts, etc.

tolerance limit (TL 10...100): The concentration of a substance that some specified portion of an experimental population can endure for a specified period of time with reference to a specified type of response; for example, T100 means that all test organisms endured the stress for the specified time; TL10 means only 10 percent of the test organisms could tolerate the imposed stress for the specified time.

tolerance limit median (TLm): The concentration of a toxic material required to kill 50 percent of a group of aquatic test organisms in a specified period, normally 96 hours or less; usually expressed as milligrams of active ingredient per liter of solution. See *LD50*.

tolerance range: The range of one or more environmental conditions within which an organism can function; range between the highest and lowest value of a particular environmental factor in which an organism can live.

tolerant association: An association of organisms capable of withstanding adverse conditions within the habitat; often characterized by a reduction in the number of species (from a clean water association) and, in the case of organic

pollution, an increase in individuals representing certain species.

tolerant species: Those species that are adaptable to (tolerant of) human alterations to the environment and often increase in number when human alterations occur.

topiary work: The cutting and trimming of shrubs and trees, especially evergreens, into odd or ornamental shapes, thus producing an effect entirely different from that produced by the natural growing habits of the plane.

topographic map: See *map*.

topography: The relative positions and elevations of the natural or manmade features of an area that describe the configuration of its surface.

toposequence: A sequence of related soils that differ one from the other, primarily because of topography as a soil formation factor. See *clinosequence*.

topping (horticulture): Severe cutback of trees and shrubs.

topsoil: Earthy material used as top dressing for house lots, grounds for large buildings, gardens, road cuts, or similar areas. It has favorable characteristics for production of desired kinds of vegetation or can be made favorable; the surface plow layer of a soil; also called surface soil; the original or present dark colored upper soil that ranges from a mere fraction of an inch to two or three feet thick on different kinds of soil; the original or present A horizon, varying widely among different kinds of soil. Applied to soils in the field, the term has no precise meaning unless defined as to depth or productivity in relation to a specific kind of soil.

top working: Changing the upper branches of a tree to another variety by grafting or budding. See *graftage*.

tornado: A violently rotating column of air, pendant from a cumulonimbus cloud and nearly always observable as a funnel cloud; on a local scale, the most destructive of all atmospheric phenomena.

torric: A soil moisture regime defined like aridic moisture regime but used in a different category of the soil taxonomy.

total annual yield: The total annual production of all plant species of a plant community.

total coliform: The Escherica coli and similar gram negative bacteria that are normal inhabitants of fecal discharges. The total coliform group is recognized in the drinking water standards of public health criteria.

total concentration: Refers to the concentration of a constituent regardless of its form (dissolved or bound) in a sample.

total digestible nutrients (TDN): A standard evaluation of the digestibility of a particular livestock feed, including all the digestible organic nutrients: protein, fiber, nitrogen free extract, and fat. The percentage of total digestible nutrients represents the approximate heat or energy value of the feed.

total dissolved solids (TDS): The total dissolved mineral constituents of water.

total hardness: The total dissolved salts in water expressed as total parts of dissolved salts in a million parts of water.

total soil water potential: The work per unit quantity of pure water that has to be done to change its energy status to that of soil water at the point under consideration; the sum of matric, gravity, pressure, osmotic, and overburden potentials.

township line: In the generally recognized public land survey, every 24 miles a station is indicated measuring both east and west from a predetermined principal meridian. Similar measurements are also taken north and south from a predetermined base line. In this manner a succession of quadrilaterals are formed, each roughly 24 miles square. Each of these is, in turn, subdivided into 16 smaller quadrilaterals roughly six miles square. In this system of grid lines, north south lines become range lines and east west lines become township lines.

toxaphene: Chemical that causes adverse health effects in domestic water supplies and is toxic to fresh water and marine aquatic life.

toxic: Poisonous.

toxicant: A substance that through its chemical or physical action, kills, injures, or impairs an organism; any environmental factor which, when altered, produces a harmful biological effect.

toxic cloud: Airborne plume of gases, vapors, fumes, or aerosols containing toxic materials.

toxic equivalent: The potency or toxicity of one substance in comparison to another.

toxic-forming materials: Earth materials or wastes that, if acted upon by air, water, weathering, or microbiological processes, are likely to produce chemical or physical conditions in soils or water that are detrimental to biota or uses of water.

toxicity: Quality, state, or degree of the harmful effect resulting from alteration of an environment factor.

toxicology: Study of the effects of poisons in living organisms.

toxic pollutants: Materials that cause death, disease, or birth defects in organisms that ingest or absorb them. The quantities and exposures necessary to cause these effects can vary widely.

toxic salt reduction: Decreasing harmful concentrations of toxic salts in soils, usually by leaching and with or without the addition of soil amendments.

toxic spoil: Acid spoil with pH below 4.0; also a spoil having amounts of minerals such as aluminum, manganese, and iron that adversely affect plant growth. See *acid spoil; spoil.*

toxic substance: A chemical or mixture that may present an unreasonable risk of injury to health or the environment.

trace elements: See *micronutrients.*

tracer: A stable, easily detected substance or a radioisotope added to a material to follow the location of the substance in the environment or to detect any physical or chemical changes it undergoes.

tracking: The movement of bulldozers and other cleated equipment up and down the face of a slope for the purposes of stabilization, compaction, erosion control, and vegetative establishment.

triazine herbicide: A class of herbicides containing a symmetrical triazine ring (a nitrogen-heterocyclic ring composed of three nitrogens and three carbons in an alternating sequence). Examples include atrazine, propazine, and simazine.

trailing: Controlled directional movement of livestock; natural trailing is the habit of livestock or wildlife to repeatedly tread in the same line or path.

training (horticulture): A procedure of judicious pruning and staking to adapt plants to limited areas or to form particular shapes; also to encourage the formation of flowers and fruit.

training samples (remote sensing): The data samples of known identity used to determine decision boundaries in the measurement of feature space prior to classification of the overall set of data vectors from a scene.

transect: A cross section of an area used as a sample for recording, mapping, or studying vegetation and its use. A transect may be a series of plots, a belt or strip, or merely a line, depending on why it is being used.

transboundary pollutants: Air pollution that travels from one jurisdiction to another, often crossing state or international boundaries. Also applies to water pollution.

transferable development rights (TDR): A land development control system in which landowners whose land is restricted because of classification as prime farmland or floodplain are awarded development right certificates to compensate for the restriction; the development right certificates acquired a market value because of a requirement that specified areas authorized for very intensive development could only build at such an intensity if the landowner bought a required number of development rights.

transhumance: Seasonal movements of domestic animals from one area to another in which different climatic conditions prevail.

translatory wave (hydraulics): A wave, such as a flood wave, whose water particles constantly progress in the direction of the wave movement; a characteristic of unsteady flow.

transmission loss: See *conveyance loss.*

transmissibility: The rate or flow of groundwater, at the prevailing temperature, through a vertical strip of aquifer one foot wide with a height equal to the saturated thickness of the aquifer and under a unit hydraulic gradient.

transmittance: The ratio of the radiant energy transmitted through a body to that incident upon it.

transparency: A photographic print on a clear base, especially adaptable for viewing by transmitted light; also the light transmitting capability of a material.

transpiration: The photosynthetic and physiological process by which plants release water into the air in the form of water vapor.

transplant (forestry): A seedling that has been transplanted one or more times in the nursery.

transportation (soils): The movement of detached soil material across the land surface or through

the air. May be accomplished by running water, wind, or gravity; soil erosion. See *detachment.*

transverse polyconic map projection: See *map projection.*

trap: See *sand trap.*

trap efficiency: The capability of a reservoir to trap sediment. See *Venturi flume.*

trash rack: See *debris guard.*

treated wastewater: Wastewater that has been subjected to one or more physical, chemical, and biological processes to reduce its potential of being health hazard.

treatment tank: A water tight tank designed to retain sewage long enough for satisfactory bacterial decomposition of the solids to take place; septic tanks and aerobic sewage treatment tanks.

tree: A woody perennial plant that reaches a mature height of at least eight feet and has a well defined stem and a definite crown shape. There is no clear cut distinction between trees and shrubs. Some plants, such as the willows, may grow as either trees or shrubs.

tree farm: A privately owned area dedicated by the owner to the production of wood crops.

tree guard: Any device placed around a tree to protect it from injury by animals, people, or vehicles.

tree seed orchard: A plantation of trees, assumed or proven to be genetically superior, that has been isolated to reduce pollination from genetically inferior outside sources, and intensively managed to improve the genotype and produce frequent, abundant, and easily harvestable seed crops. A

seedling seed orchard is established from selected seedling
progenies; a clone seed orchard is
established by setting out clones as
grafts or cuttings.

tree surgery: The corrective treatment of the bark and wood of
trees to remove decay and add
strength and also to provide a
healing surface.

tree well: A device constructed to
maintain the original grade
around an existing tree and allow
air to the roots.

tree wrapping: A prepared paper or
other material, such as burlap
straps, used to wrap tree trunks in
a spiral casing to prevent sunscald
and damage by rabbits.

tremie: Device used to place concrete or grout under water.

triangulation: A system of extending a survey from a base line of
known length by measuring the
angles in a network of triangles
which includes the base line as
one side.

triazines: Herbicides that inhibit
photosynthesis, leading to yellowing of leaves, followed by the
death of leaf tissue; uptake can
occur through leaves but there is
little movement inside the plant;
when soil applied they are taken
up by the roots and move in the
xylem to plant leaves.

tributary: Secondary or branch of a
stream, drain, or other channel
that contributes flow to the primary or main channel.

trickle tube: A small diameter pipe
to take water by gravity from a
farm pond to a drinking recepta-
cle without allowing livestock

access to the pond.

tripton: The dead suspended particulate matter in aquatic habitats;
the nonliving portion of the seston. See *detritus*.

tritium: A radioactive form of
hydrogen with atoms of three
times the mass of ordinary hydrogen; used to determine the age of
water.

trophic: Relating to the processes of
energy and nutrient transfer from
one or more organisms to others
in an ecosystem.

trophic level: The level in a nutritive series of an ecosystem in
which a group of organisms in a
certain stage in the food chain
secures food in the same general
manner. The first or lowest trophic level consists of producers
(green plants); the second level of
herbivores; the third level of secondary carnivores; and the last
level of reducers.

trophogenic region: The area of a
body of water where organic production from mineral substances
takes place on the basis of light
energy and photosynthetic activity.

troposphere: The lower part of the
earth's atmosphere in which most
weather phenomena occur;
extends from the surface of the
earth to a height of about 10 miles
(16.1 km) above the equator; at
the pole its thickness is about five
miles (eight km).

turbidity: Haziness in air caused by
the presence of particles and pollutants; a cloudy condition in
water due to suspended silt or
organic matter.

truncated soil profile: Soil profile
that has been cut down by accelerated erosion or by mechanical

means. The profile may have lost part or all of the A horizon and sometimes the B horizon, leaving only the C horizon. Comparison of an eroded soil profile with a virgin profile of the same area, soil type, and slope conditions, indicates the degree of truncation.

tubelings: Plant seedlings planted and nursery developed in reinforced paper tubes. When the root system develops, the tubeling is ready for transplanting.

tundra: The treeless land in arctic and alpine regions; varying from bare area to various types of vegetation consisting of grasses, sedges, forbs, dwarf shrubs, mosses, and lichens.

tundra soil: Soils characteristic of tundra regions; a zonal great soil group consisting of soils with dark brown peaty layers over grayish horizons mottled with rust and having continually frozen substrata, formed under frigid, humid climates with poor drainage. Native vegetation consists of lichens, moss, flowering plants, and shrubs. See *soil classification.*

turbidimeter: Device used to measure the amount of suspended solids in a liquid.

turbidity: The cloudy condition caused by suspended solids in a liquid; a measurement of the suspended solids in a liquid; conditions in the atmosphere that reduce its transparency to radiation.

turbulent flow (hydraulics): A type of flow in which any particle may move in any direction with respect to any other particle and not in a fixed or regular path. The water is agitated by cross currents and eddies.

turbulent velocity (hydraulics):

That velocity above which turbulent flow will always exist in a particular conduit and below which the flow may either be turbulent or laminar, depending on circumstances.

turnout: See *delivery box.*

turnover: See *overturn.*

turnover rate: The number of times a specific outdoor recreation unit can be expected to be used by different groups or individuals in one day.

type, forest: A descriptive term used to group forest stands of similar character as regards composition and development due to certain ecological factors, by which they may be differentiated from other groups of stands. It suggests repetition of the same character under similar conditions.

U

ubiquitous organisms: Organisms that can tolerate a wide range of environmental conditions or variation; organisms that are so active or numerous as to seem to be present or existent in all types of environments. See *tolerant association, sensitive organisms.*

udic: A soil moisture regime that is neither dry for as long as 90 cumulative days nor for as long as 60 consecutive days in the 90 days following the summer solstice at periods when the soil temperature at 50 cm is above 5 degrees C.

Ultisols: See *soil classification.*

ultraviolet radiation: Electromagnetic radiation of shorter wavelength than visible radiation but longer than X-rays; roughly, radiation in the wavelength interval between 10 and 4,000 angstroms.

umbric epipedon: See *diagnostic horizons.*

unavailable forage: Forage not available to grazing animals.

unbalanced population (fisheries): The numerical ratio between prey and predators that is not conductive to the production of quality fish and/or the quality of fishing success; for example, a population consisting of many stunted bluegills and a few large bass.

unconfined aquifer: An aquifer whose upper surface is a water table; an aquifer containing unconfined groundwater.

unconsolidated deposit: Deposit of loosely bound sediment that typically fills topographically low areas.

undercutting: Removal of material at the base of a steep slope, overfall, or cliff by falling water, a stream, wind erosion, or water action; steepens the slope or produces an overhanging cliff.

undergrazing: An intensity of grazing in which the forage available for consumption under a system of conservation pasture management is not used to best advantage. See *overgrazing.*

underground development waste: Waste rock mixtures of coal, shale, claystone, siltstone, sandstone, limestone, or related materials that are excavated, moved, and disposed of during development and preparation of areas incident to underground mining activities.

underground mining: See *mining.*

undergrowth (forestry): Seedlings, shoots, and small saplings under an existing stand of trees.

underlying stratum: See *substratum.*

underplant: To plant young trees or

sow seeds under an existing stand of trees.

understock: The rooted portion of a plant to which the scion is grafted; plants grown especially for this purpose. See *graftage*.

understory: That portion of the trees in a forest below the upper crown cover; also called underwood. See *overstory*.

underuse: Degrees of grazing use that are less than the degree deemed essential for proper grazing use.

undesirable species: Plant species that are not readily eaten by animals; species that conflict with or do not contribute to the management objectives. See *pest*.

undifferentiated soil group (mapping unit): Two or more soils or land types that are mapped as one unit because their differences are not significant to the purpose of the survey or to soil management.

unconfined aquifer: An aquifer containing water that is not under pressure; the water level in a well is the same as the water table outside the well.

uneven-aged stand: A forest stand composed of intermingled trees that differ markedly in age.

unhulled seed: Any seed normally covered by a hull, that is, by bracts or other coating, and from which the hull has not been removed.

Unified Soil Classification System (engineering): A classification system based on the identification of soils according to their particle size, gradation, plasticity index, and liquid limit.

uniform flow: A state of steady flow when the mean velocity and cross sectional area are equal at all

sections of a reach.

un-ionized: The neutral form of an ionizable compound (such as an acid or a base).

un-ionized ammonia: The neutral form of ammonia-nitrogen in water, usually occurring as NH_4OH. Un-ionized ammonia is the principal form of ammonia that is toxic to aquatic life. The relative proportion of un-ionized to ionized ammonia (NH_4+) is controlled by water temperature and pH. At temperatures and pH values typical of most natural waters, the ionized form is dominant.

unit hydrograph: A hydrograph of one inch (2.5 cm) of direct runoff occurring uniformly on a basin at a uniform rate over a specified duration.

universal soil loss equation (USLE): An equation used to design water erosion control systems: A = RKLSPC wherein A is average annual soil loss in tons per acre per year; R is the rainfall factor; K is the soil erodibility factor; L is the length of slope; S is the percent slope; P is the conservation practice factor; and C is the cropping and management factor. (T = soil loss tolerance value that has been assigned each soil, expressed in tons per acre per year).

unsatisfied demand: The difference between outdoor recreation opportunity and the capacity of existing and programmed resources, usually expressed in activity occasions.

unsaturated flow: Movement of water in a soil, the pores of which contain both air and water.

unsaturated zone: The area above the water table where soil pores are not fully saturated, although some water may be present.

unsteady flow (hydraulics): Flow in which the flow rate changes with time at a given cross-section. See *translatory wave*.

unsupervised classification (remote sensing): A computer-implemented process through which each measurement vector is assigned to a class according to a specified decision rule, where, in contrast with supervised classification, the possible classes have been defined based on inherent data characteristics rather than on training samples.

upgradient: Of or pertaining to the place(s) from which groundwater originated or traveled through before reaching a given point in an aquifer.

upland: Dry ground (i.e., other than wetlands).

upland meadow or pasture: Upland pastures are areas maintained in grass for livestock grazing; upland meadows are hay production areas.

uplift (hydraulics): The upward pressure of water on the base of a structure.

upwelling: A process whereby nutrient-rich waters from the ocean depths rise to the surface; it commonly occurs along continental coastlines.

uranium: A radioactive element with the atomic number 92 and, as found in natural ores, an average atomic weight of approximately 238; the two principle isotopes are uranium-235 (0.7 percent of natural uranium), which is fissionable (capable of being split and thereby releasing energy) and uranium-238 (99.3 percent of natural uranium), which is fertile (having the property of being convertible to a fissionable material); natural uranium also includes a minute amount of uranium-234.

urban area: An area whose character is urban in nature; towns of over 2,500 are defined as urban by the US Bureau of Census.

urban fabric analysis: An Urban Fabric Analysis is a method for determining the proportions of vegetative, roofed, and paved surface cover relative to the total urban surface in the city. To analyze the effect of surface cover modifications and simulate realistic estimates of temperature and ozone reductions resulting from such modifications, the baseline urban fabric must be quantified.

urban heat island effect: The urban heat island effect is a measurable increase in ambient urban air temperatures resulting primarily from the replacement of vegetation with buildings, roads, and other heat-absorbing infrastructure. The heat island effect can result in significant temperature differences between rural and urban areas.

urban runoff: Water from rain, melted snow, or landscape irrigation flowing from city streets and domestic or commercial properties that may carry pollutants into a sewer system or water body.

urbanized areas: A standard of urban area density used by the US Bureau of Census to delineate areas that include cities of 50,000 or more and the adjoining areas with a density of at least 1,000 persons per square mile.

urban land (soils mapping): Areas so altered or obstructed by urban works or structures that identification of soils is not feasible. A miscellaneous land type.

urban migration: The movement of people from rural areas to urban areas.

urban runoff: Stormwater from city streets and gutters that usually contains a great deal of litter and organic and bacterial wastes.

urban waste: A general term used to categorize the entire waste

stream from the urban area. It is sometimes used in contrast to "rural waste." See *waste*.

ustic: A soil moisture regime that is intermediate between the aridic and udic regimes and common in temperate subhumid or semiarid regions, or in tropical and subtropical regions with a monsoon climate. A limited amount of moisture is available for plants but occurs at times when the soil temperature is optimum for plant growth.

utility: The ability of a good to satisfy human wants.

V

vacation farm: A rural area operated as a working or simulated farm with vacation living accommodations for rent.

vadose zone: The zone between land surface and the water table within which the moisture content is less than saturation (except in the capillary fringe) and pressure is less than atmospheric. Soil pore space also typically contains air or other gases. The capillary fringe is included in the vadose zone.

valence: That property of an element that is measured in terms of the number of gram atoms of hydrogen that one gram atom of that element will combine with or displace; for

example, the valence of oxygen in water, H_2O, is two.

valley cross section: The vertical and horizontal configuration of a valley normal to the direction of water runoff.

valley fill: The placement of overburden material from adjacent contour or mountaintop mines in compacted layers in narrow, steep-sided valleys so that surface drainage is possible.

value, color: The relative lightness or intensity of color, approximately a function of the square root of the total amount of light. One of the three variables of color. See *Munsell color system, hue, chroma*.

vapor dispersion: The movement of vapor clouds in air due to wind, thermal action, gravity spreading, and mixing.

vapor flow: The gaseous flow of water vapor in soils from a moist or warm zone of higher potential to a drier or colder zone of lower potential.

vapor pressure: A measure of a substance's propensity to evaporate, vapor pressure is the force per unit area exerted by vapor in an equilibrium state with surroundings at a given pressure. It increases exponentially with an increase in temperature. A relative measure of chemical volatility, vapor pressure is used to calculate water partition coefficients and volatilization rate constants.

vaporization: The change of a substance from liquid to the gaseous state. One of three basic contributing factors to air pollution. See *combustion*.

variable costs: Costs subject to the year's production schedule. As such, they may be largely controlled by the operator. Examples are the use of fertilizer and insecticides, hauling grain, etc.

variance: In tests and experiments, a measure of the dispersion of the data from the mean of the group; in pollution, permission granted by regulatory agencies to pollute for a limited period of time, usually while corrective measures are being taken; in zoning, permission granted by zoning boards for departure from standards of the zoning ordinance.

varied flow (hydraulics): Nonuniform flow in which depth of flow changes along the length of a reach; can be either steady or unsteady. See *gradually varied flow, rapidly varied flow*.

variegated foliage: Leaves that are edged, splotched, spotted, or patterned with color other than the background color.

variety: See *cultivar*.

vector: A carrier, usually an arthropod, that is capable of transmitting a pathogen from one organism to another; a type of data using polygons, points, and lines; gives a very realistic display or map, but not good for extensive modeling due to problems of exactly matching layers of data.

vegetable crop: Vegetables grown primarily for local markets, home consumption, and distant markets.

vegetable channel: See *grassed waterway*.

vegetation: Plants in general or the sum total of plant life in an area.

vegetation type: A plant community with distinguishable characteristics.

vegetative reproduction: The propagation of plants by an asexual method, such as budding, cutting, division, or grafting. See *graftage*.

vein: A mineralized zone having a more or less regular development in length, width, and depth to give it a tabular form and commonly inclined at a considerable angle to the horizontal.

velocity head (hydraulics): Head due to the velocity of a moving fluid, equal to the square of the mean velocity divided by twice the acceleration due to gravity.

venation: The arrangement of veins in leaves, petals, and some fruit.

vent (irrigation): An air release valve or stand used to release air trapped at high points in a pipeline.

Venturi flume: Calibrated measuring flume having a contracted throat section which produces a differential head that can be related to discharge.

Venturi meter: A proprietary device for measuring the flow of fluids through pipes, consisting essentially of a Venturi tube and a special form of flow registering device.

Venturi scrubbers: Air pollution control devices that use water to remove particulate matter from emissions.

Venturi tube: A closed conduit that gradually contracts to a throat, causing a reduction of pressure head by which the velocity through the throat may be determined.

vernalization: The exposure of sees or plants to low temperatures to stimulate flower development.

vernal pool: Depressions holding water for a temporary period in the spring, and in which various amphibians lay eggs.

vertebrates: Animals that have an internal skeletal system. See *invertebrate*.

vertical interval: See *terrace interval*.

Vertisols: See *soil classification*.

very coarse sand: See *soil separates, soil texture*.

very fine (soils): See *particle size classes for family groupings*.

very fine sand: See *soil separates, soil texture*.

very fine sandy loam: See *soil separates, soil texture*.

very stony: Containing sufficient stones to make tillage of intertilled crops impracticable. The soil can be worked for hay crops or improved pasture if other soil characteristics are favorable. Stones occupy approximately 0.1 to three percent of the surface. See *stony for discussion of phase names*.

viable seed: A fertile seed capable of germination under favorable conditions. See *seed*.

viewshed: A physiographic area composed of land, water, biotic, and cultural elements which may be viewed and mapped from one or more viewpoints and which has inherent scenic qualities and/or aesthetic values as determined by those who view it.

virgin forest: A mature or overmature forest essentially uninfluenced by human activity.

virgin material: Any basic material for industrial processes that has not previously been used; such as wood pulp trees, iron ore, silica sand, crude oil, bauxite. See *secondary materials, primary materials*.

virus: A minute organism, resembling certain molecules of protein, found in the cells of other organisms and frequently cause disease.

visible wavelengths: The radiation range in which the human eye is sensitive, approximately 0.4 to 0.7 micrometers.

visit: The entry of any person into a site or area of land or water, generally recognized as providing outdoor recreation. Visits may occur either as recreation visits or as nonrecreation visits.

visitor day: Twelve visitor hours, which may be aggregated continuously, intermittently, or simultaneously by one or more persons and is a figure to determine the use of a recreation facility.

voids: A general term for pore spaces or other openings in rock. In addition to pore space, the term includes vesicles, solution cavities, or any openings, either primary or secondary; also called interstices.

volatile matter: The matter lost from a dry solid waste sample that is heated, in a closed crucible, until red hot.

volatile organic compounds (VOCs): A group of chemicals composed primarily of carbon and hydrogen that have a tendency to evaporate (volatilize) into the air from water or soil. VOCs include substances that are contained in common solvents and cleaning fluids. Some VOCs are known to cause cancer.

volatile solids: The material lost from a dry solid waste sample that is heated, in an open crucible in a ventilated furnace, until red hot. The weight of the volatile solids is equal to that of the volatile matter plus that of the fixed carbon.

volatilization: The loss of gaseous components, such as ammonium nitrogen, from animal manures.

volume reduction: To process waste materials so as to decrease the amount of space that materials occupy. Processes include: (1) mechanical, which uses compaction; (2) thermal; (3) biological, in which the organic waste fraction is degraded by biological action; and (4) chemical.

volume weight: See *bulk density*.

vulnerable zone: An area over which the airborne concentration of a chemical accidentally released could reach the level of concern.

wady: A ravine or watercourse, dry except in the rainy season; some are permanently dry; also spelled wad or wadi. See *arroyo*.

warm-season grass: Native prairie grass that grows the most during summer, when cool-season grasses are dormant.

warm season plant: A plant that completes most of its growth during the warm portion of the year, generally late spring and summer.

warmwater fish population: Fish that normally survive, grow, and reproduce in warm water, 25 degrees to 32 degrees C (59 degrees -90 degrees F).

washoff: Materials transported from a land or soil surface by overland flow, often used to describe soil materials transported off runoff test plots.

waste: Material that has no original value or no value for the ordinary or main purpose of manufacture or use; damaged or defective articles of manufacture; or superfluous or rejected matter or refuse. Some examples of waste include:

bulky waste: Items whose large size precludes or complicates their handling by normal collection, processing, or disposal methods.

construction and demolition waste: Building materials and rubble resulting from construction, remodeling, repair, and demolition operations.

hazardous waste: Those wastes that require special handling to avoid illness or injury to persons or damage to property.

wood pulp waste: Wood or paper fiber residue resulting from a manufacturing process.

special waste: Those wastes that require extraordinary management.

yard waste: Plant clippings, prunings, and other discarded material from yards and gardens. Also known as yard rubbish.

waste management system: The colleting, conveying, storing, and processing devices and structures used to handle and dispose of animal manures.

waste processing: An operation such as shredding, compaction, composting, and incineration, in which the physical or chemical properties of wastes are changed.

waste sources: Agricultural, residential, commercial, and industrial activities that generate wastes.

waste treatment: Any of the physical or chemical processes whereby the qualities of given waste are made more compatible or acceptable to man and his environment.

wastewater: Water that carries

wastes from homes, businesses, and industries; a mixture of water and dissolved or suspended solids.

wasteway: Channel for conveying or discharging excess water or wastewater.

waste utilization: Using an agricultural or other waste on and in an environmentally acceptable manner while maintaining or improving soil and plant resources.

water application efficiency: Ratio of the volume of water stored in the root zone of a soil during irrigation to the volume of water applied.

water classification: Separation of water in an area into classes according to usage, such as domestic consumption, fisheries, recreation, industrial, agricultural, navigation, waste disposal, etc.

water budget: An accounting of the inflow, outflow, and storage changes of water in a hydrologic unit.

water column studies: Investigations of physical and chemical characteristics of surface water, which include suspended sediment, dissolved solids, major ions, and metals, nutrients, organic carbon, and dissolved pesticides, in relation to hydrologic conditions, sources, and transport.

water conservation: The physical control, protection, management, and use of water resources in such a way as to maintain crop, grazing, and forest lands; vegetal cover; wildlife; and wildlife habitat for maximum sustained benefits to people, agriculture, industry, commerce, and other segments of the national economy.

water control (soil and water conservation): The physical control of water by such measures as conservation practices on land, channel improvements, and installation of structures for water retardation and sediment detention (does not refer to legal control or water rights as defined).

water cushion: Pool of water maintained to absorb the impact of water flowing from an overfall structure.

water demand: Water requirements for a particular purpose, such as irrigation, power, municipal supply, plant transpiration, or storage.

water disposal system: The complete system for removing excess water from land with minimum erosion. For sloping land, it may include a terrace system, terrace outlet channels, dams, and grassed waterways. For level land, it may include only surface drains or both surface and subsurface drains.

water enrichment: See *eutrophication.*

water horsepower (irrigation): The power required to operate a pump if the pump and drive were both 100 percent efficient.

water impoundment: A body of water created or stored by impoundment structures such as dams, dikes, and levees.

water level (stage) recorder: See *recording gage, gaging station.*

waterlogged: Saturated with water; soil condition where a high or perched water table is detrimental to plant growth, resulting from over irrigation, seepage, or inadequate drainage; the replacement of most of the soil air by water.

water management: Application of practices to obtain added benefits from precipitation, water, or water flow in any of a number of areas, such as irrigation, drainage, wildlife and recreation, water supply, watershed management, and water storage in soil for crop production. See *irrigation water management, watershed management.*

water penetration: The depth to which irrigation water or rain penetrates soil before the rate of downward movement becomes negligible.

water pollution: The addition of harmful or objectionable material to water in concentrations or sufficient quantities to adversely affect its usefulness or quality.

water purveyor: A public utility, mutual water company, county water district, or municipality that delivers drinking water to customers.

water quality: The chemical, physical, and biological condition of water released to beneficial use.

water quality criteria: A scientific requirement on which a decision or judgment may be based concerning the suitability of water quality to support a designated use.

water quality standards: Minimum requirements of purity of water for various uses; for example, water for agricultural use in irrigation systems should not exceed specific levels of sodium bicarbonates, pH, total dissolved salts, etc.

water requirement (plant physiology): In a strict sense, the ratio of the number of units of water absorbed by the plant during the growing season to the number of units of dry matter produced by the plant during that time. More generally, the amount of water lost through transpiration during the growing season, since the amount retained in the plant is very small compared to the amount evaporated from it. Water requirements vary with plants, climatic conditions, soil fertility, and soil moisture.

water resources: The supply of groundwater and surface water in a given area. water rights: The legal rights to the use of water. They consist of riparian rights and those acquired by appropriation and prescription. Riparian rights are those rights to use and control water by virtue of ownership of the bank or banks. Appropriated rights are those acquired by an individual to the exclusive use of water, based strictly on priority appropriation and application of the water to beneficial use and without limitation of the place of use to riparian land. Prescribed rights are those to which legal title is acquired by long possession and use without protest of other parties.

water rights: The legal rights to the use of water. They consist of riparian rights and those acquired by appropriation and prescription. Riparian rights are those rights to use control water by virtue of ownership of the bank or banks. Appropriated rights are those acquired by an individual to the exclusive use of water, based strictly on priority appropriation and application of the water to beneficial use and without limitation of the place of use to riparian land. Prescribed rights are those to which legal title

is acquired by long possession and use without protest of other parties.

water rights, correlative doctrine: When a source of water does not provide enough for all users, the water is reapportioned proportionately on the basis of prior water rights held by each user.

water sample: A representative part of a portion used to determine quality of a larger body of water.

watershed: The land area that drains into a stream; the watershed for a major river may encompass a number of smaller watersheds that ultimately combine at a common point.

watershed approach: A coordinated framework for environmental management that focuses public and private efforts on the highest priority problems within hydrologically-defined geographic areas taking into consideration both ground and surface water flow.

watershed area: All land and water within the confines of a drainage divide or a water problem area consisting in whole or in part of land needing drainage or irrigation.

watershed lag: Time from center of mass of effective rainfall to peak of hydrograph.

watershed management: Use, regulation, and treatment of water and land resources of a watershed to accomplish stated objectives.

watershed planning: Formulation of a plan to use and treat water and land resources.

watershed protection and flood prevention projects: A system of land treatment or soil conservation practices combined with structural measures installed to improve infiltration and reduce erosion of land within a drainage basin and to protect lands from floods.

water sports area: An area of water with facilities for swimming, boating, and water skiing.

waterspout: A tornado over water.

water spreading: The application of water to lands for the purpose of increasing the growth of natural vegetation or to store it in the ground for subsequent withdrawal by pumps for irrigation.

water sprout: A side shoot of a plant, originating from an adventitious bud on the trunk or main branches of a tree. See *adventitious bud.*

water storage pond: An impound for liquid wastes designed to accomplish some degree of biochemical treatment.

water table: The upper surface of groundwater or that level below which the soil is saturated with water; locus of points in soil water at which the hydraulic pressure is equal to atmospheric pressure.

water table, perched: The surface of a local zone of saturation held above the main body of groundwater by an impermeable layer or stratum, usually clay, and separated from the main body of groundwater by an unsaturated zone.

water tension: The equivalent negative pressure in the soil water; equal to the equivalent pressure that must be applied to the soil water to bring it to hydraulic equilibrium, through a porous permeable wall or membrane, with a pool or water of the same composition; also called

water pressure.

water use efficiency: Crop production per unit of water used, irrespective of water source, expressed in units of weight per unit of water depth per unit area. This concept of utilization applies to both dryland and irrigated agriculture.

waterway: A natural course or constructed channel for the flow of water. See *grassed waterway.*

water management: Determining the water needed for crop growth and applying that water efficiently, considering water availability, drainage, and offsite water quantity/quality impacts.

water year: The 12 month period, October 1 through September 30, designated by the calendar year in which it ends (used with streamflow data and analyses). See *climatic year.*

watt: A unit of power; the rate of energy use or conversion when on joule of energy (. 0238 calories) is used or converted per second.

watt-hour: The total amount of energy used in one hour by a device that uses one watt of power for continuous operation.

wavelength: The mean distance between maximums (or minimums) of a roughly periodic pattern; the least distance between particles moving in the same phase of oscillation in a wave disturbance; optical and infrared wavelengths are measure in nanometers (10-9 m), micrometers (10-6 m), and Angstroms (10-10 m); wavelength = velocity/frequency.

weather: The state of the atmosphere at any given time with regard to precipitation, temperature, humidity, cloudiness, wind movement, and barometric pressure.

weathering: The erosive effects of the forces of weather on the surfaces of the earth; one of the soil forming factors.

weather modification: The intentional inadvertent alteration of weather by human agency.

weed: An undesired, uncultivated plant.

weed tree: An undesirable species of tree that interferes with the development of crop trees.

weep holes (engineering): Openings left in retaining walls, aprons, linings, or foundations to permit drainage and reduce pressure.

weight method: A method of arriving at the volume of forage or herbage on a range area by clipping and weighing samples or by estimating weight.

weir: Device for measuring or regulating the flow of water.

weir notch: The opening in a weir for the passage of water.

well: A bored, drilled, or driven shaft whose purpose is to reach underground water supplies.

well graded soil (engineering): A soil consisting of particles that are well distributed over a wide range in size or diameter. Such a soil's density and bearing properties can normally be easily increased by compaction. See *poorly graded soil*.

wet digestion: A solid waste stabilization process in which mixed solid organic wastes are placed in an open digestion pond to decompose anaerobically.

wetlands: Seasonally flooded basins or flats; the period of inundation is such that the land can usually be

sued for agricultural purposes; lands transitional between terrestrial and aquatic systems where the water table is usually at or near the surface or the land is covered by shallow water; mush have one or more of the following attributes: a) At least periodically, the land supports predominately hydrophytes; b) The substrate is predominantly undrained hydric soil; and c) The substrate is non-soil and is saturated with water or covered by shallow water at some time during the growing season of each year.

Wetlands Conservation (Swampbuster): First established in 1985, the so-called Swampbuster provision states that farmers or ranchers lose eligibility for farm program benefits if they produce an agricultural commodity on a wetland converted after December 23, 1985, or if they convert a wetland after November 28, 1990, and make agricultural production possible on the land. Natural Resources Conservation Service certifies technical compliance, and USDA's Farm Services Agency administers changes in farm program benefits.

Wetlands Reserve Program (WRP): Congress authorized WRP under the 1985 Farm Act. Natural Resources Conservation Service administers the program in consultation with USDA's Farm Services Agency and other Federal agencies. WRP is funded through Commodity Credit Corporation and has an enrollment cap of 1,075,000 acres.

Landowners who choose to participate in WRP may sell a permanent or 30-year conservation easement or enter into a 10-year cost-share restoration agreement to restore and protect wetlands. The landowner voluntarily limits future use of the land yet retains private ownership. USDA pays 100 percent of restoration costs for permanent easements and 75 percent for 30-year easements and restoration cost-share agreements.

wet meadows: Meadows located in moist, low-lying areas, often dominated by large colonies of reeds or grasses.

wet milling: The mechanical size reduction of solid wastes that have been wetted to soften the paper and cardboard constituents.

wet scrubber: An air cleaning device that literally washes out the dust. Exhaust air is forced into a spray chamber, where fine water particles cause the dust to drop from the air stream. The dust laden water is then treated to remove the solid material and is often recirculated.

wetted perimeter: Length of the wetted contact between a liquid and its containing conduit, measured along a plane at right angles to the direction of flow.

wetting agent: A chemical that reduces the surface tension of water and enables it to soak into porous material more readily.

wheel track planting: Plowing and inverting the surface soil and planting in wheel tracks in a separate operation with no additional working of the soil between the operations.

white goods: Discarded kitchen and other large, enameled appliances.

wilderness: A rather large, generally inaccessible area left in its natural state and available for recreation experiences. It is void of development except for those trails, sites, and similar conditions made by previous wilderness users.

wilding: A seedling naturally reproduced outside of a nursery, used in reforestation.

wildlife: Undomesticated vertebrate animals, except fish, considered collectively.

Wildlife Habitat Incentives Program (WHIP): The 1996 Farm Act created WHIP to provide cost-sharing assistance to landowners for developing habitat for upland wildlife, wetland wildlife, threatened and endangered species, fish, and other types of wildlife. Participating landowners, with the assistance of the Natural Resources Conservation Service district office, develop plans for installing wildlife habitat development practices and requirements for maintaining the habitat for the five- to 10-year life of the agreement. Cost-share payments of up to 75 percent may be used to establish and maintain practices. Cooperating State wildlife agencies and nonprofit or private organizations may provide expertise or additional funding to help complete a project. WHIP funds are distributed to States based on State wildlife habitat priorities, which may include wildlife habitat areas, targeted species and their habitats, and specific practices.

wildlife land: Land managed or used primarily for wildlife.

wildlife management: The art of producing sustained annual crops of wildlife.

wildling: A seedling or young plant naturally produced outside a nursery and dug for use as planting stock.

wilting point: The water content of soil, on an oven dry basis, at which plants wilt and fail to recover their turgidity when placed in a dark humid atmosphere. The percentage of water at the wilting point approximates the minimum water content in soils under plants in the field at depths below the effects of surface evaporation. It is approximated by the moisture content at 15 bar tension.

windbreak: A living barrier of trees or combination of trees and shrubs located adjacent to farm or ranch headquarters and designed to protect the area from cold or hot winds and drifting snow. Also headquarters and livestock windbreaks; a narrow barrier of living trees or combination of trees and shrubs, usually from one to five rows, established within or around a field for the protection of land and crops from wind. May also consist of narrow strips of annual crops, such as corn or sorghum.

wind suitability groups: Soil groups in which the growth response of adapted trees and shrubs generally is the same for all soils if proper management is used.

wind erosion: The detachment and transportation of soil by wind.

wind erosion equation: An equation used for the design of wind erosion control systems; E = f (IKCLV) wherein E is the average annual soil loss, expressed in tons

per acre per year; I is the soil erodibility; K is the soil ridge roughness; C is the climatic factor; L is the unsheltered distance across the field along the wind erosion direction; and V is the vegetative cover.

windrowing: The composting process of sorting and shredding refuse, placing it in elongated rows usually five or six feet deep, and turning the piles for natural aeration. "Modified windrowing," a more efficient and quicker method, utilizes controlled amounts of air being blown through the material being composted.

wind stripcropping: The production of crops in relatively narrow strips placed perpendicular to the direction of prevailing winds.

wing: Any folaceous, membranous, or woody expansion, as that along the sides of certain plant stems and petioles; for example, maple seeds and winged euonymus.

wing wall: Side walls of a structure used to prevent sloughing of banks or channels and to direct and confine overfall.

winter irrigation: The irrigation of lands between growing seasons in order to store water in the soil for subsequent use by plants.

winter kill: The death of fish in a body of water during a prolonged period of ice and snow cover; caused by oxygen exhaustion due to respiration and lack of photosynthesis. See *summer kill*.

witches-broom: An abnormal growth of tufted, small, closely set branches, caused by fungi, mistletoes, viruses, insects, and mites;

occurs in many species of trees.

withdrawal: The act or process of removing; such as removing water from a stream for irrigation or public water supply.

wolf tree: A tree of little or no economic value for wood fiber production. It is usually broad crowned, short stemmed, large, and limby due to more than adequate growing space. It may have value for wildlife purposes.

woodland: Any land used primarily for growing trees and shrubs. Woodland includes, in addition to what is ordinarily termed "forest" or "forest plantations," shelterbelts, windbreaks, wide hedgerows containing woodland species for wildlife food or cover, stream and other banks with woodland cover, etc. It also includes farmland and other lands on which woody vegetation is to be established and maintained.

woodland management: The management of woodlands and plantations that have passed the establishment stage, including all measures designed to improve the quality and quantity of woodland growing stock and to maintain litter and herbaceous ground cover for soil, water, and other resource conservation. Some of these measures are planting, improvement cutting, thinning, pruning, slash disposal, and protection from fire and grazing.

woodland suitability groups of soils: A soil classification system grouping soils that are capable of producing similar kinds of wood crops, that need similar management to produce these crops, and that have about the same potential productivity.

woodland weeding: The elimination or control of undesirable weeds, vines, shrubs, or trees of poor form or less desirable or inferior species to improve the growth of desirable species.

woodlot: A relatively restricted area devoted to the growing of forest trees.

wood pulp: The basic primary material from which most papers are made. It consists of small, loose wood fibers mixed with water.

working face: That portion of a sanitary landfill where waste is discharged by collection trucks and is compacted prior to placement of cover material.

X,Y,Z

xeric: A soil moisture regime common to Mediterranean climates that have moist cool winters and warm dry summers. A limited amount of moisture is present but does not occur at optimum periods for plant growth. Irrigation or summer fallow is commonly necessary for crop production.

xerophyte: A plant capable of surviving periods of prolonged moisture deficiency.

yard waste: Grass clippings, prunings and other discarded material from yards and gardens.

yellowboy: The unsightly orangered or yellow precipitate of ferric sulfate and hydroxide observed in many streams polluted by mine drainage.

yield: The mass of material or constituent transported by a river in a specified period of time divided by the drainage area of the river basin.

yield, sustained: See sustained yield.

zenith: The point in the celestial sphere that is exactly overhead; opposite of nadir.

zero air: Atmospheric air purified to contain less than 0.1 ppm total hydrocarbons.

zero tillage: See no tillage.

Zingg bench terrace: A special type of bench terrace designed for dryland moisture conservation. It employs an earthen embankment similar to the ridge terrace; a part of the terrace interval immediately above the ridge is bench leveled. Runoff water from the sloping area is retained on the leveled area and absorbed by the soil. See terrace.

zone: 1. (ecology) An area characterized by similar flora or fauna; a belt or area to which certain species are limited. 2. (engineering) In earth dams, a segment of the earthfill containing similar materials; earth structures may be divided into two or more segments of zones to make the best use of available materials.

zone of aeration: Subsurface zone above the water table in which the soil or permeable rock is not saturated.

zone of saturation: The layer beneath the surface of the land containing openings that may fill with water.

zoning: The partition of a city, county, township, or other governmental unit or area by ordinance into sections reserved for different purposes, such as residential, business, manufacturing, or agriculture.

zoning, exclusionary: Zoning standards within a specific community that tend to keep low- and middle-income families from obtaining residences because the land are or building size requirements are exceptionally high.

zoning ordinance: An ordinance based on the police power of government to protect the public health, safety, and general welfare. It may regulate the type of use and intensity of development of land and structures to the extent necessary for a public purpose. Requirements may vary among various geographically defined areas called zones. Regulations generally cover such items as height and bulk of buildings, density of dwelling units, off street parking, control of signs, and use of land for residential, commercial, industrial, or agricultural purposes. A zoning ordinance is one of the major methods for implementation of the comprehensive plan.

zooplankton: Unattached microscopic animals of plankton having minimal capability for locomotion. See plankton, phytoplankton.

zymogenous flora: Organisms found in soils in large numbers immediately following the addition of readily decomposable organic materials.